CIVIL WAR WITNESSES
AND THEIR BOOKS

CONFLICTING WORLDS

New Dimensions of the American Civil War

T. Michael Parrish, Series Editor

CIVIL WAR
WITNESSES
AND THEIR BOOKS

NEW PERSPECTIVES ON
ICONIC WORKS

Edited by

GARY W. GALLAGHER &
STEPHEN CUSHMAN

LOUISIANA STATE UNIVERSITY PRESS   BATON ROUGE

Published by Louisiana State University Press
lsupress.org

Designer: Barbara Neely Bourgoyne
Typeface: Ingeborg

Library of Congress Cataloging-in-Publication Data
Names: Gallagher, Gary W., editor. | Cushman, Stephen, 1956– editor.
Title: Civil war witnesses and their books : new perspectives on iconic works / Edited by
    Gary W. Gallagher, and Stephen Cushman.
Description: Baton Rouge : Louisiana State University Press, [2021] |
    Series: Conflicting worlds: new dimensions of the American Civil War |
    Includes bibliographical references and index.
Identifiers: LCCN 2021005501 (print) | LCCN 2021005502 (ebook) | ISBN 978-0-8071-7580-4
    (cloth) | ISBN 978-0-8071-7635-1 (pdf) | ISBN 978-0-8071-7636-8 (epub)
Subjects: LCSH: United States—History—Civil War, 1861–1865—Sources. | United States—
    History—Civil War, 1861–1865—Personal narratives. | United States—History—Civil War,
    1861–1865—Historiography.
Classification: LCC E464 .C565 2021 (print) | LCC E464 (ebook) | DDC 973.7092/2—dc23
LC record available at https://lccn.loc.gov/2021005501
LC ebook record available at https://lccn.loc.gov/2021005502

Once again for John L. Nau III,
whose generosity continues for Civil War-era studies
at the University of Virginia

CONTENTS

CONTENTS

CIVIL WAR WITNESSES
AND THEIR BOOKS

Introduction

GARY W. GALLAGHER AND STEPHEN B. CUSHMAN

Many people who lived through the Civil War took up their pens to write about transformative events. Typical was North Carolinian Catherine Ann Devereux Edmondston, who on January 27, 1862, composed the first entry in her journal after several weeks of neglect. "I am sorry," she wrote with a degree of self-reproach, "that I intermitted the practice of keeping a Diary!" Then she got to the heart of why so many soldiers and civilians in the United States and the Confederacy found it important to write about the war: "This year of all the years of my past life I ought to have been most faithful in keeping my Record, for it is not, I hope, probable that I shall ever pass through so stirring a time again. . . ." Edmondston had "all my life been sighing for something to write about," only to conclude that her prewar diaries had chronicled actions and observations that now seemed "hopelessly inane & stupid." Secession and the outbreak of fighting had changed everything, creating a situation that justified, really demanded, careful recording and assessment. Going forward, with so much at stake, Edmondston would fill her diary with detailed and perceptive observations that, when published more than a century after their composition, became part of the legacy created by the wartime generation. In addition to those such as Edmondston who wrote in the midst of events, others recorded retrospective thoughts, swelling the size of a formidable literature that provides rich fodder for readers and scholars who would explore either the history or the memory of the Civil War era.[1]

The eight essays in this volume draw on that literary legacy and constitute the second installment of a broader project begun in *Civil War Writing: New Perspectives on Iconic Texts* (LSU Press, 2019). A third collection of essays will follow, extending our examination of significant writings by participants who lived through the conflict. Readers familiar with *Civil War Writing* know it presents assessments of texts written by civilians and combatants, men and women, northerners and southerners, including those by Elizabeth R. Varon of Joseph T. Wilson's *The Black Phalanx* and by Brenda E. Stevenson of Charlotte Forten's diaries. The third volume also will contain at least one, and perhaps two, essays on African American texts, as well as one devoted to a foreign observer's travel account. The absence of an African American presence in *Civil War Witnesses* stems from the press of commitments on potential contributors, which brought changes to the roster of books under review.

As in *Civil War Writing,* the essayists in *Civil War Witnesses* selected books, eleven in all, that have proved influential over a significant period. Some of the authors whose books lie at the center of the essays wrote primarily for their peers; others had in mind how future generations would judge the actions of the wartime generation, and one, whose diary has been much cited by historians, made her entries with no thought that they would appear in print long after her death. The authors include five men and three women, among whom were a prominent general from each side, the wives of a headline-seeking US cavalry commander and a Democratic judge from New York City, a member of Robert E. Lee's staff, a Union artillerist, a matron from the Confederacy's sprawling Chimborazo Hospital, and a leading abolitionist member of the United States Senate. Five of the authors supported the United States, three the Confederacy. In terms of genres, readers will find examples of memoir, narrative history, and a diary among the eleven titles.

Sequence can pose a problem in collections of essays, but such was not the case in this instance. The contributors chose books, three of them posthumous, that appeared between 1872 and 1962 and do not lend themselves to a chronological ordering. Instead, as in *Civil War Writing,* placement reflects an editorial sense of rhythm and equilibrium. Elizabeth R. Varon leads off by deftly setting James Longstreet's memoir *From Manassas to Appomattox* (published 1896; copyrighted 1895) against background controversies over his wartime record, his postwar career, and his public clashes with Lost Cause apologists. Longstreet's book appeared after, in some cases long after, many other generals' memoirs, among them big books by Joseph E. Johnston, William T. Sherman, Richard Taylor, John B. Hood, Ulysses S. Grant, George B. McClellan, and Philip H. Sheridan. Although every one of these books included some measure of self-justification, and in several cases personal score-settling, the writing of *From Manassas to Appomattox* presented James Longstreet with a formidable challenge. No other Civil War leader, who performed so well during the war, fell so far in public standing after it. No other leader paid so high a price for his postwar readiness to forgive and work with his former enemies. No other Confederate leader became such a consistent target for ruthless abuse by a legion of Lost Cause apostles, first and foremost among them Jubal A. Early, who died in March 1894. Carefully tracing Longstreet's literary career through the composition of his memoirs, Varon demonstrates that the former commander of the Confederate First Corps, with the help of powerful allies, deliberately set out to fashion himself into "a prophet of sectional reconciliation." At the same time Varon's essay shows that postwar reconciliation between former belligerents made up only part of the story; James Longstreet could resume his long-standing friendship with Ulysses S. Grant, to the admiration of some and the disgust of others. But every bit as charged, and in the end unsuccessful, were his attempts at reconciliation with his Confederate antagonists.

Our second essayist turns to Henry Wilson's *The History of the Rise and Fall of the Slave Power in America,* published in three hefty volumes between 1872 and 1877. William A. Blair places Wilson's sweeping indictment of slaveholders and the havoc they wreaked on the American republic in conversation with contemporary scholarship. Abolitionist, senator from Massachusetts from 1855 to 1873, and vice president during U. S. Grant's second term, Wilson crafted a narrative that extended from the colonial roots of slavery through the early stages of Reconstruction. Blair's incisive essay casts Wilson's work as "a thinly disguised form of autobiography" that engaged with the large political and social contours of an age beset by immense disruption and change—and which featured the villainous "Slave Power" as a small minority of the nation's populace that often dominated governmental actions. Blair identifies in Wilson's text much that accords with twenty-first-century scholarly interpretations, including its celebration of emancipation as the Civil War's preeminent achievement, its framing of the war with Mexico as a shameless effort to extend slavery's reach, its condemnation of Indian "removal" as further evidence of the Slave Power's inexhaustible pursuit of power and control, and its use of the term *human rights* in a decidedly modern way. In light of these interpretive elements of *The History of the Rise and Fall of the Slave Power in America,* Blair finds irony in the fact that almost no one today, even in the academic world, pays much attention to Wilson or his masterwork. He labels the trilogy "one of the most significant Civil War books that few people will ever read, written by one of the most important political figures of the era whom few people remember."

Sarah E. Gardner considers Phoebe Yates Pember's *A Southern Woman's Story* (1879), which unlike Wilson's trilogy remains widely cited, with respect both to its textual history and to its historical contexts. In 1866, Pember published "Reminiscences of a Southern Hospital" serially in four issues of *Cosmopolite,* an ephemeral periodical edited briefly in Baltimore by former Confederate civil servant Thomas De Leon Cooper. As Gardner shows, Pember's revisions, though relatively few, changed in subtle yet significant ways the manner in which she represented herself. Born in Charleston into a prominent Jewish family, Pember was a recent widow of thirty-nine in December 1862, when she assumed her duties in Richmond as chief matron at Chimborazo Hospital, with its ninety wards treating nearly 80,000 patients during the war. Readers looking for autobiographical details of Pember's comfortable antebellum life will not find them in *A Southern Woman's Story.* Nor will they learn anything about her life between 1866 and 1879, when the necessity of earning a living helped motivate her to seek a book publisher— eventually G. W. Carleton in New York and S. Low and Son in London—for her personal narrative. What they will find, and what scholars have tended to value in Pember's narrative, are vividly drawn details of Confederate medical care. They will also find a perceptive author's shrewd observations about many aspects of noncombatant life and its social complexities in wartime Richmond. To these received ways of reading Pember's story, Gardner's adds important insights into what she calls the self-fashioning of its author. As Gardner goes on to demonstrate, the authorial self-fashioning of Phoebe Yates Pember in turn reflected the shaping pressures of "the cultural moments" at which her story appeared.

Stephen B. Cushman's essay reminds us that George B. McClellan defies simplistic analysis. Superb at building an army and able to forge a powerful bond with its soldiers, "Little Mac" seemed incapable of testing the men's limits on the battlefield and consequently fumbled more than one opportunity to deliver crushing blows to Rebel opponents. Cushman's assessment of *McClellan's Own Story,* the posthumous memoir published as part of Charles L. Webster and Company's "Shoulder Strap" series in 1887, reveals a book that mirrored the general's complicated personality and record. Uninterested in aligning himself with either McClellan's fierce critics or his defenders, Cushman examines the origins and substance of *McClellan's Own Story.* A pastiche of wartime reports and official correspondence, excerpts from letters to his wife Ellen, and the general's own writings, the book found its way into print through the efforts of Democratic newspaper editor William Cowper Prime, who served as McClellan's literary executor, and Mark Twain, who owned the publishing house and had guided U. S. Grant's memoirs to impressive success. Cushman focuses on several themes, including the importance of McClellan's religious views and their presence in the book, the frequent use of self-serving counterfactuals to suggest what might have been, and the ways in which the general reciprocated his soldiers' undeniable, and much remarked on, affection for their chief. Nothing comparable to this bond between McClellan and his troops, notes Cushman, appears in the memoirs of Grant, William Tecumseh Sherman, or Philip H. Sheridan, though the last two of those Union stalwarts also had enviable relationships with their men. Prime's text offers ample ammunition for those who seek to applaud or deprecate McClellan, but it also, more tellingly in Cushman's judgment, renders it impossible to dismiss "Little Mac" with a casual wave of the interpretive hand.

J. Matthew Gallman's savvy tour of Maria Lydig Daly's *Diary of a Union Lady, 1861–1865* (1962) reveals a range of political complexities in wartime New York. As he points out, published diaries of prominent northern women, would-be Union counterparts of Mary Chesnut, are few, making Daly's acute observations and trenchant comments from her "privileged perch" all the more valuable. Maria Lydig Daly and her husband Charles, a distinguished judge of Irish descent, were wealthy New Yorkers who moved freely among the highest social and political circles of the city. Staunch War Democrats, they stood firm in their support of fighting to preserve the Union yet just as firm in their opposition to Abraham Lincoln and his policies. Admirers of George B. McClellan, the Dalys backed him in the 1864 election, despite the antiwar plank in the Democratic platform, and remained personal friends of the McClellans after the war. Maria Daly's Irish sympathies—she and her husband followed closely the fortunes of Thomas Meagher, the Sixty-Ninth New York Regiment, and the Irish Brigade throughout the war—combined with her antipathy toward Lincoln to make her writing about the 1863 New York draft riots especially compelling. That twenty-first-century readers would judge her a racist is no surprise; what is worth watching, with Gallman's guidance, is the deepening of Daly's thinking as she watches United States Colored Troops march through New York. Although unsympathetic to what she thought of as Massachusetts abolitionism, Mary Daly did not end the war thinking exactly as she did when she began her diary in January 1861. Every bit as absorbing as her observations on race are those on gender and women in New York society. Both sets of observations resist easy, reductive generalizations.

M. Keith Harris shifts the spotlight to soldiers in the ranks with his essay on John D. Billings's *Hardtack and Coffee: The Unwritten Story of Army Life* (1887). For decades after its publication, Billings's book stood with Carlton McCarthy's *Detailed Minutiae of Soldier Life in the Army of Northern Virginia 1861–1865* (1882) as pioneering accounts that sought to explain the ordinary experiences of common soldiers. A veteran of the 10th Massachusetts Battery, Billings wrote in response to a plethora of accounts from commanders who had revisited grand strategic movements and battles. He hoped his description of life in camp and on the march would resonate with veterans, who had experienced that life, as well as with civilians who had not but would be eager to form a better impression of what the Union's troops had endured. Harris explores the activities and behaviors Billings considered essential to explaining the common soldier's world and discusses how scholars have mined *Hardtack and Coffee* for day-by-day details about citizen-soldiers. His essay also highlights other valuable dimensions of the book, often ignored by scholars, including how Billings dealt with race, slavery, and reconciliation. Although Billings deployed demeaning stereotypes of African Americans common to most white Union soldiers, he placed slavery at the center of sectional strife, equated secession to treason, and left no doubt that Union armies functioned as forces of liberation. As for reconciliation, notes Harris, Billings aligned himself with the mass of Union veterans who believed they had fought for a righteous Union cause, never absolved Confederates of complicity in treason, and stood apart from those who reached across the sectional divide in the late nineteenth century without reference to which side had been right during the war.

Cecily N. Zander's exploration of Elizabeth Bacon Custer's three major memoirs—*Boots and Saddles, Or Life in Dakota with General Custer* (1885), *Tenting on the Plains, or General Custer in Kansas and Texas* (1887), and *Following the Guidon* (1890)—goes against the conventional interpretive grain. Historians seldom have been kind to "Libbie" Custer as an author. Typically dismissed as a "professional widow" whose voluminous publications sought to buttress the reputation of her problematical husband, she invites comparison to LaSalle Corbell Pickett, another widow whose writings championed a spouse with a decidedly mixed record. Well aware that Libbie Custer strove to shape public understanding of her husband and his career, especially his actions at the battle of the Little Bighorn in 1876, Zander insists that a preoccupation with that dimension of her writings obscures a more important one: namely, that the three memoirs possess considerable value as texts that illuminate many aspects of US history in the mid- and late nineteenth century. The books deal with the Civil War, Reconstruction, and the US Army's role in postwar western expansion—all from the perspective of a woman whose testimony promotes understanding of how Americans at the time connected, or did not connect, episodes and policies concerning Rebels and Indians during the war and postwar events in the South and West. Taken as a group, shows Zander, the books address important topics such as reconciliationist impulses during Reconstruction, the absence of concern about African American rights in the wake of Appomattox, morale and motivation in the postwar army, and differing public attitudes toward Civil War veterans and their Indian war counterparts. Far from a one-dimensional hagiographer of her husband, Libbie Custer emerges as an author deserving serious attention from scholars and lay readers alike.

With his closing essay on Walter Herron Taylor's two books, *Four Years with General Lee* (1877) and *General Lee, His Campaigns in Virginia, 1861–1865, with Personal Reminiscences* (1906), Gary W. Gallagher illuminates the literary origins of two foundational Lost Cause tenets. Former assistant adjutant general of the Army of Northern Virginia, a very young Walter Taylor, only twenty-three when the war began, served on Robert E. Lee's staff throughout the war. Because he worked so closely with him, Taylor witnessed much that contributed to Lost Cause exaltation of Lee as general and man. In helping to formulate this first tenet of Lost Cause orthodoxy—the Confederate commander was a superior being, both military and moral—Taylor benefited from proximity to Lee, but so did others, and Taylor did not labor alone at constructing this piece of Lost Cause iconography. By contrast, because the young adjutant oversaw preparation of the monthly manpower returns of the Army of Northern Virginia, his contribution to the second tenet—Confederate armies were vastly outnumbered throughout the war and therefore both doomed from the start and sublimely heroic in their exertions—was unique. Taylor's first book, *Four Years with General Lee,* enjoyed the added prestige of publication by the major New York house D. Appleton and Company, which brought out books by Joseph E. Johnston and William T. Sherman in 1874 and 1875, respectively, and followed with Richard Taylor's *Destruction and Reconstruction* in 1879 and Jefferson Davis's *The Rise and Fall of the Confederate Government* in 1881. In his concluding section on the reception and reputation of Walter Taylor's work, from the late nineteenth century through the early twenty-first, Gallagher helps us understand how two aspects of Lost Cause thinking evolved, how they interlocked with other aspects under construction, and how imagining the Lost Cause as a unified set of unchanging dogmas is erroneous.

Interest in the Civil War remains high as the United States enters the third decade of the twenty-first century. This phenomenon reflects the continuing attraction of compelling personalities and profoundly important political, military, and social events. It also stems from the war's ability to command popular attention in the form of sharp debates about the Confederate memorial landscape, which in turn underscores how rival memory traditions stir passion and controversy. Because the influence of iconic texts pervades all kinds of contemporary engagement with the war, there likely will be at least one more volume in this series. The writings of U. S. Grant, Frederick Douglass, John Singleton Mosby, Jefferson Davis, and perhaps Kate Edmondston, among others, invite fresh investigation.

NOTE

1. Catherine Ann Devereux Edmondston, *"Journal of a Secesh Lady": The Diary of Catherine Ann Devereux Edmondston, 1860–1866,* ed. Beth G. Crabtree and James W. Patton (Raleigh: North Carolina Division of Archives and History, 1979), 103. Edmondston's massive diary ranks among the best by any woman on either side of the conflict.

James Longstreet on his porch in Gainesville, Georgia, in 1894. He had signed the contract to write his memoirs the previous year. Collection of Gary W. Gallagher.

From Manassas to Appomattox

James Longstreet's Memoir and the Limits of Confederate Reconciliation

ELIZABETH R. VARON

"I am not sorry that I write of the war thirty years after its close, instead of ten or twenty," James Longstreet proclaimed in 1896, in the preface to his memoir *From Manassas to Appomattox*. "I believe that now, more fully than then, the public is ready to receive, in the spirit in which it is written, the story which I present."[1] In choosing these words to frame his 690-page account of the Civil War, Longstreet sought a final vindication in the protracted conflict—pitting him against ex-Confederate defenders of the "Lost Cause"—over his wartime record. Longstreet's reference to the passing of the decades was no mere literary boilerplate, but a guide to how that war of words had unfolded: The mid-1870s and mid-1880s had been flashpoints in the contest over Longstreet's reputation, moments at which his own public pronouncements, in the forms of articles, letters, speeches, and interviews, had drawn a swift backlash, leaving him determined to tell the full story of his wartime experiences and to set the record straight.

Longstreet's memoir is the key to understanding his "paradoxical popularity in the late nineteenth century," to use William Garrett Piston's phrase. Scholarly treatments of Longstreet have painted him as a social outcast, a political lone wolf, and as his own literary worst enemy—as a man so engulfed in bitterness against his various detractors, and so in over his head, that his public accounts of his own war record and of his political purposes were mired in self-defeating mistakes and misrepresentation, making him

11

an easy mark for those who sought to scapegoat him. They have also noted that Longstreet's reputation improved considerably in his last years, so much so that at the time of his death in 1904 he was widely mourned as a great hero of the Civil War. Unable to square their negative assessment of Longstreet's literary output with evidence of his improving reputation, scholars such as Piston have ventured that his popularity "came despite, not because of, his prolific writings in self-defense": Longstreet benefited in his late years from the general public fascination with the Civil War generation and the growing traction of the Lost Cause memory tradition.[2]

A close look at Longstreet's memoir and how it took shape reveals a very different story. Longstreet was not a lone wolf, but instead a man with powerful allies, in the South as well as the North: His collaboration with the editorial staff of the *Atlanta Constitution,* I will demonstrate, was the key to his improved standing in the region. Longstreet was not blinded by bitterness but instead relished the process of writing the memoir, building it from careful research and prolific short-form writings and interviews, and then preparing the public, through savvy use of the media, to receive the memoir "in the spirit in which it [was] written." Longstreet was no political naïf, who clumsily misrepresented his own wish to return southern politics to their status quo antebellum, but instead an influential Republican political operative, determined to chart a new course for the South. And he was no easy mark: His critics kept coming at him, in waves of vituperation, precisely because he was a formidable literary and political foe, who posed a clear and present threat to Lost Cause orthodoxies.

Tracing his authorial career, this essay will argue that Longstreet succeeded, to a surprising degree, in fashioning himself as a prophet of sectional reconciliation between the North and South. But the memoir's reception reveals, too, how and why Longstreet fell short of a full rehabilitation among southern whites: Reconciliation *among* Confederates, who persisted in fighting each other over the meaning and legacy of the war, proved elusive, with race relations and the memory of Reconstruction as the key points of contention.

Longstreet during Reconstruction: Hero or Pariah?

By the time Longstreet published his memoir, at the age of seventy-five, he was not only a famous Civil War veteran, but also a veteran politician and author—respected in some circles and notorious in others. Thirty years earlier, at the end of the Civil War, he had been regarded in the former Confederate states as one of the greatest heroes of the conflict, having commanded the Army of Northern Virginia's fabled First Corps. After the war, Longstreet settled in New Orleans, where he achieved economic success working as a cotton broker, and was widely admired by his fellow Confederates. But by June of 1867, Longstreet had become a pariah among former Confederates, in New Orleans and across the South, reviled as a traitor to his party, his country, and his race. This turnabout resulted from his publishing four letters, from March to June of 1867, expressing his support for the newly announced program of Congressional Reconstruction, the centerpiece of which was black voting. On March 18, 1867, Longstreet wrote to the *New Orleans Times* the following: "There can be no discredit to a conquered people for accepting the conditions offered by their conquerors, nor is there any occasion for a feeling of humiliation. We made an honest, and I hope I may say a creditable fight, but we have lost. Let us come forward, then, and accept the ends involved in the struggle." This published letter and the letters that followed ignited a public firestorm. At each turn in the ensuing conflict over Longstreet's support for Reconstruction, he doubled down rather than backing down, drawing the wrath of ex-Confederates and the admiration of northerners and southern Unionists.[3]

Stung by Confederate condemnation of his stance, Longstreet became deeply immersed in Republican Party politics. He chose, in Louisiana's bitter gubernatorial election cycle of 1873, to back the faction led by Union veterans William H. Kellogg (a white northerner) and P. B. S. Pinchback (a black southerner). In the battle of Liberty Place, on September 14, 1874, Longstreet, leading the largely black New Orleans Metropolitan police and state militia, fought to defend the Republican state government against a violent takeover by the White League, the white supremacist paramilitary arm, full of Confederate veterans, of the Democratic Party. Longstreet was wounded in the battle and taken prisoner by the White League; it took Federal troops sent by President Ulysses S. Grant to pacify the city. Longstreet could no longer remain in New Orleans after the Liberty Place imbroglio and in 1875 he resettled his family in Gainesville, Georgia. But he in no sense turned away from politics. He remained an active Republican officeholder, holding patronage posts as an internal revenue collector, postmaster, ambassador to the Ottoman Empire, US marshal for Georgia, and Federal railroad commissioner.[4]

As Longstreet fought ex-Confederates in the streets, he also fought them on the page, in a heated debate over his wartime record, especially at the battle of Gettysburg; while his detractors sought to cast him out of the Confederate pantheon and blame the Confederacy's demise on him, Longstreet struggled doggedly to defend his own military performance during the war. The opening salvos in this conflict were attacks on Longstreet by Jubal A. Early, one of Robert E. Lee's lieutenant generals, and Rev. William Nelson Pendleton, Lee's former chief of artillery. In a January 19, 1872, speech in Lexington, Virginia, commemorating the birthday of Robert E. Lee (who had died in 1870), Early pinned the Confederate loss at Gettysburg on Longstreet, charging him with delaying the crucial attack on the Federal left flank on July 2, 1863. A year later, in a Lexington speech that became the centerpiece of an ensuing lecture tour of the South, Pendleton piled on, arraigning Longstreet for failing to obey Lee's order for a "sunrise attack" on July 2. These men were soon joined in the anti-Longstreet faction by Lee staffers A. L. Long, Charles Marshall, Charles Venable, and by Lee's nephew Fitzhugh Lee and the Rev. John William Jones. They saw themselves as champions of the Lost Cause and guardians of Lee's reputation, and they worked relentlessly to immortalize Lee as a saintly, faultless marble man and to proclaim the Confederacy's righteousness and seek its vindication.[5] The public reception of these lectures reveals the toll Longstreet's political career was taking on his military reputation. The social ostracism and public condemnation of Longstreet by ex-Confederates was at its peak in the mid-1870s, as he was roundly labeled a "Judas" and a "traitor." Against this backdrop, the Democratic/pro-Confederate southern press praised Early and Pendleton for exposing not only Longstreet's failures at Gettysburg but his motives: his delay was not simply a question of poor execution but instead an act of treachery. Longstreet's detractors explicitly connected his wartime failings and postwar conduct in Louisiana—indeed, the more deeply Longstreet became implicated in Republican politics, the more receptive white southerners became to the criticisms of his war record. Referring to Pendleton's 1873 speech, the *Dallas (Texas) Herald* editorialized in October of 1874 that they had not at first believed the charges against Longstreet. But "since the appearance of Longstreet at the head of the metropolitan police, prepared to hurl his messengers of death upon the citizens of New Orleans," the editors added, "we withdraw our incredulity and are prepared now to believe that no deed of infamy could be named or conceived that [Longstreet] would not gladly be a party to."[6]

Longstreet regarded Early's and Pendleton's attacks as a smear campaign—even some of the Virginia clique admitted that there had in fact been no "sunrise order"—but he was at first reticent about countering them. At the time of Early's 1872 speech, Longstreet had already twice, fleetingly, questioned Lee's judgment at Gettysburg: once in an interview he had done with journalist William Swinton, as part of research for Swinton's 1866 book *Campaigns of the Army of the Potomac,* and a second time in an 1871 interview with the Republican newspaper the *Chicago Tribune.* In both Longstreet revealed that he thought the Confederate assaults on July 2 and 3 ill-advised and had hoped Lee would stick to defensive tactics during the Gettysburg campaign; Longstreet had favored instead, he told the *Tribune* interviewer, "the turning of the Federal position on Cemetery Ridge." Once Early and Pendleton escalated the debate over Gettysburg by impugning Longstreet's motives and honor, Longstreet knew he would have to marshal a substantial array of documents and allies in order to mount a sustained counterattack. He began collecting the "facts and figures" he would need to prove that he was not responsible for the Gettysburg loss, reaching out to some former officers and aides for their recollections, and traveling to Washington, DC, to get access to War Department archives containing official records.[7]

Longstreet Fights Back

In January of 1876, Longstreet provided the *New Orleans Republican*—a newspaper which had ardently defended his political course during Reconstruction—with a copy of a letter he had written to his uncle A. B. Longstreet from Culpeper, Virginia, on July 24, 1863, just three weeks after the battle of Gettysburg. Longstreet had then confided to his uncle that "the battle was not made as I would have had it. My idea was to throw ourselves between the enemy and Washington, select a strong position, and force the enemy to attack us." Longstreet closed the 1863 letter with the prediction that "the truth will be known in time."[8]

The conservative southern press called the *Republican*'s publication of the letter "a vain attempt" by Longstreet to restore his damaged reputation, and Jubal Early and Fitzhugh Lee led the way in assailing Longstreet for slandering Lee. Longstreet replied in early March of 1876, in the pages of the *Republican,* accusing Fitzhugh Lee of exploiting current "political prejudices" to rewrite the history of the war. A few weeks later, in a caustic piece published in the *Republican,* Longstreet unlimbered his pen and took direct aim at Early, staking another claim that would become a staple of his writings on the war: namely, that Early and his critics were attacking him and exonerating Lee so that "the drippings of [Lee's] robes may remove blemishes that hang about their names." From here on out, Longstreet's defense of his own performance would be coupled with arch attacks on the military failings of his critics.[9]

Meanwhile, a new literary alliance was taking shape for Longstreet, at the behest of Alexander K. McClure, editor of the *Philadelphia Weekly Times.* The *Times* was in the process of commissioning a series of accounts of the war by Union and Confederate veterans, in what historian David Blight has described as "an initial effort at reconciliation through recollection." Mc-Clure was in the vanguard of an ascendant national cult of reconciliation, which submerged the difficult unresolved political and racial conflicts of the war era and enshrined a narrative of shared heroism and sacrifice on the part of the blue and the gray. Articles of the kind commissioned by Mc-Clure, and then gathered together and published in the popular 1879 book *The Annals of War,* served the purpose of reconciliation by diverting public attention away from politics toward military history.[10]

McClure had been following the controversy over Longstreet and Gettysburg, and upped the ante by commissioning Walter H. Taylor to write an anti-Longstreet account of Gettysburg for the March 1876 issue of the *Times.* Taylor's charges that Longstreet had delayed on July 2 and failed to use the forces at his disposal on July 3 had the predictable result of goading Longstreet into action. McClure swept in, offering to Longstreet the chance to vindicate himself in the pages of the *Times,* and even sending to Gainesville, to assist in the writing and editing process, the rising journalistic star Henry W. Grady. The Georgia-born Grady was serving at the time as an Atlanta-based correspondent for the *New York Herald* as well as taking on freelance assignments like the one offered by McClure. Grady would go on to be a journalistic legend and icon of reconciliation in his own right, but at this stage, in 1876–77, his duty was a simple one: to make sure Longstreet finished his article in a timely fashion, so the *Times* could claim to offer its national readership "Longstreet's first public defense of his movements at Gettysburg," as McClure put it.[11]

Longstreet's November 3, 1877, article in the *Philadelphia Weekly Times,* and a follow-up article that the paper published a few weeks later, were responses not only to McClure's bait but also to provocations coming from another influential source: the pages of the recently established *Southern Historical Society Papers (SHSP)*. An outgrowth of the Southern Historical Society, which had been founded in New Orleans in 1869 to promote a pro-Confederate history of the war and which relocated to Richmond, Virginia, in 1873, the *SHSP* series was a forum for the anti-Longstreet faction. Under its head, the Rev. J. William Jones, the *SHSP* printed a slew of anti-Longstreet articles by Early and others; these included an August 1877 offering from Early, which accused Longstreet of having a "constitutional inertia, mental and physical, that very often delayed his readiness to fight."[12]

With such slanders ringing in his ears, Longstreet provided, in his first *Philadelphia Times* essay, the detailed defense the public had awaited. The article highlighted Longstreet's pre-campaign deliberations over strategy with Lee, in which Longstreet proposed that the Confederates concentrate their forces under Gen. Joseph Johnston at Tullahoma, Tennessee, for a march through Tennessee and Kentucky into Ohio; this would surely, Longstreet reckoned, take the pressure off of Vicksburg, the key Mississippi River stronghold that was under siege by Grant. Lee agreed that the time was right for an offensive that would relieve Vicksburg by drawing the Union army north to protect its own territory, but he proposed an invasion of Maryland and Pennsylvania instead. After some back and forth, Longstreet "finally assented that the Pennsylvania campaign might be brought to a successful issue if [Lee] could make it offensive in strategy, but defensive in tactics."[13]

Of the many key phrases in the *Philadelphia Times* article, this "offensive in strategy, but defensive in tactics" formulation is one that has attracted the most attention from modern scholars, and justifiably so. Here was the key to all that followed: Longstreet went on to describe how he pressed this argument on each day of the Gettysburg battle, clinging to the hope that Lee would dislodge the army from the unfavorable low ground it occupied and throw it between Gen. George G. Meade's Army of the Potomac and Washington, inviting a defensive battle, akin to Fredericksburg, on terrain favorable to the Confederates. Lee failed to take this advice, Longstreet explained, because he had been thrown off balance and lost his "matchless equipoise" as a result of both the "deplorable absence" of his cavalry chief J. E. B. Stuart and Lee's own overexcitement at the prospect of another underdog victory. Longstreet's men gave their all in their attacks on the 2nd and 3rd, he maintained, despite the fact that they had been asked to do the impossible.[14]

Longstreet's article created quite a public stir. "I have this day read your letter in the Phila. Weekly Times, Nov. 3, which I have been trying to get for a week or more; the letter was so sought after, I had to send to the office in Phil'a for a copy," Longstreet's devoted former aide-de-camp John W. Fairfax wrote him on November 12, 1877, from Prince William County, Virginia. Fairfax had closely followed Longstreet's lead during Reconstruction, as a staff officer in the New Orleans State National Guard and secretary of the Republican State Central Committee. Fairfax endorsed Longstreet's account of Gettysburg as truthful, and declared his war record to be "faultless."[15]

While such political allies were few and far between, a much larger group of former First Corps officers and rank-and-file troops defended Longstreet's military record while setting aside or rejecting his politics. This defense was partly self-interest: They understood that, whatever their partisan leanings, their own reputations were at stake—that defending Longstreet's wartime performance meant vindicating the First Corps. But many, such as former artillery chief Edward Porter Alexander and staff officers Moxley Sorrel and Thomas Goree (all Democrats), also expressed their abiding fondness for Longstreet. For example, when Longstreet wrote his former aide-de-camp Thomas Goree in the spring of 1875, asking for his recollections of Gettysburg, Goree offered his support for Longstreet's account, noting, "Although we may differ in our political opinions, yet I have always given you credit for honesty and sincerity of purpose."[16] The loyalty of his First Corps staff was gratifying. But if Longstreet had imagined that the *Philadelphia Times* articles would soften the opposition of his Virginia critics, he was sorely mistaken. Early led the way in the *SHSP*'s new round of counterattacks. For Longstreet to suggest that "he was the self-constituted 'council' of General Lee," and that Lee sought his "assent," was proof, Early charged, of Longstreet's "impudence, arrogance, and presumptuous self-conceit." The Lost Cause faithful across the South rallied to the defense of Lee. Longstreet's *Philadelphia Times* article could "not disturb the imperishable fame" of Lee, as a rebuttal that circulated in Deep South newspapers put it: Longstreet had merely shown that "Lee's matchless strategy failed to be executed by his Lieutenants." Longstreet's vindication would have to wait.[17]

The Century Essays

Longstreet's next sustained defense of his war record came in the mid-1880s, in the form of a series of five articles he published, from 1885 to 1887, in *Century* magazine. On the face of it, this assignment had much in common with his *Philadelphia Times* one—like McClure, the *Century* editorial team (lead by Robert Underwood Johnson and Clarence C. Buel) commissioned a series of veterans' reminiscences as a vehicle of sectional reconciliation. But much had transpired since Longstreet's *Times* articles appeared. Another set of interlocutors had insinuated themselves into the Longstreet-Gettysburg controversy: the editorial team of the ambitious newspaper the *Atlanta Constitution*. Two members of the *Constitution* staff, Josiah Carter and Joel Chandler Harris, were selected to help Longstreet with writing and editing the *Century* pieces. Another *Constitution* staffer, Pascal J. Moran, would eventually help Longstreet with his memoir. And the man who had aided him with the *Philadelphia Times* articles back in 1877, Henry W. Grady, had in the meantime risen through the journalistic ranks from reporter to celebrated editor-publisher, purchasing a one-fourth interest in the *Constitution* in 1880 and building it into one of the South's leading newspapers.[18]

These men brought their own distinct political spin to the project of sectional reconciliation. By the mid-1880s Grady was the premier national spokesman of the "New South" movement, which wedded the themes of "intersectional white racial brotherhood" and southern commercial and industrial development. As self-styled southern "liberals," they offered a retooled version of paternalism in which whites would support industrial education and some material improvements for blacks in exchange for their lasting subordination. Grady and his ilk, in boosterism aimed at attracting northern investors, painted a rosy picture of southern social and material progress, denying that blacks were oppressed—even as they also sought to deny blacks the right to vote and hold office, and developed new tools of oppression such as the convict-lease system. The *Constitution* clique, as the mouthpiece of Georgia's Bourbon Democrats, blended elements of the Lost Cause creed with elements of the cult of reconciliation: Grady professed to be glad that slavery was dead, while also insisting that "the South has nothing for which to apologize . . . nothing to take back." Grady was fully committed to the Lost Cause narrative in which white southerners were vindicated by their victory over Republican Reconstruction.[19]

Grady's Atlanta ring took a keen interest in James Longstreet, seeing in him—as a native Georgian, hero of the greatest Confederate victory on Georgia soil at Chickamauga, and popular figure in the North—a potential asset to the New South movement. But before Longstreet could be useful as a New South symbol, he needed to be neutralized as a political threat. The Democratic press in Georgia had initially expressed hope, when Longstreet left New Orleans in 1875, that the move betokened a retreat from the political arena. Such hopes were soon dashed. Longstreet remained active as a federal officeholder and continued to relish a role he had played during Reconstruction: as a spokesman for white southern Republicans to presidential administrations and to the northern public, using his own influence, especially over patronage appointments, to try to build the Republican Party in the South.[20]

Given Longstreet's evident determination to exercise political clout, the question for Georgia Democrats was what they could do to deter and divert him. The *Constitution* and Grady's team tried a carrot-and-stick approach to luring Longstreet away from Republican politics. In the rare moments when the beleaguered state Republicans seemed poised to gain some ground in Georgia, the *Constitution* cast Longstreet in an unfavorable light, as a party hack selling his soul for the rewards of patronage. For example, in 1881–82, as Georgia Republicans tried to forge an alliance with some anti-Bourbon "independent" Democrats around a hybrid platform of protective tariffs, fair elections, public schooling, and internal improvements, the *Constitution* worked to brand the new movement a "second attempt to Africanize the South for the benefit of the Republican party," and criticized Longstreet for trying to lure unwitting Democrats into a trap. Such tactics worked, and the Bourbons soon "regained complete control of the state."[21]

But in the long stretches of time when the Georgia Republicans were in disarray or retreat, Grady and his circle enticed Longstreet with praise, defending his war record to incentivize his political solidarity with former Confederates. Grady previewed this approach in an 1879 interview he conducted with Longstreet at the general's Gainesville, Georgia, home, for the *Philadelphia Times*. Despite his South Carolina birth, "General Longstreet is a Georgian," Grady began. Grady praised the Longstreet family as "people of intelligence and authority," and described Longstreet as the "most accomplished soldier on the Southern side of the late war" and "so thoroughly military in his habits that the soldier always rose above the partisan." Longstreet "has a charming family, a fair competency, a peaceful home," Grady observed in closing, "and will probably end a life stormy, potent and terrible in the highest degree in a placid and grateful contentment." This was less a prediction than a form of advice: Grady was implicitly suggesting that a disavowal of politics was Longstreet's path back into the affections of white Georgians.[22]

Once Grady assumed its leadership, the *Atlanta Constitution* took a similar tack. When the Hayes administration appointed Longstreet as US minister to the Ottoman Empire in 1880, some southern Democrats howled their disapproval. But the *Constitution* approved the appointment, declaring bluntly that since the South had defeated the forces of Radical Reconstruction, the paper was willing "to be rather tolerant of other people's opinions, particularly since such opinions can work no harm." It helped that Longstreet himself was willing enough to signal his commitment to the New South movement's economic agenda. "We have put aside politics in Georgia," he told the *New York World* rather disingenuously in 1883, singing from Grady's hymnal. "What we are bending all our energies to is to attract northern capital and to develop our great industrial and mineral resources."[23]

Grady and the *Constitution* encountered significant resistance within Georgia from conservative Democrats who persisted in depicting Longstreet as a tool of Radical Republicans, "always ready to prove his sorrow for his rebellious acts and, at the same time, to rub salt in the wounds of his fellow white citizens." Determined to rehabilitate Longstreet further and promote Confederate reconciliation, Grady made his most brazen move in 1886 when he orchestrated Longstreet's appearance at the unveiling of a new monument to the late Senator Benjamin H. Hill in Atlanta. Jefferson Davis was to be the guest of honor. Davis and Longstreet had long been estranged, as Davis joined in the chorus of those scapegoating Longstreet for Gettysburg, and Longstreet in return critiqued Davis's wartime leadership. Somehow Grady, master of ceremonies for the event, persuaded Longstreet not only to attend the unveiling but to ride in on horseback bedecked in his old dress uniform, in a grand dramatic gesture. In what the *Constitution* described as the "greatest occasion Atlanta ever saw," Longstreet strode to the podium and he and Davis embraced, to the roar of the crowds numbering in the tens of thousands. "The very clouds quivered with the shouts that went up," as the *Constitution* floridly put it.[24]

Read in this context, Longstreet's *Century* articles of 1885–87, prepared with the editorial help of *Constitution* staffers Josiah Carter and Joel

Chandler Harris (author of the popular *Uncle Remus* stories), seem fully consistent with Grady's agenda of sectional reconciliation and New South boosterism. The articles covered a series of major battles and campaigns (Seven Days, Second Manassas, Antietam, Fredericksburg, and Gettysburg), offering up a multitude of military opinions while steering clear of politics. Focusing on tactical details, Longstreet called attention to the failings of Union and Confederate generals alike, criticizing Union general John Pope, for example, for underestimating the Confederates at Second Manassas, and taking Jackson to task for his lateness at the Seven Days. While Longstreet's account of Gettysburg lashed out against the Early clique for scapegoating him, the article ended on an unreservedly reconciliationist note: "I thought before the war, and during its continuation, that the people would eventually get together again in stronger bonds of friendship than those of their first love," Longstreet claimed.[25]

But once again, as in the case of the *Philadelphia Times* essays, Longstreet's *Century* articles failed to silence his harshest critics, who were simply unwilling to detach his military judgments from his political record. As the *Charleston News and Courier* put it, taking umbrage at the criticism of Jackson and Lee in the *Century* article on the Seven Days: "It is unfortunate for General Longstreet that he survived the war. Had it been his lot to die in the Wilderness from the wound which he received in the moment of victory, what a halo of glory would have surrounded his name! Neither 'Gettysburg' nor 'New Orleans' would have been written against his record, and he would have been honored as Lee and Jackson are honored."[26]

Stung by such coverage but not deterred, Longstreet turned in earnest to writing his memoir—and to whetting the public's appetite for it.

Longstreet Writes the Memoir

Between 1887 when the last of the *Century* articles appeared, and 1896 when Lippincott rolled out *From Manassas to Appomattox,* Longstreet was often in the public eye, giving interviews meant to create anticipation for his forthcoming tome. An article entitled "Longstreet in Peace" by Josiah Carter in the *Constitution* in July of 1887 promised that the memoir would "be made up mainly of accounts of adventures in the wars in which Gen. Longstreet has taken part" and that it would "contain some very startling statements about the late war." Subsequent interviews by the *Washington Post* and other newspapers repeated the promise of "startling" revelations, and found Longstreet increasingly expansive in his musings about the war. Using the press as a vehicle, Longstreet emphasized two themes. The first was that Appomattox was the defining moment of his postwar career—that he took part in Reconstruction out of gratitude to Grant and in order to uphold the terms of his Appomattox parole. And the second was that "nobody but the politicians wanted the war to continue": soldiers such as he and Grant had yearned for and sought peace well before hard-liners, Jefferson Davis in particular, were willing to end the conflict. These were not new themes for Longstreet, but after Grant's death in 1885 they loomed larger in Longstreet's thinking, and had a greater public resonance. As Grant's biographer Joan Waugh has explained, "by the time of his funeral Grant had become as much a symbol of national reconciliation as he was earlier a symbol of uncompromising Union victory." During his prolonged, painful battle with throat cancer, Grant had "bask[ed] in an unanticipated but welcomed wave of tributes from former enemies"—gestures which "tipped Grant's inclination towards embracing sectional harmony." National reunion became the keynote of the national mourning and commemoration of Grant's passing. While some Lost Causers like Jubal Early remained resistant to this trend, others like Fitzhugh Lee "saluted the Christian compassion" of Grant's lenient terms at Appomattox.[27]

Longstreet, who felt the loss of Grant keenly, became more and more fulsome in his praise of his old friend and more committed to the image of Grant as a peacemaker. On July 23, 1885, the day of Grant's death, a grief-stricken Longstreet was visited in Gainesville by a *New York Times* reporter. After noting that they had been "on terms of the closest intimacy," Longstreet described Grant as "the truest as well as the bravest man that ever lived," and "the highest type of manhood America has produced." These kinds of superlatives invited the question of how Lee rated in comparison to Grant, and Longstreet obliged with an answer, telling the *St. Louis Globe-Democrat* in the fall of 1887, for example, that he rated Grant the better general than Lee on the grounds of Grant's "moral courage." Longstreet contrasted Grant's commitment to reconciliation with Jefferson Davis's stubborn defiance, saying, "Mr. Davis never did give up 'the cause' as entirely lost. He expects to be President yet." Longstreet also continued to play up a popular story for which the northern press had an insatiable appetite: the tale of how Grant and Longstreet, after the failed Hampton Roads Peace Conference of February 1865, had discussed having their respective wives ("who were as fast friends as their husbands") reach out to each other to open up an "unofficial" channel of communications between Grant and Lee, through which they could discuss moving towards peace. In Longstreet's telling of the tale, Lee unwittingly sabotaged the overture by making a "direct request" through official channels for a peace conference with Grant; Grant duly declined that request, as formally treating for peace was beyond the bounds of his authority and jurisdiction. The two sides continued fighting until April 9, 1865. The story served to foreshadow the reunion of Grant and Longstreet at Appomattox. "Grant acted as though nothing had happened to mar the ties that had existed between us before the war," Longstreet told a *Philadelphia Times* reporter in 1892. "He put his arm within mine . . . and said with the same affection as of old: 'Pete, let's go back to the good old times, and play a game of brag as we used to.'"[28]

Fighting back against the negative depictions of him as an unscrupulous placeman who had "deserted his people for the spoils of office," Longstreet also emphasized that he had not sought out political office but instead had accepted his first postwar appointment, as surveyor of the port of New Orleans, at President Grant's behest. Again and again Longstreet told the story of how Grant had forwarded Longstreet's name to the Senate; how Longstreet had demurred, for fear of causing controversy; how Grant had urged him to take the post; and how he had accepted, in order to be consistent with his Appomattox pledge to accept "reconstruction and reconciliation." In Longstreet's telling, Grant's dispensing of patronage was an "olive branch," extended, out of the goodness of his "big, generous heart, not to the individual but to the South."[29]

Many in the southern press proved surprisingly receptive to such symbolism. Indeed Longstreet found an enthusiastic collaborator in the person of Pascal J. Moran of the *Atlanta Constitution*'s editorial staff (although Grady died in 1889, the paper's leadership, under Clark Howell, remained committed to the New South agenda). Moran was a Canadian who had emigrated to the United States in 1866 and gradually earned a reputation as one of the South's most respected journalists. He seized on the idea that Longstreet and Grant had "sought a revival of the fraternal relations which should never have been broken." In a widely reprinted 1890 article by Moran, Longstreet recalled how he felt when Grant extended him the hand of mercy at Appomattox: "Great God,

I thought to myself, how my heart swells out to such a magnanimous touch of humanity. Why do men fight who were born to be brothers?" Moran editorialized, "If it were given all men to know the motives which influenced Longstreet in the year which followed the war, sympathy, if not approval, would at least be extended to him." Evidently appreciative of this relatively even-handed portrayal, Longstreet contracted with Moran in 1892 to help him edit, fact-check, and revise his memoir manuscript before it went to press.[30]

But Longstreet's detractors pushed back at such attempts to fashion him into a symbol of the fraternal bonds between blue and gray veterans. The reaction to a June 1893 interview Longstreet gave to the *Washington Post* exemplifies their tactics. The interview, in which Longstreet blamed the late Jefferson Davis (Davis had died in 1889) for mismanaging the Confederate war effort, aroused the wrath of former Confederate general Dabney H. Maury, part of the Virginia clique. In an outraged response, Maury, reaching back to Reconstruction, insisted that Longstreet tried to "sell out the South to the 'Grant party of the North,'" and that he presided as a "vice president of a negro meeting in Lafayette Square!" and later "went over body and bones to the radical party, march[ing] in procession with the negroes and baser whites." Maury was referring to two actual events—a May 1867 visit by the abolitionist statesman Henry Wilson to a Republican rally in New Orleans, which Longstreet attended but did not preside over, and an April 30, 1870, public celebration of the ratification of the Fifteenth Amendment (enfranchising African American men) in New Orleans, at which Longstreet, as a state officer and party leader, did preside. Maury's ilk regarded both events as unimpeachable evidence of Longstreet's radicalism.[31]

Longstreet published a pointed reply in the *Washington Post*. He confirmed that he had indeed ridden "in a carriage in a procession to mark the adoption of the Fifteenth Amendment to the Constitution." Reminding readers that Maury had supported the Liberal Republican faction which challenged Grant in 1872, and which supported both the Fifteenth Amendment and blanket amnesty for former Confederates, Longstreet then skewered Maury for hypocrisy, saying that "He probably thinks the back door more honorable than the front." The attack from Maury was not the only such salvo. The *New Orleans Times-Democrat* charged that Longstreet had "prostituted his knowledge of the art military to the training and drilling of a negro constabulary" in New Orleans. Defending his Reconstruction record in a *Washington Post* piece in the spring of 1894—subtitled "He Asks only a

Fair Hearing"—Longstreet emphasized that Confederates "accepted paroles of honor at the capitulation at Appomattox Court House under pledges to obey and respect the laws of Congress."[32]

To shore up further his credentials as a herald of blue-gray reunion, Longstreet participated in two major reconciliation-themed events in 1895: the dedication of the Chickamauga and Chattanooga National Military Park on September 18–20, and the famous "Cotton States and International Exposition" in Atlanta, which lasted from September to December and attracted a million spectators. His speeches on these occasions focused on the themes of sectional fraternity and reunion and were widely acclaimed.[33] But Longstreet fared less well in commemorative events focused on the Confederacy. As historian William Garrett Piston explains, such events were "almost completely controlled by his avowed enemies," and by one enemy in particular: fellow Georgian and former major general in the Army of Northern Virginia's Second Corps John Brown Gordon. After Reconstruction, Gordon had become the dominant force in state politics, serving two terms as a US senator (1873–80 and 1891–97) and one as governor of Georgia (1886–90). The animosity between Brown, Georgia's leading Democrat, and Longstreet, its most famous Republican, illustrated the obstacles to Grady's vision of a united "New South." Seeing Longstreet not only as a political opponent but also a rival for military laurels, Gordon began in the mid-1880s to ally himself publicly with Jubal Early's anti-Longstreet faction. In 1889, Gordon became the founding president of the United Confederate Veterans organization, which committed itself to "the worship of Lee and the use of Longstreet as scapegoat for Gettysburg and by extension for the loss of the war," to quote Piston. Longstreet regarded the UCV as an unabashedly political organization that did the bidding of "Solid South" Democrats; ever the loyal Republican, Longstreet regarded it "as a high compliment to be excluded" from UCV membership. On occasions when Longstreet did venture to participate in Confederate memorialization—such as the 1890 unveiling in Richmond of the Lee statue—he did so warily, and only at the special request of some of his own former troops, who insisted on his receiving an invitation even though the events' managers would have preferred that Longstreet stayed away.[34]

Longstreet hammered home one last theme in order prepare the way for his memoir: namely that his account would be scrupulously researched. He did not claim to be a historian, but he did aim to provide the raw material for future historians—a detailed account based on his own firsthand experience, informed by his deep understanding of the "art" and "science" of war, and supported by the documentary record. He found a key ally in the person of War Department clerk Leslie J. Perry, a Union veteran who rose through the bureaucratic ranks after the Civil War to become, in 1889, one of the "civilian experts" compiling the massive, 128-volume comprehensive documentary reference work titled *The War of the Rebellion: A Compilation of the Official Records of the Union and Confederate Armies*. In the ten years he worked on collecting and editing material for the *Official Records* (as the series came to be called), Perry stepped forward to burnish Longstreet's military reputation by making the case, "excluding evidence not in accord with the official records," that Lee and not Longstreet bore primary responsibility for the Gettysburg defeat. The compiling of the *Official Records* was itself an engine of sectional reconciliation—a joint effort of northerners and southerners to offer an "impartial" body of documentary evidence.[35]

By the fall of 1895, with the process of researching and writing the memoir finally coming to its conclusion, Longstreet visited Lippincott in Philadelphia in September to attend to the last details of publication. The prestigious Union League Club held a banquet in his honor, at which Union veterans "grasped General Longstreet's hand all the heartier in bearing testimony to his valor on the field." So keen was the interest in Longstreet's travails as an author that the *Washington Star* could observe, in October of 1895, that as "every one knows, he has for the past eight years been engaged in writing his memoirs," and that "next to his family and the famous old white horse, that book is nearer and dearer to the warrior's heart than anything he ever possessed during life." The memoir had been "such a constant source of pleasure to him," Longstreet's son told the *Star,* "that I don't know how he will get along now it is completed and in the hands of publishers." As advance copies and excerpts started to become available in the late fall of 1895, and as Lippincott recruited agents to hawk the book on subscription, promising "unprecedented" sales, the time had come to find out: Would Longstreet finally get his fair hearing?[36]

The Contents of From Manassas to Appomattox

"Honor to all!" This would be the theme of his account, Longstreet announced in the preface of his 690-page memoir. Insisting, as he had done for years, that "political passions and prejudices" had led to the "misrepresentation" of his war record, Longstreet pledged to readers that he would offer them "the materials of history" in a spirit of sectional reconciliation.[37] What followed was a chronological march through Longstreet's career, moving quickly through his prewar life and Mexican War adventures, and arriving at First Bull Run by page thirty-five. Early on, Longstreet established his friendship with Grant as a defining theme, observing on page seventeen, in a section on his West Point education, that Grant, "a lovable character, a valued friend," was the "man who was to eclipse all."[38]

The pace of the memoir then slowed down as Longstreet offered an intricate account of the Seven Days battles and Second Manassas, arriving at the Antietam campaign by page 200. Longstreet considered this first third of the book a "plain narrative of occurrences," emphasizing Confederate strategy and tactics, and reprising details from his *Century* articles. While he got in some passing swipes at Early and Fitzhugh Lee and Stonewall Jackson, criticizing aspects of their military performance, his tone was mostly rather dry and detached. But in chapter twenty, entitled "Review of the Maryland Campaign," Longstreet dropped his reserve and signaled that his cumulative details were adding up to an argument: He was demonstrating that Confederates lost the war not because of the Union's overwhelming numbers and resources, but instead because of their own failings. The principal failing, one that afflicted both armies at times but proved more costly to Confederates, was hubris. As he put it, referring to Lee's decision to divide his army during the Antietam campaign: "Providence helps those who can avail themselves of His tender care, but permits those who will to turn from Him to their own arrogance. That His gracious hand was with the Confederates in their struggles on the Chickahominy, and even through the errors of the Bull Run campaign, cannot be questioned. When, however, in self-confidence, they lost sight of His helping hand, and in contempt of the enemy dispersed the army, they were given up to the reward of vainglory." Indulging in some counterfactual fantasies, Longstreet imagined that if Confederates had concentrated their power at Antietam, they would have not only won the day but also forestalled "one of the decisive political events of the war," namely Lincoln's issuance of his preliminary Emancipation Proclamation.[39]

Longstreet not only called out Confederate overconfidence—"the hallucination that McClellan was not capable of serious work seemed to pervade our army," he lamented—but also traced it to its source: the leadership of Lee. Longstreet's portrayal of Lee in the first third of the memoir was paradoxical. He emphasized the two men's intimacy, proudly quoting Lee's "Here is my old war-horse at last!" line to encapsulate their mutual trust and respect. But he also foreshadowed the troubles to come, saying on page 159, "our personal relations remained as sincere after the war until politics came between us in 1867." Trying to stake a claim as a fair and balanced arbiter, not blinded by political passions or prejudices, Longstreet concluded his review of the Maryland campaign by observing of Lee and McClellan, "Both were masters of the science but not the art of war. Lee was successful in Virginia, McClellan in Maryland." He had used such phraseology in interviews before, to make the point that while Lee and McClellan, as trained engineers, were possessed of great military learning and skill, they lacked some qualities of character—self-control, calmness, adaptability, generosity of spirit—that Longstreet attributed to men he considered superior generals, namely Joe Johnston and Grant. The contrast between the "science" and "art" of war was redolent of the writings of French military theorist Antoine Jomini, whose writings on the Napoleonic art of war were conveyed to West Point cadets in the antebellum period through professors such as Dennis Mahan. Jomini's influence on Longstreet is plain to see: Jomini's emphasis on throwing force upon decisive points; on the value of the strategic offensive but potential pitfalls of the tactical offensive; and most of all his emphasis on "moral courage"—those key qualities of character that were the most essential attributes of a great leader—all echo in Longstreet's writings on the Civil War. In Jomini's view, one of the key tests of a leader's character was whether he could resist having "too great a contempt for the enemy."[40]

Longstreet's evident aim in his treatment of Lee, and of the other Confederate "marble man," Stonewall Jackson, was to demythologize them. In his description of Second Bull Run, for example, Longstreet offered humanizing details about both, noting of Jackson that he had the habit of raising his right hand not "as an invocation of Divine aid," as some of his followers liked to think, but instead because a wound from First Bull Run had left his hand partially paralyzed and impeded the blood circulation. A few lines later, Longstreet described how Lee was thrown from his horse and "pulled . . . violently to the ground," severely spraining his wrist and breaking some of the bones in his hand. Such anecdotes were meant to bring these men off their pedestals and down to earth.[41]

Longstreet's next ten chapters, covering the Chancellorsville and Gettys-burg campaigns, developed additional elements of his explanation for Confederate defeat: that Confederate leaders were often at cross-purposes with each other, and often lured into fighting battles that yielded need-lessly costly, "fruitless" victories. Longstreet provocatively second-guessed Lee's decision-making at Chancellorsville—a battle widely considered Lee's tactical masterpiece—by suggesting that if Lee had waited a few days to concentrate more troops to attack Hooker, the battle could have been a Fredericksburg-style rout. Instead, "Lee was actually so crippled by his vic-tory that he was a full month restoring his army to condition to take the field." This of course foreshadowed Gettysburg: "When the hunt was up," Longstreet observed, Lee's "combativeness was overruling." In Longstreet's view, Lee was too entranced by what military historian Cathal Nolan has recently called "the allure of battle": the view, with roots that stretched back to ancient warfare, that heroic genius—"sheer will and brilliance" on the part of generals—could produce hinge moments, in which grand-scale, decisive, iconic battles turn the tide of history. Lee would have been better served, Longstreet maintained, by the realization that the Civil War was a war of grinding exhaustion and attrition.[42]

Longstreet's account of Gettysburg in the memoir largely reprised his ac-counts in the *Philadelphia Times* and *Century* articles: Lee reneged on their agreement for an offensive strategy but defensive tactics; there had been no sunrise order on the second day; Longstreet had proposed an alternate, more practical plan; Longstreet's First Corps had given the battle their all, and performed heroically, despite lacking proper support from Lee's other two corps; Lee had assumed the responsibility for the battle's outcome and later conceded that Longstreet's plan would have been better. Longstreet continued to maintain that "Lee had lost his balance" at Gettysburg. He had used this formulation in earlier writings, observing in his 1877 *Philadelphia Times* account that Lee "lost the matchless equipoise that usually character-ized him" and was "thrown from his balance" both by overconfidence and by the failings of Stuart, A. P. Hill, Ewell and others; in his 1885 *Century* piece on the Seven Days, Longstreet added that Lee was "remarkably well-balanced—always so, except on one or two occasions of severe trial when he failed to maintain his exact equipoise." In choosing the image of balance (or its synonym "equipoise") to conjure Lee's state of mind, Longstreet was drawing on a vocabulary popular in his era for describing the characteristics of military leaders. Soldiers and civilians alike saw "equipoise" as a key attribute of successful commanders; for example, William Tecumseh Sherman, in an 1887 *Century* article, lauded the "magnificent equipoise of Gen. Grant." Military biographers such as Alfred Thayer Mahan and Theodore Ayrault Dodge praised the "equipoise"—the balance of character and intellect, and of boldness and caution—of military idols such as Napoleon and Adm. Lord Nelson. Longstreet himself deployed the term, in an 1895 interview, to compare Grant and Napoleon, observing, "Napoleon was undoubtedly brighter and quicker, but he did not have the equipoise of Grant."[43]

But Longstreet's righteous indignation at the Lee-worship of Early's crew flashed hotter in *From Manassas to Appomattox* than in his earlier accounts. Longstreet's original claim that Lee atypically lost his equipoise at Gettysburg became an altogether more stinging indictment. "[Lee] was excited and off his balance," Longstreet charged in the memoir, and "labored under that oppression until enough blood was shed to appease him." In this rendering of their Gettysburg disagreement, Longstreet seemed to attribute to Lee not overconfidence and overexcitement—an excess of qualities that in their proper measure were good and benign—but instead a willful, hubristic, and even sinister desire to impose his will and exact his tribute, no matter what the cost to his own men. In his 1877 account, Longstreet had ventured criticism of Lee while also fulsomely professing "the greatest affection" for him and "greatest reverence for his memory"; in the 1895 memoir, Longstreet again alluded to their friendship, but in a more rueful, clipped way. Asserting that he had the "kindest relations" with Lee until "interrupted by politics in 1867," Longstreet on page 401 of the memoir got to the heart of the issue: that it was Early and his ilk who had done the real damage to Lee's reputation. In dredging up Lee's alleged criticisms of Longstreet and suggesting that Lee himself sought to "shift the disaster" to Longstreet's shoulders, Early had *either* lied about Lee's postwar intentions (if Lee in truth did not seek to cast blame), *or* exposed some very unbecoming truths about Lee's own pettiness (if Lee was pretending to be Longstreet's friend while treacherously undermining him). "It does not look like generalship to lose a battle and a cause and then lay the responsibility upon others," Longstreet bluntly declared in the memoir, revealing that Early's relentless campaign had worn away at Longstreet's *own* faith in his friendship with Lee.[44]

After covering the southern army's retreat back into Virginia in a chapter wistfully titled "The Wave Rolls Back," Longstreet turned his attention, in nine chapters numbering 118 pages, to his stint in the Western theater, where he was transferred in September of 1863 to join Braxton Bragg's army in its face-off with Union general William Rosecrans. Theoretically, this move suited Longstreet well—he had, after all, been urging since the spring a grand concentration of Confederate forces in the West. But in personal terms, his contempt for Bragg augured poorly. Longstreet folded his accounts of the Confederate victory at Chickamauga in northern Georgia (which many consider his finest hour as a commander) and the disastrous Knoxville campaign in East Tennessee (by all accounts a low point) into his overarching narrative of Confederate cross-purposes, fruitless victories, and missed opportunities. Longstreet's deft generalship of the Confederate left wing on September 20, 1863, at Chickamauga had been decisive in what he called "the first pronounced victory in the West." But in his view, it was too little, too late: This western strategy should have been effected the previous spring. Recounting his October 10 meeting with Davis (who visited the army) and his offer to Davis that he resign amidst bitter Confederate infighting, Longstreet reflected in the memoirs that, "In my judgment our last opportunity was lost when we failed to follow the success at Chickamauga, and capture or disperse the Union army." Davis dismissed Longstreet's offer with a "gracious smile; but a bitter look lurking about its margin," foreshadowing the further deterioration of their relationship.[45]

Longstreet would again ask to be relieved of command, and again have that offer declined, after the "tragic debacle" at Knoxville: his failed attempt to dislodge the Federal forces under Gen. Ambrose Burnside in East Tennessee, featuring an ill-conceived and uncharacteristic frontal assault on the Union defenses at Fort Sanders. Modern scholars agree that Longstreet performed poorly in East Tennessee—he was at odds with his principal subordinates and ordered terribly mismanaged assaults at Fort Sanders. But in Longstreet's telling, the failed campaign was doomed by the poor leadership of his superiors, who left his detached units poorly supplied and provisioned, outnumbered and cut off from reinforcements. Under Davis's leadership, the Confederacy was mired in a "settled policy of meeting the enemy where he was prepared for us."[46]

Longstreet's remaining chapters on the war, covering his return to Lee's side in Virginia and the epic year-long clash between Grant and Lee that culminated at Appomattox, gave him the chance to hammer home his main contention: that Confederate failings lost them the war. Recognizing that the war was attritional in nature, Longstreet nonetheless maintained that "the power of battle is in generalship more than in the number of soldiers." The Confederates might have outgeneraled the Yankees but did not—and while infighting, ego battles, logistical failures, tactical errors, and other factors all added up, in the end it came down to Lee versus Grant. "They were equally pugnacious and plucky," Longstreet averred, but Grant had a key edge, as he was "the more deliberate." Grant not only possessed superior numbers and resources, but he knew how to use them. Quoting French Revolutionary leader Georges Jacques Danton's famous epigram "L'audace, toujours l'audace!" on the effectiveness of daring in wartime, Longstreet countered that "an Americanism which seems an appropriate substitute is *A level head, a level head, always a level head.*" "President Lincoln's good judgment told him that Grant was the man for the times," and Grant proved it, in the Overland campaign, trench warfare outside Petersburg and Richmond, and most especially with his lenient terms at Appomattox. "As the world continues to look at and study the grand combinations and strategy of General Grant, the higher will be his award as a great soldier," Longstreet concluded. Confederates should be "foremost in crediting him with all that his admirers so justly claim."[47]

This portrait of Grant stood in sharp contrast to Longstreet's treatment of his postwar critics. Recounting how he was severely wounded by friendly fire at the Wilderness on May 6, 1864, Longstreet wrote, in one of the most biting passages in his memoir, "Bad as was being shot by some of our own troops in the battle of the Wilderness,—that was an honest mistake, one of the accidents of war,—being shot at, since the war, by many officers, was worse." Refuting Fitzhugh Lee's 1878 charge that Longstreet had "lost his way and reached the Wilderness twenty-four hours behind time," Longstreet reviled him for bearing false witness. In his Appomattox chapter, Longstreet took Pendleton to task for calling a "mutinous" meeting, on April 7, 1865, of officers who wanted to suggest to Lee that he should surrender. These "knights of later days," as Longstreet called the postwar Virginia cabal, claimed that they sought to relieve Lee of the humiliation of proposing peace, but their actions, Longstreet fumed, "would not stand the test of the military tribunal."[48]

Longstreet portrayed himself in these last pages of the memoir as someone who was weary of war and open to a negotiated peace (he again retailed his story of his peace overtures with Ord in February of 1865), but also utterly determined to do his soldierly duty, and to fight the enemy and seek victory vigorously until no choice was left but to surrender. This was a more honest self-portrait than the one Longstreet had offered in suggesting that he knew the cause was lost after Chickamauga. His account of the surrender set up the memorable rhetorical flourish of Longstreet's final chapter, on the postwar years: the proposition, paraphrasing a scriptural passage in Luke 7:47, that "those who are forgiven most love the most." Longstreet had uttered this catchphrase of reconciliation in earlier speeches, to sum up his gratitude for Grant's leniency at Appomattox and for Grant's subsequent role in helping secure him amnesty under President Andrew Johnson's restoration policy. Here Longstreet pivoted to a brief but pointed defense of his Reconstruction stance, reprising his familiar arguments that he had sought a practical path towards reconciliation, and that he felt that respect for the laws of Congress—including its Reconstruction acts enfranchising black men—counted among the "obligations under which we were placed by the terms of our paroles" at Appomattox. Longstreet repeated his earlier formulation—that his appointment as customs surveyor in 1869 came from "the bigness of [Grant's] generous heart."[49]

In the final paragraph of Longstreet's memoir, he called to mind a former slave, his "old nurse" Daniel, who resided, along with other freedmen and women once owned by the Longstreet family, in Macon, Mississippi, and who "called on" Longstreet whenever the old general visited that town. During Longstreet's last visit, he explained in the memoir, Daniel, "who still claims the family name, but at times uses another," had seemed more concerned about his well-being than ever, and had asked Longstreet if he belonged to a church. Longstreet replied "I try to be a good Christian." Daniel "laughed loud and long, and said—'Something must have scared you mighty bad, to change you so from what you was when I had to care for you.'" The last two lines of the memoir read: "In a recent letter [Daniel] sent me a message to say that he is getting to be a little feeble. Blessings on his brave heart!"[50]

The anecdote about Daniel seems at first glance the kind of paternalistic sentimental cant that Lost Cause defenders of slavery, waxing nostalgic about the days before emancipation and about the affection and loyalty of their "servants," so often trafficked in. But when read in context, following as it does Longstreet's contrast between the bitter "animus" of his "latterday" Confederate critics and the openhearted generosity of Grant, another layer of meaning to the Daniel story becomes visible. Longstreet ascribed to Daniel some of the "moral courage" he ascribed to Grant: the impulse to forgiveness.[51]

Reception of the Memoir

Longstreet's campaign to fashion himself as a fair-minded arbiter and symbol of sectional reconciliation paid off in critical acclaim. Northern reviewers heaped praise on Longstreet for offering an account "so well supported by argument and evidence," as the *Milwaukee Journal* put it. The midwestern journalist Murat Halstead commented that "the value of Longstreet's journal is greatly enhanced by the value of impartiality": Longstreet had told the truth about the likes of Davis and Lee "not with petty animosity, but the solemnity of competent judgment." Generally northern reviewers did not see the book as hostile to Lee, but instead as evidence of Longstreet's "real admiration for Lee as a man and as a General." Northern reviewers delighted in Longstreet's portrayal of Grant, and accepted Longstreet's argument that the two men's friendship, rather than partisanship or ambition, provided the impetus for Longstreet's political career: "The modest office of Surveyor of Customs was bestowed upon him by Gen. Grant unasked, moved by his personal generosity," a review in *The Nation* noted.[52]

In short, northern reviews generally reflected back to Longstreet the reconciliationist image he tried to project, and confirmed his sense that the time was right for his literary offering. Writing of his memoir that "it will tend to hasten the era of good fellowship," the *Morning Democrat* of Davenport, Iowa, quoted Longstreet's opening paean to the "patriotism in all Americans" as representative of the "fine fraternal spirit" in which the book was written. "Of the old sectional bitterness there is not a trace in this book," claimed a review in the *Buffalo Evening News:* "It was indeed fortunate, as the author himself thinks, that he abandoned a design of former years and waited till that bitterness was a thing of the past before he told his story." The *Philadelphia Times,* for its part, which had done so much to launch Longstreet's defense back in 1877, commented that since his memoir was "written at a later period than any of the other important works from the leading generals of both sides, it [was] evidently more free from passion, prejudice and insensibly conceived errors than any of them."[53]

Indeed, some reviewers seemed disappointed that Longstreet's account was not more caustic. The *New York Tribune* was clearly chagrined by Longstreet's choice to offer a detailed campaign history rather than an extended polemic, commenting that "it would have been vastly more effective if those portions which are general had been strictly subordinated to the personal narrative. Then every point on which General Longstreet differs from his literary adversaries, most of whom were his companions in arms, would have been plain to the reader. As it is, many of them must escape attention until renewed criticism brings them into prominence."[54]

Predictably, though, Longstreet's literary adversaries swiftly mobilized to make sure no point of controversy escaped attention—they simply would not accept that the memoir had any veracity or merit. Fitzhugh Lee, Walter H. Taylor, and J. William Jones led the way with a host of others following, in articles with titles like "Longstreet a Traitor," "Longstreet's Book of Malice," and "Setting Longstreet Straight." Their aim was to arraign Longstreet for slandering Lee. Fitzhugh Lee mused that "advancing years have made [Longstreet's] memory vague" on Lee's record and that "proven facts" contradicted the memoir's claims. Taylor, taking issue with Longstreet's "until enough blood was shed to appease him" phrase, accused him of depicting Lee "to the world as an insatiate, cruel and bloodthirsty monster," and threatened that such a charge "will but recoil with crushing force on him who made it or approved it." Jones, for his part, commented that Lee's only fault was "that he allowed his tender feelings for his 'old war horse' to prevent him from putting Longstreet under arrest and cashiering him for disobedience of orders." Seeking to dispel the image of Longstreet as a "meek martyr," Jones charged that Longstreet himself had kept the controversy alive, fuming that "ever since Longstreet became a Republican, a partisan Republican press has labored to make him the great general on the Confederate side, and to exalt him at Lee's expense." Jones and his cabal started unfounded rumors that Longstreet's editorial helper P. J. Moran had a major hand in writing the memoir and that Moran was an untrustworthy Yankee who served as "an officer in a negro regiment." And they took aim too at War Department historian Leslie J. Perry, accusing him of "garbl[ing] the official record and adroitly manipulat[ing] the facts" with his "prejudices and unsound theories."[55]

Such critiques illustrate how inimical Longstreet's theme of forgiveness was to the Lost Cause creed. Adherents of that creed were not disposed either to offer repentance for the Confederacy's sins or to extend forgiveness to their political enemies. Even those prominent Confederate veterans, such as Edward Porter Alexander, who were relatively forthright in their appraisals of Longstreet's military record and of Lee's, were unwilling to forgive Longstreet for what they considered the worst of his excesses. As Alexander wrote, reflecting on Longstreet's memoir, Longstreet's "*great* mistake was not in the *war* but in some of his awkward & apparently bitter criticism of Gen Lee in his own book. One instance you will find on page 384 where he says that Lee was off his balance 'until enough blood was shed to appease him.' Many an old soldier will *never forgive* Longstreet such a sentiment."[56]

Many other southern critics reminded readers of Longstreet's political apostasy during Reconstruction. A Tennessean quoted in the Memphis press opined that Longstreet was "simply a renegade of the same class as Mahone and Mosby, and has received from the people of the South the same contempt that has been shown to the few Confederate renegades. For the sake of a federal position he deserted his cause." A Wilmington, North Carolina, paper professed pity for Longstreet, as he "behaved badly after the war and alienated hundreds of thousands of the strong and faithful men of the South." It added: "Every time he writes he makes it harder to forget the past and withhold censure. . . . It is pitiable to see the gangrene of jealousy so punishing an old veteran." A few southern newspapers picked up on Longstreet's closing anecdote featuring his former slave Daniel, recounting it under the headline "Privileged Darky Makes Caustic Remark to Gen. Longstreet."[57]

As much as they postured as champions of the region, these critics did not speak for all white southerners. Lippincott advertised and sold the memoir in the South, and found willing agents and promoters for it, including among Confederate veterans. Col. A. W. Moore, for example, the "special agent" in charge of selling the book in Virginia and the Carolinas, offered buyers testimonials from three former Confederate generals—John D. Kennedy, John Hagood, and John Bratton—vouching that Longstreet's memoir was a valuable first-hand account that "should be in the library of every Southerner." A few positive reviews from southern periodicals ran counter to the stream of negative reviews. Richmond, Virginia, lawyer and scholar S. S. P. Patteson, for example, published a praiseworthy commentary in the literary magazine the *Sewanee Review* of May 1896, calling Longstreet's memoir a "serious military history" which "every Southern man who loves fair play will hail with delight." Patteson attributed the unkind reviews Longstreet had received in the South to the still prevalent belief that his "change of politics . . . tended to endanger white supremacy." But Patteson urged readers to value the book for its revealing perspective on military events.[58]

Fittingly, the *Atlanta Constitution* took the lead in promoting the book among white southerners. In two lengthy reviews—one by Joel Chandler Harris's son Julian Harris, an up-and-coming editor, and the other by P. J. Moran—the *Constitution* praised both the historical value and literary merit of *From Manassas to Appomattox*. Harris took a somewhat critical line, saying that the memoir was marred in places by "apparent bitterness." But he concluded that "there is very little that demands a sweeping condemnation when the history is viewed without prejudice." In emphasizing that Lee had assumed responsibility for Gettysburg (Lee had said famously "It is all my fault"), Longstreet had "brought out the grandeur of Lee's character." Lee, in his generous acceptance of blame, had testified to humanity's fallibility: "who could not love a man like that?," Harris asked. In the final analysis, Harris found the memoir "well worth reading" and "written in a fine style."[59]

Moran, for his part, in a March 29, 1896, *Constitution* article that both reviewed the memoir and gave Longstreet the chance to answer his critics, emphasized its reconciliationist elements. The book, Moran editorialized, "discards the political interests which led to the war and deals with its military features almost exclusively." Longstreet obligingly seconded that interpretation, telling Moran, "In writing this book of the war I was dealing with a congenial subject and one which should be a matter of pride to every American heart. While it portrays the struggle of two contending armies, both of American birth and lineage, it holds them up as the highest ideals to be found in military history, and no matter to what side the reader may belong, he cannot but feel a pride that these high-minded and brave men were his countrymen."[60]

In the interest of promoting Confederate reconciliation, this review/interview had Longstreet again emphasizing his strong bond with Lee—the way that Lee had continued to repose trust in him after Gettysburg, and the fact that Lee had refrained from any critique of Longstreet's war record. Trying to give his fellow southerners a window into his own motivations, Longstreet told Moran that the memoir was "a book about the future." "My thought always was that the south should try to build up and recover somewhat of that she lost."[61]

This was the *Constitution*'s story, and in the years between the publication of the memoir and Longstreet's death in 1904, Moran and Longstreet's other "New South" defenders stuck to it. In an 1898 article subtitled "The Old Warhorse Who Stood by General Lee," Moran wrote that Longstreet's memoir had paid the "highest possible military tribute" to Lee not by "slobbering over him" but instead by "giving his true measurement with military exactness and historic accuracy." When President McKinley appointed Longstreet to the federal patronage position of US railroad commissioner (replacing the popular Confederate veteran and Democratic appointee Wade Hampton), some southern Democrats strenuously objected, but the *Constitution* defended the appointment. The objections, as the Senate confirmation debates revealed, focused both on Longstreet's record as an "oppressor of his people" in New Orleans (especially at Liberty Place in 1874), and "his criticism of General Lee in his book on the war," as Virginia's Senator John W. Daniel specified. The *Constitution* by contrast chose to cast the appointment as "gratifying to the many friends of that superb old soldier." Noting that the appointment followed on the heels of his marriage, in August 1897, to Helen Dortch (forty-two years his junior), the *Constitution* "most heartily" extended Longstreet a "double measure of congratulation." The Senate finally confirmed Longstreet by a vote of 31 to 15, with Georgia's Democratic senator Augustus Bacon voting in favor on the grounds that "disagreements which succeeded the war and the friction which resulted therefrom should be forgotten." As it turned out, Longstreet's tour of duty as railroad commissioner, which required him to travel extensively in the West on his tours of inspection, only increased his national visibility and popularity.[62]

The surge in Longstreet's popularity reached its apogee in January of 1904, when he passed away at age 87, succumbing to a combination of pneumonia, cancer of the eye, and the lingering effects of his old wartime throat wound. Thousands of mourners and well-wishers marched in his funeral procession in Gainesville, Georgia; church bells tolled, battle flags waved, and Longstreet was given full military honors, his casket bedecked in the American and Confederate flags. Tributes poured forth from the press and from veterans in the North and the South. In northern eyes Longstreet was a prophetic patriot who "put himself at once where all now stand,—on the broad, high ground of American citizenship," as the *New York Journal* put it. Anti-Confederate southerners also sang his praises: the *Southwestern Christian Advocate,* the organ of black Methodists, observed in its notice of Longstreet's passing that "he has been accused of disobeying Gen. Lee's orders at the Battle of Gettysburg, but the charge was so emphatically and success-fully refuted that it would seem none but the most prejudiced believe it."[63]

Those ex-Confederates who wanted to claim Longstreet could at last do so without having to blunt his continued prominence in Republican poli-tics. Naturally, the *Constitution* led the way in eulogizing him, recalling his wartime heroism and his 1886 reunion in Atlanta with Jefferson Davis. But to an unprecedented degree, other southern whites followed. Most south-ern papers chose to explain away, set aside, or forgive Longstreet's political choices. "Now that the stout warrior is dead and gone to eternal judgment," the *Vicksburg Herald* intoned in a typical formulation, "all should speak of his virtues, his glorious deeds of arms, without thought or reference to that sad error of judgment that, no smaller in its intent and inception than 'a man's hand,' grew to a dark cloud between Longstreet and his people." "Let the Dead Lion sleep in peace," the *Birmingham Ledger* of Alabama proclaimed. "The heroic Longstreet needs no higher eulogy than the single phrase, He was the friend of Grant and Lee." Many Confederate veterans joined in this chorus. As one First Corps veteran told the *Savannah Morning News,* the fact that Longstreet "was made collector of customs at the port of New Orleans by Gen. Grant is by no means remarkable or to be construed as proof that he was false to the South, for Longstreet and Grant had been friends before the war was begun."[64]

And yet, despite all of this eulogizing, it remained clear that Confederate reconciliation had not been fully achieved. Controversy would continue to swirl over Longstreet, as he and other prominent veterans who had com-peted for military laurels and political influence during their lifetimes were brandished, in their afterlives, as symbols and icons in partisan combat and in memory wars. A considerable number of holdouts rejected or resisted reconciliation-tinged efforts to lionize Longstreet. Opposition persisted in Richmond, where, as William Garrett Piston has noted, "the *Southern His-torical Society Papers* continued to print bitterly anti-Longstreet articles up to the eve of the First World War." It persisted, too, in New Orleans, where annual commemoration of the September 14, 1874, battle of Liberty Place brought forth waves of invective against Longstreet as one of the "hench-men" of the Radicals, trying to fasten the "despotism of negro supremacy" onto Louisiana whites.[65]

Confederate memorial culture continued to marginalize Longstreet. The Savannah chapter of the United Daughters of the Confederacy, for example, pointedly refused to send a laurel wreath to Longstreet's graveside (to the eternal disgust of Helen Dortch Longstreet); this refusal accorded with the UDC's campaign to tell the "true" history of the Confederacy, focused on Lee's infallibility and the failures of his subordinates. Revealingly, when John Brown Gordon died, within a week after Longstreet's death, in January of 1904, Confederate veterans' organizations and publications lavished much more praise on him than they had on his political rival Longstreet. Gordon, in his 1903 *Reminiscences of the Civil War* and in an article on Gettysburg drawn from the book, had renewed the attacks on Longstreet's wartime record, blaming him for losing the battle that might have won the war. Coinciding as they did, the two men's deaths invited a new round of assessments and comparisons. "Thousands and thousands more people of the South will grieve because of the death of Gen. Gordon than for Gen. Longstreet," a letter to the editor of the *Macon Telegraph* pronounced on January 13, 1904, for when during Reconstruction "it became a question of [the] negro or white man," Longstreet had chosen the "negro side of the fence" while Gordon "knew the current of thought in the masses" and "chose the popular way," and was thus able to do "more as a national harmonizer than Gen. Longstreet."[66]

Fearing that it would prove easier than ever to scapegoat a man who could no longer defend himself, Longstreet's young wife Helen Dortch stepped forward to do literary battle with his adversaries, writing and self-publishing her own account of his life. Her 1904 tome *Lee and Longstreet at High Tide* built on Longstreet's 1895 memoir, foregrounding his intimacy with both Lee and Grant. Its introduction, by former Union general Dan Sickles, described Longstreet as the "rainbow of reconciliation that foreshadowed real peace between the North and South." But Helen Longstreet's contempt for her husband's ex-Confederate detractors was palpable, and unsparing. In a message directed at her late husband, she conjured the depths of the divisions that continued to roil the South. "I would tell him," she wrote, that "his unmatched courage to meet the enemies of the peace time outshines the valor of the fields whereon his blood was shed so copiously in the cause of his country. I would tell him that his detractors are not the South; they are not the Democratic Party; they represent nobody and nothing but the blindness of passion that desires not light." No clasping of hands would seal the partisan breach that Helen referred to, and the memory wars over Longstreet's image would rage on, through Helen Longstreet's lifetime (she died in 1962) and beyond.[67]

Modern-day scholars, for their part, have readily acknowledged the historical significance of *From Manassas to Appomattox*. Longstreet's tome has had an impressive shelf life: since its original appearance in 1895, the memoir has been reprinted often and regularly, initially by Lippincott and eventually in scholarly editions with historians providing annotation and context. The most recent such edition, published in the spring of 2020 by Indiana University Press, provides a revealing window into historians' shifting assessments of Longstreet as a memoirist. The 2020 edition is a reprint of Indiana University Press's 1960 edition, which had featured an introduction by James I. Robertson Jr., then one of the leading Civil War historians in the nation. Robertson purported, in his framing of the memoir, to find a middle ground between the "slanderous" critiques offered by H. J. Eckenrode and Bryan Conrad in their 1936 Longstreet biography and the "eulogistic" take of Sanger and Hay, in their 1952 two-part biography. But Robertson nonetheless depicted Longstreet as an embittered and pathetic figure, observing that as a writer, "Longstreet proved his own worst enemy. The more he wrote, the more bitter he became." Robertson drew on the views of the renowned Lee scholar Douglas Southall Freeman, who described Longstreet the memoirist as "an old man, soured by failure."[68]

The 2020 edition of the memoir retains the Robertson introduction but adds a brief foreword by historian Christian B. Keller of the US Army War College. As Keller notes, in the decades that elapsed since the 1960 edition, scholars have continued to debate the veracity and effectiveness of *From Manassas to Appomattox*. The historian Robert Krick has taken the harshest line (describing the memoir as "mean-spirited" and Longstreet himself as "small minded"), and been challenged by Longstreet defenders such as Cory M. Pfarr, who accuse Old Pete's modern critics of perpetuating an older tradition of Lee worship. In between these interpretive extremes, modern biographers such as William Garrett Piston and Jeffry D. Wert have aimed at a historiographical "rebalancing," as Keller puts it: they have tried to move beyond Lost Cause myths and the blame-game to use Longstreet as a window into Confederate defeat and its legacies. In the spirit of rebalancing, Keller himself acknowledges Longstreet's "penchant for self-justification" but emphasizes that Longstreet was "far from alone in evaluating his experiences in the war through a personal lens." Keller praises both Longstreet's "eye for detail" and his "ability to see the big picture."[69]

What all of the existing scholarship on Longstreet has had in common, across this spectrum of opinion, is a preoccupation with the Gettysburg controversies and a tendency to overlook the other themes and broader meaning of *From Manassas to Appomattox*. It was not Gettysburg, and the endless interpretive strife over it, that lay at the heart of Longstreet's memoir, but instead Appomattox, with its promise of a lasting peace founded in the kind of forgiveness Grant had extended to Longstreet, and the gratitude Longstreet had offered in return.

NOTES

1. James Longstreet, *From Manassas to Appomattox* (1896; reprint, New York: Da Capo Press, 1992), xv.

2. William Garrett Piston, *Lee's Tarnished Lieutenant: James Longstreet and His Place in Southern History* (Athens: University of Georgia Press, 1987), 166–69; Jeffry D. Wert, *General James Longstreet: The Confederacy's Most Controversial Soldier* (New York: Simon & Schuster, 1993), 412–13, 418–19, 423–27; Donald Bridgman Sanger and Thomas Robson Hay, *James Longstreet: I. Soldier; II. Politician, Officeholder, and Writer* (Baton Rouge: Louisiana State University Press, 1952), 400, 433–36; Cory M. Pfarr, *Longstreet at Gettysburg: A Critical Reassessment* (Jefferson, NC: McFarland, 2019), 180–83.

3. *New Orleans Times,* March 18, 1867. On Longstreet's Reconstruction years, see the relevant chapters in Wert, *General James Longstreet;* Piston, *Lee's Tarnished Lieutenant;* and Sanger and Hay, *James Longstreet.*

4. On political conflict and violence in New Orleans in these years, see James K. Hogue, *Uncivil War: Five New Orleans Street Battles and the Rise and Fall of Radical Reconstruction* (Baton Rouge: Louisiana State University Press, 2006).

5. Wert, *General James Longstreet,* 422–23; Piston, *Lee's Tarnished Lieutenant,* 118–23.

6. *Dallas Herald* in *Lake Charles Echo* (LA), October 10, 1874. On Longstreet's image as a race traitor in the South in the mid-1870s, see for example *Calhoun Weekly Times* (GA), April 23, 1873; *Talbotton Standard* (GA), July 30, 1873; and Macon's *Georgia Weekly Telegraph and Georgia Journal & Messenger,* September 22, 1874. On the connections between his political and military reputation, see for example *The Southern Home* (Charlotte, NC), March 24, 1873, and *Wheeling Daily Register* (WV), April 19, 1873.

7. *Chicago Tribune,* January 29, 1871; Wert, *General James Longstreet,* 422; *Richmond Dispatch,* June 18, 1873; *Inter Ocean* (Chicago), July 16, 1875. Taylor, Venable, and Marshall, when pressed by Longstreet, all conceded that they had no recollection of a sunrise order—but they supported the idea that Longstreet's delays on July 2 had cost the Confederates the battle. See Thomas W. Cutrer, ed., *Longstreet's Aide: The Civil War Letters of Major Thomas J. Goree* (Charlottesville: University Press of Virginia, 1995), 229–30.

8. *New Orleans Republican,* January 25, 1876.

9. *Alexandria Gazette,* February 4, March 18, 1876; *New Orleans Republican,* March 26, 1876.

10. David Blight, *Race and Reunion: The Civil War in American Memory* (Cambridge, MA: Harvard University Press, 2001), 164; Piston, *Lee's Tarnished Lieutenant,* 131; Alexander McClure, *Colonel Alexander K. McClure's Recollections of Half a Century* (Salem, MA: Salem Press, 1902), 399–400.

11. McClure, *Recollections,* 399–400.

12. Blight, *Race and Reunion,* 158–60; Early, "Letter from Gen. J. A. Early," *Southern Historical Society Papers* 4 (August 1877): 50–68 [hereafter cited as *SHSP*].

13. *Philadelphia Weekly Times,* November 3, 1877, reprinted as "General Longstreet's Account of the Campaign and Battle," *SHSP* 5 (January 1878): 54–86.

14. Pfarr, *Longstreet at Gettysburg,* 22–23; "General Longstreet's Second Paper on Gettysburg," *SHSP* 5 (June 1878): 257–69. For a detailed analysis of Lee's choice of the tactical offensive on July 2, see Gary W. Gallagher, "'If the Enemy is There, We Must Attack Him': R. E. Lee and the Second Day at Gettysburg," in Gallagher, ed., *The Second Day at Gettysburg: Essays on Confederate and Union Leadership* (Kent, OH: Kent State University Press, 1993), 1–32.

15. John Walter Fairfax to Longstreet, November 12, 1877, John Walter Fairfax Papers, Virginia Historical Society, Richmond. On Fairfax during Reconstruction, see *New Orleans Republican,* January 14, 1872, and February 24, 1874. A few other prominent former Confederates who had served under Longstreet—most notably the Texan Tom Ochiltree and the Louisianan W. B. Merchant—joined the Republican Party and defended both Longstreet's wartime service and his postwar politics. On Ochiltree, see Claude D. Hall, "The Fabulous Tom Ochiltree: Promoter, Politician, and Raconteur," *Southwestern Historical Quarterly* 71 (January 1968): 347–76. On Merchant, see for example *New Orleans Republican,* August 1, 1871.

16. Thomas Jewett Goree to Longstreet, May 17, 1875, in Cutrer, ed., *Longstreet's Aide,* 158. On Alexander, see Gary W. Gallagher, ed., *Fighting for the Confederacy: The Personal Recollections of General Edward Porter Alexander* (Chapel Hill: University of North Carolina Press, 1989), 96, 110, 245, 252; on Sorrel, see G. Moxley Sorrel, *At the Right Hand of Longstreet: Recollections of a Confederate Staff Officer* (Lincoln: University of Nebraska Press, 1999).

17. Jubal A. Early, "Leading Confederates on the Battle of Gettysburg: A Review by General Early," *SHSP* 4 (December 1877): 241–302; "Reply to General Longstreet's Second Paper," *SHSP* 5 (June 1878): 270–87; *Galveston Daily News,* December 23, 1877; *Montgomery Advertiser,* November 18, 1877; *Daily American* (Nashville, TN), December 14, 1877; *Intelligencer* (Anderson, SC), January 31, 1878.

18. Blight, *Race and Reunion,* 158–60; Piston, *Lee's Tarnished Lieutenant,* 144–45.

19. William A. Link, *Atlanta, Cradle of the New South: Race and Remembering in the Civil War's Aftermath* (Chapel Hill: University of North Carolina Press, 2013), 150–53 (quotation on 152); Daniel Joseph Singal, *The War Within: From Victorian to Modernist Thought in the South, 1919–1945* (Chapel Hill: University of North Carolina Press, 1982), 47; Edward Ayers, *The Promise of the New South: Life after Reconstruction* (New York: Oxford University Press, 1992), 21; Blight, *Race and Reunion,* 200 (Grady quotation); Harold E. Davis, "Henry W. Grady, Master of the Atlanta Ring, 1880–1886," *Georgia Historical Quarterly* 69 (Spring 1985): 1–38.

20. *Savannah Advertiser* in *Atlanta Constitution,* February 11, 1875.

21. *Atlanta Constitution,* January 2 (Hill quotation), 5, February 18, March 29, 1882; John E. Talmadge, "The Death Blow to Independentism in Georgia," *Georgia Historical Quarterly* 39 (March 1955): 46 (last quotation).

22. *Atlanta Constitution,* November 3, 1877; *Philadelphia Times,* July 27, 1879.

23. *Atlanta Constitution,* May 25, 1880; *New York World* in *Columbus Daily Enquirer-Sun,* May 25, 1883.

24. *Atlanta Constitution,* January 15, 1888. On images of Longstreet as a Radical tool, see for example *Savannah Morning News,* October 27, 1881, *Bainbridge Democrat* (GA), August 24, 1882, and *Banner-Watchman* (Athens, GA), April 1, 1884. The enmity between Davis and Longstreet was exacerbated by the publication of Davis's 1881 *The Rise and Fall of the Confederate Government,* which Longstreet roundly criticized in the press. See for example his *New York Herald* and *Philadelphia Press* interviews (reprinted in the *Daily Memphis Avalanche,* June 23 and July 10, 1881).

25. James Longstreet, "The Seven Days' Fighting about Richmond," *Century* 30 (July 1885): 469–77; "Our March Against Pope," *Century* 31 (February 1886): 601–14; "The Invasion of Maryland," *Century* 32 (June 1886): 309–15; "The Battle of Fredericksburg," *Century* 32 (August 1886): 609–26; "Lee's Invasion of Pennsylvania," *Century* 33 (February 1887): 622–36.

26. *Charleston Courier and News* as quoted in *Alexandria Gazette,* July 13, 1885.

27. For example, in an 1880 interview Longstreet said, "To me the surrender of my sword was my reconstruction. I looked upon the 'Lost Cause' as a cause totally, irrevocably lost." (*New York Times,* Feb. 22, 1880.) In the *Washington Post* in July 1881, Longstreet had recounted the Ord episode, lamenting that "a little diplomacy at that time would have ended the war and been of unquestionable advantage to both sections of the country." (*Washington Post,* July 6, 1881.) See *Daily Inter Ocean,* July 10, 1893 ("nobody but the politicians" quotation); Joan Waugh, *U. S. Grant: American Hero, American Myth* (Chapel Hill: University of North Carolina Press, 2009), 237, 239, 240.

28. *New York Times,* July 24, 1885; *Philadelphia Times,* May 15, 1892.

29. *Vicksburg Herald* (MS), December 18, 1887; *St. Louis Globe-Democrat,* September 8, 1887; *Washington Post,* May 21, 1894.

30. *Atlanta Constitution,* July 6, 1888; *New York Times,* January 12, 1890; *New Orleans Daily Picayune,* July 13, 1892. On Moran's reputation, see for example *Macon Telegraph* (GA), March 12, 1892.

31. *Washington Post,* June 11, August 2, 1893; Carroll Free Press (Carrollton, GA), August 4, 1893 (reprint of Maury letter). On the 1870 celebration, see *New Orleans Republican,* May 4, 1870.

32. *Washington Post,* August 2, 1893, May 21, 1894; *New Orleans Times-Democrat,* June 15, 1893.

33. *Milwaukee Sentinel,* September 20, 1895; Link, *Atlanta, Cradle of the New South,* 164; *Atlanta Constitution,* September 22, 1895.

34. Piston, *Lee's Tarnished Lieutenant,* 141, 157, 163–65; Cutrer, ed., *Longstreet's Aide,* 176–77.

35. Longstreet interview with *St. Louis Globe-Democrat,* reprinted in *Atlanta Constitution,* June 11, 1890. On Perry, see for example *Daily Charlotte Observer* (NC), June 18, 1893, and

Philadelphia Inquirer, November 13, 1895. On the *Official Records* (commonly referred to as the *OR*), see Yael A. Sternhell, "The Afterlives of a Confederate Archive: Civil War Documents and the Making of Sectional Reconciliation," *Journal of American History* 102 (March 2016): 10, 26–27.

36. *Washington Star,* October 12, 1895; *Atlanta Constitution,* October 15, 1895. Longstreet's memoir carries a copyright date of 1895 and publication date of 1896. As Wert explains, "Longstreet expected publication by Christmas 1895, but it was delayed at the printers until early in 1896. (Wert, *General James Longstreet,* 423.) On Longstreet at the Union League, see *North American* (Philadelphia), September 30, 1895. On sale of the book by subscription, see for example *Boston Globe,* October 13, 1895; *Harrisburg Telegraph,* December 24, 1895.

37. Longstreet, *From Manassas to Appomattox* [hereafter *FMTA*], xvi–xvii.

38. Longstreet, *FMTA,* 17.

39. *FMTA,* 39, 54, 152, 196, 283–84 (quotation), 288–89. Taking issue with the "overwhelming numbers" interpretation of Confederate defeat, Longstreet indicated in an October 26, 1895, public letter on his book's purposes that "To claim that the people went apart from the union to embark in a hopeless cause will be to put them in a false light in order to conceal individual indiscretions, for events have illustrated reasonable hope of success." (*Galveston Daily News,* November 9, 1895.)

40. *FMTA,* 159 (second quotation), 220 (first quotation), 288 (third quotation); Baron Henri de Jomini, *The Art of War* (Philadelphia: Lippincott, 1862), 38, 51, 56–65. For a previous reference by Longstreet to the "art of war," see for example *Morning Oregonian* (Portland), July 5, 1893.

41. *FMTA,* 92.

42. *FMTA,* 330; Cathal J. Nolan, *The Allure of Battle: A History of How Wars Have Been Won and Lost* (New York: Oxford University Press, 2017), 4–13 (quotation on 13).

43. *FMTA,* 362, 384; *Philadelphia Weekly Times,* November 3, 1877 ("matchless equipoise" quotation); Longstreet, "The Seven Days," 477; *National Tribune* (Washington, DC), October 3, 1895. In Longstreet's view, another such occasion on which Lee lost his balance was in the Wilderness on May 6, 1864, when Lee, in the excitement of battle, began moving into the line of fire with an advancing brigade, only to be summoned back to relative safety by Longstreet and others. (*Philadelphia Times,* July 27, 1879.) On equipoise, see *St. Louis Globe-Democrat,* July 1, 1887 (Sherman quotation); Alfred Thayer Mahan, *The Life of Nelson: The Embodiment of the Sea Power of Great Britain,* vol. 1 (London: Sampson Low, Martston, 1897), 680; Theodore Ayrault Dodge, *Napoleon: A History of the Art of War* (Boston: Houghton Mifflin, 1907), 4:684.

44. *Philadelphia Weekly Times,* November 3, 1877; *FMTA,* 384, 401, 405; Lee's and Early's own assessments of blame at Gettysburg were more complex than Longstreet let on. In his postwar conversations with William Allan, Lee specifically singled out Stuart and Ewell for criticism, though he spoke more generally of "the imperfect, halting way in which his corps commanders (especially Ewell) fought the battle." See Gary W. Gallagher, *Lee the Soldier* (Lincoln: University of Nebraska Press, 1996), 13–14. Early's own large memoir, not published until 1912, had been completed by 1866 and contained almost none of the anti-Longstreet bias so evident in Early's later speeches and writings. See Jubal A. Early, *Lieutenant General*

Jubal Anderson Early C.S.A.: Autobiographical Sketch and Narrative of War between the States (Philadelphia: J. B. Lippincott, 1912).

45. *FMTA*, 456 (first quotation), 466 (second quotation), 468 (third quotation). See also Wert, *General James Longstreet*, 300, 311, 321 323, 329 (fourth quotation), 486.

46. *FMTA*, 486, 541 (quotation); Earl J. Hess, *The Knoxville Campaign: Burnside and Longstreet in East Tennessee* (Knoxville: University of Tennessee Press, 2012).

47. *FMTA*, 534 (third quotation), 551 (first quotation), 566 (second quotation). Longstreet's assessment of Grant on April 2, 1864, in a letter to Lee is at odds with much of the postwar material Longstreet produced: "If Grant goes to Virginia I hope that you may be able to destroy him. I do not think that he is any better than Pope. They won their successes in the same field. If you will outgeneral him you will surely destroy him. His chief strength is in his prestige." US War Department, *The War of the Rebellion: The Official Records of the Union and Confederate Armies*, 127 vols., index, and atlas (Washington, DC: GPO, 1880–1901), ser. 1, vol. 32, pt. 3:737.

48. *FMTA*, 568–69 (quotation on 568), 583–85, 620–21.

49. *FMTA*, 625–28, 634 (first quotation), 637 (second quotation). The biblical verse Longstreet alluded to is from Luke 7:47, KJV.

50. *FMTA*, 638.

51. Daniel had been born in Georgia and moved with Longstreet's widowed mother Mary Ann Dent Longstreet, to Macon, Mississippi, after her husband died; he appears as Daniel Johnson, age 50, in the 1870 census records for Noxubee County, Mississippi, where he worked as a farm laborer, and as Dan Longstreet ten years later in the 1880 census. The Mississippi Longstreets included the AME minister and ardent Republican J. W. Longstreet, who served as a party delegate at state conventions. (Census Records, 1870 and 1880, accessed through Ancestry.com.) On J. W. Longstreet, see for example *Weekly Mississippi Pilot* (Jackson, MS), September 18, 1875, and *Clarion-Ledger* (Jackson, MS), May 12, 1880.

52. Piston, *Lee's Tarnished Lieutenant*, 166; *Milwaukee Journal*, March 28, 1896, *Daily Leader* (Lexington, KY), March 3, 1896 (Halstead quotation); *The Nation*, February 13, 1896, p. 164.

53. *Morning Democrat* (Davenport, IA), February 2, 1896; *Buffalo Evening News*, January 22, 1896; *Philadelphia Times*, January 12, 1896.

54. *New York Tribune*, March 18, 1896.

55. *Commercial Appeal* (Memphis, TN), October 29, December 22, 1895 (Jones quotation); *Wilmington Messenger* (NC), January 24, 1896; *Weekly News & Courier* (Charleston, SC), March 11 (Lee and Taylor quotations), June 24, 1896; *Richmond Dispatch*, February 16, 1896 (second Jones quotation). On Moran, see William W. Hassler, "The 'Ghost' of General Longstreet," *Georgia Historical Quarterly* 65 (Spring 1981): 24–25. On criticism of Perry by Jones and others, see *Commercial Appeal* (Memphis, TN), December 22, 1896, and *Daily Commercial Herald* (Vicksburg, MS), August 13, 1895. As he acknowledges in its preface, Longstreet also received editorial assistance in his manuscript revisions from Alfred Matthews, a Philadelphia-based freelance writer and editor who published essays in the popular journals of the era on subjects such as the settlement of the Midwest and railroad construction. (*FMTA*, xvii; *Philadelphia Times*, January 11, 1902.)

56. E. P. Alexander to Mr. Bancroft, October 30, 1904, James Longstreet Papers, 1850–1904, Stuart A. Rose Manuscript, Archives, and Rare Book Library, Emory University, Atlanta,

Georgia. On northern arguments that peace should be grounded in forgiveness and charity and the Lost Cause creed's inversion of those arguments, see Caroline E. Janney, *Remembering the Civil War: Reunion and the Limits of Reconciliation* (Chapel Hill: University of North Carolina Press, 2013), 173, 234, 259.

57. *Commercial Appeal* (Memphis, TN), October 29, 1895; *Wilmington Messenger* (NC), January 24, 1896. On the Daniel anecdote, see *Jennings Daily Times-Record* (Jennings, LA), October 28, 1903.

58. *Daily Charlotte Observer* (NC), April 29, 1896; *Wilmington Morning Star* (NC), May 8, 1896; S. S. P. Patteson, "Longstreet and the War between the States," *Sewanee Review* 4 (May 1896): 326, 328, 333.

59. *Atlanta Constitution,* January 26, 1896.

60. *Atlanta Constitution,* March 29, 1896.

61. *Atlanta Constitution*, March 29, 1896.

62. *Atlanta Constitution*, October 30, 1897, July 20, 1898; *Weekly Advertiser* (Montgomery, AL), April 9, 1897; *News & Observer* (Raleigh, NC), January 23, 1898; *Daily Picayune* (New Orleans, LA), January 24, 1898. On Longstreet in the West, see for example *Salt Lake Semi-Weekly Tribune,* August 23, 1898, and *Portland Oregonian,* September 6, 1898.

63. Helen D. Longstreet, *Lee and Longstreet at High Tide: Gettysburg in the Light of the Official Records* (Gainesville, GA: by the author, 1904), 242; *Southwestern Christian Advocate* (New Orleans, LA), January 14, 1904.

64. Longstreet, *Lee and Longstreet at High Tide,* 231, 238, 240, 242, 316, 342; *Savannah Morning News,* January 6, 1904. On Longstreet's funeral, see also Eugene Alvarez, "The Death of the 'Old War Horse' Longstreet," *Georgia Historical Quarterly* 52 (March 1968): 70–77.

65. Piston, *Lee's Tarnished Lieutenant,* 168–69, 172. On coverage of the Liberty Place anniversary, see for example *Daily Picayune,* September 14, 1899, and *Southern Sentinel* (Winnfield, LA), September 14, 1906.

66. Alvarez, "The Death of the 'Old War Horse,'" 74; Piston, *Lee's Tarnished Lieutenant,* 168–69, 172; *Macon Telegraph,* January 13, 1904.

67. Longstreet, *Lee and Longstreet at High Tide,* 90 (last quotation), 228, 235, 238–40, 310, 316, 317 (Sickles quotation).

68. Thomas W. Broadfoot, *Civil War Books: A Priced Checklist with Advice,* 5th edition (Wilmington, NC: Broadfoot Publishing, 2000) lists Lippincott editions from 1896, 1903, and 1912, the Indiana University Press reprint in 1960, and additional reprints in 1976, 1984, and 1985. For Robertson's introduction and Keller's foreword, see James Longstreet, *From Manassas to Appomattox,* ed. James I. Robertson Jr., with a foreword by Christian Keller (Bloomington: Indiana University Press, 2020), xxii–xxiv, xxxii. See also Robert K. Krick, "'If Longstreet . . . Says So, It Is Most Likely Not True': James Longstreet and the Second Day at Gettysburg," in Gary W. Gallagher, ed., *The Second Day at Gettysburg: Essays on Confederate and Union Leadership* (Kent, OH: Kent State University Press, 1993), 58, 85; Pfaff, *Longstreet at Gettysburg,* 15.

69. Keller Foreword to Longstreet, *From Manassas to Appomattox,* xxxii–xxxiii. In the midst of contemporary debates over Civil War memorialization, commentators such as Stephen A. Holmes and Charles Lane have noted that the absence of Longstreet monuments in the South is proof that Confederate statues were intended to be symbols of Lost Cause racial politics rather

than conventional war memorials. See Holmes's op-ed at https://www.cnn.com/2017/08/23 /opinions/where-are-monuments-to-confederate-general-longstreet-opinion-holmes/index .html and Lane's at https://www.washingtonpost.com/opinions/the-forgotten-confederate -general-who-would-make-a-better-subject-for-monuments/2016/01/27/f09bad42-c536-11e5 -8965-0607e0e265ce_story.html.

"The Honorable Henry Wilson of Massachusetts." Library of Congress, Prints and Photographs Division, reproduction number LC-DIG-cwpbh-00671.

A Modern Sensibility in Older Garb

Henry Wilson's Rise and Fall of the Slave Power *and the Beginnings of Civil War History*

WILLIAM A. BLAIR

Henry Wilson entered politics because he believed that America had a problem. Slavery was not declining as the Founders had hoped, but growing. It threatened to spill beyond state borders into newly acquired territories. To Wilson, this danger existed because southern slaveowners, although a minority of the population, had become a commanding power, especially in the national government where they dominated the presidency, the Supreme Court, and Congress. They sniffed out danger from afar, mobilized agents to act on their behalf, and guarded against anything remotely compromising their interests. They were antidemocratic and brutal. They censored abolition materials in the mails, refused to hear antislavery petitions in Congress, beat to a pulp a leading senator who disagreed with them, browbeat poorer whites of their section into submission, turned the government into abettors of the kidnappers of fugitives, and displayed in general the corruption and violence of men used to wielding the lash. In other words, they trampled on the Constitution, ignoring protections of freedom of speech and the right to petition. It seemed to Wilson as if some "imperious autocrat or secret conclave" conspired to spread slavery everywhere. What was this powerful combination that was centered in the South but had northern allies? Henry Wilson and his Republican colleagues captured this menace in three simple words—the Slave Power.[1]

Those three little words provided the intellectual basis for three fat volumes of history spanning more than 2,000 pages as Wilson charted how this Slave Power came into being and how it was broken. His monumental *The Rise and Fall of the Slave Power in America* first appeared in 1872 and took until 1877 to complete. Begun in the late 1860s, it was the work of nearly a decade—work that its author did not live to see completed. Critics generally gave the books a good reception, with most of them noting their chronological sweep from the establishment of slavery through Reconstruction. The set was among the first generation of multivolume histories of the period written by an author recognized as uniquely suited for the task.[2] A dedicated abolitionist, he served for more than two decades as a leader of the political antislavery movement, helping to found the Free Soil and Republican Parties, representing Massachusetts in the US Senate, chairing the important Military Affairs Committee during the war, and serving as vice president of the United States in Ulysses S. Grant's second term. He was a man of principle, dedicated to the antislavery cause out of moral concerns, yet he was, in the words of one biographer, a practical Radical who did not push beyond what he believed was legislatively achievable.[3]

This nineteenth-century man produced a work that, in its interpretations, is in many ways in synch with the histories written in the twenty-first century. Wilson represented the coming of the war as triggered by a power struggle over whether to contain or spread slavery, not as a battle over some ill-defined or unnamed state rights. Slave masters dragooned the southern states into secession and forced the firing upon Fort Sumter.[4] In Wilson's view, emancipation was the Civil War's greatest achievement—a conclusion upheld in many historians' works today. He showed surprising sympathy for Native Americans, characterizing their removal to west of the Mississippi as a plot to advance the land holdings of the Slave Power and their treatment in general as encounters "in which the principles of humanity, honesty, and fair dealing have been so completely ignored and trampled underfoot."[5] He described the Mexican War as a naked conquest to aid the spread of slavery, and Wilson cited a legislator who called it a disgrace to the national character. He tweaked American exceptionalism, arguing that the barbarism in the United States over the slave trade exceeded that of Africa and claiming that the nation practiced a despotism that would strike horror among the monarchists of Europe.[6]

Wilson also foreshadowed more recent studies of slavery by focusing on its brutality. Though his emphasis on the Slave Power tended to put the focus on the endangerment of white liberties in the North, he still managed to attack the evils of the plantation. Wilson flatly rejected the claim by opponents of abolition that allegations of violence against blacks were exaggerated. He offered a judgment that mirrored the title of a prominent modern book on slavery by saying, "The half was never told."[7] He even unabashedly portrayed the prejudice that existed in the North, including in his own state of Massachusetts, as he catalogued the discriminatory practices throughout much of the Free States that banned black voting, immigration of black people into states, riding with white people on public transportation, and serving on juries. Similarly, he admitted to lukewarm sentiments among many members of his Republican Party when it came to black rights, indicating that they did not all share in antislavery sentiment but dreaded the domination of the Slave Power more, as well as the possibility of a divided Union. "They would accept Abolition rather than disunion," he observed, "but they did not desire it."[8]

Perhaps most surprising was his use of the words "human rights" in a distinctly modern fashion. The language of rights had been coming into its own with the Enlightenment, and the American and French Revolutions. The term "human rights" emerged in the eighteenth and nineteenth centuries to capture the sense that human beings are born deserving of certain ways of living that cannot be infringed upon or trammeled by an oppressive power. The abolition movement around the Atlantic World provided one of the earlier examples of this new thought. But as modern historians of human rights have asserted, these early manifestations of the term did not necessarily refer to all groups of people, such as Native Americans, black Americans, or women.[9]

Yet Henry Wilson displayed a modern sensibility in his belief that all individuals were entitled to the same chance to succeed in life and that the way to advance was through Free Labor. More than many of his time, he gathered under the conceptual umbrella of human rights a broader group of people. He was a champion of workers whether white or black, during a time when workers' rights faced a stiff fight. He believed in an eight-hour workday. He wrote that Native Americans deserved better treatment than they had received from Anglo Americans. After the Civil War, he introduced legislation to eliminate debt peonage in New Mexico territory, another victory in the cause of Free Labor. And although he refused to support women's suffrage in the Fifteenth Amendment, believing the stand would jeopardize ratification, he did make an unsuccessful attempt at legislation to recognize the right of women to vote in the District of Columbia.[10]

Henry Wilson's upbringing reinforced a sympathy with workers and the oppressed. Wilson grew up hard. In fact, he did not start out life as a Wilson at all but as a boy named Jeremiah Jones Colbath. He was born into grinding poverty on February 16, 1812, in the village of Farmington, New Hampshire. His father was a day laborer feeling the economic pinch of the war with England, which had strained commerce throughout the region. Winthrop Colbath does not seem to have been talented as a worker; instead, he excelled at drinking. As eight children came along, food grew scarcer. The boy knew what hunger felt like. "Dreariness and tragedy filled their days," wrote one biographer.[11] The poverty and drinking by the father caused the family to indenture Jeremiah at the age of ten as a servant to a neighboring farmer, a situation that did not end until the young man reached the age of twenty-one.

Overcoming a start that could have held him back in life, he forged himself into a success story. He read voraciously, taking advantage of any opportunity to educate himself. At the age of twenty-one, once free of his indenture, he changed his name, ostensibly a reaction against his father. Why he chose Wilson remains a matter of speculation. Not surprisingly, he pledged himself to life as a teetotaler and supported temperance efforts, connecting him with a social reform movement that also drew many into the cause of antislavery. As a free man he sold the sheep and oxen pledged to him for his indenture and used the proceeds as a grubstake for his start in life. He moved to Natick, Massachusetts, where he learned the shoe trade and, through effort, rose to manage a shoe shop of his own. By 1847, he had grown the business to 109 employees turning out more than 120,000 pairs of shoes per year.[12] This background earned him the political nickname of the Natick Cobbler, which highlighted his working-class roots.

Wilson exemplified the Free Labor ideal espoused by Abraham Lincoln and other Republicans for what was supposed to happen in a country that valued work as the way to improve not only oneself but also society. Accumulation of wealth through labor was supposed to result in social mobility. People were to rise from common laborers to shopowners. They were to escape their initial dependency on wages and become independent. The goal, however, was not just to have pecuniary or personal advancement but to ensure that the person could exercise the power of the ballot virtuously and without outside influence. When he reached a level of prosperity that allowed him to give back to society, Wilson chose politics as his instrument. His years as an indentured servant gave him an appreciation for the plight of workers, and it seems natural in retrospect that he dedicated himself to a fight against an entity that was the opposite of Free Labor, the Slave Power.[13]

One turning point may have come came in 1836 as he journeyed south to Washington to try to recover from unspecified health problems. Wilson reportedly visited slave pens where he saw people manacled, separated, sold, and whipped. He also sat in on Congress and witnessed firsthand how the slaveholding class protected its interests. Overall, the excursion appears to have been a transformative moment. A friend who became a biographer wrote about this time: "His sympathies for the bondmen, his indignation against the cruel system of human traffic carried on hard by the Capitol of a nation boastful of its freedom, were re-awakened, so that he then and there determined, that, come weal or woe, the powers which God had given him should thenceforth be devoted to the destruction of an institution so revolting to every instinct of humanity, so inconsistent with the declaration of our national independence, and so antagonistic to the whole teaching and spirit of the gospel."[14] Whether or not this was the singular episode that turned him into an activist on behalf of abolition, there is little doubt that Wilson made it a life's mission to destroy slavery.

This goal took him on a journey that began with the Massachusetts legislature and then national office; in the process, he became one of the best-known political figures of his generation. He first ran an unsuccessful campaign in 1839 on a temperance platform and then joined the Whig Party to earn state office. After becoming disenchanted with the Whigs, he helped found the Free Soil Party in 1848 as a means of blocking slavery from the western territories. In the 1850s he led a portion of that organization into the newly forming Republican Party. Later, in the Civil War—as chair of the US Senate's Military Affairs Committee—he sponsored critical legislation that mustered the resources and the soldiers to win the war. This included the controversial legislation that instituted a national draft. He provided what one scholar has termed "essential contributions" toward enacting the Thirteenth Amendment, which ended slavery. All of this activity he recorded in his three-volume history.[15]

In doing so, Wilson left a unique record of the rise of the antislavery movement and the destruction of the slaveholding class that had prospered from the ownership of human beings. The recounting of this story was eagerly anticipated in newspapers and appreciated by a reading audience. His fame as a leading political figure contributed to the enthusiasm. By 1874, one newspaper even claimed that "more babies are named for him than for any man in and out of Massachusetts, George Washington not excepted."[16] Even if this observation was in jest, that it was made at all underscored his notoriety.

Unfortunately, that notoriety did not last. *Rise and Fall of the Slave Power* is one of the most significant Civil War books that few people will ever read, written by one of the most important political figures of the era whom few people remember. It is somewhat puzzling how a person on the leading edge of his time—with beliefs and policy positions consonant with today's values—has had his magnum opus consulted only episodically and his name more often in the background than the foreground. For reasons that are unclear, Wilson's career has been overshadowed by more famous Radicals such as Senator Charles Sumner and Congressman Thaddeus Stevens. It is possible that he appeared to be too ordinary; he was known as someone who liked to mingle with common people. And he was not an imposing figure. Most described him as dark-haired, portly, and without elegance. One person said he was "rather loose and ramshackle in his manner of speech; his enunciation was not distinct, his delivery was slipshod, and he was neither precise nor fortunate in his choice of words." Scholars do reference Wilson and often use sections of the books in their own studies, but most often in footnotes. In the words of one historian, these volumes do not bear the weight that they once had with the public.[17]

Yet it is safe to say that the notion of a Slave Power itself has enjoyed an increasing presence in the literature on the coming of the Civil War. Historians have noted how Republicans used the concept to explain the need for the party's existence and to mobilize voters. The Slave Power became the way that Republican Party leaders defined the crisis of the 1850s as one that involved a growing threat to white liberties. Thus the party could have maximum appeal to masses of white voters with minimum emphasis on the plight of black slaves.[18]

Although the sensibility behind the work is modern, the length of the books and the style of writing run contrary to the reading tastes of today. There are two voices in the book: a more florid style typical of nineteenth-century romanticism—with the gaudy colors and gimcrack of a Victorian-era building—and a more tedious, minute-like accounting of debates and parliamentary procedures lifted from the *Congressional Globe* or proceedings of antislavery organizations. The descriptive passages can be compelling, such as when Wilson replicated eyewitness accounts of a slave coffle. Poorly clothed men, women, and children tumbled in carts or walked tethered by an ox-chain followed by a white man with pistols in his belt. The most vivid writing, however, more often occurred in quotations borrowed from others rather than in Wilson's original prose.[19]

The heroes of the collection were the antislavery legislators in Congress. And while the accounts of legislative maneuvering provided by Wilson are incredibly useful for learning the pros and cons of policy decisions, they often took readers into blind alleys where good intentions failed. Success for the antislavery cause came through warfare, with the Confederacy ironically contributing to its own demise as southern members withdrew from the US Congress and handed the lawmaking majority to the Republicans.

What is here, however, remains valuable because the collection represents a thinly disguised form of autobiography that connects with a much larger picture. Henry Wilson told the legislative story through public records and referred to himself in the third person as "Mr. Wilson." This approach mirrored how he appeared in the *Congressional Globe* and other legislative minutes, making it easy for him to patch in materials from those sources without having to re-create them. It also made it appear that he was not in the center of the history, when in fact he was. What made the reading public eager to read this tome was the fact that his life was inextricably bound with the rise of the Whigs, the Free Soilers, and the Republicans—and the winning of a war that ended slavery. *His* story also told *that* story. Beginning with the rise of abolition in the 1830s, Wilson was an active part of many of the events that appeared in the books. As such, his writing still conveys an understanding of what made the Republican Party tick: how it manufactured itself, presented itself, mobilized its masses, and created the mechanisms that won the war and changed the meaning of freedom in this country.

By 1869, Henry Wilson had begun collecting the material that found its way into his *Rise and Fall of the Slave Power*. Here again he was on the leading edge of his time. The historical profession was a couple of decades away from establishing itself in universities and adopting consistent methods and norms for writing history. The production of history remained in the hands of the talented amateur and especially public figures—not necessarily the professor. Neither footnotes nor critical examination of sources was common. Histories existed as a combination of creative observation and the reproduction of full letters or other documents to provide a sense of authenticity. There was little pretense to objectivity or to balancing accounts. Wilson's *History,* in fact, was blatantly partisan and sectional, leading to his devaluation by the next generation of historians—self-described professionals in academic settings—who self-consciously sought more scientific methods.[20]

To his credit, Wilson used materials that became standard in the earliest manifestations of professional history and continue to be so today. He pulled together newspaper accounts, minutes or proceedings from meetings of the antislavery organizations that formed in the antebellum period, and the legislative records of state lawmakers for the foundation of his project. The *Congressional Globe,* with entire passages lifted or summarized, became a core source. He also wrote for information to William Lloyd Garrison and Theodore Dwight Weld, as well as Secretary of State William Henry Seward. And he could consult an important secondary work: the magisterial, multivolume *History of the United States from the Discovery of the American Continent* written by George Bancroft, which came in handy for fleshing out the story of the establishment of slavery on the continent.[21]

From the start, he planned on publishing three volumes of more than 2,000 pages. Multivolume histories were the standard at the time. To help with such an effort, he employed the Rev. Samuel Hunt, a Congregationalist minister in Natick who was of the same denomination as Wilson. Hunt also served as a superintendent of the American Missionary Association charged with establishing schools for the freedpeople in the South. Wilson planned for the first volume to cover the establishment of slavery and the rise of the Slave Power through the annexation of Texas as a slave state. The next volume spanned the aftermath of the War with Mexico through the election of Lincoln in 1860. Finally, the last volume traced the fall of the Slave Power from its secession from the Union through war and the establishment of new Republican regimes in the South. The sweeping chronology that began with the establishment of slavery in British North America followed the lead of the histories by Bancroft and Horace Greeley.

Critical to the work was giving birth and shape to the Slave Power itself. It formed the chief villain throughout Wilson's history. He referred to this entity as an "it," giving it an identity lying somewhere between human and thing. And it remained in his hands a collective entity without differentiation or dissension among its ranks, an image that current historians would correct. From the opening page, Wilson articulated the corruption that gave rise to slavery in America. "From inborn indolence, conjoined with avarice, pride, and lust of power, has sprung slavery in all its Protean forms, from the mildest type of servitude to the harsh and hopeless condition of absolute and hereditary bondage." He called slavery a "subversion of the natural rights of millions."[22] Throughout the volumes, he built a picture of brutal, greedy slavemongers whom he and his colleagues depicted as a minority holding overweening power over not only their section but also the nation.

Demographics provided an important part of the indictment of the slave oligarchy as a privileged minority. Republicans in the 1850s consulted the census and concluded that only roughly 300,000 people at most owned slaves, a number that Wilson replicated.[23] As historian William Gienapp pointed out, Republicans used different figures to represent the domination of planters. Seward used the more standard 350,000, while some counted only those owning ten or more slaves. Journalist and abolitionist Gamaliel Bailey was more expansive, and closer to accurate, in estimating the Slave Power's strength at 2 million people out of 8 million southern whites. Others concentrated only on the most affluent who owned the largest number of slaves, trimming the figure to perhaps 50,000 people. Whatever the number, Wilson and his colleagues used the statistic to build the case that southern masters were antidemocratic, practicing minority rule by a slaveowning oligarchy. Antislavery forces also pointed out that this minority enjoyed unfair representation in Congress, where their numbers were inflated, as they were in southern states, by counting three-fifths of every human being that they owned—a constituency whose needs were not considered. This situation created a privileged class whose members sought to maintain power by whatever means necessary.[24]

Unfortunately, this approach by well-intentioned, antislavery writers has left historians cleaning up after them for more than a century and a half. By making the Slave Power so small, Wilson and his colleagues helped lend credence to the argument—fashioned later in the century by southern apologists—that because most white southerners did not own slaves, they could not have fought a war for slavery. Abolitionists understated the ties that bound white society to the institution. Their approach did not account for the family members within households of masters, a fact that boosted the percentage of persons directly using slaves to roughly one-third of the white South. And if we then toss in the people who rented slaves, as we should, we get closer to 40 percent of white people as having made direct use of slaves. Republicans consistently underestimated the stake that the white population had in a system of bondage built on racial caste, just as they overestimated the extent of Unionism within the Confederacy.[25]

What outraged antislavery men at the time was how this minority in the South made such a large impact on national policy. They looked at the men who served as president and held other prominent positions in the various arms of the government and saw a striking situation. As historian Leonard Richards has pointed out, "In the sixty-two years between Washington's election and the Compromise of 1850, for example, slaveholders controlled the presidency for fifty years, the Speaker's chair for forty-one years, and the chairmanship of the House Ways and Means for forty-two years." The only men reelected president during this time were slaveholders. Also, "eighteen out of thirty-one Supreme Court justices were slaveholders."[26] Southern dominance in the executive, legislative, and judicial branches was a measurable phenomenon.

Wilson and his colleagues had an equally strong case to make in depicting the Slave Power as antidemocratic. In the first two volumes of *Rise and Fall of the Slave Power,* he provided examples of how southern politicians exerted influence in Congress to clamp down on free speech, overrule the free exercise of the ballot, and support a proslavery government in Kansas which came into power through fraud at the polls and which stifled attempts by white people to speak out against slavery.

Wilson spent time on describing the proscription against antislavery petitions in Congress and the censoring of abolition materials in the US mail. The American Anti-Slavery Society (AAS) mounted a heavy campaign in 1834 to send petitions to Congress that protested the internal slave trade conducted in Washington and asked for the abolition of slavery in the capital. In 1836, the House passed a resolution commonly called the "gag rule," which automatically tabled petitions relating to slavery without giving them a hearing. It took nine years, and the persistent efforts by Representative John Quincy Adams and others, to overturn the procedure. Wilson criticized the gag rule, saying, "It struck down the sacred right of the people to petition for the redress of their grievances, by clamor, menace, and resolution, destroyed the freedom of debate, and hushed the voice of the representatives of the people."[27] It again showed that the Slave Power stifled free speech and subverted democratic procedures to protect its interests.

An arguably worse violation of free speech occurred with the banning of abolition materials from the US mails.[28] The members of the AAS had been busy again, this time flooding the South with what may have been the nation's first direct mail campaign. The AAS sent newspapers, tracts, and other information directly to key people it targeted in the South to convince masters of the wisdom of abolition. The lists of names numbered more than 20,000. The postmaster in Charleston, South Carolina, set aside a sack of mail filled with this information that appeared to him to be incendiary. On July 29, 1835, a mob broke into the post office at night to steal the mail. Instead of going after the perpetrators who attacked a federal office, the postmaster decided to hold any further such publications until receiving instructions from Washington. The government supported this position. In his annual message to Congress, President Andrew Jackson encouraged representatives to interdict such materials on the basis that they encouraged insurrection. Ultimately, Congress passed legislation that acknowledged the right of states to ban from mails publications that were judged as threatening the public peace.[29] Once again, the Slave Power had trampled on a right of everyone, including white people.

The fulcrum to Wilson's project came in volume two in the sections where he covered the years spanning 1843 to 1852. He considered the discord and changes occurring in government policy from the War with Mexico through the close of the presidential election of 1852 as having "no parallel for the intensity, variety, and disastrous results of the slavery struggle." Through designs and plots of the Slave Power, in Wilson's view, Texas was annexed to the United States. The country fought a successful war, obtained vast new territories, opened territories—which had been free of slavery under Mexico—to the pollution of the Slave Power, enacted a Fugitive Slave Law that made the Federal government support kidnappers, and elected to the presidency a northern man in Franklin Pierce whose public policies supported their intentions. At the same time, below the Federal level, states even in the North enacted discriminatory laws against free blacks as they also tightened the noose on the ability to free the enslaved.[30] In the process, the Slave Power had become emboldened. Their leading politicians and ideologues changed from sometimes conceding slavery as an evil—albeit one too dangerous to abandon without overthrowing society—to professing their institution as not only good but also as better in the treatment of a laboring class than that of northern employers.

Disturbing to Wilson and his colleagues were the new constitutional arguments that emerged in this period. It was well known that even though the founding document of government did not use the word slavery, it sanctioned the institution in three sections: rounding up fugitives, delaying the end of the African slave trade, and counting slaves as three-fifths of a person for apportionment. Political abolitionists had all but given up on finding a legal basis to compel the South to abandon slavery. Federalism allocated to the states the right to determine whether to sanction the institution. The battle became how to halt its expansion, with Wilson's cohorts digging in their heels to say that Congress could do whatever it wished with the territories, including prohibit slavery. However, this position was countered by the South's leading politicians, who asserted that the Constitution, in their view a proslavery document, allowed for carrying slavery everywhere. Wherever the Constitution went, they argued, slavery followed—Congress be damned.[31]

It was an aggressive posture, which raised suspicions among the Whigs who would become Republicans that the slavocracy had even more extravagant intentions in mind. Perhaps they wanted to make slavery truly national and open all lands in the United States, including the free states, to their foul practices.

It seems ludicrous to believe that southern planters desired to take slavery into the North, yet this became a more common assertion by members of the emerging Republican Party as the sectional crisis progressed. Wilson took pains to show any and all of the tendencies of southerners to take slavery into more northern terrain. In volume one, he mentioned how Illinois had made it possible at first to keep slaves in the newly establishing state, and then how it was finally beaten back in the 1818 constitutional debate. Because of this, he claimed that it increased the desires of southerners to turn Missouri into a slave state.[32] In volume two, he depicted the formation of Oregon as a battle over the exclusion of slavery. He indicated that the Slave Power intended to legalize slavery in Oregon, New Mexico, and California.[33] Oregon had been saved from this ruthless hunger for expansion, as had California. New Mexico was more complicated because it existed in a region that could be more conducive to slave labor, even if with less economic viability. But these were only some of the targets. Could the free states in general be vulnerable? Could a state like Illinois be in the crosshairs once again?

No less a figure than Abraham Lincoln had jumped on board this train, warning that masters wished to make enslavement national in his famous "House Divided" speech. It was a speech given in 1858 that expressed the Republican consternation over the *Dred Scott* decision by the US Supreme Court, which had declared that persons of African descent were not citizens and that Congress had no power to prohibit slavery. Early in the speech, he depicted the struggle as one between those wishing to restrict slavery and those trying to move it forward, "till it shall become alike lawful in *all* the States, *old* as well as *new—North* as well as *South.*" The *Dred Scott* decision, Lincoln asserted, was part of an overall plan to spread slavery that was being put into place through collusion among people holding the highest offices. As ring leaders in this plot he included President James Buchanan, former president Franklin Pierce, Chief Justice Roger B. Taney, and Senator Stephen Douglas. Lincoln did not use the phrase Slave Power, yet everyone knew that was what he meant. He produced no smoking gun to connect these men in designs to help the Slave Power, but he made the ties circumstantially through inference. And he made sure that he provided a vivid example of what might happen: "We shall *lie down* pleasantly dreaming that the people of *Missouri* are on the verge of making their State *free;* and we shall *awake* to the *reality,* instead, that the *Supreme* Court has made *Illinois* a *slave* State."[34] In other words, white liberties were at stake.

The senator in his *History* consistently portrayed the southern leadership as involved in a plot, scheme, or conspiracy to exert its will. And, like Lincoln, he lumped in much of the Democratic Party's *northern* leadership as complicit, only Wilson characterized these men as subservient, portraying them as unequal to their southern masters and as traitors to their region. Thus, Wilson had an answer for the question about how a minority could dominate national politics: northern men were complicit and allowed it to happen because they put their own quest for power over that of national ideals.

Among the worst of these villains was Daniel Webster, who was not a southern Democrat but a northern Whig. This Massachusetts senator delivered a famous address during the debate over the 1850 compromise that gained him praise from many parts of the country and damnation from a majority within his home state. Wilson considered Webster worse than a Democrat because he believed this Whig had betrayed the party, state, and region. Webster's speech of three and one-half hours (a bit on the short side for him) conceded that slavery existed in the South and could not be touched, and that the best way to handle the crisis of the moment and avoid disunion came through compromise. This position led to a renewed power of the Federal government to return fugitive slaves to the South.

Compromising on this issue was, to Wilson, a failure for advancing human rights. He accused Webster of selling out to the slavocracy in order to secure support for his presidential aspirations. A public meeting in Boston a little more than two weeks after the speech also repudiated Webster's position. The senator tried to defend himself; in the process, he created more anger by castigating abolitionists for their constant agitation. This attempt at self-defense wrecked Webster's political career as a senator, although he was appointed to a second term as secretary of state in the Fillmore administration—one attacked by antislavery forces as subservient to the slave interests.[35]

It seems unlikely, though, that Wilson or Lincoln saw a conspiracy in reality.[36] Lincoln never used the word openly, and Wilson was too pragmatic for that. Southern politicians supported slavery, to be sure, but had different ideas about how best to preserve it and disagreed over how desperate was the need to leave the Union when the time came. It is important to reiterate here the sound conclusions of scholars who considered this kind of conspiratorial rhetoric as not articulating internal beliefs but as a means of holding together various factions within a Republican Party in the process of defining itself. This strategy was especially useful in justifying the existence of a party that was largely sectional.[37]

It was compelling, and perhaps necessary, for Wilson to depict the Slave Power as out of step with the country's constitutional roots. Most abolitionists, including the senator, favored the statements of human rights in the Declaration of Independence and considered the Constitution a problem because it protected slavery. Wilson was a bit different. Throughout his life, he retained the view that leaders such as George Washington, Thomas Jefferson, and James Madison—even though slaveholders—never intended the institution to be permanent. They considered slavery as temporary and emancipation as a foregone conclusion, with only the time and method uncertain. As proof, Wilson and his colleagues observed that the Constitution did not use the word *slavery* and that the Congress under the Articles of Confederation enacted an Ordinance of 1787 that prohibited slavery from the Old Northwest, which embraced future states like Ohio, Illinois, and Indiana. Surely this evidence established, according to antislavery thinking, the Founders' intentions to see slavery disappear and to give the legislative branch the power to decide where it would and would not go. In a speech he delivered in 1846 to the legislature of Massachusetts, Wilson framed what was at stake: "Freedom and slavery are now arrayed against each other. We must destroy slavery, or slavery will destroy liberty. We must restore our government to its original and pristine purity."[38]

This view ignored the more complicated behavior of the men he praised. Washington was somewhat ahead of his time: he did free his slaves but not until after his death. Until then, he enjoyed the benefits of slave labor and bought and sold human beings. But even emancipation had the unfortunate repercussion of separating some families because his chattel had intermarried with that of his wife, Martha, who did not free her slaves. And while it is true that Jefferson's early career featured attempts to ban the importation and spread of slavery—including support for prohibiting it in western territories—he never emancipated his slaves and appeared to harden in his position as life went on. These nuances, however, Wilson ignored. The argument for antislavery Founders also was not as pat as Wilson made it, especially when it came to evaluating the Constitution's slant on the issue. Historian Don E. Fehrenbacher has argued that the constitutional dispute went unresolved over the decades preceding the Civil War. Garrison indeed may have had the more persuasive argument in castigating the Constitution as an "infamous bargain." More recently, historians have tended to lean toward characterizing the Constitution as a proslavery document.[39]

Struggles over the admission of Kansas as a state brought together many of the themes by which Wilson characterized the Slave Power: how it used antidemocratic practices to get its way, how it trampled on the liberties of white people, and how it routinely resorted to the brutality of an aristocracy who habitually abused human beings. In 1854, Congress tried to organize the territory under the Kansas-Nebraska Act, which allowed for popular sovereignty—residing with the people living in the territory—to decide whether it would become a slave or free state. To men like Wilson, this attempt represented an assault on the old Missouri Compromise line, which had demarcated where slavery could and could not go. Earlier in the *History,* he had criticized the compromise for perpetuating slavery, but in the context of the 1850s the 36°30′ line took on the aura of a cherished institution—one of the last lines in the sand for protecting free labor. Once that was gone, it opened the country to the possibility of no restrictions on slavery's advance, and it took Congress out of the equation for legislating a decision.

The Democratic administrations of Franklin Pierce and James Buchanan—so-called northern Doughfaces who sympathized with the South—pushed the country toward recognizing a proslavery government in Kansas, despite strong evidence of voting fraud, violence, and unconstitutional provisions against free speech. With so much at stake, both sides flooded the region with settlers and thugs. "Border ruffians," proslavery men from Missouri, stuffed ballot boxes to elect proslavery delegates to Congress and a legislature. The fraud was so rampant that no one could deny it. Then in the spring of 1856, proslavery forces dragged along five cannons to lay siege to the town of Lawrence, Kansas, the center of antislavery activity in the region. Roughly 800 men, as historian James McPherson recounted, "demolished its two newspaper offices, burned the hotel and the home of the elected free-soil governor, and plundered shops and houses."[40] Instead of punishing the perpetrators, the national government endorsed the proslavery efforts. Wilson reproduced with relish the assessment of Congressman Galusha Grow who, after visiting the territory, reported that the rights of the people of Kansas had been trampled in the dust, "the ballot-boxes violated, their houses burned, their presses destroyed, their public buildings battered down by the United States cannon under the direction of United States officers."[41] All of this was happening to white people—the key point in the Slave Power argument.

Then came the vicious assault against Wilson's colleague, Massachusetts senator Charles Sumner. For five hours over two days in May 1856, Sumner lashed out verbally at southern leaders, claiming that a Slave Power had fastened its paws on Kansas and "with loathsome folds, is now coiled about the whole land." During the speech, the senator said that his colleague from South Carolina, Andrew Butler, worshiped a harlot known as slavery. Sumner's language implied that masters maintained slavery so they could engage in forcible sexual relations with their charges. Congressman Preston Brooks, a cousin of Butler's, stewed about the slights and two days after the speech attacked Sumner in the Senate chambers, thrashing the Massachusetts senator more than thirty times with a cane and causing trauma that required roughly three years to heal. Wilson was one of the men who helped Sumner to his living quarters after the caning. He said about the attack in his *History:* "This blow at free speech, and personal safety as well, like a flash of lightning in a dark and stormy night, revealed by its lurid glare the grim facts of the situation, and the people, for good reason, trembled as they gazed apprehensively into the immediate and more remote future."[42]

Final evidence of the undemocratic nature of the Slave Power came with secession. Like many, Wilson characterized the movement as unnecessary and undemocratic. The Republicans had promised not to attack slavery where it existed. Yet the trigger for disunion had come from a presidential election that had been conducted legally and constitutionally, with no one in the South alleging that fraud had occurred. Alexander Stephens, future vice president of the Confederacy, had admitted as much as he counseled his fellow Georgians not to rush to a decision to leave the United States. Wilson also cited the conservative President James Buchanan, who during the secession winter said something near and dear to the senator's heart. Although Lincoln did not win the election with a majority of the popular vote, it had been held in conformity with the Constitution, affording no justification for "the destruction of the best system of government ever devised by mortals." There had been no overt act, he and other northerners maintained. The Slave Power had refused to accept the verdict of the ballot, the centerpiece of democratic rule. Throughout the antebellum period, they had paid lip service to democracy and then abandoned it when it no longer suited their interests.[43]

If there is a villain, then there must be a hero, and it came for Wilson in the form of the political antislavery movement. The adjective "political" makes all the difference in the world in this case. Not all abolitionists, especially the purists who shunned the electoral process and legislative action as corrupt, earned recognition by the author as the most effective champions of the cause. From the start, he had favored pursuing political, governmental solutions to abolishing the country's shame and had spent the majority of his public life helping to create the institutions that could carry on this cause. It made no sense to him that people, no matter how well intentioned, wasted time protesting in ways that had little chance of achieving the ultimate goal. He could not resist tweaking the followers of William Lloyd Garrison who "presented what appeared to their countrymen the practical solecism of endeavoring to reform the government by renouncing all connection with it; of seeking to remove a political evil by refusing all association with political parties. . . ." To him, moral suasion offered no practical weapon for defeating the Slave Power. Understandably for a man who devoted his life to politics, he considered state and national legislatures as the venues in which to combat the southern masters.[44]

Yet before he came to describing the schism within abolition's ranks, Wilson mirrored the periodization of more recent histories by dating the origins of this effort to the colonial era. For a while, histories of abolition written even in the twentieth century typically had begun the narrative in 1831 with William Lloyd Garrison's cry in the pages of *The Liberator* for immediate freedom for slaves. Even those sensitive to efforts predating Garrison tended to see a decline in abolition activity after the Revolution. More recently, historians have elongated the periodization of major events and eras. We now have the long Civil War and especially the long emancipation, the latter of which has become interpreted as a century-long, interracial, international struggle with African Americans at the center of the movement. The expanded chronology has brought back into the story the hard-fought struggles that went on continuously over slavery and abolition even after the Revolution—a period that had been neglected until the past couple of decades—while also highlighting a cast of historical agents that included African Americans.[45]

As in many recent works, Wilson located the origins of abolition in the period before the American Revolution. He took his readers back to the Germantown Quaker petition against slavery that was produced in 1688, considered to be among the first printed documents of abolition by a religious body. Located near Philadelphia, the town was settled by Quakers and Mennonites, some of whom hated the practice of slavery. Four men wrote the document, which urged forbidding the use of slaves and argued that all people enjoyed certain natural rights. Predictably, because of the attitudes of the time, the petition went nowhere. Wilson continued to feature people who spoke out against slavery, including personalities such as George Whitefield, the English evangelical who helped spread Methodism as he whipped up religious fervor in the colonies before the Revolution. Just as he did with the Founders, Wilson cherry-picked the material, choosing the minister's descriptions of brutality against slaves in 1739—thus stressing an antislavery posture—while ignoring the cleric's later staunch defense of establishing slavery in Georgia. Nonetheless, readers encountered a history of the antislavery movement that depicted uninterrupted advocacy, including the successful ending of the African slave trade in the early Republic and the work of Benjamin Lundy in Maryland, a precursor to Garrison and founder of one of the first abolition newspapers in the country.[46]

The one area in which Wilson mirrored his time, and not today, concerned his treatment of black activists. He may well disappoint contemporary scholars because he gave African Americans little attention. Black people appear in *Rise and Fall of the Slave Power,* but infrequently and with little recognition of their contributions to the movement. Black women are nowhere to be found. Nor did he refer to Benjamin Banneker or Phyllis Wheatley, both of them now staples in college textbooks describing black protest against slavery in the early Republic. And strangely for a man who hailed from Massachusetts, he nearly overlooked David Walker, a free black man originally from the South who, while living in Boston, wrote one of the more radical antislavery documents to appear before the Civil War. Published in 1829, his *Appeal* urged enslaved people in the South to use revolutionary means if necessary to free themselves from bondage. Southerners were incensed by the pamphlet and generally banned it, but even northern abolitionists had problems with its incendiary message. Wilson's handling of this seminal abolition tract by a black author came down to one sentence: "A colored man, in Boston, by the name of Walker, had published a pamphlet which was freely condemned by Mr. Lundy, in which, arraigning with terrible and merciless severity the slave-masters for their wrongs inflicted on the poor bondmen, and breathing a most vindictive spirit, he counselled the colored race to take vengeance into their own hands." Like many white abolitionists, a number of whom espoused nonviolence and nonresistance, Wilson could not countenance the thought of a black insurrection.[47]

Similarly, when recalling the work of the Underground Railroad, Wilson featured primarily the efforts of the white stationmasters instead of the perspective of the fugitives. Today, historians give credit to black people who fought on the side of the Patriots, petitioned state legislatures for rights, wrote abolition tracts, raised funds, and cooperated with white allies in forcing the antislavery cause into public discourse and politics. Fugitive slaves are now interpreted as undertaking a political act without which the Civil War and emancipation may not have come. Yet Wilson highlighted only white people in his chapter on the Underground Railroad as he detailed how stations dotted the countryside across much of the North, especially in western portions such as Ohio. Some of the people he singled out for praise included Eliza Wright, Levi Coffin, and Owen Brown, the father of John Brown. These and others he described as heroes, risk takers, and followers of knight-errantry, similar to the Minutemen who responded to dangers during the Revolution. In one sense, the focus is understandable, since the large majority of stationmasters were white people, but Wilson did little to tell readers about the slaves involved in this long-term effort.[48]

An exception to the lack of attention to black compatriots in the struggle for freedom was Frederick Douglass, to whom Wilson devoted an entire chapter in volume one. He considered Douglass a "champion" of the antislavery movement, "one who was a signal illustration, not only of self-culture and success under the most adverse circumstances, but the fact that talent and genius are 'color-blind,' and above the accidents of complexion and birth." As a person who gave speeches, Wilson admired the eloquence and oratorical skills of the refugee from bondage.[49] Much of the chapter served as a straight biography of Douglass, providing readers with details of his flight to freedom and efforts for abolition similar to those covered in the narrative that the black abolitionist had written—except for misspelling the name of his most notorious abuser as Corey instead of Covey.[50]

More interestingly, Wilson used Douglass as an example of the problem of Christianity and slavery. By the time of the writing of *Rise and Fall of the Slave Power,* Wilson had undergone a rebirth of his own Christian faith, rejoining the Congregational Church, and was aware of Douglass's background as a preacher. In 1839, as a twenty-two-year-old, Douglass had secured a license to preach at the Quarterly Conference of the A. M. E. Zion Church. And he served occasionally as a local preacher in the New Bedford area. Wilson capitalized on how Douglass's experiences of slavery highlighted the hypocrisy of the religious faith of the Slave Power. The African American's narrative, for instance, told of the brutal practices of Covey as a trainer of slaves, which meant he knew how to break them through physical violence. Douglass's actual owner and Covey, to whom he was sent for disciplining, were churchgoers. Covey, Wilson wrote, was in fact "pretentious in his church-going, praying, and psalm-singing." Historians have noted how proslavery ideologues used the Bible to support their ownership of human property and, in fact, often won the war of rhetoric by quoting passages that—because of the time in which they were written—accepted the fact of enslavement. Even though religion informed much of the abolition sensibility, some in the movement were aware of the problems that wrongheaded faith created, and there were tensions among some Garrisonians over the extent to which to trust the evangelical tradition as a potential liberating force. Still, Wilson did not turn away from religion. He ended the chapter on Douglass by calling slavery the great national guilt that had rested upon the land, and he reminded readers of Lincoln's warning in the Second Inaugural of 1864 that God might match every lash upon a slave's back with blood shed by soldiers in the Civil War.[51]

Despite this divergence from more modern treatments of abolition, Wilson's volumes provided insight into how the early antislavery organizations went about their business. Here, Wilson took the same approach in describing those institutions as he did with Congress by focusing on parliamentary procedures. Readers were inundated with every twist and turn of a group's formation, making it appear as if Wilson was a recording secretary reproducing the minutes. For a modern audience, it does not always make for easy reading, although it has its entertaining moments—albeit quite unintentionally.

Take, for example, the inauguration of the New England Antislavery Society. It took Wilson four pages to trace the evolution of the organization from idea to realization. First, in November 1831 men gathered in the office of Samuel E. Sewall, a rising Boston attorney, to test whether an antislavery society might have some efficacy. The call for immediate abolition by Garrison had angered many, but these antislavery men hoped that the cry had awakened some to the call. If they could find twelve persons who agreed with the philosophy, then an organization was viable. At that early date they could muster only nine—even in Boston. So they took no action and adjourned the meeting.

A month later they tried again. Wilson dutifully listed all ten of the persons attending, which included Garrison and his publisher. Despite being two short of the stated goal, they named a committee of three to prepare a constitution. That called for another adjournment until January 1, 1832, when they picked up additional participants. The committee reported a preamble and a constitution. The latter was adopted, but the preamble was referred to another committee to report at an adjourned meeting on the sixth of the month. Then the preamble was reported and signed—but only after an amendment. A few of the framers of the statement balked at first because they disagreed over some unnamed issue in the preamble that they, presumably, had written. Finally, all was well. The participants chose a president, two vice presidents, a corresponding secretary, a recording secretary, a treasurer, and a board of counselors consisting of six members. This must have come close to exhausting the total membership at the time. Fortunately, several unnamed black people had joined, but no women as yet.

At last, we have reached the first public meeting of the newly formed New England Antislavery Society, which occurred on January 29 at the Essex Street church in Boston. It drew a talkative group. Public addresses were made by many of the men; as usual the clergy were conspicuous. Speakers picked up on the statements of the preamble: that every person of full age and sane mind had a right to immediate freedom from bondage (not mentioning what happened to those who were young or not in their right minds); that reason, religion, and justice denied that a man could own another man as property. They vowed to use lawful and peaceful means; they condoned no forms of violence. Eminent philanthropists in the United States and England were designated as honorary members. It was not clear whether these men wished to be included, but they likely were targeted for fund-raising. The group voted to send a copy of the constitution to editors and clergy throughout New England. It was accompanied by an address that stressed the need to follow the Golden Rule; to respect the principles of the Declaration of Independence; to consider slavery as an evil *now* similar to the property owned by a thief. According to Wilson, the appeal began to draw more participants into the fold. The movement did take off and expanded relatively quickly. Recently, historian Manisha Sinha has used Garrison's report that by 1836 tracked seven state antislavery societies with more than 500 auxiliaries. By 1838, the American Antislavery Society had more than 1,000 auxiliaries with roughly 100,000 members.[52]

Time and again throughout his *History,* Wilson provided similar treatments of the meetings of antislavery forces, which contain rewards that may not be obvious at first. The accounts showed the need for money and how critical it was to identify philanthropists who would underwrite expenses for preparing, printing, and mailing tracts and information of all kinds. One can only imagine the expenses for renting halls for speakers and advertising the events. They also needed to support costs for petition drives. This was where Wilson missed a chance to do more in bringing to the forefront the involvement of women, especially African Americans who ran the baking sales, the bazaars, and the subscription drives that brought money into the movement. Not stated explicitly, but included in more recent historical works, was the need to fund the Underground Railroad: to gather the food, blankets, and other supplies to assist fleeing slaves on their way. Abolition was an expensive business, requiring a constant scrounging for resources that had to be parceled out to cover many needs and priorities. This situation created inevitable friction among those competing for those resources.[53]

It was also a dangerous business. Wilson depicted the mob actions that conducted punitive campaigns against public antislavery figures. In his opening for the Underground Railroad chapter, he baldly stated, "Violence was the essential element of slavery." He spent an entire chapter in volume one on the murder of Elijah Lovejoy, who was killed by a proslavery mob in Alton, Illinois. An ordained Presbyterian minister, he had set up a church and newspaper, first in Missouri, but faced persecution and destruction of his printing press. Moving to Illinois did not save him. In November 1837, a proslavery mob attacked the warehouse where he housed his printing press. He was killed during an exchange of gunfire. No one was punished for the crime, underscoring for Wilson and his compatriots the influence of the Slave Power even in a free state. The incident made a deep impression on the opponents of slavery. "They saw, too, that the conflict was not to be the bloodless encounter of ideas alone, but one in which might be involved scenes of bloody violence and personal hazard and harm."[54]

One more point needs to be made about Wilson's depiction of the procedures of abolition meetings. It presented antislavery leaders and their followers as employing the standard practices of a democratic political culture. They created preambles, wrote constitutions, established rules for voting and membership. In other words, they operated in a legalistic fashion. Southern whites at the time, joined by more than a few northerners, considered abolitionists to be dangerous people who resorted to extralegal means. They were fond of quoting the words of William Henry Seward from his first speech before the US Senate in 1850. Congress debated what to do about the new territories taken from Mexico. Seward, an attorney, conceded that the Constitution protected slavery where it was, but he countered the rationale of southern leaders such as John C. Calhoun that the Constitution protected slavery everywhere. Seward said the new territory was governed by a "higher law," meaning a moral law instituted by the creator. During the 1850s, abolitionists also employed violent resistance to stop slave masters from tracking down their fugitives. And, of course, there was John Brown. But in Wilson's treatment, abolitionists were deliberate, rational, democratic, and law-abiding.

Differences over methods led to a schism within the abolitionist movement by the early 1840s, especially with the rise of the Liberty Party, which ran candidates on an antislavery platform. Wilson characterized the split as a simple difference between what he called the "Old Organization" of Garrisonians committed to moral suasion that avoided governmental solutions versus those who embraced political action. He believed it was a mistake that Garrison had come out against a Union with slaveholders, meaning that it was better to have disunion than continue to live in a nation with slavery. In Wilson's opinion, this policy handed the Slave Power an additional means with which to marginalize the movement. He admitted, though, that even among members of the political wing there existed differences in approach. Some accepted the unconstitutionality of slavery; others believed that it was a local system whose extension had to be resisted through constitutional means. And some were more pragmatic than others. In his analysis of the breach, Wilson overlooked the more complicated dimensions that historians now cite, including disputes between Garrison and religious figures, as well as the furor within the American Anti-Slavery Society over the election of Abby Kelley, a woman, to the business committee—credited as one of the last straws for leading to a schism.[55]

The controversies over fugitive slaves and the extension of slavery into the Kansas-Nebraska territories tore apart the Second American Party System and paved the way for the formation of the Republican Party. Wilson called it a "new party of freedom" that collected into its fold remnants of the Whig and Free Soil Parties, as well as Democrats indignant over the removal of the 36°30´ line via the Kansas-Nebraska Act.[56] He was an enthusiastic participant, helping to form the party.

First had come a detour in Wilson's party membership that caused controversy throughout his life, including during his 1872 election campaign for vice president. He joined the American Party. It may not have been one of his better moments in public service. Congressman George Julian, a Radical Republican from Indiana, considered Wilson's joining Know Nothings in the 1850s a shameful episode that disfigured volume two "by his elaborate efforts to whitewash it into respectability."[57]

For once, Wilson seemingly had abandoned his commitment to human rights by signing on with a political movement that practiced exclusion and discrimination. The American Party opposed immigrants and Catholics and wanted to prevent these two groups from holding office or voting. The Know

Nothings—so-called because of their secretiveness—in general were anti-Catholic and anti-immigrant, hoping in Massachusetts to strip political influence from the Irish, who tended to support the Democrats. During the 1850s, they flowed into the country, fleeing famine and oppression at home. They had lent their support to defeat constitutional changes that Wilson endorsed, had defended the rendition of fugitive slaves, and had backed the Kansas-Nebraska settlement. The American Party became quite a force in Massachusetts. Know Nothings who captured the legislature wanted to exclude new immigrants from public office and from ever voting at all, but then relented to a twenty-one-year waiting period for the franchise. They also hoped to stop efforts to exclude the Bible from public schools. It was a reactionary movement.

When the party took over the Massachusetts legislature in the 1854 elections, Wilson went along with it. Although historians mostly have excused him for this—and there is merit to the argument—he also owed his first Senate seat to the move. Wilson needed American Party support to fulfill his ambitions for higher office. Senators were not elected by the people then but by state legislators. To win votes from a legislature controlled by the party, he issued in 1855 a public letter of endorsement of the nativist agenda. Historians have given Wilson a pass because he hoped to encourage the antislavery tendencies within the Massachusetts party, and he did work against the more egregious legislation, helping to prevent the twenty-one-year wait to vote. The party provided a home for antislavery activists who had few places to go during a tumultuous time in political realignment. The bottom line, however, was this: He used the organization to catapult him into the US Senate, causing some of his peers to think of him as a political adventurer.[58]

This part of his past came up in 1872, when he and Grant ran against Horace Greeley. The abolitionist editor of the *New York Tribune* had become a Liberal Republican—a reformer who claimed to eliminate corruption by "purifying" the ballot through excluding anyone less than the "Best Men" from voting. As such, the Liberal Republicans were not very far from the Know Nothings of the 1850s in wanting to prevent certain groups from voting, yet that did not stop them—as Greeley's newspaper did—from lashing out against Wilson for his transgression. Supporters of Wilson attacked such "villainy" by arguing that the politician had done so in order to ensure that antislavery remained a guiding principle of the Massachusetts organization and that the American Party was the only home that the antislavery cause could find until the Republican Party had come into being.[59]

That fledgling party did rise to prominence, with Wilson as a key player. With the help of the Civil War, it became the weapon that defeated the Slave Power.

After two and a half volumes, spanning 1,566 pages, the war finally came in *The Rise and Fall of the Slave Power*. There were no battles, no generals, no heroic soldiers within its pages. Not even Gettysburg received more than a mention. General Grant, Wilson's running mate, appeared in one sentence, despite the fact that the senator was one of the people deciding on whether to revive the rank of lieutenant general to bestow on the cigar-smoking commander. The focus of the book was far from the battlefield: It was tightly centered on Congress and political leaders. *Rise and Fall of the Slave Power* featured a war of loans, of raising troops, of furnishing supplies, and of finding the means to end slavery and discriminatory laws against free blacks. In Wilson's telling, the democratic process furnished a weapon to defeat the Confederacy; lawmaking advanced the cause of freedom and equality.

By the time Wilson worked on the third volume, he was vice president of the United States under Grant. He did not live to see either the book or his term in office finished. He had just completed volume two as his health deteriorated. A partial paralysis occurred in 1873, slightly altering his appearance and impairing his speech. He needed to lean on his personal secretary, Reverend Hunt, even more to assist with his project. One gets the sense from his biographers then and more recently that Wilson raced against mortality's clock to complete his *History,* often putting down his pen after a hard day's work at 2:00 A.M. the next morning. The final product was less enthusiastically received than the earlier work and indeed had a curious, pessimistic ending that probably was the product of Hunt.[60]

The effort was helped by reproducing, sometimes verbatim, passages from an earlier work by Wilson, which allowed the production of the book to move along more quickly than it might have while also limiting personal insights. In 1865, the senator had published a book of 400-plus pages that detailed the antislavery legislation passed by Congress during the Civil War. The Confederacy had handed over national power to the Republican Party when its congressmen resigned from their positions in the US Congress. Since most southern members had been Democrats, it tipped the scales toward the Republicans, allowing the fledgling party to enact laws that advanced the cause of freedom. In this volume Wilson dealt with issues involving slaves and free blacks, reproducing many of the debates that one can find in the *Congressional Globe.* The actions encompassed such decisions as emancipating slaves in the District of Columbia, restricting slavery in the territories, providing equal pay for black soldiers, and abolishing slavery permanently through the Thirteenth Amendment.[61]

Once again Wilson's presentation of the achievements of the war sounded very much in line with recent histories, beginning with his emphasis on emancipation as the central outcome of the conflict. He characterized it as "the great historic event of the war," adding, "It was far more memorable than any of its great battles, strategic movements, or the final surrender of the Rebel army at the Appomattox Court-House."[62] Foreshadowing most historical accounts written today, Wilson's *History* showed emancipation resulting from the work of many hands, especially military personnel who had to craft policy for handling fugitive slaves, and antislavery legislators who served as the heroes of the conflict.

Even so, he was honest about the complex motivations behind the expansion of freedom. He understood that much of the North retained notions of caste and prejudice against African Americans. Support for ending slavery occurred not for moral reasons but for military purposes: "not because it was wrong but because it was unsafe, and because it could not continue and the Union endure." He noted the irony that the Slave Power had, to a great extent, allowed this ending to happen by disarming themselves when many southern members left the US Congress in 1860–61.[63]

So where did Lincoln fit in this narrative of emancipation? Was he a Great Emancipator? In Wilson's treatment, Lincoln appeared as a hesitant, but earnest, learner. The senator was disappointed that the president in the early going would have maintained slavery if it meant preserving the Union. But Lincoln did learn. He was a good man, according to Wilson; someone who agonized his way toward emancipation, delayed his decision out of preconceived bias and concern for the Border States, but eventually came around to the right side of history. Lincoln hesitated because he believed that he had little power to abolish slavery everywhere and permanently. Once issuing the proclamation that affected slaves as the Union army progressed through the Confederacy, however, Lincoln did not falter even when facing political backlash that included a public castigation from legislators in his home state of Illinois. All told, Wilson believed that the Emancipation Proclamation had immortalized the president.[64]

However, he took Lincoln at his word that he did not control events, but that events had controlled him, with a higher power dictating the way that emancipation unfolded. This version meshed with Wilson's own Christian worldview and put him in the company of many African Americans who saw Lincoln as essential to the coming of freedom, but as an instrument guided by the Almighty.

Wilson may have been more frustrated with the president's course than he let on in his *History*. An account exists by Albert G. Riddle, who served as representative from Ohio in the Thirty-Seventh Congress, which makes Wilson appear to have been upset with the president in early 1864. Riddle had come to the White House in February and encountered a number of officials in the president's anteroom who were giving him quite the roasting. "The one most loud and bitter was Henry Wilson, of Massachusetts. His open assaults were amazing." Riddle said he confronted Wilson, indicating that the senator should challenge Lincoln openly rather than in the offices of the Executive Mansion. According to him, Wilson conceded that most of the North favored the president and that he likely would win renomination, adding: "bad as that would be, the best must be made of it."[65]

The account, though, likely overstated Wilson's discontent. At the time, Radicals were wondering about whom to support for the Republican nomination in 1864, with Treasury Secretary Salmon P. Chase—a person Wilson liked—numbered among the potential choices. Radicals in late 1863 had been unhappy with the president for his lenient formula for rejoining the nation. The day after Lincoln's "Proclamation of Amnesty and Reconstruction," a number of men gathered on December 9, 1863, who were uncommitted to Lincoln and friendly to Chase. Senator Wilson was among them. Nonetheless, Wilson worked hard in the presidential campaign to reelect Lincoln, delivering forty-two speeches in the six weeks prior to the balloting. Wilson's own reelection was up at the time, making Republican success important for his political career. When push came to shove, the senator threw his energies behind Lincoln.[66]

He also supported the president wholeheartedly in one of the more controversial areas—the political arrests of critics of the administration. The Slave Power faded as an influence in Union national governance in volume three. The chief villains became the Democrats, with Wilson failing to distinguish between those of the opposition who favored continuing the war and those calling for an armistice. Wilson particularly chastised the Democrats for their 1864 election platform that charged the government with interference in elections, suppression of freedom of press and speech, and running a failed war effort that cost thousands of lives without an end in sight. He stressed that the "political and military campaigns of that year were only different parts of the same conflict." Wilson declared that these claims in the Democratic platform "startled the loyal States. Its uncompromising hostility to the war, its unconcealed sympathy with the Rebel cause, its intensely unpatriotic demands for peace at any price, convinced all but the utterly disloyal that there was neither honor nor safety anywhere but under the Republican banner." Potentially worse than disunion for the Massachusetts senator was the prospect of a possible reunion of the country with slavery intact.[67]

Early in the conflict Wilson had signaled his support for stern measures against dissent, taking the lead in Congress to endorse the waiving of habeas corpus by the president in response to unrest in Maryland. He considered maintaining the fidelity of Maryland as one of the decisive battles of the war and applauded the arrests of supposedly disloyal public officials. In his *History,* Wilson admitted that civil strife demanded stretching the Constitution. He believed that the fundamental law "was of less importance than the Union, that the infractions of the former were less perilous than the rupture of the latter, and that the provisions of even the organic law of the government must be silent in the presence of the supreme law of the nation's safety." He added: "That they made mistakes, both the President and Congress, that they did not always see alike may be readily admitted, without calling in question either their honesty or their sagacity."[68] Constitutional flexibility aided in seizing slaves of the enemy as well as in containing dissent.

Wilson favored hard policies that stretched the Constitution not only because of his antislavery views but also because of his concerns with mobilization. Opposition from Democrats that might hurt enlistments worried many Republicans, including Lincoln and Secretary of War Edwin Stanton. It caused them to order military arrests of civilians in the loyal North who discouraged men from enlisting in the army. As chair of the Senate Military Affairs Committee, Wilson was involved with virtually every piece of legislation to raise and equip the men who fought the war. From the earliest days in 1861, he helped expand the size of the army, giving Lincoln increased powers to call for volunteer soldiers. He became known for his support of aid for soldiers.[69] In 1863, he was instrumental in crafting the infamous Enrollment Act that created a national draft, another policy that critics claimed was an unconstitutional expansion of governmental powers. His representation of these issues in his *History* affirmed that he had no second thoughts and took pride in the management of the war by Republicans.

Because of the source material, the narrative of the war and Reconstruction remained primarily a replication of the public record, with few insights into Wilson's private world. While detailing impressive and important actions, there were few, if any, revelations of political maneuvering. This was to some extent a shame, for it would have been enlightening to know the inner workings of the Military Affairs Committee. Yet Wilson neglected the deliberations that went on in executive session—meaning legally behind closed doors—over personnel matters. His committee confirmed nominations for promotions of officers, giving it extensive power to determine who rose through the ranks. This power included appointments to the quartermaster's and other bureaus within the War Department. His friend and biographer Elias Nason estimated that Wilson acted on 10,891 military nominations ranging from second lieutenants to Lieutenant General Grant. In January 1864, the *New York Times* reported 1,200 nominations on the docket with another 300 on the way. And on one day alone—May 19, 1864—the Senate agreed to confirm 400 appointments.[70]

Grant was one of the men who lobbied Wilson. In January 1864, he asked for the confirmation of the appointments of William Tecumseh Sherman and James B. McPherson to brigadier general in the regular army. Through Henry W. Halleck, then general-in-chief, Grant had learned about an attempt to scuttle McPherson's appointment on the impression that he was too much of a southern sympathizer. McPherson had few supporters in Washington. Because of this lack of support, Halleck suggested that Grant write some of his friends about the matter. He did the same later in the year with the appointment of his aide, John A. Rawlins, under less trying circumstances. Upon becoming general-in-chief himself, Grant worked with Wilson to reorganize pieces of the military apparatus, such as the Quartermaster's Bureau. None of these transactions appeared in Wilson's collection.[71]

Similarly, if Wilson's *History* served as thinly disguised autobiography, then it was—in the words of Henry Adams about his own book—"a shield of protection in the grave."[72] *Rise and Fall of the Slave Power* presented the man whom Wilson wanted the world to know while neglecting, as most human beings would, the less flattering aspects of his life. He could not hide his affiliation with the American Party, but he put the best possible face on it. When dealing with the problems in Kansas before the war, he overlooked the brutal massacre of five proslavery people with broad swords wielded by men under John Brown. In doing so, he maintained the impression that the Slave Power instigated and employed violence, not abolitionists. He did, however, recount his condemnation of John Brown's raid at Harpers Ferry, which distanced him from more radical abolition colleagues and put him in the same category as moderates like Lincoln. A newly forming party hoping to win the White House could not afford to do anything else but come down on the side of law and order.

And then there was Bull Run. Occurring on July 21, 1861, this first major encounter between North and South in the politically sensitive Washington-Richmond corridor embarrassed the Union army, which saw a near victory turn into a rout that featured a flight by many back to Washington. Wilson earned two strikes against him in this encounter: his own ignominious scramble to avoid capture (undoubtedly true) and a rumor about his connection with a Confederate spy (partially false).

First, the mostly true account. Wilson was among the politicians and socialites who traveled to the area of Centreville, Virginia, to witness what some believed would be the culminating battle of the war. Wilson was among the disorganized mass of people fleeing from the Confederate army. Congressman Alfred Ely was captured. Wilson's carriage was crushed in the retreat, yet he made it back safely. The episode earned him a few knocks in the newspapers—especially in the Border States and South. Exchanges shared the story—most likely apocryphal—that Wilson tried to commandeer the wagon of a teamster but was repulsed. Hearing that the man identified himself as the senator, the teamster allegedly replied, "Henry Wilson be d__d. I have kicked him off the wagon six times already."[73]

Now for the partially true, but mostly false account. Neglected was his rumored flirtation with Rose Greenhow, a Virginia/Washington socialite who was a spy for the Confederacy. This flirtation would have been scandalous, if true, for since 1840 he had been married to Harriet Wilson, who often stayed with him in Washington. Widowed in 1854, Greenhow moved in important circles and claimed to milk those connections for information that reputedly helped the Confederates know the Union deployments for

First Bull Run. She published an account of her activities, and subsequent imprisonment, while in London in 1863. Wilson appeared in a number of places in the book, with hints that he had furnished her important information concerning Bull Run. She also held letters from a man who signed them "H," which were reputedly written to her by the senator and remain housed today in the National Archives in Washington.[74] These expressed passion and frustration at being absent from her.

Historians, however, have doubted the authenticity of the letters and noted that a handwriting expert has passed judgment against them. Wilson did know Greenhow, and like other political figures visited her in prison in 1862, but there does not appear to have been a love affair, and the accusation that he betrayed sensitive information raises skepticism. Probably the best indication of the story's flimsy nature was that it was not deployed by opponents during his political campaigns. Reviews in the United States at the time called Greenhow's book "silly" in general and said that while she claimed to be putting one over on the government, its officials were aware of her activities as they closed the trap on her.[75]

One element missing from Wilson's account of public life was the impeachment of Andrew Johnson in 1868. A Democrat who assumed the presidency upon the assassination of Lincoln, Johnson angered many Republicans, including Wilson, for his sympathy with southerners and especially for his endorsement of discriminatory legislation against African Americans through the Black Codes. Like many of his Radical colleagues, Wilson considered the policies of Reconstruction as the duty of the legislative branch to define, not the executive. This had been a bone of contention even with Lincoln, but the tensions grew exponentially with Johnson in the White House. Wilson intended to include a chapter on the trial, but he passed away before accomplishing it. Hunt, his secretary who finished the third volume, excused not including an account of the proceedings because they were a matter of public record and "of local and temporary interest and importance" that "hardly deserves a very large space or mention in a general history of the Slave Power."[76] This was a questionable rationale and overlooked how controlling the president also provided a chance for the legislature to dictate the terms of Reconstruction and thus protect the victory over the Slave Power.

It was a victory that looked at times as if it were slipping away. Hunt's ending to volume three was decidedly pessimistic, with a tone strikingly at odds with the triumphal sentiments that dominated much of the three books. In a chapter titled "Conclusions," Hunt bemoaned the illiteracy in the late slaveholding states that he believed hampered the ability of especially the freedpeople to exercise the franchise with good judgment. He noted the continued stubbornness on the part of the defeated Slave Power in embracing its "lost cause," defending slaveholding, and accepting black suffrage only because it was forced by the federal government. The former slaveholders still contended that it was a "white man's government, in which the freedmen have no legitimate part, and from which they shall be excluded, even if violence and fraud be needful therefor." Although the demon slavery had been exorcised from the body politic, other evil spirits haunted the country.[77]

Hunt also noticed a changing of the power structure in the former Confederacy. In 1871, the governments in the reconstructed states were in the hands of loyal men, many of whom belonged to the Republican Party. The freedmen were cared for. Northern Christian philanthropy had been guiding progress in education, religion, and industry. But a "reaction has taken place. The old regime is reinstated, and everything, save legal chattelhood, is to be restored." One reviewer of the volume hoped that the melancholy prophecies would be proven false. "It is not to be believed that the American people are wearied of the task they have undertaken, and that they will consent to see in any section of this country that old regime restored which recognized race distinction and class legislation."[78] It is debatable that Wilson would have ended his work with such a dark commentary.

The mood may have reflected unsettled feelings from some within the Republican Party. It was a young institution, scarcely a decade old when the war ended. With the Slave Power defeated, the wing of the organization that included abolitionists wondered what it was going to do next. What was the next dragon to slay? Additionally, many of the old Radical guard who had brought a moral cause into the political domain had been passing away. Columnists wondered if the party had an ongoing function or should give way to a different organization with a fresh sense of mission. Horace Greeley and his followers had thought so—breaking ranks with the Republicans and forming a third party that had opposed Grant for president.

Wilson used his bully pulpit to argue against disbanding the party. *Rise and Fall of the Slave Power,* in fact, meshed with the message he delivered while campaigning for himself and Grant in 1872. His campaign theme was backward-looking, celebrating what the Republican Party had accomplished. The party stood for liberty; it burst the fetters of bondage; it saved the Union. It deserved to continue in a leadership role. "I am for preserving the Republican party, and hope it will live a hundred years for it will take a century to get the fire of slavery out of the hearts of the people; to make every drop of disloyal blood loyal; to make them remember the Providence of God and the brotherhood of the country."[79] He did not start out to write a campaign document, but *Rise and Fall of the Slave Power*—appearing when it did—served as his version of Waving the Bloody Shirt, reminding the country who had been loyal and who should lead it.

To be sure, Wilson had his detractors. Although much of the press gave him accolades over his books, now and again came stark criticism. Even though the country knew that the vice president suffered from an illness we know today as a stroke, it did not prevent the *Commercial Advertiser* in New York from calling him out for making himself a center of the anti-slavery story at the expense of others. "Those who will take the trouble to wade through his crude compilations, which he calls a history, will find that Henry Wilson overshadows all other men in that great moral revolution." To this person, Horace Greeley came across as "a shivering poltroon," which the author thought was unfair.[80] A little earlier, another critic—this time in the South—said that Wilson had failed both as a statesman and as an author. His views on the slavery question "are so narrow and contracted as to render his 'history' valueless to the student, or to the candid seeker after truth." This last, however, came from the biased pen of a man who considered the Slave Power a tower of strength to the American confederation.[81]

Even his supporters agreed that he was not a statesman. Upon his death in November 1875—three months shy of his sixty-fourth birthday—columnists rendered an assessment of the man and his accomplishments. The country still feels his legacy in many ways, including in an amendment to the Constitution and legislation that led to the creation of the Congressional Medal of Honor and the National Academy of Sciences.[82] But for all of his gifts, and there were many, Wilson was a man of one idea. Wrote one eulogist: "The man of one idea may be a man of genius, he may be a great leader (unless, as in the anti-slavery war, all the people around him are leaders); but he is not a statesman." According to this person, Wilson was guided by a simple moral imperative that required him to support the Union and the cause of antislavery. Once that choice was made, and won, it left Wilson and his compeers facing the problems of a new world for which they had few solutions.[83] This observation appeared in a Boston newspaper while Wilson was still alive, noting it was "a pity that Henry Wilson can't get to think that there are any issues now since the 'Fall of the Slave power in America.' A generation of voters are drifting without any particular political home, thinking no more of these defunct issues than of yesterday's dinner." He had, to some, become old hat.[84]

The narrative that he left in fact was narrow and triumphalist. It employed some of the source material that became a standard part of future professional histories, but it did so in a partisan way that lacked the pursuit of objectivity and fair judgment. The next generation of historians found this kind of work seriously lacking, as indeed it was. Unbridled sectionalism seemed unworthy and potentially disruptive. But from today's more distant perspective, Wilson comes across as surprisingly prescient in his focus on antislavery, emancipation, and Radical measures necessary in Reconstruction as the fundamental story of the era. Years later, these issues have become the nuts and bolts of the current generation of historians. They are the Civil War history of then and today.

NOTES

1. Henry Wilson, *The History of the Rise and Fall of the Slave Power in America,* 3 vols. (Boston: Houghton, Mifflin, 1872–77), 2:188.

2. One "history" that preceded Wilson's study was Horace Greeley, *The American Conflict: A History of the Great Rebellion of the United States of America, 1860-'65,* 2 vols. (Hartford: O. D. Case, 1864–66). For positive reviews, see *Lowell Daily Citizen and News,* November 19, 1873; *Providence Evening Press,* April 30, 1872; *New York Tribune,* June 30, 1874.

3. Ernest McKay, *Henry Wilson: Practical Radical; A Portrait of a Politician* (Port Washington, NY: Kennikat Press, 1971).

4. This was stressed by Thomas J. Pressly in *Americans Interpret Their Civil War* (1954; revised edition, New York: The Free Press, 1962).

5. Wilson, *Rise and Fall of the Slave Power,* 1:522.

6. Wilson, *Rise and Fall of the Slave Power,* 1:602 [Mexican War], 302, 303. For a modern interpretation of the Mexican War as conquest, see Amy S. Greenberg, *A Wicked War: Polk, Clay, Lincoln, and the 1846 U.S. Invasion of Mexico* (New York: Alfred A. Knopf, 2012).

7. Wilson, *Rise and Fall of the Slave Power,* 1:123. For today's title, see Edward E. Baptist, *The Half Has Never Been Told: Slavery and the Making of American Capitalism* (New York: Basic Books, 2014).

8. Wilson, *Rise and Fall of the Slave Power,* 3:233.

9. More commonly, scholars say that human rights emerged as a concept that we understand today after the Second World War, especially with the establishment of the United

Nations. See Nancy Flowers, ed., "A Short History of Human Rights," accessed December 14, 2017, http://hrlibrary.umn.edu/edumat/hreduseries/hereandnow/Part-1/short-history.htm; Charles R. Beitz, *The Idea of Human Rights* (New York: Oxford University Press, 2009). On abolition as an expression of human rights, see Manisha Sinha, *The Slave's Cause: A History of Abolition* (New Haven, CT: Yale University Press, 2016), 3.

10. On Wilson's concern over female suffrage hurting the chances for the Fifteenth Amendment, see John L. Myers, *Henry Wilson and the Era of Reconstruction* (Lanham, MD: University Press of America, 2009), 53.

11. McKay, *Practical Radical*, 7.

12. McKay, *Practical Radical*, 11 (name change), 40 (shoe business).

13. The best articulation of the Free Labor mentality remains Eric Foner's *Free Soil, Free Labor, Free Men: The Ideology of the Republican Party Before the Civil War* (New York: Oxford University Press, 1970).

14. The Rev. Elias Nason and Thomas Russell, *The Life and Public Services of Henry Wilson, Late Vice-President of the United States* (1876; reprint, New York: Negro Universities Press, 1969), 30–31.

15. For Wilson's actions concerning the Thirteenth Amendment, see Lea VanderVelde, "Henry Wilson: Cobbler of the Frayed Constitution, Strategist of the Thirteenth Amendment," University of Iowa Legal Studies Research Paper Series, No. 2017–24 (October 2017): 174–264.

16. John L. Myers, "The Writing of *History of the Rise and Fall of the Slave Power in America*," *Civil War History* 31 (June 1985): 147; *New York Herald,* August 6, 1874.

17. Description quoted in J. G. Randall, *Midstream: Lincoln the President* (New York: Dodd, Mead, 1953), 90. On the lack of his history's weight, see McKay, *Practical Radical,* 220, and Myers, "Writing of *History of the Rise and Fall of the Slave Power in America,*" 145. One of the important bibliographies of key works on the Civil War completely overlooks Wilson's books. See David J. Eicher, *The Civil War in Books: An Analytical Bibliography* (Urbana: University of Illinois Press, 1997).

18. William E. Gienapp, "The Republican Party and the Slave Power," in *New Perspectives on Race and Slavery in America,* ed. Robert H. Abzug and Stephen E. Mazlish (Lexington: University Press of Kentucky, 1986), 53. Nearly forty years ago, Michael Holt was one of the historians who accounted for the importance of the Slave Power as an ideal and tool for the party in his *The Political Crisis of the 1850s* (New York: John Wiley and Sons, 1978), 51. More recently, he continued to stress its importance in *The Election of 1860: "A Campaign Fraught with Consequences"* (Lawrence: University Press of Kansas, 2017). For a monograph that examines this issue, see Leonard L. Richards, *The Slave Power: The Free North and Southern Domination, 1780–1860* (Baton Rouge: Louisiana State University Press, 2000).

19. Wilson, *Rise and Fall of the Slave Power,* 1:99.

20. Pressly, *Americans Interpret Their Civil War,* 194.

21. Myers provides the best account of the preparation for the volumes. See his "The Writing of *History of the Rise and Fall of the Slave Power in America,*" 144–62. Also useful are McKay, *Practical Radical,* 219–20, and Nason and Russell, *Life and Public Services of Henry Wilson,* 402–5. For the foundational contemporary treatment, see George Bancroft, *A History of the United States: From the Discovery of the American Continent,* 10 vols. (Boston: Little, Brown, 1834–75).

22. Wilson, *Rise and Fall of the Slave Power,* 1:1.

23. Wilson, *Rise and Fall of the Slave Power,* 2:511.

24. Gienapp, "The Republican Party and the Slave Power," 54.

25. For insight into this numbers game, see Otto H. Olsen, "Historians and the Extent of Slave Ownership in the Southern United States," *Civil War History* 18 (June 1972): 101–16.

26. Richards, *The Slave Power,* 9.

27. Wilson, *Rise and Fall of the Slave Power,* 1:354.

28. For the assessment of the direct mail campaign, see http://postalmuseumblog.si.edu/2010/07/americas-first-direct-mail-campaign.html.

29. Wilson, *Rise and Fall of the Slave Power,* 1:322–28; Bertram Wyatt-Brown, "The Abolitionists' Postal Campaign of 1835," *The Journal of Negro History* 50 (October 1965): 227–38.

30. Wilson, *Rise and Fall of the Slave Power,* 2:174–75.

31. Wilson, *Rise and Fall of the Slave Power,* 2:175.

32. Wilson, *Rise and Fall of the Slave Power,* 1:161–63. For a recent scholarly treatment on the issue of Illinois and slavery, see Suzanne Cooper Guasco, "'The Deadly Influence of Negro Capitalists': Southern Yeomen and Resistance to the Expansion of Slavery in Illinois," *Civil War History* 47 (March 2001): 7–29.

33. Wilson, *Rise and Fall of the Slave Power,* 2:32–43.

34. Abraham Lincoln, *The Collected Works of Abraham Lincoln,* ed. Roy P. Basler, 9 vols. (New Brunswick, NJ: Rutgers University Press, 1953), 2:461–68, 462 (first quotation), 467 (second quotation), emphasis in original.

35. Wilson, *Rise and Fall of the Slave Power,* 2:252, 254, 256, 275–76.

36. McKay, *Practical Radical,* 29–30.

37. Gienapp, "The Republican Party and the Slave Power," 53; Holt, *Election of 1860,* 2.

38. Wilson, *Rise and Fall of the Slave Power,* 1:2, 33, 38, 59, 74; 2:115 (quotation), 151. Lincoln professed similar arguments about the Founders. See James M. McPherson, *Battle Cry of Freedom: The Civil War Era* (New York: Oxford University Press, 1988), 127.

39. Don E. Fehrenbacher, *The Slaveholding Republic: An Account of the United States Government's Relations to Slavery* (New York: Oxford University Press, 2001), 38–39 (quotation). Also see Earl M. Maltz, "The Idea of the Proslavery Constitution," *Journal of the Early Republic* 17 (Spring 1997): 37–59; Paul Finkelman, "How the Proslavery Constitution Led to the Civil War," *Rutgers Law Journal* 43 (Fall/Winter 2013): 405–38.

40. McPherson, *Battle Cry of Freedom,* 148–49.

41. Wilson, *Rise and Fall of the Slave Power,* 2:560.

42. Wilson, *Rise and Fall of the Slave Power,* 2:482.

43. Wilson, *Rise and Fall of the Slave Power,* 3:12.

44. Wilson, *Rise and Fall of the Slave Power,* 1:187.

45. For examples of the recent trends, see Gregory P. Downs, *After Appomattox: Military Occupation and the Ends of War* (Cambridge, MA: Harvard University Press, 2015); Ira Berlin, *The Long Emancipation: The Demise of Slavery in the United States* (Cambridge, MA: Harvard University Press, 2015); Sinha, *The Slave's Cause.* For a work that focuses on the so-called forgotten period of political abolition, see John Craig Hammond and Matthew Mason, eds., *Contesting Slavery: The Politics of Bondage and Freedom in the New American Nation* (Charlottesville: University of Virginia Press, 2011).

46. Wilson, *Rise and Fall of the Slave Power,* 1:11; David Ceri Jones, "'So Much Idolized by Some, and Railed at by Others': Towards Understanding George Whitefield," *Wesley and Methodist Studies* 5 (2013): 16; Stephen J. Stein, "Whitefield on Slavery: Some New Evidence," *Church History* 42 (June 1973): 243–56.

47. Wilson, *Rise and Fall of the Slave Power,* 1:174.

48. Wilson, *Rise and Fall of the Slave Power,* 2:63–66, 69–73. For the newer interpretations, see Sinha, *The Slave's Cause;* Eric Foner, *Gateway to Freedom: The Hidden History of the Underground Railroad* (New York: W. W. Norton, 2015); John Hope Franklin and Loren Schweninger, *Runaway Slaves: Rebels on the Plantation* (New York: Oxford University Press, 1999). John Ashworth has raised the provocative counterfactual question: if slave resistance, demonstrated by running away and other means, had not been present, could emancipation have come? If so, he wondered, "would there have been a Civil War?" See his *Slavery, Capitalism, and Politics in the Antebellum Republic: Volume 1—Commerce and Compromise, 1820–1850* (New York: Cambridge University Press, 1995), 5.

49. Wilson, *Rise and Fall of the Slave Power,* 1:499.

50. Wilson, *Rise and Fall of the Slave Power,* 1:501–2.

51. Wilson, *Rise and Fall of the Slave Power,* 1:510 [Covey], 511. On Douglass's preaching, see Lenwood G. Davis, "Frederick Douglass as a Preacher, and One of His Last Most Significant Letters," *The Journal of Negro History* 66 (Summer 1981): 140–43. On the advantages that the Bible contained for proslavery rhetoric, see Mark A. Noll, *The Civil War as a Theological Crisis* (Chapel Hill: University of North Carolina Press, 2006), chapter 3.

52. Wilson, *Rise and Fall of the Slave Power,* 1:223–28; Sinha, *The Slave's Cause,* 252–53.

53. Foner, *Gateway to Freedom,* 65–67; Sinha, *The Slave's Cause,* 276–77.

54. Wilson, *Rise and Fall of the Slave Power,* 2:61 (first quotation); 1:382.

55. Wilson, *Rise and Fall of the Slave Power,* 2:107–10. On Abby Kelley, see Sinha, *The Slave's Cause,* 286–87.

56. Wilson, *Rise and Fall of the Slave Power,* 2:408.

57. Myers, "The Writing of *History of the Rise and Fall of the Slave Power in* America," 157.

58. McKay, *Practical Radical,* 87–89, 92–93, 106; Tyler Anbinder, *Nativism and Slavery: The Northern Know Nothings and the Politics of the 1850s* (New York: Oxford University Press, 1992), 90–91, 147, 188; James M. McPherson, *Battle Cry of Freedom,* 139. Dale Baum also is forgiving of Wilson's Know-Nothing venture. Free Soilers tried to turn the American Party toward antislavery positions and reduce the illiberal measures aimed at immigrants. See his "Know-Nothingism and the Republican Majority in Massachusetts: The Political Realignment of the 1850s," *The Journal of American History* 64 (March 1978): 961, 974, 976.

59. *Massachusetts Spy,* September 6, 1872.

60. Nason and Russell, *Life and Public Services of Henry Wilson,* 417–18; Myers, "The Writing of *History of the Rise and Fall of the Slave Power in America,*" 158. There has been some debate over how much of the book was written by Hunt and whether Wilson was up to the task of creating so much prose. Myers's study gives Wilson credit for writing the lion's share of the books.

61. Henry Wilson, *History of the Antislavery Measures of the Thirty-Seventh and Thirty-Eighth United-States Congresses, 1861–65* (Boston: Walker, Fuller, 1865); John L. Myers, *Senator Henry Wilson and the Civil War* (Lanham, MD: University Press of America, 2008), 166.

62. Wilson, *Rise and Fall of the Slave Power,* 3:380.

63. Wilson, *Rise and Fall of the Slave Power,* 3:726 (quotation), 727, 729.

64. Wilson, *Rise and Fall of the Slave Power,* 3:386–88.

65. Albert Gallatin Riddle, *Recollections of War Times: Reminiscences of Men and Events in Washington, 1860–1865* (New York: G. P. Putnam's Sons, 1895), 267; Horace White, *The Life of Lyman Trumbull* (Boston: Houghton Mifflin, 1913), 219.

66. Myers, *Senator Henry Wilson and the Civil War,* 144–45, 163. For the Radical discontent with Lincoln's soft Reconstruction measures, see Wilson, *Rise and Fall of the Slave Power,* 3:534–35. For the meeting of disenchanted Republicans, see J. G. Randall and Richard N. Current, *Lincoln the President: Last Full Measure* (New York: Dodd, Mead, 1955), 95–96.

67. Wilson, *Rise and Fall of the Slave Power,* 3:543 (first quotation), 558.

68. Wilson, *Rise and Fall of the Slave Power,* 3:187–88 (Maryland), 246.

69. Myers, *Senator Henry Wilson and the Civil War,* 57, 100–101.

70. Nason and Russell, *Life and Public Services of Henry Wilson,* 339; Myers, *Henry Wilson and the Civil War,* 106, 135, 145.

71. Ulysses S. Grant, *The Papers of Ulysses S. Grant,* ed. John Y. Simon et al., 32 vols. (Carbondale: Southern Illinois University Press, 1967–2012), 10:35–36, 197, 259.

72. Quoted in Ernest Samuels, *Henry Adams* (Cambridge, MA: The Belknap Press of Harvard University Press, 1989), preface.

73. See *The Sun* (Baltimore), August 5, 1861; *Richmond Whig,* August 9, 1861; *Columbian Register* (New Haven, CT), August 10, 1861.

74. For a letter from the collection featured as a teaching document, see https://www.docsteach.org/documents/document/love-letter-from-henry-wilson-to-rose-oneal-greenhow, accessed January 19, 2018.

75. Mrs. Greenhow, *My Imprisonment and First Year of Abolition Rule at Washington* (London: Richard Bentley, 1863), 77; Myers, *Senator Henry Wilson and the Civil War,* 16–21. For reactions, see *New Haven Palladium,* December 31, 1863; *Portland Weekly Advertiser,* January 9, 1864; *San Francisco Bulletin,* January 30, 1864.

76. Wilson, *Rise and Fall of the Slave Power,* 3:734.

77. Wilson, *Rise and Fall of the Slave Power,* 3:737.

78. Wilson, *Rise and Fall of the Slave Power,* 3:740; *Portland Daily Press,* May 1, 1877.

79. *Providence Daily Press,* October 19, 1872. For another stirring speech that reflected similar themes, see *New York Herald,* March 26, 1872.

80. *Commercial Advertiser,* January 18, 1875.

81. *Augusta Chronicle,* January 28, 1874.

82. John L. Myers, *Henry Wilson and the Era of Reconstruction,* xi.

83. *Evening Post,* November 22, 1875.

84. Boston *News* quoted in the *San Francisco Bulletin,* August 15, 1874.

Detail of a panoramic photograph of Chimborazo Hospital, Richmond, Virginia, taken just after US military forces captured the Confederate capital in April 1865. The hospital's buildings spread across the hill in the background. Library of Congress, Prints and Photographs Division, reproduction number LC-DIG-ppmsca, 33629.

"The Brisk and Brilliant Matron of Chimborazo Hospital"

Phoebe Yates Pember's Nurse Narrative

SARAH E. GARDNER

In 1909 Thomas Cooper De Leon, a former Confederate officer and later secretary to Jefferson Davis, published *Belles, Beaux and Brains of the '60s,* an insider's reminiscence of Confederate movers and shakers. Of Phoebe Yates Pember, "the brisk and brilliant" matron of Richmond's Chimborazo Hospital, he had this to say: "Hers was a will of steel, under a suave refinement, and her pretty, almost Creole accent covered the power" to challenge male authority. The friction of these attributes against bumptiousness, he continued, "made the hospital the field of many 'fusses' and more fun."[1]

De Leon had more to go on than his memory of early encounters with Pember. Less than a year after the war had ended, the enterprising De Leon ran a serialized account of Pember's time as a hospital matron, "Reminiscences of a Southern Hospital," in his short-lived periodical *Cosmopolite.* Thirteen years later, Pember published a lightly revised edition of her reminiscences as *A Southern Woman's Story* with a New York publishing house. Although Pember and De Leon occasionally ran into each other in wartime Richmond, much of what De Leon gleaned about Pember's war work came from the account(s) she had made public.

Few would disagree with De Leon's brief assessment. Indeed, whether or not future generations of scholars came across De Leon's brief description of Pember, they nonetheless arrived at the same conclusion. Pember was by all accounts an efficient and dedicated hospital matron. Indeed, it would be difficult to arrive at any other conclusion. Pember *was* "the brisk and brilliant

91

matron" because she wrote herself that way. As this essay will suggest, Pember used her reminiscences not only to recount her wartime service but also to establish a persona, one that belied her familial and financial circumstances. Through her hospital work and her accounting of it, Pember attempted to create a new life for herself.

Extant records make it difficult to gauge the popularity of Pember's reminiscences at the time of their publication. But by the mid-twentieth century they had gained attention. In 1939, sixty years after the publication of *A Southern Woman's Story,* nearly seventy-five years after the Civil War's end, and at a time when much of the world was at war, Douglas Southall Freeman published *The South to Posterity: An Introduction to the Writing of Confederate History.* Freeman, who had recently received the Pulitzer Prize for his four-volume biography of Robert E. Lee, used the occasion to promote an array of primary accounts that offered what Freeman believed to be the fullest expression of Confederate sentiment. He commended *A Southern Woman's Story* for the author's refreshing forthrightness. Her account, he contended, "would be heartbreaking were it not told with an odd humor. She wrote as she talked," he observed admiringly, "always to the point."[2] By including Pember's reminiscences in his bibliography, Freeman signaled to readers its rightful place among more familiar sources that elucidate the Confederate war. *New York Times* book reviewer Charles Poore penned a glowing account of Freeman's bibliography. So too did William T. Couch, director of the University of North Carolina Press, whose equally fulsome review appeared in the *Virginia Quarterly Review.*[3] Still, even with Freeman's imprimatur, Pember did not quite achieve the fame of other chroniclers of the Confederate past, such as Mary Chesnut or Kate Stone. Neither Edmund Wilson nor Daniel Aaron, for example, saw fit to include Pember in their influential studies of Civil War literature.[4]

But even if Freeman failed to elevate Pember to canonical status, he nonetheless articulated the strengths of her reminiscences. Pember was an astute observer of her surroundings and a keen interpreter of the situation at hand. Her field of vision was necessarily narrow rather than panoramic. But she had a great deal to say about hospital work, medical care, wartime shortages, Confederate morale, and women's wartime experiences. For these reasons, *A Southern Woman's Story* has informed the authors of a number of studies on discrete subjects. In 1935, for example, Francis B. Simkins and James W. Patton drew on Pember's account for an article centered on

Confederate women's hospital work published in the inaugural volume of the *Journal of Southern History*. Pember's reminiscences proved especially relevant to their discussion of the obstacles faced by hospital matrons. "The vagaries of volunteer nurses," Simkins and Patton calculated, "the inefficiency of hospital assistants," "widespread pubic prejudice against women serving in hospitals," and the "inadequate and uncomfortable quarters" assigned to matrons conspired against women such as Pember. And yet they prevailed, the authors concluded, because of their "invincible logic," "confident spirit," and "heroism."[5]

Over the decades, historians and literary scholars have expanded on these early works. Though these studies often approach the subject matter from new vantage points, they nonetheless tend to supplement the arguments put forward by earlier scholars. Like Freeman, Mary Elizabeth Massey, in her 1966 study of Civil War–era women, highlighted the readability of *A Southern Women's Story,* describing it as "scintillating." Part of its attraction, Massey suggested, was its immediacy. Pember gave the "impression of seeing, hearing, and having opinions on everything," Massey wrote approvingly, "and she had the ability to laugh at herself and at others."[6] Other scholars have focused on the broad themes of Civil War nurses' trials and triumphs. The scholarship has become increasingly sophisticated, drawing on a variety of theoretical and disciplinary approaches.[7] Still, the larger framework of solace and hardship has remained.

This essay takes a different tack by focusing on two relatively underexplored topics that emerge from Pember's reminiscences. First, it examines the ways in which Phoebe Yates Pember presented herself to reading audiences. Because reminiscences center on a particular event in the narrator's life, the genre necessitates selectivity. Pember need not document every facet of Civil War nursing. Instead, she could focus on those moments and those episodes that conveyed what she deemed central to her wartime work, namely her loyalty to the Confederacy and her unimpeachable character.

Second, the essay examines the cultural context in which the reminiscences appeared. In addition to the two editions that appeared during Pember's lifetime—the first within months of the war's end, the second during a period of sectional reconciliation—a scholarly edition, issued by historian Bell I. Wiley, appeared in 1959, just as the modern civil rights movement was intensifying and the nation prepared to commemorate the Civil War centennial. Each of these three moments defined both the possibilities and the limits for *A Southern Woman's Story*'s cultural influence. A single text can carry only so much weight at any given time. But it can also perform different work at different periods during its lifespan. Because Pember's reminiscences appeared at three critical periods of Civil War mythmaking, it illuminates the contours of Civil War memory in ways that other texts cannot.

Pember's self-representation remains consistent in the two iterations of her reminiscences published during her lifetime. On occasion, she amplified or muted a point. But she did not substantially revise the 1879 edition based on her experiences during the thirteen years that separated the publication of the two editions. Nor did she give way to reflection. Had she thought differently in 1879 about her wartime service or about the Confederacy's war efforts, she did not let on in *A Southern Woman's Story*.

But if the text itself remained relatively stable, the context did not. The years 1866 and 1879 looked a lot different. And 1959 looked more different still. The publication venues differed, too. A startup periodical from Baltimore did not wield the same kind of influence as did the established New York publishing firm of G. W. Carleton, for example. And neither had the kind of promotion machinery that fueled the commercial press at mid-twentieth century. Granted, Wiley published his edition of Pember's diary with a small regional press. But he had earned a reputation for writing "good, accessible history" that was popular with general readers.[8] He need not publish with a large commercial press in order to be reviewed by the *New York Times*.

Pember had no control over readers' responses to her reminiscences, of course. Extant documentation is scant, but judging by contemporary reviews and by the way scholars have written about Pember's wartime service, it appears as if she succeeded in shaping readers' perception of her. In other words, readers saw her the way she wanted them to see her. And although Pember hoped to influence the cultural moments in which her reminiscences appeared, little evidence suggests that either edition was read widely or significantly influenced the immediate postwar era or the period that followed formal Reconstruction. Wiley's edition, however, certainly garnered attention, and commentators could not ignore the vexed relationship between the modern civil rights movement and the Civil War commemoration. Eighty years after Pember published *A Southern Woman's Story*, her reminiscences finally gained traction.

Author and Text

Phoebe Yates Levy (1823–1913) was born into a prominent Jewish family from Charleston, South Carolina, where her English-born mother, Fanny, was reputedly "the leader of 'the best Jewish society.'" The Levys moved to Savannah, Georgia, perhaps because the city was believed to be more tolerant of Jews. In 1856, Phoebe married Bostonian Thomas Pember; she was widowed in 1861 when her husband died of tuberculosis.[9] Pember included none of these details in her reminiscences. Nor did she mention that the death of her husband forced her to return to her family, now refugees in Marietta, Georgia. The family reunion was not a happy one. "You know how unpleasantly I have been situated at Papa's house," she stressed to her older sister, Eugenia, "and owing to his indifference I see no chance of bettering my position there." Finding the situation untenable, she sought a way out.[10] She did so by becoming chief matron of Chimborazo Hospital.

Pember provided little in her reminiscences that documented personal growth. This is not to say that she does not discuss the evolution of her duties or the expansion of her responsibilities as matron. But she does not often give into soul-searching. She is more introspective in her letters. In early 1863 she wrote to her sister Eugenia, explaining midway through the letter that she stopped to visit one of her patients who wanted her to tell him whether he was dying. The "poor fellow" barely had time to get the question out before he died. "I sometimes wonder," Pember confessed, "whether I am the same person who was afraid to look at a dead person, for I have no timidity and hardly any sensibility left."[11] In this brief moment, Pember admitted that her steely fortitude came with time, and perhaps at a cost. The war had changed her in ways that she did not anticipate. But her readers need not know that. From the opening page of the reminiscences, Pember appears fully formed.

Pember achieved that effect by remaining circumspect about her prewar life. She opened not with autobiography but with the Confederacy's need of hospitals. Because of its proximity to major scenes of battle, Pember explained, Richmond naturally "took the lead" in constructing these new, larger, and better ventilated hospitals. She let readers know how many hospital wards made up a division; how many patients a typical ward accommodated; and what kinds of "establishments" were necessary to support the workings of a hospital. "There were the carpenter's, blacksmith's, apothecary's and shoemaker's shops," she catalogued, "the ice-houses, commissary's and quartermaster's departments; and offices for surgeons, stewards, baggage-masters and clerks." "Each division was furnished with all of these," she continued, "and each hospital presented to the eye a small village."[12] Readers thus learn a great deal about Confederate hospitals in these opening pages. They learn nothing about Pember, except perhaps that she had an eye for detail.

Indeed, the very title of the 1866 version obscures authorship. It draws the reader's attention to the hospital, as if it could reminisce, rather than to the unnamed "matron" who had penned the piece. To be sure, the practice of publishing wartime reminiscences anonymously was not uncommon among Confederate women.[13] But Pember's title is a far cry from that of Kate Cumming, who in 1866 also published her nurse narrative, *A Journal of the Hospital Life in the Confederate Army of Tennessee From the Battle of Shiloh to the End of the War: With Sketches of Life and Character, and Brief Notices of Current Events during that Period.*[14] Indeed, Pember's original title does more than conceal identity. It emphasizes the action in the hospital rather than the impressions of the woman who wrote the account. The title of the 1879 version, *A Southern Woman's Story,* restores Pember to the lead role, however. Significantly, the copyright page bears her name.

In both editions, Pember becomes an actor in her own story only when she disclosed that "Mrs. R—," or, as Pember described her in the 1879 edition, "the wife of the then acting secretary of war," asked her to superintend Chimborazo Hospital. The telling of the story, however, is as important as the event that transpired. The invitation was, Pember admitted in both accounts, "rather a startling proposition to a woman used to all the comforts of luxurious life." Here, for the first time, Pember discloses some information about her prewar life. In so doing, she implies that she is a woman of standing. Although she does not elaborate on what she means, she nonetheless encourages readers to infer that she is cultured and refined. Moreover, Pember sought to conceal Mary Elizabeth Randolph's identity, either by giving only her last initial in the 1866 edition or by referring to her as the wife of a prominent cabinet member in the 1879 account.[15]

In playing down her own role in the narrative and by protecting the identity of Mary Randolph, Pember conformed to southern class and gender norms. In speaking of elite Confederate women's willingness to aid the cause, for example, Pember clarified, "there was no parade of generosity; no published lists of donations, inspected by public eyes. What "was contributed," she stressed, was given unostentatiously."[16] Women of standing, Pember suggested, did not broadcast their charitable works. Neither did they work for wages.[17] Pember, of course, did both. In writing her reminiscences, she publicized her wartime work. And as a hospital matron, she earned wages. Pember thus performed a literary sleight of hand, skillfully deflecting attention away from those aspects of her story that might garner criticism and redirecting it to that which was laudable, namely, her sensibilities and her dedication to the Confederate cause.

Pember framed her decision to become chief matron at Chimborazo as born out of patriotism, not need. But that was not quite the case. "You may imagine how frightened and nervous I feel concerning the step I am about to take and how important in its small way it will be to me," she confided to Eugenia. "I look forward with pleasure to any life that will exempt me from daily jealousies and rudeness" that she experienced in her father's house. She closed the letter by assuring her sister that "nothing but the strongest pressure could force me out into the world in such a painful and laborious life."[18] That is not the image that she presented to her readers.

Indeed, nothing in Pember's reminiscences suggests vulnerability. Instead, Pember presented herself as self-possessed, confident in her ability to discharge her duties, and in control of her domain. Perhaps the most often-cited example of Pember's assertiveness centers on her insistence that she, the hospital matron, dispense alcohol to her patients, as mandated by law.[19] That the Confederacy approved a bill that obligated matrons to assume such a task, historian Libra Rose Hilde concluded, "suggests fairly widespread problems with alcohol abuse" among the surgeons and officers.[20] Unsurprisingly, then, the head surgeon was not amused. Although "proverbially sober himself," Pember wrote, the surgeon well understood—as did Pember—that commissioned and noncommissioned officers would surely rebel against the new order of things. "So, the printed law being at hand for reference," Pember stated, "I nailed my colors to the mast, and that evening all the liquor was in my pantry and the key in my pocket."[21]

That said, Pember's battle was not easily won. As Wiley noted, the opening skirmish "was only the beginning of a long and bitterly waged contest for control of a commodity which . . . eventually became a symbol of authority in a tussle between the male and female contingents of the hospital staff."[22]

Pember continued to face resistance from assistant surgeons and nurses, who harassed her with officious notes of complaint. Pember found these exchanges draining as well as insulting. "They were difficult to understand and more difficult to endure," she admitted. "Accustomed" as she was "to be treated with extreme deference and courtesy" by high-ranking members of the Confederacy, "moving in the same social grade I had always occupied when beyond hospital grounds, the change was appalling." But she also understood the importance of picking her battles. "My pen was certainly ready enough," she acknowledged resignedly, but she wondered whether she should "waste my thunderbolts in such an atmosphere."[23]

Pember was not the only hospital matron who assumed the duty of dispensing whiskey. "Yet few . . . commented" on this part of their work or on alcoholism in hospitals. Only Pember, Hilde observed, "recorded considerable conflict over hospital liquor."[24] Pember's inclusion of this protracted conflict is thus significant, especially since, according to Hilde, her refusal to bow down to male authority indicated that she had "overstepped the bounds of Southern womanhood."[25] Unlike Pember's earlier efforts to stay within the gendered expectations for women of her class, in this instance she seemingly courted censure. For someone who carefully monitored how much she disclosed to her reading public, such a move seems uncharacteristic.

But if Pember risked alienating her audience by broadcasting her apparent disregard for gender conventions, she countered by emphasizing her dedication to her patients. In other words, she did not flout gender hierarchies to call attention to herself. Rather, she crossed the line because her patients' lives were at stake. In so doing, she appealed to her readers' sense of justice and to their patriotism. Surgeons who stole whiskey from the sick and the wounded compromised their charges' ability to recover, Pember believed. And those who were intoxicated as they treated patients did even greater damage. Near the end of her reminiscences, she told the story of a soldier who had been admitted to Chimborazo with a crushed ankle. The patient had been attended to before he arrived but developed a burning fever "and complained of the fellow leg rather than the injured one." Although the attending surgeon ordered the patient to remain undisturbed, Pember "determined to look" at the leg "in spite of orders." His suffering proved too great for her to ignore. A quick examination showed a healthy splinted leg. Pember then examined the fellow leg. "It was a most shocking sight—swollen, inflamed and purple," Pember wrote, underscoring the severity of the soldier's wound. "[T]he drunken surgeon had set the wrong leg!"[26] The soldier soon died. Pember's anger is palpable. Once again, she had bucked male authority. But she had done so out of concern for her patient. And once again, she had proven the more dedicated Confederate.

Pember rarely missed an opportunity to emphasize her loyalty to the Confederate cause. But she often did so by writing of Confederate women collectively. Early in her reminiscences, for example, Pember boasted that "[t]he women of the South had been openly and violently rebellious" from the moment the North violated their "states' rights." They "incited the men to struggle in support of their views," she continued, "and whether right or wrong, sustained them until the end." They had borne crushing hardships and unstintingly given of their time and resources. "No appeal was ever made to the women of the South," Pember asserted, "either individually or collectively, that did not meet with a ready response."[27] She returned to the selflessness of Confederate women later in her reminiscences, this time singling out those "anxious wives, mothers and sisters" who sent what little they had to their menfolk confined to Chimborazo. "The silent tears dropped over these tokens will never be sung in song or told in story," Pember lamented.[28] And although Pember did not write of herself in these passages, she most assuredly counted herself among the Confederacy's staunchest supporters. This strategy allowed Pember to establish bonds with her imagined readers without drawing attention to herself.

Pember courted solidarity with her readers not only by asserting her uncompromising dedication to the Confederate cause, however. She also signaled her level-headedness, her efficiency, and her ability to solve problems creatively. Her first meeting with the head surgeon, a "cultivated, gentlemanly man, kind-hearted when he remembered to be so, and very much afraid of any responsibility resting upon his shoulders," did not go particularly well. Pember wished to discuss practical matters. He commenced "an aesthetic conversation on belles lettres." Although Pember certainly could have held up her end of the conversation, she was more interested in practical matters. While the head surgeon droned on, Pember faced a pressing problem, one that needed an immediate solution. Despite an understocked larder and an ill-equipped kitchen, Pember had six hundred men to feed. "Just then my mind could hardly grope through the darkness that clouded it," she admitted. At last the answer came to her: chicken soup. "For the first time," she confessed, "I cut up with averted eyes a raw bird, and the

Rubicon was passed."[29] In this one episode, Pember demonstrated her quick wit, her ability to take charge, and her willingness to engage in domestic duties beneath her station.

To be clear, Pember had never butchered a chicken. She did, however, know Caesar's commentaries on the Gallic wars. Without ever mentioning her prewar life, Pember thus revealed something about her upbringing. Yet she concluded with a deflection, turning attention away from herself and focusing it back on Confederate hospitals. Although this move seems especially calculated for the 1866 edition, Pember left it in the 1879 version as well. "My readers must not suppose that this picture applies generally to all our hospitals, or that means and appliances so early in the war for food and comfort were so meagre," she explained. Pember particularly wished to clear up the misunderstanding between her and the head surgeon, noting that the confusion stemmed from differing interpretations of the Confederate law that outlined matrons' duties. Above all, she did not want her postwar reading audience to assume that mismanagement was endemic and had somehow compromised patients' care. She then turned back to herself, closing this anecdote by noting, "Nature may not have intended me for a Florence Nightingale, but a kitchen proved my worth."[30]

Later, Pember likened her vigilant supervision of the hospital's alcohol to "the dragonship of the Hesperides,—the guarding of the liquefied golden fruit to which access had been open to a certain extent before her reign—and for many, many months the petty persecutions endured from all the small fry around almost exceeded human patience to bear."[31] Pember spoke of herself in the third person, thereby aligning herself with all Confederate matrons who faced a similar task. But the analogy was her invention. By comparing herself to the beast that protected the golden apples, she not only suggested the magnitude of her task, but she also demonstrated her familiarity with Greek mythology. Hercules eventually slayed the dragon, allowing the apples to be stolen. Pember implied that she would not be similarly defeated.

In another instance, Pember recounted her efforts to discipline a subordinate, referred to as No. 2, who had cordoned off part of the ward for her own private quarters. Pember tried to reason with the woman, explaining that each patient had been granted "by law, a certain number of feet. [E]very inch taken therefrom," Pember continued, "was so much ventilation lost." No. 2 was unmoved. A "*coup-d'etat* became necessary." While calling for the carpenter to tear down the partition, Pember admitted that she "felt the spirit of Boadicea." It was, she tells her readers, *"un fait accompli."*[32] Only those well versed in British folklore would pick up on the reference to the Celtic queen who had led an unsuccessful uprising against the Roman Empire. In this case, Pember was similarly defeated. "The victory was not gained," she admitted, "only the fortifications stormed and taken." Amidst the "dust and flying splinters," her nemesis remained "among her seven trunks enthroned like Rome upon her seven hills."[33]

Pember included this anecdote not merely to describe the vexations she faced as a hospital matron. Nor did she simply welcome the occasion to drop another classical allusion in her reminiscences, as was her wont. Pember included it because it allowed her to distance herself from No. 2, a woman whose material circumstances were not so very different from her own. Pember had complained privately to her sister that she took on extra work, "copy writing for the Department," because she needed the money. Congress's appropriations for matrons, she explained, barely covered expenses.[34] Pember did not, however, mention her late-night work in the reminiscences, likely because she was attuned to censure that "befell" elite women who worked for and accepted wages.[35] Charitable work was one thing; wage work something else altogether. By couching wartime service as an expression of her commitment to the Confederate cause as well as the fulfillment of an obligation to perform acts of charity, Pember shielded herself from criticism.

Perhaps for that reason, Pember did not mask her disdain for strivers. Throughout her reminiscences, she signaled the class status of her colleagues and her patients. As historian George C. Rable has pointed out, Pember "contemptuously described the 'inefficient and uneducated women, hardly above the laboring classes' who worked in Confederate hospitals."[36] In so doing, she simultaneously projected her own superior breeding. Often, she used dialect to mark inferiority. "No. 2," for example, entreated the medical director after her contretemps with Pember, enlisting "his sympathy by a plausible appeal and description of her desolate condition. 'A refugee,' or 'refewgee,' as she called herself," Pember sneered, "'trying to make her living decently.'"[37] Because "refugee" and "refewgee" share the same pronunciation, the only reason Pember had to spell the word phonetically was to suggest that the antagonistic nurse was illiterate. And for many mid-nineteenth-century Americans, illiteracy marked both socioeconomic inferiority and a deficient intellect.[38] Pember and her insubordinate nurse were in the same financial boat. But Pember could never suggest as much to her readers.[39] By impugning No. 2's reputation she shielded her own. Significantly, although Pember recalled this incident in the 1866 version of her reminiscences, she did not use "refewgee" to ascribe cultural inferiority to her antagonist in that account.[40] Whatever concerns Pember might have harbored about readers' perceptions of her status became heightened in the intervening thirteen years. Readers needed to understand that she and No. 2 were not cut from the same cloth.

Pember was less contemptuous of the common soldiers she treated, though she still found their class status worthy of commentary. "The mass of patients were uneducated men," she wrote, "who lived by the sweat of their brow." Untutored in the finer arts of sociability, these soldiers were incapable of expressing gratitude to those who cared for them. "Common natures look only with surprise at great sacrifices and cunningly avail themselves of the benefits they bestow, and give nothing in return,—not even," she ruefully continued, "the satisfaction of allowing the giver to feel that the care bestowed has been beneficial." That said, she found many of her interactions with patients "pleasant," noting they could, at times, counteract the disappointments and "lighten duties."[41]

Pember also used dialect to render the speech of common soldiers. Here, too, she distanced herself from the unlettered, although her motives differed from those that impelled her to draw attention to her subordinate's drawl. Pember had censured No. 2 for putting on airs, for appealing to the privileges of class and station that did not belong to her. Pember's soldier-patients, however, had earned her respect. That nurses such as Pember idealized the common soldier but "lack[ed] . . . sympathy for their socially inferior coworkers," literary scholar Jane E. Schultz observed, "hints at the powerful hold that reverence for manhood exerted over wartime society."[42] Indeed, Pember found the common soldiers far more admirable than "the young surgeons," many of whom were not "gentlemen, although their profession should have made them aspirants to the character."[43]

When Pember recounted a soldier's query, "Kin you writ me a letter?" for example, she did so to suggest the soldier's plain speech.[44] Pember quickly acquiesced, and included in her reminiscences for the benefit of her readers the letter the soldier had dictated to his mother. It is worth noting when Pember abandoned standard spelling to reflect the soldier's pronunciation and when she did not; when she violated rules of grammar to suggest his patterns of speech and when she relied on common usage. "'I hope this finds you well," she wrote for the soldier, "as it leaves me well, and I hope I shall git a furlough Christmas, and come and see you, and I hope that you will keep well, and all the folks be well by that time, as I hopes to be well myself. This leaves me in good health, as I hope it finds you—."[45] "Get" becomes "git," to suggest the soldier's Georgia dialect. "Furlough," however, remains unchanged. Pember did not pen the equivalent of "refugee/refewgee" because she had no need to do so. Pember did not consider the soldier her equal. And he never pretended to be. Pember could thus afford to be generous and respectful, as her social upbringing had taught her.

Indeed, Pember intervened, believing it necessary to help the soldier craft a story that comported with epistolary conventions. Fearing his letter lacked forward movement, she asked him a series of questions that yielded "some material to work upon." She filled up the sheets of paper, for "no soldier would think a letter worth sending home that showed any blank paper." The soldier was stunned at the result. "'Did you writ all that?'" he asked. Yes, she replied. "'Did *I* say all that?'" he wondered. "'I think you did,'" she answered kindly.[46]

Pember's framing of this episode emphasized her eagerness to help a common soldier craft a letter worthy of reading. In so doing, she underscored her attention to the art of writing. The soldier's story went around in circles, Pember noted. It lacked a beginning, middle, and end. There was no rise and fall of action. Her rewriting of the Georgia soldier's letter makes clear her concern for the way a story unfolds and her insistence that the author must work to maintain readers' interest.

Louisa May Alcott recorded a similar scene in *Hospital Sketches,* her thinly veiled account of her brief stint as a nurse at a Union Hospital in Georgetown, DC.[47] "[H]aving got the bodies of my boys into something like order," Alcott recorded, "the next task was to minister to their minds, by writing letters to the anxious souls at home. . . . The letters dictated to me, and revised by me," she contended, "would have made an excellent chapter for some future history of the war."[48] Alcott drew attention to the literary quality of these edited letters by likening them to those penned by "Ensign Spooney" to his parents "just before Waterloo" in William Makepeace Thackeray's *Vanity Fair.* Her soldiers' letters, too, were "full of affection, pluck, and bad spelling."[49] Alcott had published short fiction in *The Atlantic Monthly* as early as 1860. By the time she wrote her sketches, she was well attuned to literary conventions. As far as we know, Pember was a novice when she wrote of her wartime service. Although she never admitted to her readers that she aspired to write professionally, she might have considered her reminiscences as a way to practice her craft.

George Rable, who wrote an introduction for an edition of *A Southern Woman's Story* published in 2002, calculated that Pember began drafting her narrative "almost immediately after the war."[50] It is possible that she began the work earlier, however. In an 1863 letter to her sister Eugenia Philips, Pember explained that she spent her evenings "writing for the magazines."[51] It is unclear whether Pember referred here to what would become "Reminiscences of a Hospital." Unless De Leon had formed and disclosed his plan to launch a magazine at the war's end, Pember could not have anticipated the emergence of *Cosmopolite*. Still, she might have imagined her reminiscences appearing in any number of venues. Alcott, for example, published what became *Hospital Sketches* serially in Franklin Sanborn's abolitionist newspaper *Boston Commonwealth* in 1863. Thomas Wentworth Higginson published parts of *Army Life in a Black Regiment* (1870) in the *Atlantic Monthly* near the war's end.[52] Although Pember did not travel in the same circles as the Concord literati, it is nonetheless conceivable that she wrote with publication in mind soon after starting her work at Chimborazo.

Like Alcott, Pember was drawn to the war's pathos. Her attraction to the war's emotional pull is evident throughout her account, but it is especially pronounced in her vignette of an "educated and gentleman[ly]" patient who hoped Pember might wield her influence and secure him a furlough. The Alabamian immediately won Pember's "sincere sympathy." He wished to see a young woman to whom he was briefly engaged, but the war had interrupted the couple's plans. Pember interceded on the patient's behalf, but to no avail. The furlough was denied; "every man was needed in the field," she was told. Pember then linked the soldier's story to "all stories in time of war." Pember's former patient "was killed while repelling with his brigade the attack on Petersburg," she reported, "and the little history confided to me resolved itself into a romance one night that found shape and form."[53] She included a poem she had penned—with a German title, no less—*in memoriam*. As her reminiscences suggest, wars might be about many things, but the poem reminds readers that death and loss are ever present. The poetic form presumably allowed Pember to compose "Ich Habe Gelebt Und Geliebt" quickly, in one night, she claimed. And it allowed her to tap into a popular form of expression as she explored yet another genre.[54] Finally, Pember used the occasion to demonstrate that war work had not unsexed her. As Rable noted, women nurses "were supposed to be brave and strong but at the same time remain loving and refined; endurance and perseverance" competed with assumptions about women's delicate sensibilities. The poem suggests that nursing had not eroded her ability to form bonds of sympathy. The "brisk and brilliant matron of Chimborazo Hospital" did not threaten conventional gender norms.

Texts and Contexts

At the time Pember published "Reminiscences of a Southern Hospital," two competing narratives of Confederate defeat dominated the literary landscape. One strand catered to northern readers, desperate for confirmation that erstwhile Confederates had accepted Union victory. Travel literature penned by journalists and reformers proved particularly popular with northern readers. Classics of the genre include John Townsend Trowbridge's *The South: A Tour of Its Battlefields and Ruined Cities,* published in 1866 and reissued in 1868 as *A Picture of the Desolated States and the Work of Reconstruction;* John Richard Dennett's, *The South As It Is,* which appeared originally in *The Nation* as part of its commitment to publish "trustworthy information as to the condition and prospects" of the South; and Whitelaw Reid's *After the War: A Southern Tour.* Reid had calculated that because northern readers had clamored for explanations of Confederates' "boundless confidence and overwhelming contempt of their antagonists," they would "want to know [. . .] something of the temper and condition in which these communities came out of the struggle."[55]

None of these works offered readers a confused or ambiguous message. All emphasized the destruction the war wrought, pointed to a swath of erstwhile Confederates who accepted defeat and expressed a keen desire to be reintegrated into the Union, and suggested a measure of confidence that though the work would be difficult, reunification was possible. Trowbridge learned, for example, that "never was a rebellious class more thoroughly subdued." Reid declared, "The whole body politic was as wax. It needed but a firm hand to apply the seal. Whatever device were chosen, that community would at once be molded to its impress."[56] Both had grossly overstated the case.

These travel accounts stood in marked contrast to Carl Schurz's "Report on the Condition of the South," submitted to Andrew Johnson in late 1865 at the president's behest. A German émigré, Union general, and prominent member of the Republican Party, Schurz was hardly sanguine about the South's willingness to accept even the most lenient terms of Reconstruction. "The Southern people have not abandoned their proslavery sentiments," he wrote to a friend a few weeks before he toured the Deep South. "They accept the abolition of slavery because they must. As soon as the former slave states shall have achieved state autonomy the status of the former slaves will be fixed in a way as near slavery as possible."[57] His tour of the former Confederacy confirmed what he already sensed. As David M. Oshinsky has explained, Schurz returned home greatly worried "about the rising tide of white anger he saw . . . directed mainly against blacks, the traditional victims of violence and exploitation in the South."[58] The *New York Tribune* reprinted lengthy excerpts from the report, although its target audience was more circumscribed, one that would ultimately shape Reconstruction policy. But if his report did not receive a wide readership, its findings—that the former Confederacy rejected any reading that suggested the white South had been subdued—still found their way in the literary marketplace.

In 1866, journalist and Confederate apologist Edward A. Pollard published *The Lost Cause,* the urtext of postwar Confederate mythmaking. Despite defeat, he argued, "the Confederates have gone out of this war with the proud, secret, deathless, *dangerous* consciousness that they are THE BETTER MEN, and that there was nothing wanting but a change in a set of circumstances and a firmer resolve to make them the victors." The memory of defeat, coupled with this belief that theirs was a nobler cause, encouraged former Confederates to invent what Pollard termed "a deathless heritage of glory." In this way, defeat did not render "'sacred things profane.'" Instead, the war "left the South its own memories, its own heroes, its own tears, its own dead." Nurtured by the stories former Confederates told themselves, he continued, "sons will grow to manhood," prophetically noting that "lessons sink deep that are learned from the lips of widowed mothers." Pollard had issued a call to arms. "A 'war of ideas' is what the South wants and insists upon perpetuating," he declared.[59]

Pollard understood that he needed to get ahead of the Union narrative by reminding defeated southerners what the war had determined and what it had not. In so doing, he gave the defeated both a blueprint as well as the language to deny the victors the authority to equate superiority on the battlefield with superiority of principles, thus emboldening former Confederates to resist any and all efforts to recalibrate their interests along national lines.[60]

In this war of ideas, Pember published *Reminiscences of a Southern Hospital* in a magazine that disclaimed sectional partisanship.[61] She was hardly acrimonious, and her memoir displayed none of the vitriol found in other accounts penned by former Confederates.[62] That said, she picked her battles. In the fall of 1864, for example, Pember registered her contempt at Union treatment of Confederate POWs. "Can any pen or pencil do justice to those squalid pictures of famine and desolation," she asked. She went on to portray "Those gaunt, lank, skeletons with dried yellow flesh clinging to bones. . . . Those pale, bluish lips and feverish eyes, glittering and weird when contrasted with the famine-stricken faces,—that flitting, piteous, scared smile which greeted their fellow creatures." The image of the poor, emaciated, enfeebled Confederate prisoner could never be erased from the mind's eye, Pember asserted.[63]

To be sure, Union prisoners had suffered, too. But Pember explained away their sickly condition, reminding readers that the Confederacy "had been blockaded, our harvests burned, our cattle stolen, our country wasted." The Union had no excuse, she accused—it could have fed its prisoners "upon milk and honey." For northerners, "it would seem that Christianity was but a name—that the Atonement had failed, and that Christ had lived and died in vain."[64] Odd words for a Jew, even one who was not particularly devout. But she knew her audience. And an accusation of the Union's false religiosity would likely go a long way with southern readers still weeping the bitter tears of defeat.[65] More to the point, Pember's decision to include this discussion suggests she was attuned to a broader war of words about POWs, which had origins in the war years and explained the execution of Henry Wirz, commandant of the Confederacy's infamous prisoner-of-war camp at Andersonville, Georgia, in 1865.[66]

Pember punctuated, rather than littered, her memoir with these kinds of comments. She was more likely to affirm the righteousness of the Confederate cause than to denigrate the enemy. Pember championed southern white women's unyielding dedication. She extolled the simple virtues of the common soldier. And she castigated northerners for their crassness and lack of propriety. Her commentary was pointed even if it (mostly) lacked fiery rhetoric. She closed her memoir by thanking the Confederate women of Richmond who had sustained her during her four years there. "My only wish was to live and die among them," she wrote, "growing each day better from contact with their gentle, kindly sympathies and heroic hearts." Finally, she begged her patients "to believe that whatever kindness my limited powers have conferred on the noble soldiers [. . .] has been repaid tenfold, leaving me with an eternal, but grateful obligation."[67] However much she might have muted her hostile sentiments, she clearly and unequivocally identified as a Confederate.

In 1879, Pember published *A Southern Woman's Story*, with G. W. Carleton & Co. The publisher had been in the industry for more than two decades and had "developed a profitable specialty in women's novels." Particularly noteworthy, Carleton became the northern publisher of Augusta Jane Evans, one of the South's most popular authors. Beginning in the winter of 1866–67, Carleton "was able to offer *Beulah, Macaria,* and *St. Elmo's* together on his list," which turned out to be something of a literary coup, especially given *St. Elmo's* tremendous financial success.[68] That said, Carleton was ecumenical when it came to his authors. In 1864, he issued Epes Sargent's antislavery novel, *Peculiar: A Tale of the Great Transition.* That same year, he also reprinted Raphael Semmes's *The Cruise of the Alabama and the Sumter,* originally released as a Confederate imprint by Richmond's West and Johnston. And in 1867, Carleton published Sallie A. Brock Putnam's wartime memoir, *Richmond During the War: Four Years of Personal Observation.* In a brief discussion of "the noble matrons and nurses of Richmond's hospitals," Brock singled out "the accomplished and gifted Mrs. Pember."[69] Whether Pember chose to publish with Carleton because he had a long track record of publishing southern authors, or because Putnam had achieved some measure of success with his firm, or for some other reason entirely, is unknown.

What is clear, however, is that by the late 1870s Pember aspired to a literary career and financial stability. Four months after she published *A Southern Women's Story* with Carleton, her first short story appeared in the *Atlantic Monthly.*[70] The acceptance letter is telling. In addition to expressing enthusiasm for the work, the magazine's editor regretfully clarified that he could not offer Pember "any hope of its early publication" but reassured her that the copyright rested with the author. That the editor raised these two points suggests that Pember had inquired about them. It seems likely, then, that she was looking out for her budding literary career.

Pember continued to ply her craft, submitting at least three stories to *Harper's Monthly* in the early 1880s.[71] Henry Mills Alden, the magazine's editor, was hardly impressed with Pember's efforts, imputing one of her stories for threatening to corrupt the morals of "innocent well-bred" girls. He suggested instead that she try her hand at a "good sketch . . . having for its subject some phase of Southern character, familiar to you: not a descriptive article," he made clear, for "we have had Southern live oak, magnolia, Spanish Moss . . . *ad nauseam.*"[72] The South was in vogue with northern publishers, although the subject matter's repetitiveness was beginning to wear thin. But copy is copy, and Alden published three of Pember's stories despite his initial reservations.

Pember thus reissued her wartime reminiscences as she embarked on her new (albeit short-lived) profession. By the time Pember published *A Southern Woman's Story* and her short stories, the Lost Cause myth was beginning to change from a combative articulation of Confederate grievances to a reconciliationist narrative that drew in white northerners, as Alden's letter to Pember suggests. As historian Robert J. Cook explained, Lost Cause adherents "acquiesced to reconciliation . . . on the condition that Yankees conceded that white southerners had fought as brave American patriots to defend the original Constitution."[73] Because Pember had been rather circumspect in her 1866 memoir, she did not need to revise much for the 1879 edition. Even the scene in which she described Union occupation of Richmond remained largely unedited. "There was hardly a spot in Richmond not occupied by a blue coat," she wrote calmly, "but they were quiet, orderly and respectful. Thoroughly disciplined and careful of giving offense, they never spoke unless addressed first; and though the women of Richmond contrasted with sickness at the heart the difference between the splendidly equipped army and the war-worn, wasted aspect of their own defenders, they were grateful for the consideration shown to them; and if they remained in their homes with closed doors and windows, or walked the streets with averted eyes and veiled faces, it was that they could not bear the presence of invaders, even under the most favorable circumstances." Pember changed "careful of giving offense" to "warned not to give offence" in the 1879 edition; she added the modifier "sad" to describe Richmonders' homes, but in sentiment and tone, the passage reads the same in both editions.[74]

In a few cases, however, Pember excised provocative language. In the same section that documented Union occupation, Pember grudgingly wrote, "Despite the courtesy of manner—for however despotic the acts, the Federal authorities maintained a respectful manner—the new-comers made no advance towards fraternity. They spoke openly and warmly of their sympathy with the sufferings of the South, but advocated acts that the hearers could not recognize as 'military necessities.'" Except for hyphenating "new-comers" for the 1879 edition, this passage is identical to the one that appeared in *Cosmopolite*. Yet a few sentences later, Pember elaborated on this point, noting that Federal soldiers "could not be made to understand that their presence was offensive, that the acts they excused as 'military necessities,' were the barbarous warfare of midnight burnings and legal murders." The 1879 edition reads simply, "They could not be made to understand that their presence was painful."[75] Whether Pember's position had softened over the past decade or whether she sought to reach a broader reading audience is unclear. Given Pember's literary ambitions, the second scenario seems more likely. But if she sought to earn her reputation as a writer, her hopes were dashed. Her reminiscences never received that kind of acclaim.

In 1959, Bell I. Wiley sought to redress this oversight. A well-regarded scholar whose works appealed to general audiences and scholars alike, Wiley issued a new edition of *A Southern Women's Story* with the supposition that it had remained largely inaccessible to general readers. He did not know the publication's run but assumed it was small.[76] Wiley's hunch was not necessarily off base. On March 8, 1879, *Publishers' Weekly,* the book industry's trade journal, duly noted the book's publication, although it did not list its initial print run. Two weeks later, it listed *A Southern Woman's Story* under "Recent Prominent Publications." Curiously, it miscategorized Pember's memoirs as fiction.[77] And that was all *Publishers' Weekly* had to say about Pember's memoir.

Historians have generally accepted Wiley's supposition. John Edmund Gonzales, who reviewed Wiley's edition for the *Journal of Southern History,* attributed "the extremely limited sale of the first and only previous edition" of Pember's "story" to the "fact" that it "was uncensored in its original publication (1879)." Of course, neither of these statements is true. The version Wiley worked with was not the first and only edition of the memoir, and although *A Southern Woman's Story* was not censored, Pember did revise her work, if only lightly, to mute the more acerbic statements that appeared in the *Cosmopolite* edition. Any number of factors might have contributed to a limited print run—assuming it was in fact small—including residual effects of the economic depression of the 1870s.[78]

Wiley's initial assumption was important because his edition of the reminiscences was closely associated with his work on the Civil War Centennial Commission (CWCC). Along with fellow historians and CWCC colleagues, Allan Nevins and Bruce Catton, Wiley promoted the publication and dissemination of accessible scholarship. As chair of the CWCC's Committee on Historical Activities, Wiley recommended a number of initiatives designed to elevate the field of Civil War studies, including a call for the "preparation and publication of a comprehensive . . . guide to Civil War history" that would meet "the highest standards of scholarship." In addition to monographs and other printed works, the guide should list "important manuscript collections." Wiley understood the magnitude of the proposed undertaking, noting that it would require "the collaboration of a number of outstanding scholars" and several years to complete. The committee also recommended that "state archives and other major depositories" begin the extensive and costly work of microfilming manuscript material as well as collecting, collating, and filming newspapers "published during the war years." With its emphasis on collection management, publication, and access, the Activities Committee ultimately strove to promote greater understanding of the Civil War era among students, scholars, and the general public.[79]

A number of factors conspired against the committee's efforts, including opposition from other members of the CWCC as well as insufficient funding. But some work did emerge, prompting one reviewer of Wiley's edition of Pember's reminiscences to observe that the Civil War Centennial had the salutary effect of prompting a "publication splurge" that reprinted "many contemporary accounts that for decades have been unavailable to historians and Civil War students."[80]

But just how unavailable *A Southern Woman's Story* was is less clear than Wiley and others intimated. In an omnibus review that appeared in the *New York Times Book Review* of ten recent Civil War publications, Earl Schenck Miers referred to "Mrs. Pember's unvarnished chronicle" as "long one of the classics of the war." Wiley's contribution comes not from reissuing the volume, Miers implied, but from his inclusion of the "nine hitherto unpublished letters that shed fresh light upon life in Confederate Richmond." If Wiley had not recovered a lost gem, the reviewer suggested, Richard Barksdale Harwell had with his edition of Kate Cumming's 1866 nurse narrative, *Kate: The Journal of a Confederate Nurse.* In offering his comparative assessment of the two women's accounts, Miers commended Harwell for rendering "a distinct service" in rescuing Cumming's journal "from obscurity." Miers wrote for a broad audience, for those "Civil War buffs" who engaged in "armchair maneuvers." His review thus suggests that Pember's memoir was a staple of Civil War literature, having already made its way outside the academy and into the studies and parlors of general readers.[81]

That said, Wiley's inclusion of the manuscript letters changes what readers know about Pember's wartime service. Most of the letters document Pember's steadfastness to the Confederate cause, a theme that runs through Pember's published accounts. But two letters, both written in the fall of 1863, deserve attention. The first displays a kind of unguarded vindictiveness not expressed in the memoir. "The feeling here against the Yankees," she wrote to Eugenia, "exceeds anything I could imagine, particularly among the good Christians." Pember singled out one woman who claimed to keep a pile of Yankee bones conveniently "lying around" so that she might see them first thing in the morning. Another woman wondered whether Phoebe could fetch her a "'Yankee Skull' to keep her toilette trinkets in." Pember did not recoil. Instead, she tells her sister that she chimed in "and congratulated myself at being born of a nation, and a religion, that did not enjoin forgiveness on its enemies, that enjoyed the blessed privilege of praying for an eye for an eye, and a life for a life." She then claimed to have invited these women to join "the Jewish Church, let forgiveness and peace and good will alone and put their trust in the sword of the Lord and Gideon."[82]

Pember did not record this incident in either edition of her memoirs. As religious studies scholar Diane Ashton noted, Pember hesitated to "display her own Jewish identity before the Christians upon whom she depended, unless she could present her Jewishness in a manner that underlined her loyalty to a shared Southern community."[83] In a small setting, Pember took the risk, calculating what better way to affirm her Confederate bona fides than to swing the conversation around to a theological disquisition on divine retribution.[84] But that conversation need not be broadcast to the public. Pember's tactic was strategic, for anti-Semitic sentiment was rife in wartime Richmond.[85] Given that Pember published the first iteration of her memoir only months after the Confederacy's collapse, she had good reason to leave this incident out of her account. And because Pember did not supplement the 1879 edition with any episode she had not included in the 1866 version, she had no reason to make this incident the exception. The telling of the story, then, was for her sister alone.

The second letter sheds light on Pember's defensive maneuver that concluded her reminiscences. Her last two paragraphs defended women's wartime work against accusations that contact with male bodies eroded female "delicacy and reticence." She found such allegations preposterous. "How can this be?" she exclaimed. "There is no unpleasant exposure under proper arrangements, and if even there be, the circumstances which surround wounded man, far from friends and home, suffering in a holy cause and dependent upon a woman for help, care and sympathy, hallow and clear the atmosphere in which she labors."[86] As Schultz explained, Pember spoke directly to "a conservative public made uneasy by the social dislocations of war, where contact between men and women that would seem inappropriate during peacetime was necessary." Although Pember universalized women nurses' wartime experience in this passage, a letter Wiley included in his edition makes clear that she was addressing personal attack.[87]

Pember had become incensed when "an acquaintance imputed to her the desire to work."[88] She read the accusation as a betrayal. Mrs. L—y knew the circumstances that had forced Pember to take up hospital work. "[All] this is very bad and very malicious," she unloaded in a letter to Eugenia. "[M]y life is irreproachable now as it morally always has been," she insisted. "[T]here is nothing in the past or the present to touch it." Pember genuinely feared for her reputation. In this letter Pember gave voice to the "popular view of work prevalent among women of her class." Outraged at her friend's betrayal, she asked her sister, "Who would suppose or believe that days passed among fever wards and dying men, in a hospital away from the city, with no comforts and every privation, was voluntary!"[89] Pember's respectability—a form of social currency—was on the line. Rather than address directly the woman who had impugned her character, Pember instead defended all women nurses.

Indeed, in the reminiscences' final paragraph, Pember argued that hospital work ennobled women. "If the ordeal does not chasten and purify her nature," she exhorted, "if the contemplation of suffering and endurance does not make her wise and better, and if the daily fire through which she passes does not draw from her nature the sweet fragrance of benevolence, charity, and love,—then indeed a hospital has been no fit place for her."[90] She thus ended her reminiscences with a counterargument that her entire account had disproved.

By appending these two letters to Pember's reminiscences, Wiley highlighted the difference between private and public stories and, in so doing, he drew attention to what Pember chose to include and what she chose to leave out. Equally important, Wiley proved a larger point, one that was central to his work with the CWCC, about the imperative to disseminate a wide body of archival and printed primary sources to varied reading audiences. Pember's memoir tells us a lot, but it does not tell us everything. If scholars can benefit from reading those nine previously unpublished manuscript letters, so too can general readers. Wiley believed history should be accessible; monographs should be written for nonspecialists and manuscript material should not be locked away, reserved only for the credentialed.

If *A Southern Woman's Story* was not a classic before the publication of Wiley's edition, it has likely earned that status in the ensuing sixty years, in part because Pember is a commanding figure. Deceptively slim, her account has a great deal to say about her efforts at self-fashioning at a time in her life when traditional markers of identity—familial connections, class position, and religious affiliation—were threatened. Pember became an exemplar of Civil War nursing because she wrote herself that way. To her sister she confessed her anxieties and her doubts. To her readers she demonstrated her quick wit, her resourcefulness, and her compassion. "A woman *must* soar beyond the conventional modesty" during unconventional times, Pember had claimed.[91] The reminiscences leave no room for doubt. Pember soared.

NOTES

1. T. C. De Leon, *Belles, Beaux and Brains of the '60s* (New York: G. W. Dillingham, 1907), 385. For brief biographical sketches of De Leon, see Bryan Giemza, "Thomas Cooper de Leon," in *Southern Writers: A New Biographical Dictionary,* ed. Joseph M. Flora and Amber Vogel (Baton Rouge: Louisiana State University Press, 2006), 102; John S. Sledge, "De Leon, Thomas Cooper," in *South Carolina Encyclopedia,* accessed June 23, 2020, http://www.scencyclopedia.org /sce/entries/de-leon-thomas-cooper/.

2. Douglas Southall Freeman, *The South To Posterity: An Introduction to the Writing of Confederate History* (1939; reprint, with a new introduction by Gary W. Gallagher, Baton Rouge: Louisiana State University Press, 1998), 115.

3. Charles Poore, "Books of the Times," *New York Times,* December 29, 1939, 13; William T. Couch, "Why the Confederacy Failed," *Virginia Quarterly Review* 16 (Spring 1940): 307. Not everyone was convinced. Carter G. Woodson, for example, argued that "Books like this . . . have no historical value; but on the contrary, they do the cause of modern historiography much harm among persons who learn history only from biased newspapers of the Lost Cause." See Woodson, [Review of *The South to Posterity*], *Journal of Negro History* 25 (July 1940): 385–86.

4. See Edmund Wilson, *Patriotic Gore: Studies in the Literature of the American Civil War* (New York: Farrar, Strauss and Giroux, 1962) and Daniel Aaron, *The Unwritten War: American Writers and the Civil War* (New York: Oxford University Press, 1973).

5. Francis B. Simkins and James W. Patton, "The Work of Southern Women Among the Sick and Wounded of the Confederate Armies," *Journal of Southern History* 1 (November 1935): 482–86.

6. Mary Elizabeth Massey, *Women in the Civil War* (1966; reprint with new introduction by Jean V. Berlin, Lincoln: University of Nebraska Press, 1994 [original titled *Bonnet Brigades: American Women and the Civil War*]), 188.

7. A partial list includes Massey, *Bonnet Brigades* (New York: Alfred A. Knopf, 1966); Bell I. Wiley, *Confederate Women: Beyond the Petticoat* (Westport, CT: Praeger, 1975); George C. Rable, *Civil Wars and the Crisis of Southern Nationalism* (Urbana: University of Illinois Press, 1989); Drew Gilpin Faust, *Mothers of Invention: Women of the Slaveholding South in the American Civil War* (Chapel Hill: University of North Carolina Pres, 1996); Cheryl A. Wells, "Battle Time: Gender, Modernity, and Civil War Hospitals," *Journal of Social History* 35 (Winter 2001): 409–28; Jane E. Schultz, *Women at the Front: Hospital Workers in Civil War America* (Chapel Hill: University of North Carolina Press, 2004); David J. Coles, "Richmond: The Hospital City," in *Virginia at War, 1862*, ed. William C. Davis and James I. Robertson Jr. (Lexington: University Press of Kentucky, 2007): 71–92; Libra R. Hilde, *Worth a Dozen Men: Women and Nursing in the Civil War South* (Charlottesville: University of Virginia Press, 2012); Brian Craig Miller, *Empty Sleeves: Amputation in the Civil War South* (Athens: University of Georgia Press, 2015); Marie S. Malloy, *Single, White, Slaveholding Women in the Nineteenth-Century South* (Columbia: University of South Carolina Press, 2018); Stephen V. Ash, *Rebel Richmond: Life and Death in the Confederate Capital* (Chapel Hill: University of North Carolina Press, 2019).

8. Robert J. Cook, *Troubled Commemoration: The American Civil War Centennial, 1961– 1965* (Baton Rouge: Louisiana State University Press, 2007), 21.

9. Dianne Ashton, "The Shifting Veils: Religion, Politics, and Womanhood in the Civil War Writings of American Jewish Women," in *Jews and the Civil War*, ed. Johnathan D. Sarna and Adam Mendelsohn (New York: New York University Press, 2010), 288.

10. Phoebe Yates Pember to Eugenia Phillips, Marietta, Georgia, November 29, 1862, reprinted in Wiley, ed., *A Southern Women's Story*, 149–50.

11. Pember to Phillips, Richmond, Virginia, January 30, 1863, reprinted in Wiley, ed., *A Southern Women's Story*, 156.

12. [Phoebe Yates Pember], "Reminiscences of a Southern Hospital," *The Cosmopolite*, January 1, 1866), 70; Phoebe Yates Pember, *A Southern Woman's Story* (New York: G. W. Carleton, 1879), 11–12. See also Coles, "Richmond: The Hospital City."

13. See for example [Judith B. McGuire], *Diary of a Southern Refugee During the War. By a Lady of Virginia* (New York: E. J. Hale and Son, 1868) and [Sallie A. Brock Putnam], *Richmond During the War; Four Years of Personal Observation. By a Richmond Lady* (New York: G. W. Carleton, 1867).

14. See Kate Cumming, *A Journal of the Hospital Life in the Confederate Army of Tennessee From the Battle of Shiloh to the End of the War: With Sketches of Life and Character, and Brief Notices of Current Events during that Period* (Louisville, KY: J. P. Morton, 1866).

15. [Pember], "Reminiscences," 71; Pember, *A Southern Woman's Story* (1879), 14.

16. [Pember], "Reminiscences," 71; Pember, *A Southern Woman's Story* (1879), 14.

17. David J. Coles explained, "[M]any local women volunteered their time writing letters, reading, and generally comforting the sick and wounded while others, black and white, worked as laundresses and cooks." In this formulation, there are two sorts of women who do war work: those who volunteer their time as an expression of their commitment to the cause and those who, out of necessity, work for wages. Pember, by virtue of her privileged upbringing, belonged among the elite. But she was paid for her labor. As Coles explained further,

"Southerners contended that white women, particularly from the middle and upper classes, had no business working in the horrific conditions often encountered in military hospitals." See Coles, "Richmond, The Confederate Hospital City," 78.

18. Pember to Phillips, Marietta, Georgia, November 29, 1862, reprinted in Wiley, ed., *A Southern Woman's Story*, 149–50, 152.

19. In early 1862, the Confederate Congress approved "An Act to Provide for the Sick and Wounded of the Army in Hospitals," which, among other things, categorized liquor "with other 'luxuries' and placed them under the control" of hospital matrons. See Carol C. Green, *Chimborazo: The Confederacy's Largest Hospital* (Knoxville: University of Tennessee Press, 2003), 53. For references to this turf war, see for example Coles, "Richmond, The Confederate Hospital City," 78; Faust, *Mothers of Invention,* 100; Hilde, *Worth a Dozen Men,* 163; Schultz, *Women at the Front,* 38.

20. Hilde, *Worth a Dozen Men,* 163.

21. Pember, *A Southern Woman's Story* (1879), 31–32.

22. Bell I. Wiley, "Introduction," in Wiley, ed., *A Southern Woman's Story,* 6.

23. Pember, *A Southern Woman's Story* (1879), 4.

24. Hilde, *Worth a Dozen Men,* 163.

25. Hilde, *Worth a Dozen Men,* 163.

26. Pember, *A Southern Woman's Story* (1879), 160.

27. Pember, *A Southern Woman's Story* (1879), 13–14.

28. Pember, *A Southern Woman's Story* (1879), 61.

29. Pember, *A Southern Woman's Story* (1879), 19–20.

30. Pember, *A Southern Woman's Story* (1879), 20–21. See also [Pember], "Reminiscences of a Southern Hospital," 73.

31. Pember, *A Southern Woman's Story* (1879), 33.

32. Pember, *A Southern Woman's Story* (1879), 51–53.

33. Pember, *A Southern Woman's Story* (1879), 41, 112, 74.

34. Rable, *Civil Wars,* 122.

35. Schultz, *Women at the Front,* 40; Pember to Phillips, Richmond, Virginia, January 30, 1863, reprinted in Wiley, ed., *A Southern Women's Story,* 155.

36. Rable, *Civil Wars,* 123; Pember quotation from *A Southern Women's Story* (1879), 13.

37. Pember, *A Southern Woman's Story* (1879), 54.

38. See Beth Barton Schweiger, "The Literate South: Reading before Emancipation," *Journal of the Civil War Era* 3 (September 2013): 331–59.

39. As Schultz persuasively argued, Confederate "women's hospital experience revolved around their perception of class differences," at least in part because they were "accustomed to interracial labor." See Schultz, *Women at the Front,* 4–5. But slavery had also created a "mudsill class," below which no white southerner could sink. The same did not hold true for class distinctions. Pember could never be confused for an enslaved woman. But she could be considered poor. She thus guarded her status by projecting refinement, cultivation, and intelligence.

40. [Pember], "Reminiscences of a Southern Hospital," 85.

41. Pember, *A Southern Woman's Story* (1879), 36–37.

42. Schultz, *Women at the Front,* 5.

43. Pember, *A Southern Woman's Story* (1879), 32.

44. On common soldiers' letter writing, see Christopher Hager, *I Remain Yours: Common Lives in Civil War Letters* (Cambridge, MA: Harvard University Press, 2018); Peter S. Carmichael, *The War for the Common Soldier: How Men Thought, Fought, and Survived in Civil War America* (Chapel Hill: University of North Carolina Press, 2018), 130–31.

45. Pember, *A Southern Woman's Story* (1879), 38.

46. Pember, *A Southern Woman's Story* (1879), 39.

47. Alcott's account first appeared in book form in 1863 as part of James Redpath's series of dime novels, titled "Books for the Camp Fires," designed for Union soldiers who had "more time than money on their hands, hoping to provide them with inexpensive popular literature with . . . socially progressive content." See Ezra Greenspan, *William Wells Brown: An African American Life* (New York: W. W. Norton, 2014), 403. See also John R. McKivigan, *Forgotten Firebrand: James Redpath and the Making of Nineteenth-Century America* (Ithaca, NY: Cornell University Press, 2008), 86–87. Six years later, *Hospital Sketches* was reissued by a Boston firm, supplemented with eight short stories, two of which had been previously published: "My Brothers," which appeared in *Atlantic Monthly* in 1863 under the title "The Brothers," and "An Hour," which appeared in the Boston *Commonwealth* in late 1864. See Alcott, *Hospital Sketches and Camp and Fireside Stories* (Boston: Roberts Brothers, 1869).

48. L. M. Alcott, *Hospital Sketches* (Boston: James Redpath Publisher, 1863), 43.

49. L. M. Alcott, *Hospital Sketches,* 44. The line from Thackeray reads, "full of love and heartiness, and pluck and bad spelling." See William Makepeace Thackeray, *Vanity Fair. A Novel Without a Hero* (London: Bradbury and Evans, 1853), 193. See also Elizabeth Young, *Disarming the Nation: Women's Writing and the American Civil War* (Chicago: University of Chicago Press, 1999), 84–85.

50. Phoebe Yates Pember, *A Southern Women's Story,* with a new introduction by George C. Rable (Columbia: University of South Carolina Press, 2002), xv.

51. Pember to Phillips, Richmond, Virginia, January 30, 1863, reprinted in Wiley, ed., *A Southern Women's Story,* 155. Pember explained to her sister that she wrote because she needed the money.

52. Louisa May Alcott, "Hospital Sketches I. A Day," *The Commonwealth* 1 (May 22, 1863), 1; "Hospital Sketches II. A Night," *The Commonwealth* 1 (May 29, 1863), 1; "Hospital Sketches III. Off Duty," *The Commonwealth* 1 (June 12, 1863), 1; "Hospital Sketches IV. A Postscript," *The Commonwealth* 1 (June 26, 1863), 1; Thomas Wentworth Higginson, "Leaves from an Officer's Journal I," *Atlantic Monthly* 14 (November 1864), 521–29; "Leaves from an Officer's Journal II," *Atlantic Monthly* 14 (December 1864), 740–48; "Leaves from an Officer's Journal III," *Atlantic Monthly* 14 (January 1865), 65–72.

53. Pember, *A Southern Woman's Story* (1879), 80–81.

54. Pember, *A Southern Woman's Story* (1879), 81.

55. See, "Founding Prospectus," *The Nation* 1 (July 6, 1865), https://www.thenation.com/article/founding-prospectus/; Whitelaw Reid, *After the War: A Southern Tour. May 1, 1865, to May 1, 1866* (Cincinnati: Moore, Wilstach & Baldwin, 1866), 9.

56. John Townsend Trowbridge, *The South: A Tour of Its Battle-Fields and Ruined Cities* (Hartford, CT: L. Stebbins, 1866), 189; Reid, *After the War,* 297.

57. Quoted in Michael Burlingame, introduction to Carl S. Schurz, *Report on the Condition of the South* (1865; reprint, New York: Arno Press and the New York Times, 1969), iii.

58. David M. Oshinsky, *"Worse Than Slavery": Parchman Farm and the Ordeal of Jim Crow Justice* (New York: The Free Press, 1996), 13.

59. Edward A. Pollard, *The Lost Cause: A New Southern History of the War of the Confederates* (New York: E. B. Treat, Publishers, 1866), 750–52.

60. See Jack P. Maddex Jr., "Pollard's The Lost Cause Regained: A Mask for Southern Accommodation," *Journal of Southern History* 40 (November 1974): 599.

61. [Thomas Cooper de Leon], "Salutatory," *Cosmopolite* 1 (January 1866), 2–3.

62. See for example Jubal A. Early, *A Memoir of the Last Year of the War for Independence in the Confederate States of America* (1866; reprint with a new introduction by Gary W. Gallagher, Columbia: University of South Carolina Press, 2001); Belle Boyd, *Belle Boyd in Camp and in Prison,* with an introduction by George Augustus Sala (New York: Blelock, 1867).

63. Pember, *A Southern Woman's Story* (1879), 121. On prisoner exchanges late in the war, see David Silkenat, *Raising the White Flag: How Surrender Defined the American Civil War* (Chapel Hill: University of North Carolina Press, 2019), 168–88; on prisoners and Civil War memory, see Benjamin Cloyd, *Haunted by Atrocity: Civil War Prisons and American Memory* (Baton Rouge: Louisiana State University Press: 2010).

64. Pember, *A Southern Woman's Story* (1879), 98.

65. Historian George C. Rable, in introducing an edition of Pember's diary in 2002, found Pember's remarks "cryptic." He wondered whether her marriage to a Christian had eroded whatever commitment she had to Judaism. "There is no evidence that she converted," he clarified. But he nonetheless suggested that this passage "casts doubt on Pember's religious convictions." Given that Pember never mentioned her religious faith in her memoir, that argument seems unlikely. If she tried to establish points of connection with her readers, Pember had every reason to appeal to Christianity. In the immediate aftermath of war, as Confederates tried to make sense of sacrifice and defeat, Pember articulated a question that one imagines many of her readers asked themselves. (Rable, "Introduction," *A Southern Woman's Story,* xv.)

66. See Cloyd, *Haunted by Atrocity,* 2, 31–55.

67. [Pember], "Reminiscences of a Southern Hospital," *The Cosmopolite* 1 (April 1866), accessed October 9, 2020, http://www.mdgorman.com/Hospitals/pember_memoir_partIV.htm.

68. Melissa J. Homestead, "The Publishing History of Augusta Jane Evans's Confederate Novel 'Macaria': Unwriting Some Lost Cause Myths," *Mississippi Quarterly* 58 (Fall 2005): 695–96. One of Evans's early biographers claimed that *St. Elmo* was among the top three bestselling books "of all time," following *Uncle Tom's Cabin* and *Ben Hur.* See William Perry Fidler, *Augusta Evans Wilson, 1835–1909: A Biography* (Tuscaloosa: University of Alabama Press, 1951), 129–30; Rebecca Grant Sexton, *A Southern Woman of Letters: The Correspondence of Augusta Jane Evans Wilson, 1859–1906* (Columbia: University of South Carolina Press, 2002), xxix.

69. [Putnam], *Richmond During the War;* 318. Although Putnam was disappointed in the book's modest sales, she took solace in its "favorable critical reception." See Sarah E. Gardner, *Blood and Irony: Southern White Women's Narratives of the Civil War, 1861–1937* (Chapel Hill: University of North Carolina Press, 2004), 53–54.

70. See [Phoebe Yates Pember], "Miss Magdalena Peanuts," *Atlantic Monthly* 44 (September 1879): 288–99; Editorial Office of *Atlantic Monthly* to Phoebe Yates Pember, March 17, 1879, in the Phoebe Yates Pember Letters #2232-z, Southern Historical Collection, The Wilson Library, University of North Carolina, Chapel Hill [collection hereafter cited as Pember Letters SHC].

71. See [Phoebe Yates Pember], "The Ghost of the Nineteenth Century," *Harper's Monthly* 60 (January 1880): 251–59; "Mr. Witherton's Romance," *Harper's Monthly* 60 (April 1880): 731–36; "A Virginia Visit," *Harper's Monthly* 68 (December 1883): 110–21, in Pember Letters SHC.

72. H. M. Alden to Phoebe Yates Pember, New York, April 15, 1880, in Pember Letters SHC.

73. Cook, *Civil War Memories,* 53.

74. [Pember], "Reminiscences of a Southern Hospital," *The Cosmopolite* 1 (April 1866), accessed October 9, 2020, http://www.mdgorman.com/Hospitals/pember_memoir_partIV.htm; Pember, *A Southern Woman's Story* (1879), 173

75. [Pember], "Reminiscences of a Southern Hospital," *The Cosmopolite* 1 (April 1866), accessed October 9, 2020, http://www.mdgorman.com/Hospitals/pember_memoir_partIV.htm; Pember, *A Southern Woman's Story* (1879), 176.

76. Wiley, "Introduction," in Wiley, ed., *A Southern Women's Story,* 16. Reviewers found Wiley's reasoning persuasive. *A Southern Woman's Story* "was first published in an extremely limited edition in 1879," ran one such review. Another noted that Pember's memoir was "rare and long out of print." A third conjectured that the book "did not sell well." See William F. Tompkins's review in *Virginia Magazine of History and Biography* 68 (April 1960): 222; John Edmund Gonzales's review in *Journal of Southern History* 26 (August 1960): 403; unsigned review in *Georgia Historical Quarterly* 45 (March 1961): 103.

77. "Weekly Record of New Publications," *Publishers' Weekly* 15 (March 8, 1879), 276; "Recent Prominent Publications," *Publishers' Weekly* 15 (March 22, 1879), 384.

78. On the effects of economic depressions on the book trade, see Scott E. Casper, "Introduction," in *A History of the Book in America: The Industrial Book, 1840–1880,* ed. Scott E. Casper et al. (Chapel Hill: University of North Carolina Press, 2009), 3:1–39.

79. Bell I. Wiley, "Report of the Activities Committee to the Civil War Centennial Commission," *Civil War History* 5 (December 1959): 375, 378.

80. Gonzales, review of *A Southern Woman's Story,* 403.

81. Earl Schenck Miers, "When Men Gave to the Cause Their Last Full Measure of Devotion," *New York Times Book Review,* March 6, 1960, 22.

82. Phoebe Yates Pember to Eugenia Phillips, Richmond, September 1863, reprinted in Wiley, ed., *A Southern Women's Story,* 168. On Richmond white women's support for the Confederate war effort, see Ash, *Rebel Richmond,* 14, 187–88, 209.

83. Ashton, "Shifting Veils," 291.

84. It seems improbable, then, that Pember was "horrified" by the Richmond women's confessions. Instead, Pember inserted herself into a conversation that was already designed to "exhibit . . . intense hatred" of Union soldiers. See Janney, *Remembering the Civil War,* 22.

85. Ash, *Rebel Richmond,* 151; J. B. Jones, *A Rebel War Clerk's Diary at the Confederate State Capital,* 2 vols. (Philadelphia, J. B. Lippincott, 1866), 1:221.

86. Pember, *A Southern Women's Story* (1879), 191–92.

87. Schultz, *Women at the Front,* 51–52.

88. Schultz, *Women at the Front,* 49.

89. Schultz, *Women at the Front, 49*; Pember to Phillips, Richmond, Virginia, September 13, 1863, reprinted in Wiley, ed., *A Southern Women's Story,* 169.

90. Pember, *A Southern Women's Story* (1879), 192.

91. Pember, *A Southern Women's Story* (1879), 192.

Statue of George B. McClellan by Frederick William MacMonnies, dedicated in
Washington, DC, in 1907. Library of Congress, Prints and Photographs Division,
reproduction number LC-DIG-npcc-30413.

George McClellan's Many Turnings

STEPHEN B. CUSHMAN

Tell me, Muse, about the man of many turns.
—Homer, *Odyssey*

A Tale of Two Monuments

In the small public park bounded by California Street, Columbia Road, and Connecticut Avenue in northwest Washington, DC, stands an equestrian statue of George Brinton McClellan. One of nine equestrian statues of US Civil War generals in the District, that of McClellan, perhaps on Dan Webster, the horse he called most trustworthy, is the work of Frederick William MacMonnies, graduate of the École des Beaux-Arts and choice of a commission advised by fellow artists Daniel Chester French, Augustus Saint Gaudens, and Charles Follen McKim. At the unveiling on Thursday, May 2, 1907, not quite twenty-two years after McClellan's heart failed him at age fifty-eight, President Theodore Roosevelt gave the address to a crowd that included Mrs. George B. McClellan, called Nelly by her husband, and their son, George B. McClellan Jr., known to his family as Max, then serving his second term as mayor of New York. Addressing "Men of the Army of the Potomac" in attendance as "you men of the great war," Roosevelt exhorted his auditors and subsequent readers to live active lives of strenuous effort and endeavor in the performance of challenging duty, not lives of "effortless ease, of mere material comfort." This particular chapter in the muscular and masculine gospel according to Theodore Roosevelt moved beyond the equestrian statue before him into panoramic national vision: "America will stand for much provided only that it treats material comfort, material luxury, and the means for acquiring such, as the foundation on which to build the real life, the life of spiritual and moral effort and achievement."[1]

Roosevelt's speech runs about ten pages in published form. Of those ten pages George McClellan himself received exactly one paragraph, the fourth, which consists of two sentences:

> To General McClellan it was given to command in some of the hardest fought battles and most important campaigns of the great war of this hemisphere, so that his name will be forever linked with the mighty memories that arise when we speak of Antietam and South Mountain, Fair Oaks and Malvern; so that we never can speak of the great Army of the Potomac, without having rise before us the figure of General McClellan, the man who organized and first led it. There was also given to him the peculiar gift, one that is possessed by but very few men, to combine the qualities that won him the enthusiastic love and admiration of the soldiers who fought under him, and the qualities that in civil life endeared him peculiarly to all who came in contact with him.[2]

Many things stand out here, among them one of Roosevelt's favorite adjectives, "mighty," which appears two other times in the same address; the selective listing of McClellan victories out of chronological order, as they also appear on the plinth of his statue; and the familiar description of McClellan as an excellent organizer much loved by the rank and file he organized. By the time of Roosevelt's speech, this description had established itself as orthodoxy in public memory of the Civil War, even among McClellan's critics. With the appearance in 1901 of Peter S. Michie's biography *General McClellan* in the Great Commanders series, published in New York by D. Appleton and Company, the orthodoxy became available to Roosevelt, sworn in after the assassination of William McKinley that year, in this neatly compressed, one-sentence form: "But whatever may be the judgment that history will ultimately formulate with regard to McClellan's qualifications in the domain of strategy and tactics, there will be no divided opinion with respect to his talents and attainments for the organization of armies, and the wonderful power that he possessed of implanting in the hearts of his soldiers a personal affection and devotion that has never been excelled."[3]

MacMonnies's equestrian statue of George B. McClellan, with the general's right arm akimbo and a fisted hand on his hip, faces stoutly south, down Connecticut Avenue, presumably to keep a green oxidized eye on Virginia and its troublesome siblings, although in the 1862 campaigns of the Peninsula and Sharpsburg-Antietam McClellan usually found himself turning toward some combination of north and west. In facing south today, however, the bronze commander also stares unblinking at a much nearer monument to his place in popular memory, one that sits only about five hundred yards away, near the intersection of Connecticut with Florida Avenue. It is a snugly dim, wood-featured tavern with the archly punning name *McClellan's Retreat*. On its web site, beneath an image based on one of Mathew Brady's photographs of McClellan, right hand hidden inside his partially unbuttoned coat, appears this three-sentence summary of McClellan's tortuous career—if rhetorically less august than Theodore Roosevelt's, surely now more frequently read:

"Major General George B. McClellan (Dec 1826–Oct 1885) aka 'Young Napoleon' & 'Little Mac,' was a high-ranking Union commander extraordinarily beloved by the men under his command. General McClellan was responsible for the reorganization of the Army of the Potomac after the defeat at Manassas. As the war progressed, he became known for frequently delaying his attacks, giving his opponents time to retreat, while giving his army time to rest and refit."[4]

The first two sentences repeat the orthodoxies embedded in Peter S. Michie's 1901 biography and Roosevelt's 1907 speech, as though praying aloud with them in unison, whereas the third swerves off into loosely creative improvisation. Missing from its account is any acknowledgment of the relative brevity of McClellan's hour upon the stage. In a war that lasted forty-eight months, McClellan headed the Army of the Potomac in active campaigning for five or six, depending on how one defines "active." He served as general-in-chief of United States armies a little over four months before the start of the Peninsula campaign. As a soldier, he had nothing to do with how the war progressed over the twenty-nine months from Fredericksburg in December 1862 to Appomattox in April 1865, reappearing during that stretch as a civilian candidate for president in 1864. Also notable in the summary of its patron saint's career is the absence of any reference to McClellan's own retreating, of which he left us one and only one example, the disciplined, skillful withdrawal—"cleverly executed," in the words of Robert E.

Lee's nephew Fitzhugh—to Harrison's Landing on the James River, under-taken after the battle of Gaines Mill on June 27, 1862. Instead, the web site speaks of Confederate retreats McClellan allowed, presumably referring to Joseph E. Johnston's withdrawal from Manassas in March 1862, an unwel-come surprise to Jefferson Davis, or to the retreat of the Army of Northern Virginia after Sharpsburg-Antietam in September 1862, unpursued by the Army of the Potomac. Behind its gently muddled, softly fuzzy historical makeover is the suggestion that this bar is a congenial retreat in which to rest and refit from the struggles of civilian life.[5]

McClellan's Dark Side

Abridged and predictable as these two summaries of McClellan's career may be, they avoid negative, hyperbolic caricatures of him in wide circulation, beginning with wartime newspapers and political cartoons, continuing in recent memory with Ken Burns's documentary *The Civil War* (1990), and still flourishing today. In March 1862 Nathaniel Hawthorne, along with publisher William D. Ticknor, traveled from Massachusetts to Washington "to look a little more closely at matters" there and subsequently published his account of the trip as the controversial essay "Chiefly about War-Matters," printed in the July 1862 *Atlantic Monthly,* where the author signed himself "A Peaceable Man." In this essay, which some read partly as a tongue-in-cheek hoax, especially in its fictional footnotes, Hawthorne noted meeting McClellan against the backdrop of "a most fierce and bitter outcry, and detraction loud and low, against [him], accusing him of sloth, imbecility, cowardice, treasonable pur-poses, and, in short, utterly denying his ability as a soldier, and questioning his integrity as a man." In contrast, Hawthorne offered his own more fa-vorable endorsement, taking his cue from the cheers of McClellan's soldiers as the general rode past them: "If he is a coward, or a traitor, or a humbug, or anything less than a brave, true, and able man, that mass of intelligent soldiers, whose lives and honor he had in charge, were utterly deceived, and so was this present writer; for they believed in him, and so did I; and had I stood in the ranks, I should have shouted with the lustiest of them."[6]

Since Hawthorne put the dark side of McClellan's reputation on public record in 1862, it has remained alive and well, despite formulaic, often token hom-ages to his ability to organize soldiers who loved him. Deriving their authority from the ascendancy and prestige of psychoanalysis, McClellan's harshest critics have attempted to account for the dark side of his reputation by subjecting McClellan himself to unsparing, if not anachronistic, psychiatric examination. In his judiciously balanced study *George B. McClellan and Civil War History* (1998), Thomas J. Rowland efficiently summarized the various pseudoclinical damnations of McClellan that had accumulated by the close of the twentieth century. Rowland opened his survey of diagnoses, in a chapter tellingly titled "A Foray into the Twilight Zone," with the sentence, "Clearly, the most damaging flaw attributed to George McClellan is that he labored under innate psychological defects so severe as to preclude him from ever attaining excellence as a military leader." From there Rowland proceeded to inventory writings by Irving Stone, Kenneth P. Williams, Allan Nevins, T. Harry Williams, Stephen W. Sears, Harold Holzer, and Joseph T. Glatthar, compiling a formidable train of terms and descriptors for McClellan's innate psychological defects: manic depression, arrogant confidence, wretched self-abasement, vanity, instability, inherent lack of discipline, pathological lying, unrestrained ego, delusions of grandeur, possession by demons, psychosis, morose view of life, dark fatalism, martinet tendencies, innate querulousness, persecution complex, messianic complex, paranoid personality disorder, and finally, in a quaint nod to the prepsychoanalytic worldview of Aristotle's *Poetics,* tragic flaw. Having taken his grim inventory, Rowland moved to refute the thinking behind it: "A specious line of reasoning underlies these conclusions." He countered that these historians "have acted upon their own prejudices and invoked a form of inductive reasoning to ferret out evidence for preordained conclusions," in particular the conclusion that McClellan was a failure whose failure can only be explained by employment—Rowland's word is "exploitation"—of psychological reasons "for the a priori condition of McClellan's failure."[7]

Those interested in the full scope of Rowland's exposition should consult his book. But even without it, a little garden-variety skepticism and homegrown critical thinking should lead the student of George McClellan to keep in mind a few basic considerations. For one, it is not a self-evident truth that he was a failure. Whether we call the battle of Sharpsburg-Antietam a draw or a US victory, McClellan's achievement there had large consequences, national and international, for the development and advancement of northern war aims, especially with respect to the timing of Abraham Lincoln's Emancipation Proclamation and its preempting of British intervention. After McClellan was relieved of command in November 1862, the army he built and trained managed to survive disasters under Ambrose E. Burnside and Joseph Hooker, remaining intact until the appointment of George G. Meade before Gettysburg and the advent of Ulysses S. Grant before the Overland campaign. None of these commanders had to build an army from scratch, and every one of them owed something to McClellan's exhaustive work during the latter part of 1861 and the first part of 1862.

Then there is the question of exactly who failed at what before and during the Peninsula campaign. Until January 14, 1862, George McClellan's boss was Lincoln's first secretary of war, Simon Cameron, and no one has argued that he was a success in this position. Nor has anyone argued that Cameron's successor, Edwin Stanton, set new standards for transparency, truthfulness, plain-dealing, and mental health. Just as important, the US commander-in-chief, newly elected, raw, untested Abraham Lincoln, was not yet the non-interfering, deferentially supportive war president he would become by the time he brought Grant east as general-in-chief in March 1864. All these men, along with their Confederate counterparts, began 1862 with naïve assumptions about the nature of the war they had started, about its intensity and its duration. They did not and could not imagine that by the cessation of fighting in 1865 they would have assisted in transforming war into something for which the terms "home front," "shell shock," "refugee crisis," "war crime," "weapons of mass destruction," "collateral damage," and "posttraumatic stress disorder" had not yet been invented but soon would need to be. In this sense, they were all failures, at least as of early 1862. There are other considerations, too. Was the collapse of the Peninsula campaign wholly due to McClellan's failure, or did any of it have to do with Robert E. Lee's success? The wound that disabled Joseph E. Johnston at the battle of Seven Pines brought to Confederate command someone who by the end of the war had a solid record of defeating, or at least checking, the numerically superior Army of the Potomac, and there is no reason to assume that Lee's success against McClellan was either anomalous or entirely a matter of McClellan's weakness. Finally, the supposed failure of McClellan's retreat to Harrison's Landing, from which he wrote his superiors recommending it for future operations, looks less delusional or self-serving when one considers that three years later, in the final phase of the war, Ulysses S. Grant also would make the same stretch of the James River his base of operations, though on the opposite shore.[8]

Publisher, Editor, and McClellan's Own Story

This discussion comes neither to bury George McClellan under more censure nor to try to praise him up and out from under it. Rather, the aim here is to set aside for a moment both censure and praise in order to examine an understudied event in the military-literary history of the Civil War, one that repays dispassionate scrutiny apart from the controversies in which it originated and which it in turn has helped to perpetuate. That event was the posthumous publication in 1887 of the one-volume memoir *McClellan's Own Story* by Mark Twain's Charles L. Webster and Company in the Great War Library, informally known as the Shoulder Strap series.

The first thing to say about George McClellan's posthumous memoir, the full title of which is *McClellan's Own Story: The War for the Union, The Soldiers Who Fought in It, The Civilians Who Directed It, and His Relations to It and to Them,* is that it was largely the work of McClellan's literary executor, Democratic newspaper editor William Cowper Prime, whose popular 1857 travel book *Tent Life in the Holy Land* was lampooned by Mark Twain in *The Innocents Abroad* (1869), in which Twain interspersed quotations from William C. "Grimes" with disparaging comments about him. Any twenty-first-century reader of *McClellan's Own Story* interested in Prime's role in its formation owes a large debt to Stephen W. Sears for his thorough detective work into the provenance, editing, and reception of the book. Sears's biography *George B. McClellan: The Young Napoleon* (1988) closed with a brief epilogue summarizing this research and culminating in the conclusion, "Historians have been grateful enough to Prime, certainly, but if his wish [that McClellan would have approved of his editing] was ever granted, it required truly saintly forgiveness on McClellan's part." Meanwhile, a much fuller version of the research and argument behind Sears's epilogue appeared in an essay he published in the June 1988 issue of *Civil War History.*[9]

From Sears we learn that McClellan began his narrative in the summer of 1865 in Switzerland, where he was living in self-imposed exile after his defeat in the 1864 election. He worked on it until 1868, when he returned to the United States, and resumed it in the mid-1870s, when memoirs by Joseph E. Johnston and William T. Sherman appeared. McClellan completed his narrative in 1881, after his term as governor of New Jersey, and then traveled to Europe for six months, only to return in October 1881 to news that the warehouse in which he had stored the manuscript had burned.

Having recovered gamely from discouragement, McClellan set about re-writing his story and was still working on it as late as February 1884, but by the time he died at the end of October 1885, he had completed only 166 manuscript pages, which brought the Army of the Potomac to the battle of Hanover Court House, May 27, 1862. William Prime then took up the task of filling out a book of nearly seven hundred pages, a task he discharged by assembling a pastiche of McClellan's second manuscript, his 1864 *Report on the Organization and Campaigns of the Army of the Potomac,* dispatches or letters to and from various soldiers and civilians, and, most controversially from Sears's point of view, eleven chapters of excerpts from McClellan's letters to his wife, Nelly.[10]

Sears's appraisal of *McClellan's Own Story* was understandably mixed. On the one hand, he endorsed the assertion of *Atlantic Monthly* reviewer John C. Ropes that he "was not moved by the arguments McClellan raised on his own behalf and had little sympathy for him"; Mark Twain himself shared with his wife a similar opinion. No doubt there are fair-minded readers, among the few who still look into *McClellan's Own Story,* who will concur in this judgment, and it is improbable that historians, academic or not, who are already convinced of the dark side of McClellan's psyche will find enough in the book to budge them. On the contrary, it is this very book that has provided them with abundant grist for their psychoanalytic grinding. On the other hand, Sears conceded that "no other major Civil War figure disclosed so much of himself" as McClellan did in what Prime chose to include, and, in the words of a formulation echoed at the end of his biography, "[c]ertainly history is grateful to have General McClellan so revealed."[11]

Can one have it both ways? Can one damn, censure, and repudiate the "bastardized" product of William Prime's "protective editing" and still gobble up, with a good, hearty appetite, the fruits of Prime's labor? If integrity and fairness are to be the measures of our endeavors, especially when it comes to the research and writing of history, then why not disregard improperly presented evidence, as a judge would instruct members of a jury to do? At this point one can imagine Mark Twain, or Samuel Clemens in his busi-ness persona, hearing out Sears's case against Prime and then asking Sears, with a barely suppressed smile, So what? When it came to the business of making and selling books, Clemens was no neophyte, and he knew what he was about. In a letter of February 3, 1875, he wrote his friend P. T. Barnum a sentence that could serve as the invisible, understood epigraph for any book he authored or helped to publish. Two weeks before, Barnum had sent Clemens passes to the "Greatest Show on Earth," along with a request that the author of *The Innocents Abroad* and *Roughing It* (1872) write something to help boost publicity. In his reply Clemens declined, explaining that he had been ill and adding, "I couldn't write the article, anyway, for any price, because it is out of my line; & you know, better than any other man, that success in life depends strictly upon one's sticking to his line."[12]

When it came to Charles L. Webster and Company, and to the publishing of the Shoulder Strap series of memoirs by US generals, Clemens's line was getting marketable books out of people who were not professional writers and whose deadline was often death itself, as in the cases of Grant, Sheridan, and Sherman, each of whom died just before or soon after Webster published his book. In the cases of Winfield Scott Hancock and George Armstrong Custer, that mortal deadline had passed, and there could be no question about whose pen produced the book. The title page of *Reminiscences of Winfield Scott Hancock* (1887) states that the book is "By His Wife," Almira, not identified until a picture facing the copyright page, and the title page of *Tenting on the Plains, or General Custer in Kansas and Texas* (1887) reads quite clearly, "By Elizabeth B. Custer / Author of 'Boots and Saddles.'" Samuel Crawford was the lone Shoulder Strap author who outlived his book, *The Genesis of the Civil War* (1887), by several years.

It is only in the case of *McClellan's Own Story* that there could be any ambiguity or room for controversy. The title page reads "By George B. McClellan / Late Major-General Commanding the Armies," while the name William C. Prime does not appear until page xiii, which introduces the "Biographical Sketch / of / George B. McClellan / by / W. C. Prime, LL.D." In the final pages of his biographical sketch, Prime offered a plain statement of his editorial procedure and his editorial aspirations: "In editing this volume for the press I have tried to do that which my friend would approve. The discretion he gave me was ample. I have exercised it by omissions, not by changes." As for his use of McClellan's letters to Nelly, Prime was also direct: "I confess that I hesitated very much about giving any part of these letters, written in the most sacred confidence of life, to the public eye. Others advised that, as he belonged to his country, and innumerable citizens and soldiers loved him with devout affection, they could well be allowed, had indeed a right, to read portions of these letters which reveal McClellan the man, as his narrative shows McClellan the soldier."[13]

Having quoted both these passages, Stephen Sears dismissed them, in the first case pronouncing that Prime's "judgment failed his good intentions." Sears may think so, condemning Prime for his omissions, but in a statement dated November 8, 1881, placed before the first chapter of *McClellan's Own Story*, McClellan anticipated and authorized the "judicious pruning to fit [his account] for public use," claiming that he had "no present intention of publishing anything" during his lifetime. If this statement was true, then McClellan never intended to see his story through publication. He knew any publication would have to be posthumous, and he knew that "judicious pruning" had to be a part of the process. In the case of the second quotation, Sears commented that "it is difficult to understand why Prime believed publishing these letters would enhance his friend's memory." Nevertheless, if Prime believed that would happen, he was not necessarily alone. The exact parts played by McClellan's wife and daughter, Nelly and May, remain unclear, but Sears's assertion that there "is no indication that Ellen McClellan had any role in the preparation of her husband's memoirs" cannot satisfy. As Candace Shy Hooper has pointed out, it was Nelly who preserved McClellan's letters, so they did not go up in smoke with his original manuscript in the burning warehouse. More important, Nelly was the general's legal executrix, and it is hardly credible that while living under the same roof with her mother, May could or would have copied out excerpts for Prime without her mother's knowledge and cooperation, or at least her acquiescence.[14]

Both of Sears's dismissals represent opinions, not facts, and clearly Samuel Clemens did not agree with either. Just as clearly, he was not hoodwinked by Prime, whom he called a "gushing pietist": "Seldom actually drunk with holiness but always on the verge of it, always dizzy, boozy, twaddlesome." Clemens knew his man, having confronted him more than fifteen years earlier in *The Innocents Abroad*: "I love to quote from Grimes, because he is so dramatic. And because he is so romantic. And because he seems to care but little whether he tells the truth or not." Swipes such as this one helped make *The Innocents Abroad* an orgy of irony, but this particular swipe contained more than a little self-description of Samuel Clemens himself, publishing entrepreneur, master of the tall tale, and literary counterpart of P. T. Barnum. Clemens would have been hard-pressed to show that William Prime was any more a mercenary catering to popular taste than he himself could be at times. If anything, he could have counted on Prime's popularity as a writer, along with his election to first vice president of the Metropolitan Museum of Art in 1874 and to department chair of Art History at Princeton in 1884, as credentials that could only help sales of *McClellan's Own Story*.[15]

And sales were what mattered, both to Clemens and to Prime. "How many McClellans sold?" the former jotted in his notebook. In the words of Clemens's first biographer, Albert Bigelow Paine, the success of Ulysses S. Grant's *Personal Memoirs,* which followed close upon that of *The Adventures of Huckleberry Finn,* Webster's first publication in 1885, "had given the Webster business immense prestige," so much so that the stationery of Charles L. Webster and Company soon carried on it, at the top left, "Personal Memoirs of U. S. Grant" and "Mark Twain's Works." No other title in the Shoulder Strap series equaled the success of Grant's, nor could it be expected to, particularly as the public appetite for Civil War memoirs became surfeited during the rest of the decade. Writing to Clemens as "Uncle Sam" on a piece of his office stationery, dated March 20, 1886, Charles Webster anticipated a new publishing project, *The Life of Pope Leo XIII,* authorized by the pope himself and eventually published in 1887, year of *McClellan's Own Story* and the Crawford, Hancock, and Custer titles: "I find all my letters are read by the Vicar General to His Holiness and many of them by His Holiness himself. I have managed to get the *promise* of an autograph letter stamping the book as—authentic & genuine written and signed by the Pope for the purpose of fac-simile in the book. If we get all that is promised me we will the beat the record on Grant by a great distance."

As it turned out, Webster's heady predictions about the pope's book did not come true; nothing ever beat the Grant record for the publishing company that failed in 1894. In the mid-1880s, however, Clemens felt he had the Midas touch: "I am frightened at the proportions of my prosperity. It seems to me that whatever I touch turns to gold." With respect to the Shoulder Strap series, he believed, at least for a few years, that anything "bearing the stamp of personal battle experience was considered literary legal-tender."[16]

William Prime's interest in book sales was no more hidden or subtle than the interest of his publishers. Writing to Clemens on January 24, 1886, when the two men were anticipating a meeting in New York, Prime did not sound like someone simmering with resentment of the lumps he took in *The Innocents Abroad;* he sounded like a clear-eyed, competent businessman playing his cards skillfully:

I may say frankly that having decided to publish on the subscription plan, I am not going to negociate [*sic*] with the numerous publishers who have written to me. Harpers want to do the book—on the subscription plan. I have had some more conversation with them as to their facilities &c. nothing more. The condition of Gen. McClellan's estate makes it imperative that I give prominent consideration to the money question—the value of the book—in advising Mrs. McClellan as to a publisher. My desire is to be so informed that I can advise her who in my opinion will best ensure her a successful sale of the book.

Not only does this letter challenge the parody of Prime in *The Innocents Abroad* as a twaddlesome, sentimental romantic; it shows that Nelly McClellan was hardly sequestered from the hardball played during the publication of *McClellan's Own Story*. Two months later Charles Webster opened his letter of March 20, 1886, to Uncle Sam Clemens with the report, "I have signed the contract with Mrs. McClellan & Dr Prime and have the manuscript in the safe. I have paid $5000.00 of the $10,000 which they are to have, this was all they asked for at present, but I expect I won't have to wait long for a call." In the end *McClellan's Own Story* did net a profit for Webster—in a notebook entry dated September 1, 1887, Clemens recorded it as $15,000 to date—distinguishing Prime's work from Samuel Crawford's *The Genesis of the Civil War* and the life of Pope Leo XIII, both of which lost money.[17]

A Different Kind of Memoir

It is at this point that literary history and military history need to talk. Just as no thorough military historian of Grant's Overland campaign could tell the whole story of its progress without factoring in the parts played by Quartermaster General Montgomery C. Meigs or Chief Quartermaster Rufus Ingalls, so no thorough historian of *McClellan's Own Story*, military or literary, can tell the whole story without reference to Charles Webster, Samuel Clemens, and what William Prime called "the money question." Logistics count for much in the military and in publication (as book-publishing historians know perfectly well with respect to their own careers), and historians who approach McClellan's book for the sole purpose of psychoanalyzing him, without reference to how the logistics of publication shaped what they are analyzing, risk doing so naively and through a glass darkly, or at least through a one-way mirror. If Civil War historians read *McClellan's Own Story* in order to damn either McClellan or his editor or both, there is no law prohibiting them from doing so. But one hopes they would acknowledge that damning the former would be more difficult without the work of the latter, and the work of the latter did not emerge in a social or economic vacuum.

To expect the posthumous editing of William Prime to result in something like the memoirs of Sherman, Grant, and Sheridan is to make a mistake of generic classification. If we imagine a spectrum, with an ideal of pure written transcription of Civil War events at one end and an ideal of pure literary invention at the other, then it should be obvious that *The War of the Rebellion: A Compilation of the Official Records of the Union and Confederate Armies* (1880–1901) would be closer to the first end and Stephen Crane's *The Red Badge of Courage* (1895) would be closer to the other. Among other differences between them, the Government Printing Office did not publish the *Official Records* with any thought of their strength as literary legal-tender, whereas D. Appleton and Company published *Red Badge of Courage* with that thought uppermost. Memoirs of Sherman, Grant, and Sheridan would fall somewhere between these extremes, as would memoirs written by their Confederate counterparts and published by powerful New York firms, memoirs of Joseph E. Johnston and Richard Taylor, for example. All these memoirs pay homage to standards of factual accuracy as embodied in a written record while bowing to pressures of the literary marketplace. Inevitably the results were hybrids, grafting rhetorical skill and readable presentation for the sake of contemporary sales onto material mined by future historians for documentary evidence in campaign narratives or biographies.

The genre of *McClellan's Own Story* differed from that of books by Sherman, Grant, and Sheridan only in comprising not a memoir authored by the principal but something closer to an anthology of his writings assembled by an editor. In this way it was more like *Recollections and Letters of General Robert E. Lee,* assembled by Robert E. Lee Jr. and published in New York by Doubleday, Page, and Company in 1904. During the Civil War centennial Edmund Wilson wrote of this last work, "We can only come at all close to Lee through the volume of personal documents compiled by his son, Captain Robert E. Lee." But how close was that? *Recollections and Letters* was, in the phrasing of Gary W. Gallagher, the first book about Lee Sr., "to explore the private man" (in 1875 D. Appleton and Company had published a precursor, *Personal Reminiscences, Anecdotes, and Letters of Gen. Robert E. Lee,* edited by the Rev. J. William Jones), but the explorations carried out by Robert E. Lee Jr. could not have been less protective of his father than William Prime was of George McClellan. Although Douglas Southall Freeman called *Recollections and Letters* a "delightful book," it had critics too, among them Thomas L. Connelly (who pointed out deletions of controversial passages from Lee's letters), Richard B. Harwell, and Robert W. Johannsen, who judged the book "rather disjointed and sentimental." In the cases of both *McClellan's Own Story* and *Recollections and Letters of General Robert E. Lee,* the twenty-first-century reader must work to recover the implied understanding among editor, publisher, and a particular general readership of more than a century ago.[18]

If we think of *McClellan's Own Story* as an anthology of McClellan's writings in different genres rather than the unified narrative he might have written had he survived long enough to leave something more substantial to the posthumous pruner he anticipated, and if we consider that Prime's presentation of McClellan was not necessarily more selective or protective than Sherman's or Grant's or Sheridan's self-presentations, we stand a much better chance of appreciating the readable revelations of George McClellan that William Prime aimed, with Samuel Clemens's benediction, at a book-buying audience. That audience included, at least hypothetically, veterans of the Army of the Potomac who, in Prime's words, "loved him with devout affection." It also included more than 1,800,000 citizens who voted for McClellan in the 1864 election, as well as those living in the South, or sympathetic to it, who valued the prospects of McClellan's election for negotiating their independence.

Pruning the Story

What shape did the narrative in *McClellan's Own Story* take for the 1887 readership of the book, and what shape can it take for us now? Privately tutored in Greek and Latin, the young McClellan may not have progressed far enough to read Homer in the original language, but his early exposure to the classics must have included an encounter with some English version of the first line of the *Odyssey:* "Tell me, Muse, about the man of many turns." Among numerous English translations made since the early seventeenth century, this one by Albert Cook comes closest to a literal rendering of Homer's adjective for his eponymous hero, πολύτροπον or *polytropon,* which means "much-turned," as in much-traveled or much-wandering. The George McClellan revealed by William Prime in *McClellan's Own Story* was likewise a man of many turns, some of them whiplashingly sharp. True, the same could be said of hosts of people who led twisting, turning lives much less publicly than McClellan. In McClellan's case, though, the many turnings often caused or accompanied major turnings in the Civil War during the span of his service from April 1861 to November 1862, which is also the narrative span of the book. In rebuttal one could argue that William T. Sherman, Ulysses S. Grant, and Philip H. Sheridan were men of many turnings, too. True again, but Sherman's and Grant's narratives of the war itself showed them turning upward once, from respective nadirs before and after the battle of Shiloh in 1862, and never looking back as they moved toward victory, while Sheridan's wartime turnings, at least as he wrote about them, included none that led downward.

McClellan's story, by contrast, was one of drastic ups and downs. The first editor of his Mexican war diary, William Star Myers, a professor of history and politics at Princeton and the colleague there of George B. McClellan Jr., appointed professor of economic history in 1912, put it this way: "His life covered barely fifty-nine years, his services of national prominence only eighteen months, but during this time he experienced such extremes of good and ill fortune, of success and of failure, as seldom have fallen to the lot of one man." Unusual extremes of fortune compressed into unusually short periods of time are the stuff of good stories and have been since the beginning of storytelling, as the tale of Job, which may have originated in ancient Near Eastern folk tradition, makes clear. Some of these extremes had their origins in McClellan's life before the opening of *McClellan's Own Story* in 1861 but had important consequences for his wartime career. One, from the Mexican war, was malaria, which he called his "Mexican disease" and which came back to afflict him in August 1861 and during the Peninsula campaign. Nor was this the only illness that adversely affected his career. In December 1861, having been called as the first witness to appear before the Joint Committee on the Conduct of the War, McClellan fell seriously ill with typhoid fever and could not appear to defend himself against or influence the terms of debate from the outset. Then there was McClellan's European tour, from April 1855 to April 1856, with a military commission authorized by Franklin Pierce and sent by Secretary of War Jefferson Davis to study the major armies of Europe and observe the war in the Crimea. The report McClellan prepared in Philadelphia during the spring of 1856, published by Congress in 1857, established his authority on matters of military organization. The experience and knowledge behind the report provided the foundation for the later organization of the Army of the Potomac and for McClellan's subsequent legacy in this context.[19]

As for the many turnings of April 1861 to November 1862, a significant portion of 1887 readers already would have known that McClellan's story began with minor successes in the West Virginia campaign, followed by the summons to Washington because of them. Then came the fortification of the capital and the beginnings of army organization. After the lapse at Ball's Bluff, there was the appointment to general-in-chief and Joseph E. Johnston's evacuation of Manassas. The organization of the army corps, the removal from his position as general-in-chief, and the opening of the Peninsula campaign continued the narrative, leading to the Peninsula campaign, during which McClellan fought the battle of Williamsburg, described by him as "one of the most brilliant engagements of the war." But a long stretch of dismal, rainy weather that swelled the creeks and rivers followed, as did the wrangling over assignment of Irvin McDowell's corps to service in the Shenandoah Valley. Then came the Seven Days' battles, the retreat to Harrison's Landing, and the controversial letter written there to Abraham Lincoln, along with the withdrawal from the Peninsula and transfer to Washington. The familiar plot turned next to the reassignment of a large portion of the army to John Pope before Second Manassas-Bull Run, the restoration to command, and the move into Maryland. Next the story moved to the serendipitous recovery of lost Special Order 191, the battle of Sharpsburg-Antietam, and Burnside's poor performance. Finally, McClellan's decision not to pursue Lee across the Potomac after the battle brought relief from command and the farewell to the army with which *McClellan's Own Story* concludes.[20]

Among Civil War generals who produced books after the war, or who had books associated with them, the career of McClellan's friend Joseph E. Johnston came closest to approximating the dramatic ups and downs of McClellan's, though Johnston's drama unfolded over all four years of war, which brought him to the age of fifty-eight, whereas McClellan's was compressed into a year and a half, which brought him not quite to thirty-six. The more familiar of McClellan's many twists and turns have generated copious commentary, beginning with coverage in wartime periodicals and continuing into the twenty-first century with Ethan S. Rafuse's *McClellan's War* (2005), John C. Waugh's *Lincoln and McClellan* (2010), and Chester G. Hearn, *Lincoln and McClellan at War* (2012). This vast body of commentary could not help but influence general readers. But *McClellan's Own Story* also has striking features that have escaped much or most commentary, features that could help to shape the way the book has been read by many. Here we will consider three.[21]

McClellan and the Almighty

The first feature is God. Another of McClellan's prewar turnings was that of his conversion—or in the words of Stephen Sears his "evangelical religious regeneration"—toward the Presbyterianism, or "rigid Calvinism," of Nelly's family during the seven months of their engagement from October 1859 to May 1860. In his 1901 biography Peter Michie gave a single sentence to this moment in McClellan's life and then said no more about the marriage, Christianity, or their effects on McClellan: "It proved to be a union of two minds that were counterparts of each other, and of two souls whose mutual love was continually strengthened by the powerful influence of a Christian faith." In his introduction to the 1917 edition of McClellan's Mexican war diary, in which the word "God" appears only once, William Starr Meyers was similarly succinct: "In after years he became extremely serious, deeply and sincerely religious, sometimes oppressed by a sense of duty." True as these statements may be, the truth behind them has not had a large effect on popular memory of the Civil War, in which the temperate Episcopalian Robert E. Lee and the zealous Presbyterian Stonewall Jackson are prominent fixtures. After them Leonidas Polk, William S. Rosecrans, and Oliver Otis Howard might come to mind. But few twenty-first-century students of the Civil War think first of Christianity when they think of George McClellan, and few popular images of him suggest the connection. There is nothing about it, for example, in Theodore Roosevelt's 1907 speech, Ken Burns's documentary, or the web site of McClellan's Retreat.[22]

Without looking into *McClellan's Own Story,* one would have no reason to distinguish McClellan in this context from the more secular-sounding William T. Sherman, Ulysses S. Grant, and Philip H. Sheridan. In Sherman's memoir "God" appears twenty-five times, either in quotation from someone else (for example, in John Bell Hood's side of the correspondence about treatment of the civilians of Atlanta), in the legal phrase "act of God," or in interjections such as "for God's sake" or "Great God!" In Grant's *Personal Memoirs* "God" appears only six times, always in quotation, direct or indirect from someone else. In Sheridan's memoir it appears four times, twice in quotations and twice in an oath prescribed in the text of the 1867 act "to provide for the more efficient government of the rebel States." Even Joseph E. Johnston, baptized by Leonidas Polk during Sherman's Atlanta campaign, used "God" only three times in his *Narrative of Military Operations,* once in quotation of Jefferson Davis, once in quotation of Braxton Bragg, and once on his own behalf in closing a letter to the Confederate president, "But the hand of Almighty God has delivered us in times of great danger!"[23]

Readers of *McClellan's Own Story* will find the word "God" appearing ninety-two times, seven in Prime's biographical sketch and eighty-five in the rest of the book, most often in excerpts from letters to Nelly. Following the lead of Mark Twain, some might say that this high number reveals the editorial hand of William Prime, the gushing pietist. Following the lead of Stephen Sears, others might say that here is incontrovertible evidence of McClellan's messianic complex. Meanwhile, Thomas Rowland and Ethan Rafuse have provided more balanced readings of McClellan's religious sensibility and its social background. Rowland has argued that to "the predominantly secular society of today" McClellan's "stark expression of Calvinist theology and highly stylized piety reverberates discordantly," whereas he was not out of line with the millennialist spirit that characterized "the religious mainstream of his day," and Rafuse has maintained that there was nothing about McClellan's new Presbyterianism incompatible with the Philadelphia Episcopalianism of his upbringing, his inclination toward Whig politics, and a "worldly ambition" that promoted self-improvement, progress, social stability, and "the values of rationalism, moderation, and order."[24]

At least since the adoption of the first amendment to the Constitution, the United States has had a complex and ambivalent relationship to the use of religious language in public places. Add to this complex ambivalence the chasm that divides, on the one hand, relative comfort and familiarity with public language influenced by Judeo-Christianity in the nineteenth century from, on the other, often strong antipathy toward the same in the twenty-first, and many twenty-first-century readers of *McClellan's Own Story* stand little better chance of evaluating its frequent references to God than they do its occasional phrases in Latin. For many contemporary readers the use of religious rhetoric is toxic; there is no getting past it and no appraising its nuances. But religious rhetoric is like any other rhetoric; some people use it in more interesting, significant ways than others, and two skillful rhetoricians can use it in very different ways. Lincoln, for example, often wielded rhythms and images straight from the Bible, while remaining evasive about his religious convictions, whereas McClellan, outspoken about his religious convictions, did not echo or allude to the Bible, at least in the material that comprises *McClellan's Own Story*.

"McClellan could write." The truth of this three-word formulation by William Starr Meyers does not rule out the truth of Meyers's next sentence: "In fact his pen was too ready and in later years [after the Mexican war] it often led him into difficulties." McClellan's rhetorical readiness, along with the difficulties it sometimes caused him, cannot be separated wholly from his frequent references to God. Several examples from *McClellan's Own Story* illustrate the point, among them some passages sent privately to Nelly, one order issued publicly to the Army of the Potomac during the Peninsula campaign, and one letter addressed to Abraham Lincoln but subsequently published to the world.[25]

Those who maintain that George McClellan's conversion brought him under the spell of a messiah complex either have to ignore some revealing moments in the correspondence excerpted in *McClellan's Own Story* or massage the word "messiah" to suit their own purposes. Nowhere in the New Testament does the Messiah—the Greek uses *Messias* only twice, both times in the gospel of John, otherwise rendering the Hebrew concept of the anointed one with some form of *Christos*—say anything that sounds like either of these vulnerable moments:

> I appreciate all the difficulties in my path: the impatience of the people, the venality and bad faith of the politicians, the gross neglect that has occurred in obtaining arms, clothing, etc.; and, above all, I feel in my inmost soul how small is my ability in comparison with the gigantic dimensions of the task, and that, even if I had the greatest intellect that was ever given to man, the result remains in the hands of God. (October 31, 1861)

> I hope and trust that God will watch over, guide, and protect me. I accept most resignedly all He has brought upon me. Perhaps I have really brought

it on myself; for while striving conscientiously to do my best, it may well be that I have made great mistakes that my vanity does not permit me to perceive. When I see so much self-blindness around me I cannot arrogate to myself greater clearness of vision and self-examination. (July 17, 1862)

If McClellan sounded like anyone in these passages, the first written ten days after the fiasco at Ball's Bluff, the second six days after Henry W. Halleck was named to replace him as general-in-chief, it was not Jesus, the anointed one, but Paul, apostle to the Gentiles, who called himself the worst of all sinners (1 Timothy 1:15–16) and spoke figuratively of having a thorn in his flesh that kept him from becoming conceited in the course of his missionary work around the eastern Mediterranean in the middle of the first century (2 Corinthians 12:7). The Messiah or Christ about whom he preached never refers in the gospels to his own small ability, his great mistakes, his vanity, or his blindness. In three of the gospels, Matthew, Mark, and Luke, Jesus prays in Gethsemane that the cup of death be removed from him, and in Luke only he quotes from the cross the opening of Psalm 22, "My God, my God, why hast thou forsaken me?" (King James Version). But these are very different utterances from Paul's or McClellan's, and they are conspicuously absent from John, the most Messianic or Christological of the gospels.[26]

Writing to Nelly in these moments, McClellan showed himself, in his mid-thirties, to be human, all too human, and, to his credit, aware of it. Even his reference to the uselessness of having the greatest intellect that was ever given to man showed disarming self-awareness. In his biography of his uncle, Fitzhugh Lee stated in a footnote, "General Lee said, after the war, that he considered General McClellan the most intellectual of the Federal generals," but as both Lees learned after Grant assumed overall command in 1864, the most intellectual general and the most effective general are not necessarily the same. In context the footnote followed the statement that "General Lee . . . was sorry to part with McClellan" in November 1862. The cynical reading would be that Lee was sorry to part with someone he bested in the Peninsula campaign, if not in the Maryland one. In fact Fitzhugh Lee took his uncle's reference to his adversary's intellectual superiority to mean "that as long as McClellan was in command everything would be conducted by the rules of civilized warfare." For his part, McClellan knew that his intellectual power often made him vain, arrogant, and, in the memorable formulation of William Starr Meyers, "one of the worst subordinates and best superiors that ever lived." At least McClellan's frequent invocations of God included some that acknowledged this truth.[27]

It is not clear that readers in our own moment of digital solipsism, especially those unaccustomed to questioning the concealed premises of secularism or how it establishes its authority or why it can be as rigidly dogmatic as any religion, are equipped to appreciate the nuances of McClellan's references to God and the rhetoric of his faith. By contrast, many readers of 1887 would have been able to notice distinct features of those references, or more accurately, distinct absences from them. Nowhere in *McClellan's Own Story* did McClellan mention Jesus. He never used the word "Messiah" or "Christ" or "Savior." He never referred to the resurrection or, in a theological context, salvation. He never quoted or alluded to the Bible. He spoke of sin exactly twice, as in a letter to Nelly of August 8, 1862, when he referred to it in a context that would have gratified Robert E. Lee—that of taking "the highest Christian ground for the conduct of the war"—but not in the context of redemption from personal sins, such as sloth, lust, avarice, gluttony, pride, envy, or wrath: "I will not permit this army to degenerate into a mob of thieves, nor will I return these men of mine to their families as a set of wicked and demoralized robbers. I will never have that sin on my conscience." People do not have to call themselves Christians to use the word in this familiar, idiomatic way.[28]

We can begin to appreciate the distinct quality of McClellan's Christian rhetoric when we contrast it with that of Robert E. Lee, also writing privately to his wife, Mary, in a letter of November 15, 1856, sent from Fort Brown, Texas:

> It was pleasant to join in the prayers again, & Mr P gave us a plain but good sermon. I see though he has brought to this wilderness the colouring of the high church which had much better be left behind. There is already enough of Romanism in this country inherited from Mexico, & there is more want of "the worship of spirit & of truth" in all the beauty of its sincerity & holiness. When I see its perversion by man from the purity preached by our Saviour, there is an inward rebellion over which I have no control, & I think it better for me to remain in the wilderness from whence I came & adore the Great God with all the power & all the strength he has given me free from the detraction, & disturbing forces around me.

Lee's distaste for Mexican Catholicism imprinted this letter, though during the Civil War many of his Baptist, Methodist, and Presbyterian soldiers no doubt associated his own Episcopalianism with "the colouring of the high church." Nevertheless, Lee's particular brand of rebellious Calvinist Protestantism came through loud and clear in this letter, with his insistence on "the purity preached by our Saviour"; the biblical allusion to the wilderness, here associated not with the Judean desert and Isaiah's image of a voice crying out there or the rebellious protest of John the Baptist, but with sparsely populated Texas; and the imperfectly remembered quotation of John 4:24 in the King James Version: "God is Spirit: and they that worship him must worship him in spirit and in truth." These rhetorical features, along with Lee's references to divine spirit and private adoration of "the Great God," have no counterparts in McClellan's letters to Nelly.[29]

The religious faith of Robert E. Lee and his world figured indirectly in *McClellan's Own Story,* where it inspired homage. Chapter twenty-two of the book opens with McClellan's account of coming upon White House in mid-May 1862, "a very fine plantation belonging to Mrs. Gen. Lee" and "the residence of Mrs. Custis when she was married to Washington." Having visited St. Peter's Church there, "a lonely old building beautifully placed on a command hill," McClellan gave his posthumous readers a small glimpse of his inmost religious impulses: "Finding one's self alone within that historic building, it was a natural impulse to invoke the aid of God to enable me to serve the country as unselfishly and truly as did the great man who had often worshipped there." In context McClellan meant Washington, but Lee, for whose ability McClellan said he had "the highest respect," must have worshiped in St. Peter's too, and his presence hovers over the passage. The account of this solitary moment was significant enough to McClellan for him to refer to it both in a letter written to Nelly on May 16, 1862, and in the narrative he knew one day would be made public. In the letter he wrote that "I could not help kneeling at the chancel and praying that I might serve my country as truly as he did." Among guides to his spiritual interior, this one is more reliable than many, and what it suggests is that for McClellan God was primarily to be invoked or petitioned in the context of service, duty, and ethical conduct; God was not primarily to be praised and adored out of self-forgetting, worshipful love that had no practical or instrumental value.[30]

To say so is not to judge McClellan's Christianity negatively. It is to demonstrate that it operated within a limited bandwidth usually involving pragmatic attitudes and behavior more characteristic of fretfully busy Martha, in the gospel of Luke, than of her sister, quietly contemplative Mary

(Luke 10:38–42). For readers of *McClellan's Own Story*, both now and in 1887, this aspect of McClellan's personal faith becomes or became especially significant against the background of public debate, beginning in 1862, about what it meant to wage Christian warfare. To testimony by Fitzhugh Lee we have already seen, we can add two sentences that appear early in *McClellan's Own Story*, the second of which displays the disciplined syntactic organization characteristic of the writer who built the Army of the Potomac: "Since the war I have met many of my late antagonists, and have found none who entertained any personal enmity against me. While acknowledging, with Lee and other of their generals, that they feared me more than any of the northern generals, and that I had struck them harder blows when in the full prime of their strength, they have all said that I fought them like a gentleman, and in an honorable way, and that they felt nothing but respect for me."

As with his ready pen he so often did, in this passage McClellan mixed boastfulness and self-justification with pathos and some important truth. It is easy to think about Ulysses S. Grant's relentless Overland campaign and scoff at McClellan's implicit pride in being most feared, but the qualification "when in the full prime of their strength" should give the scoffer pause. Although he himself labored under delusions about the strength of his enemy, not all of which were his fault, during the Seven Days' battles the Army of Northern Virginia, with somewhere around 90,000 soldiers, bristled with its greatest wartime strength. At the beginning of the Overland campaign two years later, with about the same number of troops McClellan had on the Peninsula, Grant faced approximately two-thirds of this number. More to the point at hand are the words, "I fought them like a gentleman, and in an honorable way."[31]

One might prefer not to have McClellan testifying so baldly in his own behalf, but Fitzhugh Lee seconded the statement, and he added the relevant term: "McClellan was always and everywhere a gentleman, who believed in conducting war in a Christian and humane manner." For all the boastfulness and self-justification so off-putting to McClellan's critics, past and present, the pathos and the truth of his many wartime turnings are that his turnings coincided exactly with a seismic shift in US strategy during the Civil War. The shift meant discarding an ineffectual ideal of fighting in the respectful, conciliatory manner of a humane, Christian gentleman and adopting a newer, more expedient ideal of making war as humane as possible by making it as brief as possible, while making it as brief as possible by making it as hard as possible. The most famous apostles of this new creed were Grant, Sherman, and Sheridan, and, at least from the point of view of the loyal states, their success confirmed the new reasoning. To twenty-first-century readers of *McClellan's Own Story,* some of whom may recollect that the same reasoning preceded the atomic bombing of Japan, the 1862 turning point in American military history may not feel comfortable, but from the perspective of today it cannot help but look inevitable. To readers of 1887, however, with the Spanish-American War still a decade away and the wars of the twentieth century inconceivable, the turning point was recent enough, and postwar reconciliation difficult enough, thanks in part to hard-war policies, that some could still think of McClellan as the champion of another kind of lost cause.[32]

Take for example McClellan's General Orders No. 7, on the subject of the Sabbath, issued in Washington on September 6, 1861, when he was still thirty-four years old:

> The major-general commanding desires and requests that in future there may be a more perfect respect for the Sabbath on the part of his command.

> We are fighting in a holy cause, and should endeavor to deserve the benign favor of the Creator.

> Unless in the case of an attack by the enemy, or some other extreme military necessity, it is commended to commanding officers that all work shall be suspended on the Sabbath; that no unnecessary movements shall be made on that day; that the men shall, as far as possible, be permitted to rest from their labors; that they shall attend divine service after the customary Sunday morning inspection, and that officers and men shall alike use their influence to insure the utmost decorum and quiet on that day. The general commanding regards this as no idle form; one day's rest in seven is necessary to men and animals; more than this, the observance of the holy day of the God of Mercy and of Battles is our sacred duty.

The word "holy" appears in *McClellan's Own Story* three times, once in an ironic reference to the South declaring its peculiar institution "a holy ordinance" and twice in these orders. Whereas Lee wrote to Mary of holiness in the context of private adoration and worship, McClellan referred to public observance of the fourth commandment, as numbered by Presbyterians,

Episcopalians, and denominations that follow Calvin: "Remember the sabbath day, to keep it holy" (King James Version, Exodus 20:8). His emphasis fell on duty, described as "sacred"; on form, insisting that it not be "idle"; and on outward decorum and quiet. That Jesus had pointed out in the Sermon on the Mount (Matthew 5) how one could keep the letter of the commandments outwardly and still violate their spirit inwardly does not seem to have concerned McClellan, whose legalistic focus on Sabbath-keeping resembled that of the scribes and Pharisees more than that of the upstart Galilean they sought to kill for Sabbath-breaking.[33]

"I will not fight on Sunday if I can help it." Ken Burns's documentary helped to link such a statement to popular memory of Stonewell Jackson, who nevertheless fought on Sundays at First Manassas-Bull Run, First Winchester, Cross Keys, and Savage's Station. Had he not been mortally wounded the night before, he would have fought on Sunday at Chancellorsville as well. But in fact this statement was made by McClellan to Nelly in a letter of May 23, 1862, written before he did have to fight on Sundays at Seven Pines and Savage's Station. That statement was not a casual or an idle one; McClellan's wish to observe the Sabbath was real, even anxious. But with the first major battle of the war having been fought on a Sunday, with the second day of Shiloh haven fallen on a Sunday, and with all the battles still to occur on or include Sundays—Resaca, Spotsylvania, Trevilian Station, Second Kernstown, Fort Fisher, Hatcher's Run, Bentonville, and the final capture of Confederate works at Petersburg—his dutiful fidelity to the Sabbath and his desire to impose its weekly rhythm on fighting that could not be constrained by it reflects a larger disjunction between his ideas of waging Christian warfare and the new kind of warfare erupting before him. To his critics this disjunction could point toward a kind of reactionary nostalgia for the theocratic order of Moses leading the Israelites through the wilderness. To more sympathetic readers it could suggest the pathos of a prophet crying out in the wilderness to an unheeding host of straying apostates.[34]

Nowhere did the mismatch between McClellan's idea of waging Christian warfare and the new exigencies of the Civil War that would emerge after the turning points of the Seven Days and the subsequent withdrawal of the Army of the Potomac to Harrison's Landing, also called Harrison's Bar, appear more sharply than in McClellan's 850-word letter to Lincoln of July 7, 1862. McClellan got his letter off to a tactful enough start, broaching his large subject with this carefully segmented, complex sentence: "I cannot but regard our condition as critical, and I earnestly desire, in view of possible contingencies, to lay before your excellency, for your private consideration, my general views concerning the existing state of the rebellion, although they do not strictly relate to the situation of this army or strictly come within the scope of my official duties." In light of what followed, both in the letter itself and in the history of the war, many have come to view the Harrison's Landing letter as not merely one more distasteful instance of McClellan's arrogance but as damning evidence of his gross insubordination. In undertaking to lecture Lincoln that the "time has come when the government must determine upon a civil and military policy covering the whole ground of our national trouble," McClellan overstepped his purely military authority in ways that anticipated William T. Sherman's exceeding of his authority in drafting the initial surrender agreement with Joseph E. Johnston on April 17, 1865, in North Carolina. But though the two instances of soldierly overreaching share some outward similarities, there are important differences between them. Whereas Sherman was outwitted and outmaneuvered, in face-to-face negotiations, by the canny duo of Joseph Johnston and Confederate Secretary of War John C. Breckinridge, McClellan confronted only himself, his own "mind and heart," and he took a long, deliberate time to do so, having first sought permission two and a half weeks earlier, on June 20, to offer his suggestions. Although Lincoln replied at the time that he had concerns about the security of such a communication, he did not deny McClellan the permission he sought, and McClellan postponed the communication until he could hand the letter to Lincoln in person at Harrison's Landing.[35]

Another important difference is that there is no evidence it occurred to Sherman at the time that he was wholly out of bounds, and he was blindsided by the furious, negative response from Washington to his first surrender agreement with Johnston, whereas McClellan showed clear signs of understanding in advance that he was on shaky ground, conceding that his views "do not strictly relate to the situation of this army or strictly come within the scope of my official duties." Unlike Sherman, McClellan was not composing a public document or a binding agreement; he was asking to share his views with Lincoln in private communication. There are many who might maintain that McClellan was still out of line, especially those who already detest him enough to find their aversion confirmed by the self-dramatizing closure of the Harrison's Landing letter, which included the only appearance of the word "forgiveness" in *McClellan's Own Story:* "I may be on the brink of eternity; and as I hope forgiveness from my Maker, I have written this letter with sincerity towards you and from love for my country." But in fact as the war went along, and as Lincoln found generals he trusted, he did ask them to share their views frankly in private, as various accounts of his final meeting with Grant, Sherman, and Adm. David D. Porter aboard the *River Queen* clearly show. In itself a general sharing his private views with his commander-in-chief was not anathema.[36]

The composition and delivery of the Harrison's Landing letter was surely a turning point for McClellan himself. Having read the letter in McClellan's presence, Lincoln did not respond at length, and the letter did not find its way into public circulation until McClellan submitted his official report on the Peninsula campaign, dated August 4, 1863. But in the meantime Lincoln did show the letter to members of his cabinet, and it helped to turn opinion against McClellan. Within two weeks, for example, Salmon P. Chase was urging the president to remove his general. Beyond its immediate implications for his career, however, McClellan's letter captured in microcosm a major turning point of the war itself. Invoking "the highest principles known to Christian civilization" and "the influences of Christianity and freedom," McClellan positioned these Christian principles and influences in opposition to the shifting policies emerging around him. Eleven days before the date of the Harrison's Landing letter, John Pope had been named commander of the new Army of Virginia, and within the next month Pope's infamous General Orders No. 5, 6, and 7 indicated that the treatment of white Virginia civilians would no longer correspond to McClellan's idea of conciliatory Christian warfare, the characteristics of which he spelled out explicitly for Lincoln in his letter:

> It should not be a war looking to the subjugation of the people of any State in any event. It should not be at all a war upon population, but against armed forces and political organizations. . . . In prosecuting the war all private property and unarmed persons should be strictly protected, subject only to the necessity of military operations. All private property taken for military use should be paid or receipted for; pillage and waste should be treated as high crimes; all unnecessary trespass sternly prohibited, and offensive demeanor by the military towards citizens promptly rebuked.

Within a year Ulysses S. Grant and William T. Sherman would be prosecuting a different brand of warfare in Mississippi, and by the end of the war Sherman's campaigns through Georgia and South Carolina and Sheridan's treatment of the Shenandoah Valley, all endorsed or ordered by Grant, would mark how sharp the turn after the Peninsula campaign had been.[37]

The Harrison's Landing letter, and the particular vision of Christian warfare it encapsulated, also pointed to another turn, one that had been under way since Confederate victory at First Manassas-Bull Run and would accelerate ten days after McClellan handed his letter to Lincoln beside the James River. Staunchly maintaining that the "Constitution and the Union must be preserved," McClellan was equally unequivocal in exhorting Lincoln not to tamper with slavery: "Neither confiscation of property, political executions of persons, territorial organization of States, or forcible abolition of slavery should be contemplated for a moment. . . . A declaration of radical views, especially upon slavery, will rapidly disintegrate our present armies." Behind these sentences hovered debate and passage of the First and Second Confiscation Acts, signed into law on August 6, 1861, and July 17, 1862, respectively. One could argue that the unfavorable results of McClellan's Peninsula campaign pushed Congress to reach a compromise on passing the Second Confiscation Act, as one could argue that the results of the Peninsula campaign advanced the progress of the Emancipation Proclamation. But the turn toward policy aimed at the disruption of slavery had begun weeks before McClellan took command of the Army of the Potomac in August 1861. Although the vicissitudes of his tenure as commanding general may have helped to shape the timetable of emancipation policy, they did not initiate the disruption of slavery. If readers of 1887 came to *McClellan's Own Story* with open-mindedness, they would have found in William Prime's presentation of the relevant documents, especially those pertaining to McClellan's vision of Christian warfare and its implications for the treatment of white southern civilians, abundant food for thought.[38]

McClellan and What If?

The second feature of *McClellan's Own Story* that has escaped much notice or commentary has to do with the language of turning points, their causes, and their effects. In discussions of any turning point in Civil War history, reasonable, well-informed people can disagree about what constitutes a particular set of causes or a particular set of effects. The many turnings of George Mc-Clellan's life and career are no exception. A specific subset of turning points, long pondered among professionals and amateurs, are those that pertain not to things that happened but to those things that did not. These are the "what ifs" or the counterfactuals, and their distinct rhetorical flavor arises from heavy seasoning with the grammatical mood we call the subjunctive: What if Joseph E. Johnston or P. G. T. Beauregard had pursued routed US soldiers back to Washington after First Manassas-Bull Run and captured the capital? What if Stonewall Jackson had not been mortally wounded at Chancellors-ville? What if William F. "Baldy" Smith and Winfield Scott Hancock had co-operated to move more quickly and efficiently into Petersburg in mid-June 1864? What if John Frederick Parker had stayed at his post at the entrance to Lincoln's box at Ford's theater, instead of adjourning to a nearby tavern? Skeptical pragmatists might dismiss such speculations as trivial indulgences in thought experimentation, but they are not; they are an inevitable part of the process of sorting out the welter of converging contingencies into histor-ical narratives. What events or developments really do make major differ-ences? When it came to composing his own narrative, or the different narra-tives William Prime pieced together to make *McClellan's Own Story,* no one resorted to subjunctive counterfactuals more often than McClellan himself. Here is one example from relatively early in the book: "In the light of the experience of the twenty-two years which have elapsed since this Memoran-dum was so hastily prepared, and after full consideration of all the events of the long and bloody war which followed it, I still hold to the soundness of the views it expressed. Had the measures recommended been carried into effect the war would have been closed in less than one-half the time and with infinite saving of blood and treasure."[39]

The memorandum to which McClellan referred here was a lengthy one of August 2, 1861, "submitted to the President at his request" and later in-cluded in *McClellan's Own Story.* The memorandum outlined McClellan's grand strategy for prosecuting the war on all fronts, not only in Virginia, and it offered his alternative to Winfield Scott's Anaconda Plan, which relied heavily on naval blockading of southern ports and on the eventual workings of Unionist sentiment in the Confederate states. By contrast McClellan's memorandum did not mention blockading at all; it focused on Virginia, Mis-souri, Kentucky, and eastern Tennessee. It advocated "a strong movement to be made on the Mississippi." It recognized the construction of railroads as having "introduced a new and very important element into war." It ventured "to suggest the policy of an ultimate alliance and cordial understanding with Mexico," and for "the main army of operations" it estimated a total force of 273,000 men. Most important for the discussion here is that unlike several of McClellan's other counterfactuals, some of which appeared in documents composed in the heat of the moment, the subjunctive formulation, "Had the measures recommended been carried into effect the war would have been closed in less than one-half the time and with infinite saving of blood and treasure," was one to which he still held in the full hindsight of rewriting the manuscript lost in the warehouse fire.[40]

Not all McClellan's counterfactuals were created equal. To be sure, there are many among his subjunctive had-X-happened statements that smack of sour grapes to set the teeth of McClellan critics on edge, such as this one: "Had Gen. McDowell joined me by water I could have approached Richmond by the James, and thus have avoided the delays and losses incurred in bridging the Chickahominy, and could have had the army united in one body instead of being necessarily divided by that stream." This sentence commented on a letter from Stanton dated May 18, 1862, in which the secretary of war informed McClellan that McDowell's force would be needed to defend against movements by Stonewall Jackson in the Shenandoah Valley and could not reinforce him. In itself it is not particularly objectionable, but when read in light of a sentence nine lines above, it becomes harder to accept: "Herein lay the failure of the campaign." Although McDowell's arrival by water could have made unnecessary the laborious bridging of the rain-swollen Chickahominy, it did not necessarily follow that the entire Peninsula campaign had to fail because he did not join McClellan in May 1862.[41]

The problem for discerning readers is that McClellan's habitual resistance to accepting blame—and he was not unique among Civil War generals in this respect—inevitably led him to make frequent use of self-justifying counterfactuals, and it can become too easy to dismiss those counterfactuals as all of a piece and all reminiscent of the boy who cried "Wolf" once too often. But the power of Aesop's original fable is that eventually the real Wolf does attack. That McClellan defaulted to counterfactual statements too often in his own defense does not mean that he never had grounds for self-defense. His counterfactual subjunctives about Ambrose Burnside's poor performance at Sharpsburg-Antietam, for example, have something to them:

If this important movement had been consummated two hours earlier, a position would have been secured upon the heights from which our batteries might have enfiladed the greater part of the enemy's line, and turned their right and rear. Our victory might thus have been much more decisive. . . . I have only adverted to the very pernicious effects of Burnside's inexcusable delay in attacking the bridge and the heights in rear. What is certain is that if Porter or Hancock had been in his place the town of Sharpsburg would have been ours, Hill would have been thrown back into the Potomac, and the battle of Antietam would have been very decisive in its results.[42]

"Nothing is certain in war." McClellan had written this sentence to Edwin Stanton in a letter of February 3, 1862, which appeared in *McClellan's Own Story*, as it had in the 1864 *Report on the Organization and Campaigns of the Army of the Potomac*. One does not have to be a Presbyterian Calvinist to embrace such a sentiment, and in light of McClellan's frequent statements about bowing to the will of God, it is odd that in this particular counterfactual of Burnside's lapses at Sharpsburg-Antietam he could have asserted any alternative human scenario as "certain." Nevertheless, McClellan had a point: Had someone more aggressive been in command at Burnside's bridge, the battle of Sharpsburg-Antietam might well "have been very decisive in its results." Had the battle been very decisive in its results, Lincoln's frustration with what he saw as McClellan's failure to pursue Lee to the Potomac might not have arisen. Had Lincoln's frustration not arisen, Ambrose Burnside might not have been in command at Fredericksburg. Had Burnside not been in command at Fredericksburg . . . and so on.[43]

What is particularly compelling about the use of counterfactuals is that they are, among other things, clear signs that no matter how often we intone the apparent truth that nothing is certain, in fact most of us find it nearly impossible to live amidst complete uncertainty. In the language of the English Romantic poet John Keats, very few of us are equipped to demonstrate *"Negative Capability,* that is, when a man is capable of being in uncertainties, mysteries, doubts, without any irritable reaching after fact and reason." Certainly, few historians are so equipped, as the writing of history consists of nothing so much as the reaching after facts and reasons operating behind events; nor was George McClellan, for all his professed submission to the will of God. It is all very well, and all too easy, to censure McClellan for his often irritable reaching after fact and reason in his own defense. But the complicated pathos of McClellan's Civil War service was and is that he has been the object of tremendous criticism leveled at him by people who are no more capable of living in uncertainty than he was. This statement is especially true in the realm of popular memory, which rarely shows affection for uncertain complexity. Familiar images of McClellan as an over-cautious whiner always crying out for reinforcements exhibit their own reductive counterfactuality: Had McClellan shown a "little of the nerve . . . which the Romans displayed during the campaign against Hannibal," he "would have settled the fate of Richmond in very few weeks."[44]

In fact, these words were McClellan's own, and he used them to criticize his civilian superiors for the failure of the Peninsula campaign: "A little of the nerve *at Washington* which the Romans displayed during the campaign against Hannibal would have settled the fate of Richmond in very few weeks" (emphasis added). Although mutual recrimination is rarely edifying, once again McClellan had a point, which can get lost in the general disparagement of his memory: not all the loss of nerve was his. Many people in Washington were uncertain about what was true in the spring of 1862, and they displayed their uncertainty with their own versions of caution, not infrequently at McClellan's expense. For many readers of 1887, "what if" counterfactuals, whether they emanated from McClellan or from Washington, were not merely hypothetical thought experiments, as they are today. They bore directly on the lives of numerous late nineteenth-century readers. The final counterfactual of *McClellan's Own Story* underscores the point: "Late on the night of the 7th [November 1862] I received an order relieving me from the command of the Army of the Potomac, and directing me to turn it over to Gen. Burnside, which I at once did. . . . Had I remained in command I should have made the attempt to divide the enemy, as before suggested; and could he have been brought to a battle within reach of my supplies, I cannot doubt that the result would have been a brilliant victory for our army."[45]

Before writing off this moment as yet one more instance of arrogance blended with sour grapes, one would do well to consider that although there is no convincing proof for McClellan's bold claim, neither is there any sure proof for its converse. For all we know, he may have been able to achieve a brilliant victory sometime after November 7, 1862; he was learning, too, along with the Lincoln administration, and we cannot know what might have happened. He managed the Maryland campaign better than he had managed the Peninsula one, and it is difficult to believe his next performance would have been worse than Burnside's at Fredericksburg or Joseph Hooker's at Chancellorsville. What matters more, at least when it comes to accounting for Samuel Clemens's winning bet on the success of *McClellan's Own Story,* is the effect such a statement could have had on a reader in 1887, someone for whom a brilliant victory by McClellan in 1862 might have meant that the losses of 1863, 1864, and 1865 were in some way diminished. Even the hypothetical fantasy of such a victory, with the mitigation of loss that might have followed, could have had compelling power. If some large, personal bereavement had followed November 7, 1862—and hundreds of thousands, even millions, of them did—then this particular counterfactual, and the light in which it cast the turning point of McClellan's relief from command, could have haunted with unavoidable force. McClellan's earlier counterfactual about his memorandum of August 1861, "Had the measures recommended been carried into effect the war would have been closed in less than one-half the time and with infinite saving of blood and treasure," may sound like so much bloviating wind-baggery nearly a century and a half later, but to someone who suffered loss of blood or treasure, directly or indirectly, in the immediate wake of McClellan's relief from command, the specter of "what if" could have been hard to shake off.

McClellan's Heart

The third and final feature of *McClellan's Own Story* that could have appealed to readers Samuel Clemens envisioned in 1887 more than to readers of today involved not so much a turning point as it did a returning, and it returns us to one of the familiar orthodoxies about McClellan that appeared in Peter Michie's 1901 biography, later echoed in Theodore Roosevelt's 1907 dedication speech at the equestrian statue in Washington: McClellan possessed "the wonderful power . . . of implanting in the hearts of his soldiers a personal affection and devotion that has never been excelled." Nearly a hundred years after the publication of *McClellan's Own Story,* Michael Shaara drew on this particular aspect of McClellan iconography in the early Joshua Lawrence Chamberlain chapters of his Pulitzer-prize-winning novel *The Killer Angels,* which had sold approximately three and a half million copies as of 2013. That many of the soldiers who served under George McClellan had deep affection for him has not been news since Nathaniel Hawthorne published his account of his 1862 visit to Washington. What may be news, and what emerged in William Prime's editing, are the many instances in *McClellan's Own Story* showing how fully McClellan returned his soldiers' affection and devotion. One can argue that if he had been able to detach himself from his affections, he might have been a more aggressive and effective combat leader. One can also argue that some of the expressions of McClellan's affections in *McClellan's Own Story* border on sentimentality, which can be the kiss of death for a twenty-first-century reader. But nineteenth-century readers differed in this respect, as Samuel Clemens knew very well, and William Prime could deliver in this area, as Clemens also knew.[46]

By the 1950s the phrase "bleeding heart" had become a pejorative term, especially in the adjectival form "bleeding-heart liberal," but when George McClellan wrote to Nelly in the aftermath of the debacle at Second Manassas–Bull Run, on the day Lincoln instructed him to reassume command after the Confederate invasion of Maryland, such language had no such negative connotations for him:

> Sept. 5, [1862,] 4 P.M.—. . . It makes my heart bleed to see the poor, shattered remnants of my noble Army of the Potomac, poor fellows! and to see how they love me even now. I hear them calling out to me as I ride among them, "George, don't leave us again!" "They sha'n't take you away from us again," etc., etc. I can hardly restrain myself when I see how fearfully they are reduced in numbers, and realize how many of them lie unburied on the field of battle, where their lives were uselessly sacrificed. It is the most terrible trial I ever experienced. Truly, God is trying me in the fire. . . .

Readers of 1887 could have known this passage only through the editorial offices of William Prime. It did not appear in McClellan's 1864 *Report,* and he had not reached September 1862 in his rewritten manuscript when he died. Confided to Nelly alone, this passage, with ellipses identical to those of the version in Stephen Sears's 1989 edition of McClellan's Civil War papers, revealed the young commander in the grip of overwhelming emotion, hardly able to restrain himself, presumably from some outward display, such as weeping or howling or cursing or all of them at once. That a psychoanalyzing critic looking over his shoulder one hundred fifty years later might take exception to McClellan's focus on himself ("the most terrible trial I ever experienced," "God is trying me in the fire") only confirms the unguardedness of his outpouring to the wife who shared his theological language. There is no passage about the love between commander and soldier as powerfully raw in the memoirs of Sherman, Grant, and Sheridan, although Sheridan did describe the emotional leave-taking from his soldiers when he was ordered east in 1864.[47]

But there is an analogous passage in *Recollections and Letters of General Robert E. Lee,* and the congruence is significant. Also writing to his wife, on Christmas Day 1862, in the wake of his victory at Fredericksburg and three months after McClellan's letter to Nelly, Lee spoke of his gratitude "to Almighty God for His unspeakable mercies" and then adopted a different tone: "But what a cruel thing is war; to separate and destroy families and friends, and mar the purest joys and happiness God has granted us in this world; to fill our hearts with hatred instead of love for our neighbors, and to devastate the fair face of this beautiful world! . . . My heart bleeds at the death of every one of our gallant men."

Even permitting the anachronism, no one could rightly call Lee a bleeding heart, and the similarity between the confessions of the two generals to their wives makes all the more poignant and remarkable another moment that readers of 1887 could have known only because of Prime's inclusion of a letter to Nelly of July 22, 1862, written from Harrison's Landing:

I am about doing a thing to-day which will, I suppose, cause the abolitionists and my other friends to drive the last nail in my official coffin. You know that our sick and wounded in Richmond are suffering terribly for want of proper food, medicines, and hospital supplies. I have ordered a boatload of all such things—lemons, tea, sugar, brandy, underclothing, lint, bandages, chloroform, quinine, ice, etc., etc.—to be sent up to Gen. Lee to-day, to be used at his discretion for the sick and wounded of both armies. I know he would not, and could not, receive them for our men alone, therefore I can only do it in the way I propose, and trust to his honor to apply them properly—half and half. I presume I will be accused now of double-dyed treason—giving aid and comfort to the enemy, etc. What do you think of it? Am I right or wrong?[48]

"Am I right or wrong?" McClellan's disarmingly vulnerable appeal to Nelly's judgment put before 1887 readers a McClellan unknown to most of us now. The Greek term for this conflict in the soul is *psychomachia* (spirit battle or mind combat), and there is no hint of it in the equestrian statue on Connecticut Avenue, nor is there much acknowledgment of it among the harshest critics of McClellan. And yet there it was on full display for the Shoulder Strap Series readership, the tightly knotted entanglement of political awareness, principled commitment to waging Christian warfare, and harrowing compassion for his soldiers that characterized McClellan as much as arrogance or caution. Was he right or wrong? His 1887 editor believed him right, consensus now believes him largely wrong, and critical thinking should guard against any easy oversimplification or reduction. It should also ask McClellan's own question of the thousands of soldiers who loved him: Were they right or were they wrong? Was their devotion wholly misguided? Was it some kind of collective delusion? Did it signify nothing?

At the very least it suggests that George McClellan had some real gift, one we associate with the word *charisma*. Although used mostly in secular contexts now, this term has biblical connections as well, and those connections could not be wholly lost on biblically literate readers able to associate McClellan's visits to wounded soldiers in the hospitals with ministrations to the ailing and afflicted in first-century Palestine:

> I have been through the hospitals, where are many of our own men and of the rebels. One Virginian sent for me this morning and told me that I was the only general from whom they expected any humanity. I corrected this mistake. (May 6, 1862)
>
> . . . Went on the hospital-steamer. . . . I saw all the officers and men on board, and tried to cheer them up. The visit seemed to do them a great deal of good, and it would have done you good to see how the poor, suffering fellows brightened up when they saw me. . . . (July 20, 1862)
>
> . . . This morning I visited the general hospital not far from here, and went through it all, finding the patients comfortable and all improving in health. They are nearly all in hospital-tents and are well provided for; in truth, they are about as well off as they could be away from home, and many of them doubtless better off than they would be there. I find the men more contented than the officers. I confess that the men enlist my sympathies much more warmly than the officers. They are so patient and devoted. They have generally entered the service, too, from higher and more unselfish motives. Poor fellows! I can never willingly break the link that unites me to them, and shall always be very proud of them and of their

love for me, even if it is not decreed by Providence that I am to lead them to Richmond. (July 31, 1862)[49]

Readers of the Shoulder Strap series encountered nothing like these moments in the memoirs of Grant, Sherman, and Sheridan. We have other powerful images of hospital visits during the Civil War—Abraham Lincoln at City Point, Walt Whitman and Louisa May Alcott in Washington, Phoebe Yates Pember in Richmond—but we do not have them in the memoirs of other Civil War generals. And they would not have reached the public when they did, if not for William Prime working in cooperation with Samuel Clemens. Was George McClellan telling the truth when he confided to his wife that he would remain very proud of his soldiers and of their love for him, "even if it is not decreed by Providence that I am to lead them to Richmond"? If so, then he could be rightfully proud for the remainder of his life. Were George McClellan's hospital visits or the devotion they signified enough to answer all the charges of all his critics, then or now? No, they are not. But they were and are a large part of *McClellan's Own Story* and its continuing power; to overlook them or to underestimate them is to slight history and bow to amnesia.

NOTES

1. George B. McClellan, *McClellan's Own Story: The War for the Union, The Soldiers Who Fought in It, The Civilians Who Directed It, and His Relations to It and to Them* (New York: Charles L. Webster, 1887), 327; Theodore Roosevelt, "At the Unveiling of the Statue to Major-General George B. McClellan at Washington, May 2, 1907," *Presidential Addresses and State Papers*, 8 vols. (New York: The Review of Reviews, 1910), 6:1231–32. A bill for the appropriation of $50,000 "[f]or the preparation of a site and erection of a pedestal for statue of late Major-General George B. McClellan" was introduced in the House of Representatives by George Washington Ray, Republican of New York and a Civil War veteran, as H. R. 8072 on February 5, 1900, and in the Senate as S. 3272 on February 21, 1900. The Senate amended the bill with the addition, "Provided, That said statue shall not be located in the grounds of the Capitol or Library of Congress." The amended bill having passed the Senate on February 6, 1901, it became H. R. 14018, referred to the Committee on Appropriations and ordered to be printed on February 13, 1901. For copies of these bills and their accompanying reports, see *McClellan Statue at Washington* [Washington, DC: Government Printing Office, 1900–01], the binder's title of a slim volume in the Huntington Library, San Marino, California, call number E467.1.M2 U5. The other eight equestrian statues are those of generals Ulysses S. Grant, Winfield Scott Hancock, John A. Logan, James B. McPherson, Philip H. Sheridan, William T. Sherman, Winfield Scott, and George H. Thomas.

2. Theodore Roosevelt, "At the Unveiling," *Presidential Addresses,* 6:1229.

3. Peter S. Michie, *General McClellan* (New York: D. Appleton, 1901), 472.

4. McClellan's Retreat web site, accessed February 20, 2020, http://www.mcclellansretreat.com.

5. Fitzhugh Lee, *General Lee* (1894; reprint, with an introduction by Gary W. Gallagher, New York: Da Capo, 1994), 166.

6. Nathaniel Hawthorne, "Chiefly about War-Matters, by a Peaceable Man," *Atlantic Monthly,* July 10, 1862, 43, 51–52. For a reading of this essay and the self-awareness shown in Hawthorne's fictionalized editorial notes, see James Bense, "Nathaniel Hawthorne's Intention in 'Chiefly about War Matters,'" *American Literature* 61 (May 1989): 200–220.

7. Thomas J. Rowland, *General George B. McClellan and Civil War History: In the Shadow of Grant and Sherman* (Kent, OH: Kent State University Press, 1998), 16–18.

8. For recent treatments of Simon Cameron and Edwin Stanton, see Paul Kahan, *Amiable Scoundrel: Simon Cameron, Lincoln's Scandalous Secretary of War* (Lincoln, NE: Potomac Books, 2016), and William Marvel, *Lincoln's Autocrat: The Life of Edwin Stanton* (Chapel Hill: University of North Carolina Press, 2015). For a discussion of how much Lincoln had learned as commander-in-chief by the spring of 1862, see Gary W. Gallagher, "'You Must Either Attack Richmond or Give Up the Job and Come to the Defence of Washington': Abraham Lincoln and the 1862 Shenandoah Valley Campaign," in John Y. Simon and Harold Holzer, eds., *The Lincoln Forum: Rediscovering Abraham Lincoln* (New York: Fordham University Press, 2002), 34–47. Gallagher argues that Lincoln reacted admirably to Jackson's campaign, showing a sound grasp of strategy and none of the nervous panic sometimes attributed to him. There still remains the question of why McClellan retreated to Harrison's Landing after his victory at Malvern Hill. Brian K. Burton has argued that he was "following the train of thought that haunted him for months. He had insisted that the Confederates outnumbered him, and he had decided he should not risk the army." See Burton, *Extraordinary Circumstances: The Seven Days Battles* (Bloomington: Indiana University Press, 2001), 366–68.

9. Stephen W. Sears, *George B. McClellan: The Young Napoleon* (New York: Ticknor and Fields, 1988), 403–6, and "The Curious Case of General McClellan's Memoirs," *Civil War History* 34 (June 1988): 101–14.

10. George B. McClellan, *Letter of the Secretary of War, Transmitting Report on the Organization of the Army of the Potomac, and of Its Campaigns in Virginia and Maryland, under the Command of Maj. Gen. George B. McClellan, from July 26, 1861, to November 7, 1862* (Washington, DC: Government Printing Office, 1864); subsequently published with an additional section on the West Virginia campaign as *Report on the Organization and Campaigns of the Army of the Potomac, to which Is Added an Account of the Campaign in Western Virginia, with Plans of Battle-Fields* (New York: Sheldon, 1864). For McClellan's somewhat coy letter to William C. Prime about translation of this report into French, see Stephen W. Sears, ed., *The Civil War Papers of George B. McClellan: Selected Correspondence, 1860–1865* (New York, Ticknor and Fields, 1989), 567: "It is immaterial to me whether it is translated or not—tho' I suppose it would be very well to have it circulate in as many languages as possible, not omitting Sanscrit & Chinese."

11. Sears, "The Curious Case," 109, 110, 113. The phrases quoted in the following sentence are from 109 and 111.

12. Samuel L. Clemens to P. T. Barnum, February 3, 1875, *Mark Twain's Letters: A Publication of the Mark Twain Project of the Bancroft Library,* Robert H. Hirst, gen. ed., 8 vols., *Letters 1874–1875,* ed. Michael B. Frank and Harriet Elinor Smith, vol. 6 (Berkeley: University of California Press, 2002), accessed February 20, 2020, http://www.marktwainproject.org /xtf/view?docId=letters/UCCL01188.xml;query=p. t. barnum;searchAll=;sectionType1=;section Type2=;sectionType3=;sectionType4=;sectionType5=;style=letter;brand=mtp#1.

13. McClellan, *McClellan's Own Story,* 22, 23.

14. Sears, "The Curious Case," 108, 109; McClellan, *McClellan's Own Story,* 27; Candace Shy Hooper, *Lincoln's Generals' Wives: Four Women Who Influenced the Civil War—for Better and for Worse* (Kent, OH: Kent State University Press, 2016), 145.

15. Bernard DeVoto, ed., *Mark Twain in Eruption* (New York: Harper and Brothers, 1940), 349; Mark Twain, *The Innocents Abroad* (New York: Library of America, 1984), 532; quoted by Hooper, 143.

16. *Mark Twain's Notebooks & Journals,* Frederick Anderson, gen. ed., Robert Pack Browning, Michael B. Frank, and Lin Salamo, eds., 3 vols. (Berkeley: University of California Press, 1975–79), 3 (1883–91), 273; Albert Bigelow Paine, *Mark Twain: A Biography,* 3 vols. (New York: Harper, 1912), 2:831–33; Hooper, *Lincoln's Generals' Wives,* 142; Charles L. Webster to Samuel L. Clemens, March 20, 1886, New York, (UCLC 42905) Catalog entry, Mark Twain Project Online (Berkeley, Los Angeles, London: University of California Press, 2016). I am grateful to Robert L. Hirst and Melissa Martin for a copy of this letter, as I am for the one in the note following.

17. William C. Prime to Samuel L. Clemens, January 24, 1886, New York, (UCLC 42868) Catalog entry, Mark Twain Project Online (Berkeley, Los Angeles, London: University of California Press, 2016); Charles L. Webster to Samuel L. Clemens, March 20, 1886; *Mark Twain's Notebooks & Journals,* 3:310.

18. Edmund Wilson, *Patriotic Gore: Studies in the Literature of the American Civil War* (New York: Oxford University Press, 1966), 329 (originally published in 1962); Gary W. Gallagher, introduction to *Recollections and General Robert E. Lee by His Son Captain Robert E. Lee* (Wilmington, NC: Broadfoot Publishing, 1988), n.p. (the 16-page introduction lacks pagination). The sentence summarizing opinions of Freeman, Connelly, Harwell, and Johannsen borrows heavily from and is wholly indebted to Gallagher's introduction.

19. William Starr Meyers, ed., *The Mexican War Diary of George B. McClellan* (Princeton, NJ: Princeton University Press, 1917), 1. For more on McClellan's 1855–56 European tour, see Sears, *George B. McClellan: The Young Napoleon,* 44–49, and Matthew Moten, *The Delafield Commission and the American Military Profession* (College Station: Texas A&M University Press, 2000), on which Ethan S. Rafuse has based his subsequent treatment in *McClellan's War: The Failure of Moderation in the Struggle for the Union* (Bloomington: Indiana University Press, 2005), 61–66.

20. McClellan, *McClellan's Own Story,* 331.

21. Rafuse, *McClellan's War,* cited above; John C. Waugh, *Lincoln and McClellan: The Troubled Partnership between a President and His General* (New York: Palgrave Macmillan, 2010); and Chester G. Hearn, *Lincoln and McClellan at War* (Baton Rouge: Louisiana State University Press, 2012).

22. Michie, *General McClellan,* 50.

23. Joseph E. Johnston, *Narrative of Military Operations, Directed, During the Late War between the States, by Joseph E. Johnston, General C.S.A.* (New York: D. Appleton, 1874), 496.

24. Sears, *George B. McClellan: The Young Napoleon*, 106–7; Rowland, *George B. McClellan and Civil War History*, 26, 28; Rafuse, *McClellan's War*, 27, 81.

25. Meyers, ed., *Mexican War Diary*, 3–4.

26. McClellan, *McClellan's Own Story*, 172, 450.

27. Fitzhugh Lee, *General Lee*, 220; Meyers, ed., *Mexican War Diary*, 3.

28. McClellan, *McClellan's Own Story*, 463–64.

29. Robert E. Lee to Mary Anna Randolph Custis Lee, November 15, 1856, Lee Family Digital Archive, accessed February 20, 2020, http://leefamilyarchive.org/papers/letters/transcripts -adams/a045.html. Transcribed in Francis Raymond Adams Jr., *An Annotated Edition of the Personal Letters of Robert E. Lee, April, 1855–April, 1861*, 2 vols., diss., University of Maryland, 1955, 1:204–8.

30. McClellan, *McClellan's Own Story*, 358, 360, 554.

31. McClellan, *McClellan's Own Story*, 35.

32. Fitzhugh Lee, *General Lee*, 220. One of the newest and best additions to the vast and growing literature on hard war and the ethical considerations it raised is D. H. Dilbeck's study of the Lieber Code, *A More Civil War: How the Union Waged A Just War* (Chapel Hill: University of North Carolina Press, 2016). See especially the pages under the entry "Christianity and Just War Ideas" in the index.

33. McClellan, *McClellan's Own Story*, 37, 445.

34. McClellan, *McClellan's Own Story*, 295.

35. McClellan, *McClellan's Own Story*, 487–88. Many have commented on McClellan's attraction to the military theories of Antoine-Henri Jomini; see for example Rafuse, *McClellan's War*, 3, 34, and Sears, *George B. McClellan: The Young Napoleon*, 36, 99, 130, 241, 390. While it is true that McClellan learned about Jomini at West Point under Dennis Hart Mahan, visited Jomini in 1868, and published the essay "General Jomini" in *The Galaxy* 7 (June 1869): 876–88, nothing in Jomini's best-known writings anticipated McClellan's Harrison Landing letter. In *The Art of War*, an English translation of Jomini's *Précis de l'art de la guerre* (1838) published the year of the Peninsula campaign, the word *Christian* appears six times and never in the context of ethics; see *The Art of War*, trans. George H. Mendell and William P. Craighill (Philadelphia: Lippincott, 1862), 362–81. Meanwhile, Jomini's name never appears in *McClellan's Own Story* or in Sears, ed., *The Civil War Papers of George B. McClellan*. This absence supports the argument—that Jomini's influence has been overestimated—in Carol Reardon, *With a Sword in One Hand and Jomini in the Other: The Problem of Military Thought in the Civil War North* (Chapel Hill: University of North Carolina Press, 2012).

36. McClellan, *McClellan's Own Story*, 489. See also the long footnote William Prime introduced at this point with an asterisk: "Pure devotion to duty, without thought of self, is incomprehensible to the average politician. . . . And it is beyond doubt that the radical difference between his own views and those of the self-seeking men who surrounded him led Mr. Lincoln to the despairing state of mind in which, a few weeks later, he desired to resign." Prime may have over-idealized both Lincoln and McClellan, but his characterization of many of the "men who surrounded Lincoln" is difficult to dispute.

37. McClellan, *McClellan's Own Story*, 488. See also Mark Grimsley, *The Hard Hand of War: Union Military Policy toward Southern Civilians, 1861–1865* (New York: Cambridge University Press, 1995), 86–87. For McClellan's report on the Peninsula campaign, see US War Department,

The War of the Rebellion: The Official Records of the Union and Confederate Armies, 127 vols., index, and atlas (Washington, DC: GPO, 1880–1901), ser. 1, vol. 11, pt. 1, 5–105; the Harrison's Landing letter appears on pp. 73–74. For a public version of McClellan's testimony before the Joint Committee on the Conduct of the War, see *New York Times,* vol. 12, no. 3621, Sunday, May 3, 1863, 2–3. This testimony did not mention the letter, but the paper did publish the full text of the Harrison's Landing letter eight months later; see *New York Times,* vol. 13, no. 3832, Tuesday, January 5, 1864, 5. The letter subsequently had wide circulation during the 1864 presidential campaign. It is included, for example, with a bound volume of 1864 campaign documents in the Huntington Library. This copy of the letter was published by E. B. Patten, 35 Park Row, New York, call number 36370.

38. McClellan, *McClellan's Own Story,* 488–89. In his essay "A Civil War Watershed: The 1862 Richmond Campaign in Perspective," Gary W. Gallagher points to a letter by Charles Sumner, dated August 5, 1862, connecting passage of the Second Confiscation Act to "pressures from our reverses at Richmond." Gallagher comments, "Had McClellan been the victor in July 1862, he certainly could have pressed his case for a softer policy more effectively." See Charles Sumner, *The Selected Letters of Charles Sumner,* ed. Beverly Wilson Palmer, 2 vols. (Boston: Northeastern University Press, 1990), 2:122, and Gary W. Gallagher, ed., *The Richmond Campaign of 1862: The Peninsula and the Seven Days* (Chapel Hill: University of North Carolina Press, 2000), 16–17, 26n23.

39. McClellan, *McClellan's Own Story,* 105.

40. In the heat of one moment, for example, McClellan wrote to Edwin M. Stanton from Savage's Station at 12:20 A.M. on June 28, 1862: "Had I twenty thousand (20,000), or even ten thousand (10,000), fresh troops to use to-morrow, I could take Richmond"; see McClellan, *McClellan's Own Story,* 101–5, 424.

41. McClellan, *McClellan's Own Story,* 346.

42. McClellan, *McClellan's Own Story,* 406, 408.

43. McClellan, *McClellan's Own Story,* 236; *Report on the Organization and Campaigns of the Army of the Potomac,* 107. McClellan's invocation of Fitz John Porter was not without complexity, as it was Porter who did not want to commit his Fifth Corps reserves to the fighting on the left flank at Sharpsburg-Antietam. See Stephen W. Sears, *Landscape Turned Red: The Battle of Antietam* (1983; reprint, New York: Warner Books, 1985), 322–23.

44. John Keats to George and Thomas Keats, December 22, 1817, *Letters of John Keats to His Family and Friends,* ed. Sydney Colvin (London: Macmillan, 1925), 48; McClellan, *McClellan's Own Story,* 346.

45. McClellan, *McClellan's Own Story,* 648, 650.

46. Michael Shaara, *The Killer Angels* (1974; reprinted, New York: Ballatine Books, 1975), 124, 166; Phil Leigh, "Making 'Killer Angels,'" *New York Times,* June 28, 2013, accessed February 20, 2020, https://opinionator.blogs.nytimes.com/2013/06/28/making-killer-angels/?_r=0.

47. Robert L. Chapman, ed., *American Slang,* 2nd edition (New York: HarperCollins, 1998), 32–33; McClellan, *McClellan's Own Story,* 567; Sears, ed., *Civil War Papers,* 435.

48. Robert E. Lee Jr., *Recollections and Letters of General Robert E. Lee* (New York: Doubleday, 1904), 89; McClellan, *McClellan's Own Story,* 453–54.

49. McClellan, *McClellan's Own Story,* 353, 452, 458–59.

"The Riots at New York—the Rioters Burning and Sacking the Colored Orphan Asylum."
Harper's Weekly offered readers this illustration of the riots that swept through parts of
the city in mid-July 1863. In her diary entry for July 14, Maria Lydig Daly recorded that
"Negroes were hung in the streets!" *Harper's Weekly,* August 1, 1863, p. 493.

Maria Lydig Daly

Diary of a Union Lady 1861–1865

J. MATTHEW GALLMAN

The Book

Diary of a Union Lady has a heft to it. My copy, a first edition, was published by Funk and Wagnalls in 1962, in the midst of the Civil War centennial. It runs to nearly 400 numbered pages, with an additional forty or so pages of introductory material. Allan Nevins, the great Civil War historian, wrote the foreword.[1] Readers might have reasonably concluded that the diarist was an important figure, and in various senses she was.

Maria Lydig Daly was a wealthy resident of New York City during the Civil War. Her husband, Charles, was a distinguished judge and one of the city's most prominent public citizens. They lived on Clifton Place, a few blocks above Washington Square, where they entertained a steady stream of interesting and important people. Most important for our purposes, Maria kept a diary throughout the war. She commented on people and events from this privileged perch. Her wit was dry; her comments sometimes ran to the caustic. And as a prominent New Yorker, she had a distinctive perspective on national and local politics and on the city's famed draft riots.

Daly's diary offers a valuable corrective to some common ideas, and a useful case study of a host of values and beliefs. Charles and Maria Daly provide us with a window into how these prominent New York Democrats thought about politics and partisan affairs. They supported the Union without reservation, but that enthusiasm never led them to waiver from their support for the Democratic Party or their visceral hostility towards the Lincolns. Maria almost never spoke of "copperheads," and their extended social circle rarely included the city's most notorious antiwar Democrats, including editors or politicians. She was a War Democrat, while declining to use that label.[2] Charles Daly was a second-generation Irish American, in a city with a huge population of working-class Irish Catholic immigrants. Both Dalys never wavered in their commitment to Ireland and to Irish Americans.

The Daly diary is a marvelous source for historians of the North during the Civil War. There are many published diaries of southern women during the war, including Mary Chesnut's famed *Diary from Dixie,* and libraries and archives are well stocked with the diaries and letters of Civil War soldiers, but there really are not that many important published diaries from the northern home front.[3] Daly's stands alongside the diaries of fellow New Yorker George Templeton Strong (1952), and Philadelphian Sydney George Fisher (1968), as the most prominent published volumes. All three appear in dozens of histories of the war, providing pithy quotes about individuals or events.[4] All were wealthy, and none was particularly typical of their cohort. But they make wonderful reading, and historians seeking to add flavor to their narratives cannot resist dipping into their pages.

The historian Harold Earl Hammond edited *Diary of a Union Lady.* Hammond had completed his doctoral degree under Nevins, and wrote his dissertation on Charles Daly, a volume that he published in 1954.[5] In the large world of published diaries, Hammond's edited volume stands out for the lengths he took to contextualize the volume for his readers. He included a lengthy section on "Personalities in the Diary," summarizing the lives of many of the key figures the reader would encounter, and he added a wealth of citations identifying the famous and the obscure. Perhaps Hammond was less punctilious than some editors in capturing the flavor of the diarist's prose. As he explains it, he and his wife, Helen Stegman Hammond, spent long hours "translating" Daly's diary, producing a transcript that cleaned up such "incidentals as punctuation, sentence structure, and spelling."[6] Although the text includes periodic ellipses, Hammond gives no indication that he removed extraneous materials. The text is a somewhat more readable version of the pages as the diarist intended them. For the general reader, that is a positive feature. But by not following more modern editorial conventions, Hammond failed to include any notations of strikeouts or spelling errors or other hints at the diarist's writing process. Hammond occasionally injects interludes in italics, where he summarizes the war's principal military and political events not fully covered in the diary and notes. These are particularly helpful when the diarist skips weeks or even months, filling in gaps in the war's larger military and political chronology.

Some wartime diarists, including Strong, had been keeping diaries long before the conflict began. Others seemed moved to start a journal at the outset of the war. Some picked up the habit at some point in the midst of the Civil War. Emilie Davis, a working-class African American woman in Philadelphia, began charting daily events in January 1863, with Lincoln's announcement of the Emancipation Proclamation.[7] Maria Lydig Daly was particularly prescient. Recognizing that she lived in momentous times, Daly began writing in a large volume in January 1861.[8] Occasionally she would note that she began keeping her journal specifically to provide an account of these years so that she could relive them in her old age. Nothing suggests that she had thoughts that her words would be published. *Diary of a Union Lady* opens with her extended comments from late January, spanning events before the war began. Hammond opted to publish the diary through the end of 1865.

So the published diary stands as a valuable tale of life in New York during and immediately after the Civil War. But like all good stories, there is an important backstory.

The Diarist and the Judge

Maria Lydig was born in 1824, the first child of Philip and Catherine Lydig. The family had Germanic roots and a long history in New York City and its environs. Both of Maria's parents came from considerable wealth, largely in mills and manufacturing. Lydig first met Judge Charles Daly in 1855. At the time both were fairly old for having never been married. He was 39 and she was 32.

Charles Daly was far from the same sort of blue blood. Daly's parents had emigrated from Ireland two years before he was born. They were Irish Catholics in a historic moment when Catholics faced considerable prejudice. Maria was an Episcopalian whose class and religion never provoked prejudice. By 1855, when the two met at a party, Charles had risen to considerable status in the city. He had served on the Court of Common Pleas in New York City since 1844, and he would remain on the bench until 1885. In addition to establishing an important reputation as a judge, Daly had invested wisely in midwestern land holdings, accumulating comfortable personal wealth. But he was nowhere near the status of Maria Lydig and her family, a fact that was not lost on Lydig's parents.

It appears that Charles and Maria each saw a kindred spirit when they met, and soon they were in regular contact and moving towards marriage. Philip Lydig was not pleased. Presumably he resisted the match because of some combination of Charles's religion, ethnicity, and family status. Here is where the narrative, as pieced together by Hammond from various correspondence, gets interesting. At some point Philip apparently banned Charles from the Lydig home, hoping to squash the romance. But Maria was no child and pushed ahead with marriage plans without her parents' consent. Finally, Philip consented to meet with Charles. In advance of that gathering Maria admitted to Charles that "Father, I fear, is a little insane." But she urged him to resist any effort to block the marriage, adding that "I am no one's chattel and my marriage is only of my own contracting." Finally, after months of wrangling, Maria reported that Philip had relented, and soon after Catherine Lydig wrote to invite Charles to their home, assuring him that he would always be welcome.

Once the Lydigs were on board with their daughter's wedding, they threw themselves into the project. Philip presented Charles Daly with a $20,000 dowry, and after a bit of investigation they settled on a townhouse at 84 Clinton Place, which they purchased outright for the couple for $12,000. This new home (on what had been 8th Street) was just a few blocks north of Washington Square and a short walk from Fifth Avenue. For decades their home would be the site for elegant dinner parties and a stopping place for a seemingly unending string of travelers. During four years of war the Dalys entertained a long list of military officers and their wives, as well as an impressive assortment of politicians, educators, artists, and other members of New York society.

Maria's diary gives every indication that she and Charles enjoyed married life, living as loving partners. Daly regularly praised "the judge's" professional acumen and accomplishments, periodically musing about how he might aspire to higher elected office. In December 1863, after enduring weeks of illness, Daly wrote an uncharacteristic diary entry about her married life. "The judge has been very kind and indulgent," she wrote. "Has anyone so good a husband as I have, or so loving a one?" After eight years of marriage "he is the same now as on our wedding day" (p. 269 in *Diary of a Union Lady*; future references to page only). Daly did not devote her diary to regular comments on the state of her personal life, but she surely seemed content on Clinton Place.

In the four years between their wedding and the outbreak of the Civil War, Charles and Maria Daly established themselves as prominent figures in New York's social and associational life. Always an advocate for Irish American interests, Charles served on the executive board of the Emigrant Aid Committee, and he took an important hand in funding St. Patrick's Cathedral on Fifth Avenue. In 1860 he became the first president of the Friendly Sons of St. Patrick in the city.[9] Maria had her hand in various philanthropic organizations, establishing patterns that would expand during and after the war. Charles Daly was a committed Democrat. In 1860 he supported Democrat Stephen Douglas for the presidential nomination. It was a decision that reflected loyalty to both the party and to the Union. Douglas represented a possible bulwark against the upstart Republican Party and its candidate, Abraham Lincoln. Although not a friend of abolitionism, Daly wanted no part of his party's proslavery southern wing.

With the election of Abraham Lincoln, and the impending secession of at least a portion of the southern states, the Dalys recognized ominous times were ahead. Maria picked up a large volume and began jotting down her thoughts on the events of the day.

A Civil War Narrative

Diaries, and certainly Civil War diaries, can be read in various ways. The historian might mine a good wartime diary for nuggets about moments or people, asking questions that apply to broader topics. One of the nice features of Civil War diaries is that they were more likely to find their way into archives, and even into print, than journals from earlier or later decades. Thus, historians interested in other mid-century themes find these wondrous sources invaluable for concerns unrelated to the war itself.

But diaries are particularly appealing because they tell a story from a distinct perspective. They are usually rich with characters who come and go. And, unlike writers of fiction, the authors tell their story day to day without knowing what the next day might bring. Thus, we read a tale where we all find out what happens together. Sometimes the reader knows the wartime history well enough to know what is coming next, which adds its own sense of drama. Of course, even the best diarist sometimes caught the flu or went on vacation and neglected that precious diary, just when unaddressed events called out for commentary. Mary Lydig Daly did that occasionally. The diary has gaps, particularly in the last months of the war, and she neglects topics she might otherwise have mentioned. But those gaps are rare.

A Nation Goes to War

Every diary from the northern home front tells a distinctive story, reflecting the individual and the place, and often just the ways in which the diarist chose to write. But at the same time, they all have a very familiar narrative. A person who has read a few dozen quickly sees patterns, as if everyone is telling the same story, just from different perspectives. And in a very real sense they are.

Daly began writing on January 31, 1861, but that one dated entry really covered far more terrain, summarizing her life up until late May. With the secession crisis mounting, Maria and Charles (whom she routinely called "the judge" in her entries) travelled to the nation's capital, where they encountered some of the cast of characters who would play important roles in the national crisis. Daly liked Maryland senator Anthony Kennedy, who pleased her for "holding Unionist sentiments."[10] She also approved of Mrs. Kennedy, "a lively, clever woman" (3). While in Washington, Maria and Charles spent much of their time in the Senate, catching speeches by Illinois Democrat Stephen Douglas and New York Republican William Henry Seward, among others. They came away particularly impressed by Kentucky senator John J. Crittenden, who was busily attempting to build support for his famed compromise.

While in the capital they saw President James Buchanan, who had yet to relinquish the position to President-elect Abraham Lincoln. Daly noted that "I have never seen so incapable a face as Buchanan's," and in fact she came away generally unimpressed with most of the men serving in both houses of Congress (7). She saved her most colorful invective for Texas senator Louis Wigfall, who would soon don a gray uniform and serve with the Confederacy. They also dined with—and were impressed by—Maryland's Reverdy Johnson, who would soon replace Kennedy in the Senate.

Later in this same long entry Daly recorded that "Fort Sumter has been fired upon!" (10). She continued with a short paragraph of careful detail, but without the anxiety that marked some northern journals. Like most diarists, Daly noted that the attack had seemed to bring the nation together in a surge of patriotism. An important page had been turned, and the North felt that impact immediately. For a moment at least, political divisions about possible compromises had given way to national unity (or so it seemed), as northern communities turned their attention to raising and outfitting new regiments of US troops. Daly, a Unionist Democrat, blamed Massachusetts and its radical abolitionists for the conflict, adding that she was "no friend to free blacks" and certainly no fan of abolitionism (14). Like most white northerners, and nearly all northern Democrats, Daly felt a fairly strong antipathy towards African Americans, whether enslaved or free, although she did not use the pages of her diary to record unpleasant racial invectives or racist jokes, and in fact she only rarely mentioned race at all. Nor did she fill her entries with attacks on abolitionists, although she blamed them for the national crisis. Now that the fight had begun, all were on the same side.

As was commonly the case across the nation, Maria and Judge Daly focused much of their attention on a particular regiment. In their case the choice seemed obvious: Their eyes turned to the 69th New York Regiment. The 69th marched out of New York in early May; before they departed Daly presented them with a new battle flag, following a path that would become adopted by patriotic women across the North. She received a gracious reply from the regiment's Col. Michael Corcoran. The 69th, and Corcoran, would remain central to the Dalys' interests for years to come.

Over the next few months, Daly remained absorbed with martial matters. She reported on other women sewing flags and banners for different regiments, while she joined a group sewing havelocks for the 69th. In June, the Dalys joined a small group in a water excursion to observe the celebrated Hawkins' Zouaves, and then continued on to visit the equally well-known California Regiment, under the command of Colonel E. D. Baker. Other excursions to military camps followed in the weeks to come. Meanwhile, the judge—now in his 40s—had begun drilling with other men, with some thoughts of joining the ranks himself. In each of these actions in those first weeks of war the Dalys acted out their personal impulses, while joining with civilians across the North similarly absorbed with war matters, applauding departing troops and enjoying excursions to witness the men training in local camps.

Maria Daly, like many women and men in both the United States and the Confederacy, soon became swept up in military matters, noting news from the battlefield besides discussions of dinner parties and other social events. For home front observers in the North and the South, the military stakes came into focus when two substantial armies clashed on July 21 at Bull Run, near Manassas Junction in Virginia, thirty miles southeast of the nation's capital. For many observers, the first battle of Bull Run—as it eventually came to be called—signaled that this would not be a short conflict, settled with one grand battle. The following day Daly recorded a lengthy description of the battle, wildly overstating the number of Federal dead but correctly describing a substantial Union rout. Her next entry corrected the number of deaths and worried about reports that Michael Corcoran and Thomas Meagher of the 69th Regiment were missing. Meagher had a notorious history as an Irish nationalist, long before the outbreak of the war gave him a new uniform and cause. The following week Daly noted that the flag she gave to the 69th was a casualty of the conflict, although the soldier who dropped it had survived unscathed, a point the diarist found annoying. That October Meagher and his wife dined at Clinton Place, as the brash officer prepared to deliver a recruiting address as the original 69th began reenlisting and became the basis for New York's Irish Brigade.

Charles and Maria continued to show an interest in the Irish Brigade, assisting in raising funds and making efforts to replace the lost flag. But, as would often prove to be the case, Daly lost patience with the visitors in her midst. By October 14 she had concluded that "I do not like Mrs. Meagher's manner, and I think that she rather desires to keep all the glory and renown to herself and her husband," rather than sharing that limelight with the likes of the Dalys. "She would have been quite willing," Daly concluded, "that I should have stayed away, as I had so much to do with the 69th" (63–64). In just so many words, Daly had demonstrated her own insecurities and her tendency to lash out at women in her circle.

With Corcoran in a Confederate prisoner of war camp, the Dalys remained interested in the internal intrigue that seemed to follow their friends in the Irish Brigade. James Shields, an Irish-born judge and soldier who had been brigadier general in the Union Army since early in the war and had been a long-term friend and confidant of Maria Daly, had hopes of taking a position in the Irish Brigade. But in January 1862 Daly reported that Shields had returned only to learn that he "had been superseded by the crafty Meagher" (93). Back in the East, Shields stayed with the Dalys, providing Maria with opportunities to record various cracks about Shields's young bride and his equally young recent lover. The following month, several released prisoners from the 69th dined with the Dalys, and they regaled the couple with unflattering portrayals of Meagher's behavior at Bull Run, including the widely shared belief that Colonel Meagher had been drunk during the battle while his comrades—including Colonel Corcoran—had been captured. In his new status as the regiment's brigadier general, Meagher became a regular target of the diarist's ire and wit.

Celebrated Union officers and their spouses remained a staple on the Dalys' social calendar, and Daly continued to share her thoughts about the couples in her private journal. Early in the war, John C. Frémont's political and military stock rose, as he achieved early successes in Missouri. Frémont, a famed explorer and outspoken abolitionist, had been the Republicans' presidential standard-bearer in 1856, and in the early months of the war the general pushed the administration to embrace his antislavery positions as part of his western command. Charles Daly was unimpressed. Maria confided that the judge found Frémont to be an "incapable, obstinate, selfish, conceited, and unscrupulous man" (56). The ambitious Frémont had married Jessie Benton, the quite brilliant daughter of Missouri senator Thomas Hart Benton. Maria took the measure of the highly public Jessie Frémont and found her—and her husband—lacking. Daly saw them both as "very ambitious, and between them they might be looking to the main chance rather than the good of their country" (57). It was an uncharitable assessment, although perhaps not far off the mark. Two years later the couples dined together again, and Daly still found Jessie Frémont to be an "enterprising, ambitious woman," while she pronounced the general "rather a shy man" with a "soft, tender, blue eye" (276). For the remainder of the war the couples periodically ran into each other in social settings. Daly's diary never failed to note Jessie Frémont's intelligence and calculating manner.

Of the many other military couples in the Dalys' social orbit, the diarists most persistent comments were reserved for Gen. George B. McClellan and his wife, Mary Ellen. Early in the war General McClellan's battlefield successes caught Daly's eye, prompting her to praise him by name in her journal long before they had met. She especially liked his battlefield dispatches in the papers, which she found properly "modest and brief" (35). In September 1861, a family friend told them that the military officers unanimously hoped that McClellan would replace Gen. Winfield Scott as the Union's leading military figure if the need arose. By early 1862, Daly's tune had shifted a bit, as she recorded rumors that McClellan was eyeing the presidency, "instigated by his wife" (98). Later that day she penned a note to Mrs. McClellan—whom apparently she had still not met—urging her to steer her husband down a patriotic path. Before long the two would become fast friends.

In November 1861 Daly introduced yet another military couple, Francis Channing and Arabella Barlow. Maria and Arabella were old friends, and as was the case with so many women in her life, the diarist assessed Barlow and her marriage with a critical eye. The Barlows had recently married and Frank had promptly gone off to war, where he would have a distinguished military career. But the thing that bothered Maria was that her friend was ten years Frank's senior. This would be another theme running through the diary: Daly had very strong opinions about the proper behavior of young women, but also about proper marital partnerships.

1862: Political Affairs and Thoughts of Voluntarism

In November 1861, Daly—who always kept up with the news—reported the arrest of two rebel agents, James Mason and John Slidell, who had been bound for England on a British merchant ship. For a time the "Trent affair" threatened to erupt in international warfare as the British questioned why an American naval vessel had interfered with a British vessel. The diarist followed these developments carefully, perhaps because Charles had journeyed to Washington to provide Secretary of State William Henry Seward advice on the matter. Seward listened and ordered the agents released from a Boston prison, and Charles earned some public respect for his judicious role in the whole matter.[11] As the Civil War entered its second year, the North settled into life in wartime, and civilians responded to a continuous series of new events and periodic rumors. Meanwhile, the Dalys lived lives as important—and wealthy—public New Yorkers and strong defenders of the Union.

That January the war changed for Maria when her brother Phil marched off to war. For the remainder of the conflict Daly recorded news from Phil's regular letters and detailed accounts of dinnertime chats when he was home on furlough. As it happened, Philip Lydig performed well in uniform and his sister was pleased to describe favorable reports from visitors from the front. Unlike so many other home front diarists, Daly never faced news of injury, capture, or death from her closest sibling or any other family member.

The Civil War moved thousands of northern women to pursue some form of voluntarism, in addition to the huge numbers of working-class women who sought employment from war contractors or the military. In November

Daly had had a long conversation with her close friend Harriet Whetten, who seemed intent on becoming a military nurse. Whetten had even made plans to visit Dorothea Dix, the superintendent of army nurses, to inquire about a position. Privately, Daly disliked Whetten's ideas. She felt sure that Harriet was not physically strong enough for the work, and she did not "believe in dilettante nursing" by young women (77). But Whetten pressed on and soon discovered that she had a true calling. The two remained close. In fact, no other female friend so consistently met with Daly's approval. And perhaps the rewards Harriet found in her work struck a nerve with Maria.

In mid-May 1862, Daly went with a friend to the Park Barracks in City Hall Park to visit recently arrived wounded soldiers. She devoted a long entry to her conversations with several ailing men, and then spent that evening gathering clothing to bring on her next visit. Daly returned to the Park Barracks a few days later and did her best but complained that the regular volunteers "did not seem to like to be interfered with" while the men "make much fun of us women" (131). The following day, perhaps moved by her previous venture, Daly followed a slightly different impulse when she learned that patients in the City Hospital needed visitors to read to them or help them write letters. Daly resolved to visit the hospital to do her part. But her benevolent plans stalled when she learned that the hospital housed "typhoid fever patients," prompting her to think better of the project. Having changed course, Daly filled the remainder of her entry with comments on those women who chose to brave the fever. She noted that Mrs. Charles Strong was quite clever, but also a "fast, worldly woman" of a suspect nature. Daly found the other volunteers at the City Hospital to be "clever women" but with "a want of serious purpose," and in need of activities "to occupy their minds and hearts." "Thank God," she concluded, she had no such void in her own life, and "I trust that if there was pressing need for my services, even in dangerous cases, I should not be found wanting" (132). Instead, Daly resolved to begin twice weekly visits to the Park Barracks as well as a weekly stint at the city's Central Relief Association, helping to prepare packages to send to the front. On the 16th Daly learned of another arriving vessel full of wounded men and vowed to once again do her part. But then she reconsidered, concluding that other women were more experienced in working with the wounded, making her own contributions unnecessary.

The following day Daly reported on her latest trip to the Park Barracks, noting that in fact there were "plenty of nurses for the transports and for the hospitals," but that "the ladies" told her they might need assistance when the weather grew warm. She came away pleased, adding that "I had no mania for being useful" and she could now carry on "with a clear conscience, since I had offered my services." Meanwhile, Daly reported that Mrs. George Strong had showed up at the Park Barracks "with rouge pot, crinoline, and maid," and proceeded to depart "having washed the faces of seven men" (134).[12]

It had been an impressive flurry of activity over several days, but Daly seemed to conclude that her impulse to hospital voluntarism was best kept under wraps, leaving nursing labors to the women who were experts, or at least those who really needed the gratification. Although she would throw herself into all sorts of benevolent activities, Daly never again mentioned the Park Barracks in her diary, apparently leaving the nursing to folks like Harriet Whetten. That September Harriet stopped by Clinton Place, where she regaled Maria with tales of her summer working in military hospitals. A favorite story concerned her brief visit to Harrison's Landing, Virginia, where Whetten met Arabella Barlow living "very comfortably at government expense at the hospital" (173) where Frank Barlow was stationed. Apparently the men in the hospital told Harriet that Arabella spent her days lounging on a sofa rather than ministering to the wounded. No doubt the story reinenforced Daly's notion that real hospital work was best reserved to the truly called.

As a widely known public figure, holding an elected position as a New York City judge, Charles Daly had strong ties with the city's Democratic Party and its Tammany Hall political machine. While both Dalys were ambivalent about Abraham Lincoln, they generally aligned with the administration for the first year of the war. Although no supporter of abolition or abolitionists, the judge approved of the First Confiscation Act (August 1861), which laid the groundwork for Union forces taking enemy property, including slaves, in the name of the war effort. By July 1862, northern politics had begun to take a more partisan turn, as the Lincoln administration had taken measures to silence some political dissent and had begun laying the groundwork for conscription and perhaps even emancipation. In July the party invited Judge Daly to deliver an important address at Tammany Hall. As testimony to the couple's political partnership, the diarist wrote that she had been busily "writing out [the] oration" Charles would deliver on July 4th (157). By that summer New York City Democrats had begun to divide, with one camp opposing not only the Lincoln administration but also the war. Charles Daly rejected such ideas, firmly aligning himself with the party's Unionist wing, while also declining to cast any doubt on his allegiance to the party itself.[13]

Maria was pleased with her husband's effort. "It is time the Democrats had something to say," she wrote (157). Charles's hosts at Tammany Hall presented Maria with a large bouquet, and the entire evening left observers with a sense that the northern Democrats were preparing to push back against Republican rule. The following month the North began conscripting troops under the auspices of the State Militia Draft, a policy that Maria credited Charles with instigating. But there were limits to how far the Dalys would go in supporting the administration and the Union. In late September a dinner guest spoke of arming black troops, a notion with "which the Judge disapproved" (177). A few days later, when another guest revealed that Lincoln had announced his Preliminary Emancipation Proclamation without consulting his cabinet, Maria called it an act of "supreme impertinence," and Charles agreed (179).

As 1862 neared a close, Democrats—both nationally and locally—geared up to challenge the administration and the Republican Party in the polls. The war was a year and a half old, with no evidence that the conflict was nearing a close. Meanwhile, northern citizens balked at conscription and emancipation, and chafed at talk of war profiteering and corruption. For well over a year Daly had barely mentioned partisan politics in her journal, but in October she wrote that "The whole North seems to be going for the Democrats" (191). And immediately after election day the following month, Daly proudly reported that Democrat Horatio Seymour had won the state's gubernatorial race, and an impressive number of party congressmen and senators had been elected. The Democrats had done well, reflecting some combination of war weariness, public resistance to particular measures—most notably emancipation—and simple political calculus. Parties out of power generally do well in off-year elections, and in these elections the northern Democracy seemed to rouse itself out of its political slumber to become a more vocal party of opposition.

But Democratic victories partially masked significant divisions within the wartime party of opposition, particularly in New York. Daly assessed those New York returns with a judicious eye. Although Seymour was her party's choice, Daly would have preferred a candidate "who exerted himself for the war" more aggressively. Worse, Daly felt that the party should not "have nominated those two scamps, Fernando Wood and his foolish, unprincipled brother [Benjamin] for Congress." Daly found the elections of the two brothers "a blot upon the party" and suggested that Fernando had paid "handsomely" for his victory (195). Daly's long election-day entry mapped out where the state's Democratic Party found itself in late 1862. On the one hand, city politicians such as the Wood brothers had become more outspoken in resisting the war and the Lincoln administration. On the other hand, many New York Democrats—like Judge Daly and Maria—remained staunchly in favor of the Union and the war effort, despite rising doubts about the president and his administration. In the days after the elections, Daly recorded various dinnertime conversations about local politics, mostly concluding that the Wood brothers were a disaster. Privately, Daly considered the judge's abilities and popularity and mused that "I sometimes wish that Charles were more ambitious," perhaps pursuing a seat in Congress or the Senate.

New York in Early 1863

Almost immediately after the 1862 election, Abraham Lincoln removed George McClellan from command of the Army of the Potomac, replacing him with Gen. Ambrose Burnside. Although McClellan's Army of the Potomac had stopped Robert E. Lee's invading Army of Northern Virginia at the bloody battle of Antietam, the general's critics—including the president—felt disappointed that he had failed to destroy the Confederate army and hasten the end the war. Daly had documented the battle and its aftermath with care. Her various military confidants did not treat McClellan badly after Antietam. Maria and Charles liked the deposed general, and he had been a favorite among politically minded northern Democrats, but Daly's diary did not indulge in the sort of angry rhetoric that followed McClellan's removal in other Democratic diaries. Just a few days later, writing from the front, Phil noted that he was sorry to see McClellan go but he had the highest respect for Burnside. Not long after the general had been removed of his command, George and Ellen McClellan made a grand trip to New York City, staying at the Fifth Avenue Hotel. Daly called on Ellen and her mother, Mary Marcy. She enjoyed the visit, which she described as a small reception stocked with local political dignitaries, including powerful Democrat August Belmont. This was at least the second occasion when the Dalys had met the McClellans. During the first, the previous May, Daly described Ellen as "a really refined, graceful, sprightly woman, and very pretty." She found Mrs. Marcy to be somewhat less annoying than she had feared (127). The personal and the military continued to intersect the following month, when Daly entertained a visit from Mrs. Ambrose Burnside, only a week before the general's troops fought the bloody—and disastrous—battle of Fredericksburg. Maria wrote that Mrs. Burnside was "pleasant, . . . lively . . . and, I should think, clever" (204).

Throughout that winter, as Union losses mounted and, in the Army of the Potomac, Ambrose Burnside gave way to Gen. Joseph Hooker, political talk in New York City grew more intense. Even at this early stage, many Democratic eyes turned to the popular George McClellan as a possible presidential candidate. The McClellans spent considerable time in the city, making the circuit of prominent social gatherings, while declining to talk politics. Still, Daly worried that the general "had injured himself by too much tampering with the ultra-Democrats."[14] When Governor Seymour delivered his annual message, Daly read it carefully, finding it "very able and patriotic" (213). Although Daly routinely commented on the content of dinnertime political discussions, she often could not resist mocking the women in her circle. On the day before she read Seymour's message Daly made a round of visits, coming home to conclude that "it was amusing to hear the political views of the ladies. Such vapid, inconsistent, violent expressions!" (213). Although Daly was unimpressed with what her female friends—both Democrats and Republicans—said about politics, there was no doubting that home front conversations had grown increasingly political.

That winter Daly, although a woman of great family wealth, periodically took notice of the war's economic impact on the city's less fortunate, and the wild economic disparities that characterized home front life. In February August Belmont, a wealthy financier and party leader, hosted a massive masquerade ball. She found the whole thing unseemly and felt that it would be "somewhat undignified" for the judge to make an appearance. In a lengthy entry Daly mused on "how apathetic our people are about the war" (218), and that despite continual bad news from the front, it seemed that the New York social set were throwing even more parties than usual, and "the women dress as extravagantly as ever" (219). Meanwhile, opera-goers flocked to see the greatest stars, and the city seemed enraptured by the nuptials between "General Tom Thumb" and "Lavinia Warren," two celebrated dwarves who had been brought to the public attention by P. T. Barnum. In the midst of all this opulence, gold prices rose, and real incomes dropped. "What is to become of the poor?" the heiress asked.

In March, sixty leading New Yorkers gathered at the Cooper Institute to promote patriotic spirit and combat the competing extremes of "copper-headism" and unbridled abolitionism. Judge Daly spoke against the excesses of the Lincoln administration, while others denounced the worst antiwar extremists in the Democratic Party. They emerged with the foundations of the new Union League, a body dedicated to promoting the Union and the war effort, while skirting explicit partisan wrangling. Judge Daly accepted a position as vice president.

While political discourse heated up, and Judge Daly's public role expanded, both Dalys persisted in their concern for Irish affairs, both locally and internationally. Throughout the war, Daly's diary had included regular reports on the Irish Brigade, and the inner machinations and rumors about their flamboyant officers. Since the previous spring, Charles had served as the chairman of the Committee for the Relief of Ireland, a body dedicated to assisting victims of famine in Ireland. The judge remained an enthusiastic member, and for a time the president, of the city's Friendly Society of St. Patrick. The couple routinely hosted visits from Irish officers, and Daly commented on the admirable traits of the Irish soldier. In December they attended a ceremony where the Irish Brigade received new flags to replace those worn and tattered by war. Meanwhile, although she was an Episcopalian, Daly regularly recorded praise for local Irish Catholic priests, often remarking that she wished she herself were Catholic. Those passions—for the Irish and for Catholics—often intersected, particularly in the person of Father Bernard O'Reilly. Father O'Reilly was the chaplain for the 69th Regiment, and he soon became one of Daly's closest intimates, visiting frequently and sending regular letters from the field. In April 1863 Maria took a substantial role in a large fund-raising ball to collect more funds for the starving in Ireland. In the midst of the Civil War, both Dalys maintained deep commitments to the associational life of New York's Irish. They were hardly alone. The attendees at the Irish Ball included Meagher, McClellan, and Bishop John Hughes.

Gotham Explodes

The events of July 1863 are crucial to the Civil War narrative, even more central to the wartime history of New York City, and vital to the wartime story Maria Daly told. In the first three days of the month, Union forces under Gen. George Meade clashed with the Army of Northern Virginia, commanded by Gen. Robert E. Lee, in the hills surrounding Gettysburg, Pennsylvania. The results were inconclusive, but the huge battle stalled Lee's invasion of the United States, prompting celebration throughout the North. The following day the nation celebrated Independence Day, and the Confederate stronghold of Vicksburg fell to Union forces under Ulysses S. Grant, giving the US forces control of the vital Mississippi River. A week later, New York's wards began implementing the new federal draft.

The draft required individual congressional districts (usually towns or city wards) to meet predetermined conscription quotas. Following local practices, draft commissioners or their agents drew the names of eligible men from preestablished lists. There were in fact multiple routes for these draftees to avoid military service, including receiving medical exemptions, hiring a substitute, and—most controversial—paying a $300 commutation fee. Rather than following a single national draft day, northern conscription unfolded piecemeal. New York's draft commissioners began selecting names on July 11. Rioting soon broke out, yielding days of destruction and death.

The story behind the New York City draft riots is too complex to revisit here, but we should know that the destruction was extraordinary, shocking New Yorkers and causing cities nationwide to change their conscription practices. Although it became a riot of largely working-class civilians who resisted conscription and decried emancipation, the rioting began with irate Irish New Yorkers, and observers came to see it as an Irish riot. An event that began with assaults on public buildings soon expanded to attacks on a wide range of buildings, with particular focus on African Americans and African American institutions, including the Colored Orphan Asylum on Fifth Avenue. The death toll has never been accurately estimated, but surely over one hundred New Yorkers—including many African Americans—died in the rioting. In her July 14 entry, Daly gave a vivid sense of the riot, noting particularly the murderous assaults on black civilians. "Negroes were hung in the streets!" she declared. Daly seemed particularly appalled by the news that furniture had been carried from the colored orphan asylum "by *women*." The asylum was over thirty blocks from the Daly home, but she worried that the rioters might visit a black "tenement house some blocks below us," as they had burned others. It was an entry full of concern for African American victims, but also for her own safety. Still, once again the wealthy New Yorker revealed some interesting class empathy. "I did not wonder," she wrote, "at the spirit in which the poor resented the three-hundred-dollar clause." Later she returned to the same point, opining that the city's laboring classes had every reason to object to the commutation fee (246).

The following week Daly recorded a long and reflective entry about the riots. In this case she noted that "three or four Negroes were hung and burned," suggesting a true horror but minimizing the overall casualties. Daly returned to her broader gender theme in pointing out that "the women assisted and acted like furies by stimulating the men to greater ferocity." Later in the same entry Daly seemed to pick away at the notion that this was an Irish riot. One friend told her that they looked "like Germans" to her. Another report claimed that some of those killed and wounded were upper-class men with "delicate hands and feet," who had gone into the streets disguised as laborers. Most of the rest, Daly argued, "were boys, and I think they were Americans" and not Irish. Meanwhile, the city's Catholic priests deserved credit for quelling some acts of violence. After one friend visited the Dalys and "talked in the most violent manner against the Irish and in favor of the blacks," Daly wrote that "I feel quite differently." Although she was "much outraged at the cruelties inflicted," she hoped that the whole affair "will give the Negroes a lesson, for since the war commenced, they have been so insolent as to be unbearable." Although Daly's wartime diary entries rarely revealed her core racism, on this day she indulged herself, concluding that "I cannot endure free blacks. That are immoral, with all their piety" (251).

The New York City draft riots marked a huge event in the Civil War and in the state of wartime dissent. For Daly it was a moment where the war's dangers came much closer to home. With rioters roaming the streets, Judge Daly insisted on grabbing his pistol and taking measures to protect his home. Not too far away, Daly learned that her father's African American maid had let fifteen blacks hide in his home (until he ordered them out). During and immediately after the riot the diarist wrote extensively, revealing some unsettling opinions. Those were days that saw Daly—at least in her private journal—reveal the depth of her hostility to African Americans, while also demonstrating a surprising empathy for laboring whites as well as her ongoing support for the city's Irish population. The following March Daly attended a dinner party and sparred with a gentleman who spoke ill of the Irish rioters, defending the Irish and praising the Catholic priests whom she credited with saving the city.

Immediately following those July entries, Daly did not turn to her diary again for two months. And for the remainder of 1863 she recorded only occasional entries. She did note Union military successes in Chattanooga and Virginia, but in no particular detail. Closer to home, Daly remained struck with the economic inequalities around her, even as she lived amidst the city's home front opulence. In September the arrival of a substantial Russian fleet broke the wartime monotony. The following month the city staged a massive banquet in the Russians' honor. The judge attended (and spoke) but Maria had a cold and stayed home. Later that month she attended a fundraiser for the United States Sanitary Commission, which featured the great actress Charlotte Cushman and the equally famous Edwin Booth. Daly applauded the event and the Commission but could not resist noting that while it did much good it also had "allowed many rascals to enrich themselves at the expense of our poor soldiers without their suffering so much." "It is almost a disgrace to get rich by this dreadful war," she added (260).

The city and state elections at the end of the year were something of a national bellwether as Democrat Horatio Seymour, a persistent critic of Abraham Lincoln, lost his bid for reelection, along with many of his fellow Democrats in the state house. Daly noted these returns but her political eye—and ire—focused more on the local political machines and the rising stench of corruption. Again she worried about Charles's electoral future and she longed for her husband to pursue higher office with a loftier role.

For the Dalys and their circle, 1863 ended like a Shakespearean tragedy. Shortly after Christmas, Gen. Michael Corcoran of the 69th Regiment had been visiting General Meagher, another celebrated figure in the Irish Brigade. Two years of war and an extended period as a prisoner of war had weakened the general, but Corcoran still insisted on riding his horse. On this occasion he fell and died soon after. Meagher, who had a sometimes-tenuous relationship with the Dalys, sent the judge a long eloquent telegram about the loss of his comrade. Daly devoted her final entry of the year to Corcoran's death and funeral. The diarist was not particularly gracious. Corcoran had been married to an unusually young woman, and Daly had found that inappropriate. Now she concluded that somehow the pressures of "a young wife to humor" had been "one of the causes of his death." Daly copied the full text of Meagher's telegram, but suggested that he probably sent it to the judge in hopes that it would get into the newspapers (it did not). On the day of the funeral, Meagher served as the lead pallbearer, and Daly acknowledged that despite talk of Meagher taking over Corcoran's command, the general was judicious enough to wait before taking that step. But Daly recalled Meagher's poor behavior at Bull Run, and his subsequent actions that had ruined the career of General Shields. With Corcoran gone,

Meagher was set to be "the representative of the Irish brave," but on a day devoted to the memory of Corcoran, Maria could not resist finishing her year's journal by venting about Meagher (270–71).

1864–65: Three Celebrated Men

Each New Year's Day the Dalys threw a large open house to ring in the near year. Their 1864 party was smaller than some, but the Dalys still welcomed 70 guests. In late November Capt. Adam Badeau had visited for dinner, and Badeau had declared that "the rebels were effectually conquered," but while there was reason for hopes of a happy conclusion, the war dragged on into the spring (267).

Back at home, New Yorkers prepared for the huge Sanitary Fair to fund the United States Christian Commission. Daly approved of the event and the larger cause, but she repeatedly commented that volunteering in such public venues was not her cup of tea. She was content to donate to the Fair and not be in the public eye in some sort of elaborate volunteer's uniform. When New York women formed the Women's Patriotic Association for Diminishing the Use of Imported Luxuries, Daly gladly took on the presidency of the organization. The Association's focus on reducing unseemly excess in time of war appealed to Daly's sensibilities, and her role in charge of the new organization met her goals of service outside of the public eye.

Meanwhile, the goings-on within the Fair gave Maria ample opportunities to comment on gendered behavior she found objectionable. These were not new themes for the diarist. She had earlier remarked on female nurses whose behavior she questioned, and general patterns of excessive makeup or frivolity among young New York socialites. In March Daly described an animated conversation she had with two older women about the social excesses they were witnessing in the city, including "married women supping with gentlemen at Delmonico's without their husbands, and the rompishness of the younger ladies." There was also, she added, "a clique of fast young married women in New York who are very much loosening the reins of good and decorous manners" (280–81). Although her comments seemed particularly rigid, Daly generally had grounds for her opinions. In this case she was talking about Mrs. Mary E. Strong, the wife of Peter R. Strong. After much social commentary about Mrs. Strong's public actions it came to light that she had been having an affair with Strong's brother for two years. "Society seems to have gone mad," Daly wrote. The Strongs' divorce trial became one of the more celebrated in the city.[15]

In March, Daly witnessed the first regiment of black soldiers marching out of the city. Earlier in the war she had expressed doubts about arming black men, and she had given voice to her fundamental hostility towards African Americans, but while other Democrats mocked this grand occasion, the diarist seemed moved. "It was a very interesting and touching sight," she wrote. And while others questioned the manhood of black troops, Daly declared that "they were a fine body of men and had a look of satisfaction in their faces." Black men and women lined the streets "with tears in their eyes as if they saw the redemption of their race afar off but still the beginning of a better state of affairs for them." Daly, always inclined towards self-examination, admitted that "though I am very little Negrophilish and would always prefer the commonest white that lives to a Negro, still I could not help feel moved" (278).

Much of the northern perspective on the political and military history of the Civil War, and especially the conflict's final year, is told around the lives of three crucial men: Abraham Lincoln, George McClellan, and Ulysses S. Grant. All three men, and their wives, played substantial roles in the Daly diary, particularly in that last year. The Dalys had not supported Lincoln and his party in 1860 and did not support him throughout the war. But while they opposed emancipation, they recognized the need for conscription, and they remained loyal to the Union and the war effort. In 1861 Daly had found the new president "a man of little practical ability," but she found him "straightforward and honest" (23). She persisted in that general assessment throughout that first year, reserving her less gracious remarks for Mary Lincoln, whom Daly found "behaves in the most undignified manner possible" (86). But a year later Daly seemed pleased to report that the president was growing in the job, and not unduly swayed by outside influences.

Generally speaking, the New York blue blood was unimpressed with the president's homespun mannerisms, and even less pleased with his Kentucky spouse. But unlike other Democratic diarists or editors, Daly rarely indulged in rhetorical excesses about tyranny and the like. It was really not until the election of 1864 approached that Daly focused on the need to remove the Republican from office. By that point Lincoln's political future rested largely on the military success of General Grant.

Whereas Daly seemed quite aware of George McClellan and his military prowess from the first months of the war, the diarist initially noted Grant's early military successes in the West without naming the rising star. She first recorded Grant by name in May 1863, as his Union forces threatened Vicksburg. That November Daly wrote a longer comment about the general and his successes at Chattanooga, which she declared "brilliantly done" (265). The following spring Lincoln elevated Grant to command of the nation's entire military effort, and the general moved east, where he would accompany the Army of the Potomac in Virginia. Meanwhile, Adam Badeau received a promotion and took a role in Grant's staff. Badeau had become a great friend and loyal correspondent, and from his new position he provided Daly with regular updates on the army. That spring, as Grant dueled with Robert E. Lee across Virginia, Daly recorded approving comments and the latest letters from Badeau.

As 1864 neared an end, Abraham Lincoln's political future became increasingly intertwined with Grant's military successes on the battlefield. That September Daly joined the rest of the North in shifting focus towards national politics. At the end of August the Democratic Party had convened in Chicago, where they nominated McClellan as the party's standard-bearer, while saddling the general with an essentially antiwar platform. The notorious peace platform left McClellan riddled with uncertainty as he struggled with how to respond. Maria watched events from a privileged vantage point, as Charles had served as a New York elector in Chicago and had later consulted with the nominee on how to navigate the political terrain. In the end, after consulting with the judge, McClellan issued a formal letter accepting the nomination while distancing himself from the peace talk in the platform. The whole affair unsettled some pro-Union Democrats, but Daly reported on September 11 that "McClellan's letter made a great commotion, frightening the Republicans, dissatisfying the peace men, but contenting the moderate people" (302). The following week Daly attended a huge Democratic rally in Union Square, where Charles was one of the featured speakers. The diarist was pleased with the day, although she worried that Charles's explicit antiadministration stance might hurt him in the long run.

With the election only a few months away, Daly had become much more partisan, accusing the Lincolns of mistreating the McClellans and sending off pieces to the local press attacking the president. Lincoln, she insisted, "is a clever hypocrite under the mask of boorishness" who was "eminently disqualified" for the office he held (305). A month later Daly wrote that "Lincoln is cheating as hard as he can," assisted by Democrats who had abandoned their party (306). Days before the election she called the "rail-splitter and his wife, two ignorant and vulgar boors" (307). When the election returns revealed that Lincoln had been reelected by a healthy margin, Daly worried about "Poor McClellan!" who had paid the price for "the instability of popular favor and of fair-weather friends" (313). Like many Democrats who had supported McClellan to the end, Daly complained about election irregularities, and she persisted in criticizing those "fair-weather friends," including General Meagher, who had cast their lot with the Republicans. In early January the Dalys set out in a search through three New York social gatherings until they finally located General and Mrs. McClellan only days before they left the city. Daly found the general looking well, and the couple preparing for a European trip. They would be gone for three years.

In another three months the war would be over. In March Abraham Lincoln delivered his Second Inaugural Address. It was by many lights one of the greatest speeches ever delivered by an American. Daly, not yet ready to forget the election, found the speech "more like a sermon" than a presidential address, and more worthy of Henry Ward Beecher than Lincoln, and the inauguration was "more like an orgy than anything else" (343). But when Richmond fell the following month, the diarist was unambiguous in her enthusiasm. Daly noted that members of the United States Colored Troops had played a major role in the occupation, without injecting any critical commentary. Soon the war was over, and the Union had been preserved.

Endings

Histories of the Civil War commonly point to four moments that mark the end of four years of carnage. The first was Lincoln's Second Inaugural address, in which he laid out his thoughts about how the nation should proceed towards reconciliation and peace. The next three moments occurred on consecutive weeks in April 1865: the fall of Richmond, Lee's surrender to Grant at Appomattox Courthouse in Virginia, and the assassination of Abraham Lincoln at Ford's Theater in Washington, DC. It is hard to avoid describing the four moments as a series of cinematic events leading to a grand tragedy.

For wartime diarists, events unfolded differently. Daly noted the Second Inaugural, but she was hardly impressed with the rhetoric or affected by its implications. The fall of Richmond and Lee's surrender to Grant earned enthusiastic diary entries, although nothing particularly momentous. Daly paid attention to the military developments in those last few weeks, praising generals and anticipating victory. But it was news of the assassination of Abraham Lincoln, and the subsequent commemorations, that moved Maria Daly to long, contemplative, entries.

"What dreadful news! President Lincoln assassinated; Secretary Seward's throat cut!" Daly wrote on April 15, 1865, beginning a long entry describing the events in Ford's Theater in journalistic detail. "God save us all. What may not a day bring forth!" she concluded (353–54). A few days later Daly recorded a lengthy, more introspective entry. After attending church on Easter Sunday, the diarist reported that the clergymen were asserting that "he was sacrificed on Good Friday." She demurred, arguing that she deferred to nobody in her patriotism, but insisted that the Union's "success must be ascribed to God alone" and not the fallen president. In this entry, only days after Lincoln's death, Daly added a long discussion of Lincoln's many failures as a president and commander-in-chief, noting that "[a]ll this will be forgotten in this shameful, cowardly act of his assassination" on the eve of peace. And, in a surprising moment of historic reflection, the judge's wife pointed out that "it was the rejection of Douglas by the Charleston Convention four years ago that elected Abraham Lincoln and Jefferson Davis, and it was not any fault of Abraham Lincoln. Nor can we blame him that when elected by a legal majority, he accepted the Presidency. Every American feels competent for any place" (354–56). In this moment of national tragedy, Daly leaned towards a generous assessment of the fallen president, but she refused to call him a martyr or a saint.

Nearly a week later, when the funeral procession reached New York and Lincoln lay in state at City Hall, Daly wrote that "I shall not go to see the show," but she would allow the servants to attend. "I am sick of pageants." But she did add, "Poor Mrs. Lincoln!," temporarily setting aside four years of hostility towards the uncouth first lady (356–57). On April 25th Daly attended the funeral procession in the city, providing future historians with a detailed description of the "most imposing" affair. But she could not resist pointing out that the assassinated president had stolen the election from George McClellan (358).

A book framed around literary conventions could easily have ended with Maria Daly writing about Lincoln's funeral procession through New York. After all, the war was safely won, the McClellans were off in Europe, and Daly had found some balance between her distaste for the fallen president and her sadness at his death. But Hammond did not choose to end *Diary of a Union Lady* there, opting instead to give the reader Daly's diary through 1865. The entries continued to appear less frequently than they had in the first years of the war, but they still tell a story about her life, the life of New York City, and her observations about national events. Closest to home, brother Phil returned from the war, apparently unscathed by the experience. In May he announced that he was engaged to be married, and his sister anticipated that "we shall like her very much" (363). In July the Dalys attended the wedding and Maria remained pleased with the bride. That October the judge—supported by "all shades of the Democracy"—successfully won renomination, once again navigating New York's thorny political world (369).

By continuing the publication for another eight months, Hammond—and Daly—put Ulysses S. Grant and Julia Grant at center stage for much of the final stanza of *Diary of a Union Lady.* In four years of war Maria Daly had not only met many of the Union's leading military and political figures, but time and again she had socialized with those men and their spouses. Often she found the famous women she met lacking, and on other occasions she took aim at the husbands who did not seem to match their ambitions. Despite some early reservations, Maria had come to like Ellen McClellan. She did not really know Mary Lincoln well, and thought little of what she did know. But in Julia Grant, Daly found a public woman who stood up to her harsh scrutiny, both during the war and in the months after.

Although Daly had praised Grant's generalship and character repeatedly over the previous many months, the couples first met in mid-November when the Dalys went to call upon the great general and his spouse. Both impressed Daly. She found Julia "simple, natural, not handsome, but pleasant looking, a slight cast in her yet but fine teeth, and a pleasant, honest smile" (371). The judge issued Grant a formal invitation to a grand reception in his honor at the Fifth Avenue Hotel. The following night both couples attended the same opera, and Mrs. Grant sent Badeau to invite the Dalys to join them in their proscenium box. Once again Maria came away pleased with Julia's simple western honesty, and she did not seem to mind that neither Grant pretended to know a thing about opera.

A few mornings later Daly visited one of her favorite haunts, the studio of the famed landscape artist Albert Bierstadt. On this occasion she admired Bierstadt's latest painting of a storm over the Rocky Mountains. There she met Republican senator and former governor Edwin D. Morgan and his wife, "a great stout dressy matron of fifty-four or five" (374). The three chatted about the Grants, and specifically Julia Grant's admitted ignorance of opera. Mrs. Morgan suggested that Mrs. Grant might just as well acknowledge her lack of culture since "'Everybody knows it and can see it.'" But Daly recorded that "I think Mrs. Grant as much of a lady as herself" (374). Apparently Daly felt a bit protective of her new friend. Still, having met the Morgans for the first time, the diarist concluded that she should eventually call on them.

On the 20th, New Yorkers gathered for the grand Grant reception, with Charles Daly playing a key role as a member of the Committee on Arrangements. Maria was pleased, if a bit embarrassed, that Julia invited her to be among the four women to accompany her on the platform. Once again, the diarist—who so rarely had much positive to say about the public women she met—wrote effusively about Julia Grant, whom she described as "natural and unaffected" with a "ladylike self-possession which is pleasing." She ended the night describing it as "an event in my life" and "the first time I had been on any platform" (376–77).

As 1865 came to a close, Maria Daly had begun throwing herself into the financial health of the new Union Home and School for soldiers' children. That summer the judge had taken a position on the Union Home's board of directors, and before long Maria was serving as its president. On Christmas Eve she wrote that she had spent the entire day at the Union Home preparing for a Christmas banquet for the fatherless soldiers' children. Both Dalys attended the dinner and came away quite pleased. On December 30, Daly wrote that she had devoted much of the week to "getting an appropriation passed for the Union Home and School," and was "at last successful" (382). A few visitors came to dinner that evening, and the diarist brought 1865 to a close.

A Diarist and a Source

Civil War diaries offer compelling windows into momentous events, providing readers with a sense of the flow of a narrative we too often read weighted down by hindsight. The best remind us that ordinary people lived ordinary lives, even while absorbing chaotic and sometimes incomprehensible news. No one person can be representative of an entire population, and Maria Lydig Daly—with her considerable wealth and reputation—was less representative than most. Still, *Diary of a Union Lady* is more than just a treasure trove of quotations for historians in search of pithy descriptions and sometimes unkind capsule portraits of celebrated women and men.

Daly's diary reminds us of the war's political complexities. Charles and Maria Daly were loyal Democrats and also devoted Unionists. But even when the Democratic Party approved an antiwar platform in 1864, neither Daly questioned their support of George McClellan for president. They lived in a crucial northern city, where Republicans and Democrats sometimes clashed bitterly, and where Democrats divided among themselves. Yet the diarist did not adopt the partisan labels commonly used by her peers to define dueling Democrats. Maria was a wealthy woman with real sympathy for the working-class Irish in her city.

Although surely a "racist" by any modern sense of the word, even when compared with many of her contemporaries, Daly's open hostility to African American appeared only occasionally in her diary, and never accompanied by the sort of offensive language that appeared regularly in much of the Democratic press. Moreover, although she never explicitly renounced her earlier opinions, Daly's later observations about African Americans in uniform suggest a mind that was slowly evolving. As a New Yorker with deep Germanic roots, Daly had married a second generation Irish Catholic and completely adopted his concerns for Ireland and Irish Americans. These considerations included very occasional comments about social and economic inequalities. Daly lived a life of overwhelming privilege and yet on occasion she seemed aware of common ethnic and racial hypocrisies, chafing at New York society's worst excesses in the midst of war.

Then there is Maria Lydig Daly the observer of gender and society. The Dalys surely seemed to be devoted spouses and committed partners, and the story of their courtship and marriage speak to a woman unwilling to march to gender conventions or familial hierarchies. But as an observer of New York society, Daly sometimes revealed her disgust with the behavior of young women pushing the boundaries of polite gender behavior. And when couples she knew married out of love, she felt free to judge them (in her diary) if their ages were too far apart or in some other way they seemed to be an inappropriate match. Daly also had the startling habit of recording sharply critical discussions of women whom she thought of as friends and confidants. Sometimes, as with Jesse Benton Frémont, she suspected a scheming character behind the intelligent and charming façade. Those harsh judgments were not always far off the mark. And, in a fortunate trick of wartime narrative, Daly became friends and strong defenders of two of the North's most prominent military wives of the Civil War: Mary Ellen McClellan and Julia Grant. Thus the diary provides the reader and the historian with charming glimpses into the wartime worlds of both women and their husbands.

More broadly, Maria Lydig Daly's diary opens vast avenues for historians who wish to understand the lives of wartime women. She wrote frequently of nursing and voluntarism, both assessing her own impulses and the actions of others. She records her own activities in a wealth of New York institutions, most run by women. She offers an elite woman's perspective on the public actions of younger women, challenging gender conventions. And, perhaps most noteworthy, she unveils a world of New York women reading about, and debating, political and military affairs, both among themselves and with men.

Diary of a Union Lady is also a distinctive "primary source" for scholars of the Civil War, in that it is really one source folded into another. In its essence it is a source for the personal thoughts of a New York woman during the Civil War. But Hammond's front matter, notes, and italicized interludes become a source in themselves. Written in the midst of the war's centennial, these extensive materials are a window into the state of scholarship roughly sixty years ago. Hammond's notes and biographical sketches are extensive, leaning heavily towards political and military figures and events. The discussions of crucial home front issues and particularly those involving the wartime roles of women, including in the United States Sanitary Commission and in nursing, are not generally incorrect, but they are thinner than his treatment of more familiar topics.[16] Hammond's notes on local politics are generally accurate, but they do reflect a particular understanding of the Democratic political landscape. It is noteworthy that Daly only used the term *copperhead* on one occasion in her diary, although she often had choice words for local Democrats who opposed the war. She referred to herself and Judge Daly as "Union Democrats," and very rarely used the label "War Democrat," even though that label would seem to apply to the position that both Dalys took. As the editor Hammond used "copperhead" freely, including nine times in the text and in notes, usually when describing an individual. In the introduction he explains that although the Dalys were Union Democrats, the judge "numbered among his personal friends important Copperheads."[17] That was, and is, common usage in describing wartime Democrats, but the label was quite imprecise and its meaning murky, both during the war and in subsequent analysis. It is interesting that Daly, living in that divided Democratic world, did not use it.

And even while taking his subject and her diary seriously, Hammond sometimes views Daly's behavior through unsettling gendered lenses. In discussing Daly's political beliefs, Hammond explains that the diarist "acquired most of the political attitudes she expresses . . . by association with the Judge and his friends," later adding that "her marriage to the Judge made her . . . liberal." In commenting about Daly's opinions on other women, Hammond notes that "she was malicious toward most members of her own sex—especially the very attractive ones—she was very human and very much a woman. It was quite natural for her to resent women who were able to make themselves more attractive than she." Hammond went on to suggest that Daly was particularly close to Harriet Whetten because she was similarly unattractive.[18] Certainly there were better ways to understand and explain how Daly came to her political beliefs, and what led her to judge some other women harshly.

Allan Nevins wrote a short foreword to the original volume, no doubt as a favor to his doctoral student. Nevins, who would have been just over 70 at the time, revealed his own notions about women as historic actors and observers. The brilliant historian paid homage to Daly's "clear-eyed observations" and "occasional flashes of insight," noting her astute portraits of Jesse Benton Frémont, Fernando Wood, and a few others. But he could not resist describing Daly as "an inimitable purveyor of the feminine gossip of New York," assuring readers that the diary—"if read tolerantly"—will be "endlessly entertaining." Nevins added that Daly "was a very silly woman at times," despite "her occasional flashes of shrewd insight." Nevins noted that Daly was sometimes "catty," a characterization that was not entirely unfair even if the term itself was disturbingly gendered. And no doubt she occasionally gossiped or wrote "silly" things, but surely Daly—in her personal journal—was no more inclined towards "gossip" than fellow Civil War diarists George Templeton Strong and Sydney George Fisher.[19]

Contemporary reviewers approached *Diary of a Union Lady* with similar presuppositions. Brooks Atkinson, the one-time theater critic for the *New York Times*, wrote a long joint review in the *Times*, commenting on Daly and Mary Chesnut. Atkinson found that both were "incandescent women," who shared much in common. Both diarists disliked slavery, abolitionists, and both Lincolns, he wrote (never mind that Daly never appeared to be particularly bothered by slavery). Like Nevins, Atkinson noted that both women loved to "gossip." The *Journal of Southern History,* a leading scholarly journal, reviewed *Diary of a Union Lady* alongside a new edition of George Templeton Strong's wartime diary in a short, combined review. Strong, the author found, "pulled no punches in describing what he observed," while Daly too often "dealt in rumor or pure gossip," leaving a record of "much less importance" than her fellow New Yorker.[20] Wayne Temple, writing for the *Journal of the Illinois State Historical Society,* not surprisingly took umbrage at Daly's harsh treatment of Abraham Lincoln. Temple appreciated the historic value of the diary but added that much of it was "devoted to gossip, and her stories concerning Mary Lincoln are easy to disprove."[21]

The truth is that Maria Lydig Daly recorded her thoughts and activities, and occasionally summaries of interesting conversations. Unlike many diarists, she only rarely used the pages of her journal to record her personal emotions. The fact that each of these contemporary male readers described Daly's published diary as full of "gossip" makes one wonder if they had ever previously encountered a diary in any form. It would seem that readers of this rich primary source will find what they are looking for.

NOTES

1. Maria Lydig Daly, *Diary of a Union Lady 1861–1865,* ed. Harold Earl Hammond (New York: Funk and Wagnalls, 1962).

2. The diary is, among many other things, a valuable source for the history of the wartime Democrats. The scholarship on northern Democrats is vast, although in some ways limited. The classic history is Joel H. Silbey, *A Respectable Minority: The Democratic Party in the Civil War Era, 1860–1868* (New York: W. W. Norton, 1977). For an innovative recent treatment see Mark Neeley Jr., *Lincoln and the Democrats: The Politics of Opposition in the Civil War* (New York: Cambridge University Press, 2017). For a forthcoming study, see J. Matthew Gallman, *"The Union as it was, The Constitution as it is": Northern Democrats and the American Civil War* (Charlottesville: University of Virginia Press, 2021). Neither Silbey nor Neely made use of the Daly diary.

3. On the diaries of southern women, and on how to read wartime diaries, see Steven M. Stowe, *Keep the Days: Reading the Civil War Diaries of Southern Women* (Chapel Hill: University of North Carolina Press, 2018).

4. George Templeton Strong, *The Diary of George Templeton Strong,* ed. Allan Nevins and Milton Halsey Thomas, 4 vols. (New York: Macmillan, 1952); Sidney George Fisher, *A Philadelphia perspective; the diary of Sidney George Fisher covering the years, 1834–1871,* ed. Nicholas B. Wainwright (Philadelphia: Historical Society of Pennsylvania, 1967).

5. Harold Earl Hammond, *A Commoner's Judge: The Life and Times of Charles Patrick Daly* (Boston, 1954).

6. Daly, *Diary of a Union Lady,* vii–viii. Nearly forty year after *Diary of a Union Lady* appeared, Bison Books issued a valuable paperback reprint, with a new introduction by the historian Jean V. Berlin. This new edition reproduced the Hammond edition precisely, with the same pagination. See Mary Lydig Daly, *Diary of a Union Lady 1861–1865* (University of Nebraska Press, 2000).

7. Emilie Davis, *Emilie Davis's Civil War: The Diaries of a Free Black Woman in Philadelphia, 1863–1865,* ed. Judith Giesberg (Penn State University Press, 2014).

8. Unlike many other diarists, who recorded their notes in year-long volumes published for the purpose, Daly wrote in a large book that contained all her notations spanning the entire year. In fact, she did not initially get the hang of keeping dated entries. The first in the volume is dated January 31, 1861, and the next is dated May 26, 1861. Both entries span large chunks of time.

9. Antebellum history from Hammond, *A Commoner's Judge,* 112–20, 127, 131. Quotations are from undated letters from Maria Lydig to Charles Daly, 1856, cited by Hammond; originals are in the Charles P. Daly Papers, New York Public Library, New York City.

10. Kennedy was a Democrat, a fact Daly did not note.

11. Hammond, *A Commoner's Judge,* 154.

12. Various women named Strong, usually unrelated, appear in Daly's diary. Here she was mocking the wife of New York diarist George Templeton Strong.

13. The diary entry is unclear about whether Maria took an active hand in shaping the speech, or whether her role was entirely in transcribing it for public delivery. See Hammond, *A Commoner's Judge,* 163.

14. Daly, *Diary of a Union Lady,* 212. Here again, Daly adopted an odd usage, referring to "ultra-Democrats" rather than "copperheads" or "Peace Democrats."

15. Daly, *Diary of a Union Lady,* 281n6; *New York Times,* March 17, 1865.

16. As just one example, in June 1864 Daly mentioned Louisa Lee Schuyler in passing. Hammond's note explains that Schuyler "was a prominent social worker active in the Sanitary Commission." (Daly, *Diary of a Union Lady,* 299.) That was true, but neglects Schuyler's crucial role in forming and running the Woman's Central Association of Relief. Nearly all of the scholarship on Schuyler and the WCAR appeared long after 1962.

17. Daly, *Diary of a Union Lady,* xxxviii–xxxix.

18. Daly, *Diary of a Union Lady,* xlviii, li, lii.

19. Daly, *Diary of a Union Lady,* xv–xvi.

20. J. H. Parks, book review, *The Journal of Southern History* 29 (August 1863): 401–2.

21. Wayne Temple, book review, *Journal of the Illinois State Historical Society* 55 (Winter 1962): 470–71.

FRYING HARDTACK.

"Frying Hardtack." This sketch by Charles W. Reed depicted one of the many aspects of soldier life that John D. Billings discussed in his book. John D. Billings, *Hardtack and Coffee: The Unwritten Story of Army Life* (Boston: George M. Smith & Co., 1887), 117.

John D. Billings's *Hardtack and Coffee*

A Union Fighting Man's Civil War

M. KEITH HARRIS

Veteran US Army artillerist and Massachusetts man John D. Billings explained in the preface to *Hardtack and Coffee: The Unwritten Story of Army Life* precisely why he wrote his book. A former private in the 10th Massachusetts Volunteer Light Artillery Battery, Billings recalled an evening in 1881 at a White Mountains resort where he and another Union Civil War veteran entertained "from twelve to twenty lads, varying in age from ten to fifteen years" with stories from the war "as [he] saw it."[1] For Billings, the war *as he saw it* reverberated as the recollection of "a trifling piece of personal experience" and led to the compilation of what Billings stated were "facts too commonplace for the general histories of the war."[2] Billings's work is unusual in this regard. He was among the first veterans of the Civil War to detail the common experiences of war from the perspective of an enlisted man.[3] He wrote to describe the life of a soldier to those who had not experienced the war. "It would have interested a civilian to observe . . . ," as Billings pointed out, the various things associated with daily soldiering.[4] Historians and other avid readers of Civil War veterans' writings have mined this treasure trove of soldierly detail in Billings's work to help piece together the day-to-day activities of a typical fighting man in camp and on campaign—the experiences of the so-called "common soldier." Knowledge that his book has been consulted extensively undoubtedly would have pleased Billings a great deal.

Hardtack and Coffee is also noteworthy for its affirmations of sectional ideology. Billings meant to complement the popular war narratives of his era—the general histories to which he refers in his opening passages—for the benefit of the civilian public. Adding an ideological angle was a bold tack for a former enlisted man writing for popular consumption in the 1880s. In some ways his sectionalism emulated the memoirs of such distinguished Union officers as Ulysses S. Grant and William Tecumseh Sherman—whose writings formed part of what one might call veteran Union commemorative literature, a distinctive genre that honored the Union cause specifically.[5] Both Grant and Sherman acknowledged the courage and fortitude of their former enemies but clearly positioned the Union cause as the more virtuous. Many prominent veterans would echo such sentiments during speeches at public dedications and similar events. Other veteran authors reserved ideology for literature written primarily for other Civil War veterans.

But what might have been commonplace in commemorative literature, public monument dedication speeches, and more exclusive veteran commemorative publications did not always appear in the popular war narratives of the 1880s, which were often written with a reconciliationist spirit and meant to appeal to a national audience. While Billings wrote with the stated intention of describing the ordinary objects and activities associated with soldiering, he likewise did a great deal to capture the essence of the Union cause and the sentiments within the ranks of enlisted men concerning his and his comrades' former Rebel enemies—points modern scholars and others often overlook. In *Hardtack and Coffee*, Billings explained the war from an undeniably Union perspective. Vivid imagery of ordinary soldiering coupled with clear and resolute sectionalism made *Hardtack and Coffee* a notable publication.[6]

Billings not only tailored *Hardtack and Coffee* for civilians but also for those who lived through the grand ordeal and sought to rekindle the excitement of their days under arms. Billings addressed his fellow veterans personally, commenting that "these pages will appeal to a large number of whom the Civil War is yet something more than a myth . . . they are confidently put forth . . . with the full assurance that they will partially meet a want hitherto unsupplied."[7] Billings catalogued and explained the typical experiences of the common soldier for his fellow veterans interested in the subject. Knowing that Billings wrote partly with his former comrades in mind, it would stand to reason that he would include content that reflected a sectional sentiment and commemorated the Union cause. Divisive Civil War–era issues may not have been the focus of *Hardtack and Coffee*, but they unquestionably provided the backdrop for the stories of enlistment, campaigning, and fighting for the Union cause. Sectionalism most certainly would have resonated with veterans and other readers familiar with commemorative literature. Those among his civilian audience versed mainly in the language of popular war narratives would have found it exceptional.

Students of Civil War–era soldiery should question whether or not one might satisfactorily describe any individual soldier as "common" in terms of his commitments to nationalism, his ideology, or even his thoughts concerning the war in both the immediate and broader contexts. Billings certainly had his own ideas about soldiers' ideological leanings. Perhaps, when it comes to military commonality, it might be best to think in terms of typical experiences with which veterans of the US armies would be familiar. Billings clearly thought in terms of shared experiences. Irrespective of social class in civilian life, ethnic background, religious affiliations, or rank in the army, Billings underscored such things as vermin infestations, the writing of letters home to family and other loved ones, boredom in camp, incessant drill, winter camp, and the various games enjoyed by all soldiers.[8]

Hardtack and Coffee's public accounting of ordinary Civil War experiences illuminated topics virtually unknown except to those who had lived through the tumult of 1861–65. Billings was among the first veterans to write in this particular style for the general public. He set a tone that stood in stark contrast to the sweeping Civil War narrative available to the public in the late 1880s. Billings surmised that the simple trappings of a soldier's life would resonate more clearly with his veteran comrades than would grand strategy and military logistics, but he also must have known—or at least assumed—that the civilian reading public would find such things engaging, especially those who had sent a husband, son, brother, or father to war while they remained behind the lines. "It is believed," Billings wrote, "that what is herein written will appeal largely to a common experience among soldiers. In full faith that such is the case, they are now presented to veterans, their children, and the public as an important contribution of warp to the more majestic woof which comprises the history of the Great Civil War already written."[9]

Dividing his book into twenty-one easily digestible chapters, Billings did provide a more personal warp. With Billings's book in hand, any reminiscing soldier or curious civilian who might inquire about military experiences could find voluminous information about life in tents, about rations, and about uniforms. They might be amused by stories of stubborn army mules, or impressed with descriptions of the military efficiency (or lack thereof) of wagon trains and soldiers on the march, or they might learn to appreciate the logistical difficulties involved in crossing a river or communicating over long distances. Whatever one's fancy in regard to the everyday life of a Union soldier, *Hardtack and Coffee* almost certainly would suffice. At the very least, as historian Henry Steele Commager noted in the mid-twentieth century, *Hardtack and Coffee* illuminated how "Civil War soldiers . . . were endlessly resourceful. They had to be. Their resourcefulness appeared not only in such contrivances as [*Hardtack and Coffee*] described, but in the creation of new weapons and new techniques of warfare." It is no wonder that, according to Commager, Billings's work was "one of the most entertaining of all Civil War books" not only during the author's own lifetime but long after the first printing appeared.[10]

Modern readers acknowledge *Hardtack and Coffee* as the Civil War era's fundamental source about all things military. And rightfully so. Billings left no stone unturned in regard to various items one might connect to the common soldier's life in the Union army. *Hardtack and Coffee* broadened Americans' understanding of the war far beyond logistics, strategy, and the sweeping movements of regiments, brigades, divisions, corps, and armies. In fact, the book personalized the war and added the human experiences, anecdotes, and trifling matters that distilled the big picture down to the rank and file. By filling in these missing elements, Billings did a great service for the overall narrative. One could imagine contemporary readers following along and vicariously experiencing the enlisted man's life through Billings's words.

Readers certainly discovered that life in the army lacked most of the comforts of home. Sleeping arrangements on campaign, for example, must have seemed profoundly unpleasant to those unfamiliar with the army. "There was [a] tent, the most interesting of all," observed Billings, "which was used exclusively in the field, and that was *Tente d' Abri*—the *Dog* or *Shelter Tent.* Just why they called it a shelter tent I cannot say . . . there is little shelter in this variety of tent. I can imagine no other reason for calling it a dog tent than this, that when one is pitched it would only comfortably accommodate a dog, and a small one at that . . . this was *the* tent of the rank and file."[11] Living arrangements for those who shared accommodations resembled the comforts of home life even less, especially if one were from a family of means. "[Bell] tents were comfortably capacious for a dozen men," Billings wrote. "In cold or rainy weather, when every opening is closed, they are most unwholesome tenements, and to enter one of them during a rainy morning from the outer air, and encounter the night's accumulation of nauseating exhalations of twelve men (differing widely in their habits of personal cleanliness) was an experience which no old soldier has ever been known to recall with any great enthusiasm." Still, soldiers grouped together in tents did the best they could to replicate a happy social setting. Although crowded together, uncomfortable, often with no room for standing or moving about, observed Billings, "these little knots [of men] were quite family like and sociable."[12]

Disease affected Civil War soldiers in horrific ways, which further emphasized the distance between home and battlefield. Many suffered from malaria, measles, dysentery, chronic diarrhea, and a number of other afflictions, which often led to an unpleasant death far from home. This so-called "bad death" occupied the thoughts of many Civil War soldiers, as their letters home would attest.[13] *Hardtack and Coffee* illuminated the reality of suffering in the ranks by harnessing the conventional gender assumptions common in the Victorian era. But most important, Billings illustrated how a painful death away from home most certainly struck a chord of sadness among the living:

> I can see my old comrades now, God bless them! Sterling fellows, soldiers to the core, stalwart men when they entered the army, but, overtaken by disease, they would report to sick-call, day after day, hoping for a favorable change; yet, in spite of medicine and the nursing of their messmates, pining away until at last they disappeared—went to the hospitals, and there died. Oh, if such men could only have been sent to their homes before it was too late, where the surroundings were more congenial and comfortable, the nursing tender, and more skilful, because administered by warmer hearts and the more loving hands of mother, wife, or sister, thousands of these noble souls could have been saved to the government and their families . . . but it was not to be, and so they wasted away, manly battling for life against odds, dying with the names of dear ones on their lips . . . [14]

Billings acknowledged the vast reach of disease within the ranks but explained it differently from modern historians. Scholars have concluded that lack of tolerance to disease, especially among rural men who had never traveled far from home and thus had not built up immunities, accounted for many of the disease-related deaths in the ranks. Billings, in contrast, found fault with the US government: "It has always struck me that the government should have increased the size of the marching ration. If the soldier on the march had received one and one-half pounds of hard bread and one and one-half pounds of fresh meat daily with his sugar, coffee, and salt, it would have been more than marching men require to keep up the requisite strength and resist disease."[15]

Apart from his compaint about the marching ration, Billings accorded considerable attention to how the Union fed its soldiers. Unsurprisingly, he pronounced food in camp to be far more abundant than food on the march, though many among his comrades would claim otherwise. "I have been asked a great many times whether I always got enough to eat in the army," he reported, "and have surprised inquirers by answering in the affirmative. Now some old soldier may say who sees my reply, 'Well, you were lucky, I didn't.' But I should at once ask him to tell me for how long a time his regiment was without food of some kind."[16] According to Billings, the army, except when on the march, did the best it could to provide for the men. The food was both plentiful and meant to replicate nutritious fare soldiers might have enjoyed before the war.

"Unwholesome rations," claimed Billings, "were not the rule, they were the exception." Of course, soldiers discussing hardtack brought the issue of "wholesomeness" into question. Despite the general grumbling among his peers about hardtack—the soldiers sang in chorus: "O hard crackers, come again no more!"—Billings had agreeable words to say about this ubiquitous army ration. Indeed, he thought it important enough to include "hardtack" in the title of his book, while still acknowledging the cracker's dubious reputation. "I presume the word 'hardtack' suggests to the uninitiated a piece of petrified bread honeycombed with bugs and maggots," he confessed, "so much has this article of army diet been reviled by soldier and civilian . . . it is a rare occurrence for a soldier to allude to it, even at this late date, without some reference to its hardness, the date of its manufacture, or its propensity for travel." But, as Billings countered, "hardtack was not so bad an article of food, even when traversed by insects, as may be supposed."[17] One could surmise that in all likelihood, Billings had a fondness, or at least a sense of nostalgia, for the cracker, as he spoke of it frequently and associated it with the creativity and resourcefulness of his former comrades—he even kept a few pieces as mementos.[18] Crumbled in coffee, fried with pork fat in a dish known as "skillygalee," consumed with raw salt pork, or eaten with sugar or a sauce made from apples, hardtack certainly left an impression. Some soldiers thought it may even have been good for weak bowels.[19]

Vermin were as common an experience in the army as nearly anything else and drew the ire of all in the ranks. Lice, known to the Union soldiers as "graybacks," were a particular nuisance. In a democratizing spirit, these tiny parasitic insects saw no distinction between class and rank. Rather, as Billings pointed out, they infested the bodies and belongings of all. "The historic 'grayback' . . . like death, it was no respecter of persons. It preyed alike on the just and the unjust. It inserted its bill as confidingly into the body of a major-general as of the lowest private. I once heard the orderly of a company officer relate that he had picked *fifty-two graybacks* from the shirt of his chief in one sitting. Aristocrat or plebian it mattered not." Soldiers took to "skirmishing" or "(k)nitting work"—euphemisms for attacking their clothes and bodies with the intent of massacring as many of the insects as the soldier could discover. "Feelings of intense disgust aroused by the first contact with these creepers soon gave way to hardened indifference, as the soldier realized the utter impossibility of keeping free from them." The impossibility of soldiers completely ridding their bodies of insects revealed Billings's sense of humor despite the unpleasant circumstances. Cleanliness consumed the thoughts of some (though certainly not all) soldiers, and lice seemed to have done their best to compromise soldiers' sanitary efforts. Billings jokingly observed soldiers' sense of near hopelessness with keeping free from vermin: "I think there was but one opinion among the soldiers in regard to the graybacks; *viz.,* that the country was being ruined by *overproduction.*" These vivid descriptions of bug infestations and the work soldiers undertook to rid themselves of pests would have been common knowledge among veterans. They must have been unsettling for civilian readers.[20]

Along with sketches of accommodations in camp, food, and insects, among other things denoting a typical soldier's experiences, Billings's descriptions of the enlisted man's everyday equipment distinguished *Hardtack and Coffee* from most other Civil War literature. He tended to enumerate the ordinary items. "A soldier's table furnishings," read a typical passage, "were his tin dipper, tin plate, knife, fork, and spoon." Billings also concerned himself with soldiers' efforts to keep their mess kits clean. "When [the sol-

dier] had finished his meal," readers learned, "he did not in many cases
stand on ceremony, and his dishes were tossed under the bunk to await
the next meal . . . Sometimes he was satisfied to scrape his plate out with a
knife, and let it go at that. When they got too black to be tolerated . . . there
was no cleansing process so inexpensive, simple, available, and efficient as
running them vigorously into the earth a few times."[21]

Billings was particularly adept at describing the many clever uses of
army issue equipment. "That necessity was the mother of invention," he
reminded his readers, "nothing can more clearly and fully demonstrate than
war." In the case of frying pans, for instance: "The soldier called in his own
ingenuity to aid him here as in so many other directions, and consequently
the men could be seen by scores frying the food in their tin plate, held in
the jaws of a split stick, or fully as often an old canteen was unsoldered and
its concave sides mustered into active duty as fry-pans." To light their tents,
men relied on another common piece of equipment: "As to the candlesticks,
the government provided the troops with those by the thousands. They were
of steel, and very durable, but were supplied only to the infantry, who had
simply to unfix bayonet, stick the points of the same in the ground, and
their candlesticks were ready for service." Soldiers, consistently improvising
to increase their comfort the best they could, utilized the abundant wood
from hardtack boxes to build bunks, tables, and hinged doors for winter
quarters.[22]

Billings suggested that life at home occupied his comrades' minds. Many
men, especially at the beginning of the conflict, enlisted in the army with
great enthusiasm, seeking adventure away from their dull civilian lives.
But life in the military, as many soldiers quickly understood, could wear an
individual thin. And so thoughts turned to home, family, and civilian life.
This was as common an experience as any—underscored by Billings's many
references alluding to the conveniences of home. "Taps ended the army day
for all branches of the service," he wrote, "and . . . the soldiers were left to
their slumbers; or, what was oftener the case, to meditations on home; the
length of time in months and days they must serve before returning thither;
their prospects of surviving the vicissitudes of war. . . ." Letters and boxes
from loved ones behind the lines naturally delighted soldiers, especially in
winter, when inactivity made soldiers particularly homesick: ". . . in winter quarters [infantry and artillerymen] accumulated a large assortment
of conveniences from home, sent on in the boxes which so gladdened the

soldier's heart." Soldiers considered these boxes the nearest thing to home, and when the army stopped for any length of time, the men went straight to work to acquire one. Writing a family member listing in careful detail the required items, they would wait with anticipation for the arrival of these small tastes from home. "If there was a red-letter day to be found anywhere in the army life of a soldier," Billings began one chapter, "it occurred when he was the recipient of a box sent to him by the dear ones and friends he left to enter the service."[23]

As already noted, Billings filled in the missing pieces of the war's story that many accounts written about high politics or military strategy and battles had ignored. He also imparted to his readers a sense of the importance of devotion to the Union cause among men in the ranks, a dimension of his book that paralleled themes found in veterans' commemorative literature. Very little concerning the everyday lives of Civil War soldiers was available in the late 1880s. One could assume that such literature was in short supply because the American audience thirsted for general histories penned by some of the war's prominent personalities—stories defined by sweeping narrative and grand strategy. Many such authors manned the literary ranks as contributors to the "Century War Series" in *Century Magazine.* That magazine's editors, who assumed a reconciled national orientation among potential readers, generally avoided causes and consequences to play down sectional bickering and encouraged their authors to emphasize battlefield valor and glory. By 1888, the series' circulation had risen to 225,000.[24] The Century Company ultimately compiled a selection of these accounts as the four-volume *Battles and Leaders of the Civil War,* an immensely popular set that sold well and featured accounts from both Union and Confederate leadership.[25] Such publications did little to personalize the rank and file or to illuminate the shared experiences of soldiers fighting a war in which millions served and between 620,000 and 850,000 died.[26]

For the role of ideology and sectionalism in the conflict, one needed to turn to veteran commemorative literature. Among the most well-received and popular publications of this genre were numerous memoirs—published in the 1870s, 1880s, and 1890s—written by such luminaries as Generals William T. Sherman and Ulysses S. Grant. These books were without question war narratives, but they also revealed the authors' resolute position that the Union cause was the more virtuous. In this sense the personal memoirs were sectional in orientation. Among works by second-tier leaders, Benjamin F.

Butler's personal reminiscences typified titles that combined personal memoirs, war narrative, and a staunch grounding in Union ideology.[27] Publishing houses meant for these books to appeal to a wide audience, including civilians.

Veterans, when speaking to or writing for former comrades, tended to fuel the sectional flames even further. Immediately after the war, Union veterans formed fraternal organizations to commemorate their fight. Together they worked to honor their dead, acknowledge their sacrifices, and preserve their wartime memories for posterity. Indeed, most organizations included in their institutional bylaws a mission statement written to ensure that the nation would remember efforts to preserve the Union.[28] In such groups, veterans had many chances to reminisce and recall their lives in the army. By the 1880s, fraternal military organizations such as the Military Order of the Loyal Legion of the United States (MOLLUS) and the preeminent veterans' organization, the Grand Army of the Republic (GAR), were in full swing with membership rosters numbering in the thousands and posts in every loyal state and some in the former Confederacy.[29]

Billings was quite familiar with the efforts of fraternal veterans' organizations. He belonged to and was very active with Grand Army of the Republic Post 94 in Canton, Massachusetts. He did not limit his work with veterans' affairs to the small town in Norfolk County, but rather broadened his role to the state level. In 1884, he served as the GAR Department of Massachusetts commander. In this capacity, he nominated GAR officials, made a number of procedural motions, and contributed to the crucial decision to compile and preserve Massachusetts GAR records.[30] Billings also served as the acting, then official, secretary of The Society of the Army of the Potomac, another prominent veterans' group. Taking on this role in 1878, he would eventually assume the rank of "colonel" and rise to be the organization's historian later in the 1890s.[31]

Published speeches and announcements at veterans' gatherings aligned with the conventional military narrative and often included paeans to national integrity. MOLLUS "companions" and Grand Army "comrades" were likely to recount the deeds of their brothers at arms and tended to do so in sweeping terms. For example, in a report on the uses of cavalry written in 1887 for MOLLUS's *Glimpses of the Nation's Struggles,* D. M. Gilmore focused less on the minutiae and more on the strategies surrounding the action at Kelly's Ford and Gettysburg in 1863. Yet MOLLUS companions were just as likely to use their platforms to reflect on the prevailing Unionist sentiment in patriotic fashion typical of the veterans' gatherings. A little over a decade after Gilmore's report, Allen B. Morse noted before his commandery in Grand Rapids, Michigan: "Our free institutions can never die while this spirit of patriotism, this unselfish love of country, is kept alive." Like many of his fellow veterans writing in the late nineteenth century, Morse had plenty to say about patriotic gallantry but little about the day-to-day lives of an enlisted soldier.[32]

Veterans' organizations designated officers to record the minutes of local and national meetings, many of which made it into print through the published MOLLUS and GAR Journal proceedings. These publications most certainly gushed with tributes to individual heroes and regiments, but they were generally restricted to veteran subscribers and published in small quantities with limited civilian access. In addition, much of the material focused on camp activities, readings of general orders, and official business of veteran posts. Leafing through pages of motions, awards, and honors as well as the endless proceedings would most certainly have bored the average civilian reader. Ordinary nonveteran citizens were unlikely to take an interest in the rites and rituals of fraternal veteran organizations.[33]

Regimental histories offered a more compelling look at the Civil War story. At least fifty regimental histories appeared in the first year after the war and many more thereafter. Veterans, who were avid readers of the late nineteenth-century commemorative literature and often interested in the local or community aspects of Civil War history, would have welcomed the various regimental histories published between the end of the war and the late 1880s. The war came to life within the pages of the regimentals through examinations of unit integrity and stalwart bravery, but again with little concern for the particulars of the common man. More typical were near poetic tributes to the unit, as Ezra D. Simons noted of his fellow New Yorkers before the Confederate trenches at Petersburg: "Again you hurled yourselves against the enemies works; you were the hammer that smote the anvil, but, alas, the hammer had heart and life, and it was bruised in pain by the heavy blows."[34]

Until recently scholars have vastly underutilized these histories as a means to reconstruct the perspectives of veterans and their organizations' sentiments concerning the war. Former soldiers who authored commemorative literature not only crafted exciting battle narrative but also noted the profound antebellum sectionalism and the various issues at stake leading up to the war, the causes for which they fought, their reasons for enlisting, and—at least in the case of Union veterans—their celebrations of triumphantly saving the Union and emancipating slaves.[35]

Regimental histories, though useful, present a set of problems. For one, authors wrote their books well after the fact and could have missed important details as memory faded over time. More important, regimental historians, collaborating with other veterans and writing for posterity, their former comrades, and their families, understood that their unit's reputation was on the line.[36] Veterans writing postwar accounts naturally wanted to show their regiments in the best light, reveal their comrades to have the most honorable of intentions, and accentuate their regiment's unblemished war record. Historians who have mined other postwar writings for nuggets of fact and fiction have generally warned readers of the tendency to enhance the truth when writing for the public, just as they have cautioned readers of wartime correspondence and diaries to be aware of biases.[37] Problems aside, Union regimentals did two important things: first, they captured a sentiment that was unquestionably present at the beginning of the war—the rush to the colors with the stated purpose to preserve the Union and punish southern traitors. Second, as historical artifacts, they illustrate the thoughts and concerns of veterans *at the time of writing*. In addition, they often note the sectional rift over slavery as the cause for southern secession. This phenomenon would suggest that Union veterans did not lock arms with former Confederates and present a history of the war on southern terms as so many historians conclude. As such, readers should review these books less as impartial histories and more as carefully crafted monuments to Union veterans and their sentiments during the postwar decades.[38]

By the late 1880s, few of these works, whether printed specifically for veterans' consumption or for a larger reading audience, dealt with the minutiae of war in anything more than a superficial way.[39] Rarely did veteran authors investigate the details well known to the common soldier—the things that one might not even consider, unless of course that person had experienced the soldier's life. Tents and ticks and tins in which soldiers boiled their desiccated vegetables might have seemed out of place in the memoirs, narratives, and personal reflections written by high-ranking generals or other prominent Union officers; they also might have seemed odd in spread-eagle regimental histories.

John D. Billings thus stood out by framing his military service as an experience in which quotidian events and commonplace equipment took center stage. And to help clarify his descriptive language, he leveraged the talents of illustrator Charles W. Reed, himself a veteran of the 9th Massachusetts Battery and a topographical engineer on General Gouverneur K. Warren's staff in the Army of the Potomac's Fifth Corps. Reed's illustrations added realism and a visual connection to the human experience to Billings's vivid descriptions of army life.

Academic historians focusing on the experiences of common soldiers have acknowledged Billings's attention to soldierly detail. James M. McPherson, for example, couples *Hardtack and Coffee* with such notable personal memoirs as Confederate Sam Watkins's *"Co. Aytch"* and notes that these "old soldiers" were "looking back on the most intense experience of their lives" while providing "valuable insights into the minds and experiences of Civil War soldiers."[40] Many historians have agreed with these sentiments. Bruce Catton cited *Hardtack and Coffee* frequently in *Mr. Lincoln's Army,* the first volume in his Army of the Potomac Trilogy. Jeffrey N. Lash, in his biography of Gen. Stephen Augustus Hurlbut, used *Hardtack and Coffee* to help understand the frequency of drunkenness among the Union officer corps. Uzal W. Ent, writing about the Pennsylvania reserves, noted that "Billings and [illustrator] Charles Reed offered unprecedented insight into the soldier's daily life," and Larry Logue's assessment of the Civil War's rank-and-file called *Hardtack and Coffee* "one of the best accounts devoted solely to the daily life of the soldiers."[41]

While Billings's attention to everyday material has been a great boon to academic historians who want analysis and insight into the life of a regular soldier, other authors have found his work useful as well. In his look at Jewish contributions to the Confederate cause, historian Marc Jordan Ben-Meir traced the Yiddish infusion into common soldierly parlance by looking closely at Billings's characterizations of problematic Union army soldiers: "Some were called Jonahs because of their bad luck and many were referred to as Schlemiels and Schlimazels. Both Yiddish words refer to a man who is clumsy, experiences bad luck, or is otherwise constantly getting into trouble." Authors of children's literature and mystery novelists alike have found Billings a welcome resource, whether discussing the "godsend of coffee" or observing how *Hardtack and Coffee* is "an excellent source of contemporary Civil War detail."[42]

Hardtack and Coffee today also finds its way into the camps of living historians, many of whom expend a great deal of effort re-creating the look and feel of a campaigning Civil War soldier. So-called "hard core" reenactors are particularly meticulous about creating an authentic-to-the-stitch look replicating period uniforms and accoutrements. Many seem to care more about appearance than battles.[43] Reenactors naturally turn to Billings as a reference guide. Or rather, as historian, reenactor, and Pennsylvania native John Heckman comments, the book is "a tool to understand camp life." Heckman describes *Hardtack and Coffee* as a valuable guide that helps "build a personal impression," and he especially appreciates descriptions of the "equipment and how they cooked . . . it's what he liked to do in the field." Still, as living historian and California native Larry Kelsey remarks, Billings published *Hardtack and Coffee* over two decades after the fact, and so reenactors must take his word "with a grain of salt . . . Billings is an excellent source, but we must leave room for possible mistakes." Although the passage of time between the war and when Billings wrote left room for error, Kelsey appreciates the book as "intimate and personal," with special attention to India rubber blankets, the unkemptness of people, and general uncleanliness. Kelsey reminds us of the significance of *Hardtack and Coffee* as a record of the soldier's daily routines: "Every person who goes through this experience should remember to write down the intimate details. That stuff can be lost through time . . . that's what makes Billings so important . . . so invaluable."[44]

Some of the detail about the everyday soldier's life in *Hardtack and Coffee* had appeared in Billings's earlier book, titled *The History of the Tenth Massachusetts Battery of Light Artillery in the War of the Rebellion* and published in 1881. Fellow veteran John B. Apthorpe initially intended to write the unit history, but the task passed to Billings. The subsequent publication drew on Apthorpe's original manuscript, Billings's personal diary, upwards of 300 personal letters written home during the conflict, and the official reports of, among others, Winfield Scott Hancock and William H. French, commanders of the Army of the Potomac's Second Corps and Third Corps respectively, in which the 10th Massachusetts Battery served. Billings devoted considerable attention to the battery's battles but also, to a degree unusual among such works, covered such subjects as tents, uniforms, and, of course, hardtack.[45]

Although Civil War scholarship in the twentieth and twenty-first century has credited *Hardtack and Coffee* as a pathbreaking work on common soldiers, the book receives little recognition as part of the commemorative literature that explores the issues propelling men to enlist and fight in the Union army. This seems a striking omission considering that Billings's reflections about life in the Civil War embraced how the conflict's sectional and political opinions resonated with a veteran writing two decades after the fact. Sadly, the most influential scholarly books on Civil War memory all but ignore Billings's contributions in this regard. Those who seek to understand the sentiments—both sectional and national—expressed by Union soldiers should situate *Hardtack and Coffee* in the larger field of Civil War memory scholarship.[46]

Billings did not whitewash his account of the Civil War for the sake of national reconciliation. In fact, he began his book with a statement concerning political divisions over slavery. His clarity is instructive. Long the source of national friction, slavery had divided the Democratic Party into sectional factions. This factionalism allowed the youthful Republican Party to elect Abraham Lincoln to the presidency in 1860. While Republicans promised not to "meddle" with slavery where it existed, they opposed its extension into the territories. Southern slaveholders, aware of this fact, "long before the election took place . . . began to make threats of seceding from the Union if Lincoln was elected." Without any hint of equivocation, Billings decried the "impetuous leaders at the South" who committed treason against the Union without waiting to see if southern fears about Lincoln's policies held true. Overt reconciliationists likely existed among the legions of Union veterans in the 1880s, but Billings did not number among them.[47]

Neither was Billings tolerant of opposition to the Republican Party in the North. In his opening pages, he described northerners who associated Republican "Lincolnites" with so-called "Black Republican" abolitionists. As a gesture of good will, Billings absolved his "neighbors and friends" who had once condemned "[William Lloyd] Garrison and [Wendell] Phillips" as "lunatics" who drove the South to desperation. It was these antislavery men, the Republican Party's antagonists suggested, who should be made to "fight for the niggers" in the front ranks. Here one does observe a spirit of reconciliation among *northern* factions. Billings particularly praised those who had once attacked the Republican Party but changed their attitudes and "afterwards went to the field. They became "changed men . . . in light of later experiences."[48]

While it is difficult to tell whether Billings was an abolitionist, he certainly sympathized with abolitionists who insisted sectional divisions over slavery would ultimately lead to war. Praising Massachusetts Republican war governor and abolitionist John A. Andrew for his foresight, Billings noted that as early as January 1861 Governor Andrew "issued an order which had for its object to ascertain exactly how many of the officers and men in the militia would hold themselves ready to respond immediately to any call which might be made upon their services by the President."[49] In the opening pages of *Hardtack and Coffee,* he linked slavery directly to sectional strife and observed that the "leading Abolitionists had argued that the South was too cowardly to fight for slavery." In subsequent passages, Billings exposed the folly of this prediction. He drew a distinction between northern attitudes toward the South and toward slavery. Northern soldiers foraging on southern soil were less vindictive than their Confederate counterparts, he claimed, because the "South hated the Yankees, but the North hated only slavery."[50]

Billings likewise provided instructive clues as to the nature of the war from the perspective of slaves behind enemy lines. He never went as far as to describe "self-emancipation" in any analytical sense, nor did he precisely quantify the number of slaves taking it upon themselves to seek freedom across the southern states at the appearance of Union armies.[51] Billings specifically mentioned neither the Emancipation Proclamation nor what it meant to the evolving nature of the Union cause. He did describe one scene of exodus, perhaps leaving it to his readers to determine both enslaved people's motivations and the implications of Abraham Lincoln's pronouncements of January 1, 1863. "In 1863 . . . after the memorable Mud March [immediately after the battle of Fredericksburg]," he noted, "large numbers of colored refugees came into camp. Every day we saw some old cart . . . unloading its freight of contrabands, who had thus made their entrance into the lines of Uncle Sam and freedom."[52]

Other black people occupy the pages of *Hardtack and Coffee* beyond the mention of refugees. After all, Billings spent nearly all of his active service on southern soil, and it stands to reason that his unit would encounter black people as slaves in service to their masters (and thus the Confederate war effort) and as free persons in the employ of the Union army.[53] His descriptions of black people conformed to the attitudes shared by many in the North and especially those of Union soldiers toward African Americans they encountered on campaign. Billings acknowledged the presence of black people in his account of a slaveholders' war but did not weigh in on the plight of the enslaved. Nor did he express any personal affinity toward slaves. Billings's text aligns him with typical white Union soldiers who understood the roots of secession but enlisted to preserve the Union rather than risk their lives to free any slaves. Though many Union soldiers ultimately embraced emancipation once they observed slavery in action or as a means to hasten the war's end, Billings neither openly supported nor rejected the idea in *Hardtack and Coffee*.[54]

Narrative episodes featuring black people often simply described scenes. Others took on comical tones that, however harsh they seem to modern readers, show how Union soldiers, seeking respite from the trials of war, laughed at the expense of persons in bondage. One example of such humor described a black man and his "fight" with an army mule, a notoriously obstinate draft animal. Shortly after the battle of Antietam in September 1862, Billings styled this altercation as a mutual understanding between black man and beast. He even offered a reconciliatory coda to the tale after the mule's swift kick and the return clubbing by the black mule driver: "A truce was declared, and driver and mule were at peace and understood each other."[55]

Billings apparently found it necessary to add another scene of black man versus mule, as if to provide additional support for his previous story. In this case, a black cook in the employ of the 60th New York Regiment found himself in a bind with a stubborn mule that did not appreciate being loaded down with the unit's wares. After an argumentative back-and-forth and the mule's "premonitory blast of his nasal trumpet," the animal kicked the kitchen equipment and the hapless cook into the Potomac River. One can only imagine how the reading public enjoyed such antics, told at the expense of the black people involved. The illustration included with the story sought to add to the hilarity.[56]

Only a few other black people appeared in *Hardtack and Coffee,* one of whom was Black Mary, the "colored servant" of a secessionist who offered to cook up a few meals for foragers. Lastly, Billings acknowledged the service of the United States Colored Troops (USCT) by placing a colored division on guard duty with the Army of the Potomac between the Rapidan and James Rivers in 1864 and briefly again when he described corps insignia. Billings offered no account of USCT units in action nor did he evaluate their fighting prowess. Likewise, he failed to offer insight into what the presence of black troops might have suggested to a population well acquainted with the racial hierarchies of the nineteenth century. Readers learned that black men fought for the Union cause, and that was all.[57]

What did Billings offer his *Hardtack and Coffee* readers in terms of Union soldiers and antislavery ideology, and how is he situated in modern (twentieth-century) scholarly assessments of soldiers' ideological commitments? Bell Irvin Wiley's celebrated account of the Union soldier titled *The Life of Billy Yank* (1952), the companion volume to *The Life of Johnny Reb* (1943), suggests that US soldiers loved the Union but were not prone to enlist for ideological reasons, especially those connected to emancipation. "In marked contrast to those whose primary interest was in freeing the slaves," Wiley argues, "stood a larger group who wanted no part in a war of emancipation. . . . Some Yanks opposed making slavery an issue of the war because they thought the effect would be to prolong the conflict at an unjustifiable cost in money and lives." Wiley notes, "The issuance of the Emancipation Proclamation aroused opponents of a 'Negro War' to the highest level of bitterness." This sentiment frames Wiley's ideological assessment of Union soldiers in regard to black people: "One who reads letters and diaries of Union soldiers encounters an enormous amount of antipathy towards Negroes. . . . Many whites remained deeply antagonistic to the end of the war."[58]

James M. McPherson's Lincoln Prize–winning *For Cause and Comrades* offers something rather different. Reviewing similar testimony to that which appears in *The Life of Billy Yank,* McPherson does find ideology to be a motivating factor for enlistment. Though many who enlisted did not mention slavery, those who did, he insists, "were outspoken in their determination to destroy the 'slave power' and to cleanse the restored Union of an evil they considered a mockery of American ideals." As the war progressed, many more Union soldiers became convinced that "the goal [of Union] was unattainable without striking against slavery." And in regard to self-emancipation, McPherson argues that "attempts by masters to reclaim runaways turned many soldiers into practical abolitionists."[59]

Billings, who explicitly positioned himself to represent the typical enlisted man, does not line up perfectly with either Wiley or McPherson regarding emancipation. His readers most certainly would have taken notice that he connected secession to slaveholders' fears of Republican aims, that he showed how Union armies, whether intentionally or not, served as liberators, and that he stopped short of embracing the emancipationist cause. Scholars have gone to great lengths to weave together the varying threads of ideological commitment—or lack thereof. Billings's words should at least move readers to consider what a veteran of the conflict thought about slavery and ideology twenty years after Appomattox.

Equally instructive is how *Hardtack and Coffee* relates to twentieth- and twenty-first-century scholarly assessments of Union veterans' attitudes toward reunion and sectional reconciliation. Historians built much of the literature on Civil War memory and veterans' activities published between the 1980s and the early 2000s on the framework of reconciliation between white people, including veterans, North and South. As the argument goes, by the 1880s Civil War veterans involved in commemorative activities, ranging from writing war narratives to dedicating monuments, had put aside their differences for the sake of national unity. Veterans supposedly commemorated a Civil War memory while at the same time constructing a version of "history" devoid of the contentious issues that had pushed men to war.

The studies of Gaines M. Foster, Stuart McConnell, and Edward Tabor Linenthal all fall in line with this approach. Much of this work challenges older studies, such as Paul Buck's Pulitzer Prize–winning *The Road to Reunion, 1865–1900* (1937) that had lauded the breakdown of sectional animosities in the postwar years and paved the way for a "promise of ultimate peace." Linenthal, for example, examines Civil War commemorative activity through the lens of "tacit forgetfulness" and describes "elaborate rituals of reconciliation" as indicative of a "moral myopia that ignored the real legacy" of the conflict. These scholars collectively recognize a fading of veterans' bitterness based on the dismissal of the sectional contentions over slavery and emancipation and the shared racist sensibilities of veterans of the North and South. McConnell reminds readers that "the question of blacks and slavery received scant mention in celebrations of the war's outcome.[60] The most compelling iteration of this idea is David W. Blight's *Race and Reunion: The Civil War in American Memory,* published in 2001. Blight convinced legions of historians and students that Union and Confederate veterans—for reasons of shared racism—had agreed to write slavery, the most divisive issue of all, out of the war.[61]

Blight's assertions, however, are flawed. For instance, he ignores the lion's share of veterans' commemorative activities, while instead focusing on the scripted "blue-gray" reunions at Gettysburg and elsewhere. Blight and others have described these events as the preeminent commemorative affairs of the late nineteenth and early twentieth centuries. Had Blight looked more carefully at the hundreds of other events that took place in remote communities away from the scrutiny of the national press—on courthouse lawns and in private meeting halls throughout the reunited states—he would have noticed a profoundly different sentiment of lingering bitterness and a clear resonance of wartime sectionalism.[62]

Where does Billings fit in this reconciliatory framework? If readers of *Hardtack and Coffee* are to believe those who stand behind the reconciliation premise, then one might assume Billings would have embraced his former enemies and dismissed the issues of slavery, emancipation, and treason. This, as noted earlier, certainly was not the case. But did Billings craft a message of long-standing sectional resentfulness for his reading public? An uncritical or cursory read of *Hardtack and Coffee* reveals little overt animosity. A more careful look at the sections on causation and the spirit of the men in the ranks similarly reveals little in the way of a reconciliatory tone. In fact, while avoiding explicitly hostile statements, Billings clearly took a sectional stance. He limited incendiary language directed toward individual Confederate fighting men, and one might conclude that Billings tried not to ruffle too many feathers. As James McPherson notes in *For Cause and Comrades,* veterans' publications suffered "from a critical defect: they were written for publication."[63] Authors of this type of commemorative literature often tailored their words specifically for the widest possible public and thus sometimes avoided unconcealed hostility. But even if these were his intentions, Billings was not especially generous with praise for his former adversaries. On only one occasion did he dignify a specific Confederate unit and one of its officers, simply reporting: "I met at Chattanooga, Tenn., recently, Captain Fort, of the old First Georgia Regulars, a Confederate regiment of distinguished service." This modest praise was all Billings could muster for the Rebels.[64]

Confederate soldiers, referred to simply as "rebels," the "enemy," or an occasional "secesh," appear as antagonists pushing the narrative along. Billings reminded readers that "the view which the average soldiers took was, in substance, that the people of the South were in a state of rebellion against the government . . . they had been duly warned to desist from the war and return to their allegiance." Noting how some southerners might assume a victim's status to their advantage, Billings recalled that "so many who really were 'secesh' claimed to be good Union men." When alluding to strategy or combat, Billings did not mince words, frequently referring to Confederates as the enemy. Typical phrases such as "the railroad had been wrested from the enemy," "the trees were felled with their tops toward the enemy," and "the Union army was greatly superior to the enemy," peppered the book as reminders that fellow Americans had once been adversaries of the federal government.[65]

Billings's history of the 10th Massachusetts Battery followed a similar path with regard to his former foe. When discussing battle, something he attended to much more thoroughly in *The History of the Tenth Massachusetts Battery of Light Artillery in the War of the Rebellion* than he did in *Hardtack and Coffee,* he repeatedly used terms associated with enemies, not wayward fellow Americans. Resisting reconciliationist euphemisms, Billings favored wartime language such as, "the enemy were drawing their lines closer about us," "our cavalry under Buford found the enemy in force," and "cannonading in the distance announced to us that the enemy had been found." As these passages indicate, the similarities between Billings's writing for fellow veterans and for a nonveteran audience are striking.[66]

Billings noted that the point of the war was to coerce white southerners back into the Union, and he criticized President James Buchanan's explanation for failing to take action against treason on the grounds that, as the chief executive put it, he had "no right to coerce a sovereign state."[67] But even if favoring the reunion of states suggests he tacitly accepted reconciliation, as it did with many of his fellow veterans, Billings did so only with an understanding that the Union cause had been virtuous, and that Confederates were unequivocally on the wrong side of the fight. Here *Hardtack and Coffee* echoed Grant's and Sherman's memoirs. He followed a similar path in his regimental history: "How can one do otherwise than admire a devotion to a cause! We must pay tribute to Rebel patriotism even while we disapprove of and condemn the convictions which prompted it."[68] For Billings, reconciliation could come only with acknowledgment that Union victory represented a triumph over disloyalty—over what many Union veterans denounced as "the greatest conspiracy of all times."[69]

Billings's unwavering clarity on war causation would have been a troubling bone of contention for his Confederate counterparts, and it is here where he waded into the deepest sectional waters. A more forgiving reconciliationist than Billings, like those described by so many scholars, simply might have blamed a few fire-eating southern leaders for steering the South astray and thus forgiven an otherwise virtuous people who fought for what they considered a just cause. Billings's ideas concerning treason suggested an unreconciled veteran harboring ill will against his former Confederate enemies. Like those who were willing to acknowledge the courage of their Confederate foes, such as GAR Adjutant Gen. W. T. Collin, Billings would agree that "mere courage never ennobled treason." Veterans such as himself were "stirred by patriotic impulse to enlist and crush out treason, and hurl back at once in the teeth of the enemy the charge of cowardice and accept their challenge to the arbitrament of war." Billings further attacked James Buchanan for failing to act and "prevent treason and secession" while the "people at the North stood amazed at the rapidity with which treason against the government was spreading."[70] Dismayed by Buchanan's inaction, the "loyal people of the North" acknowledged that the "Rebels [had to be] punished for their treason without delay." While President Lincoln was "beset night and day" to achieve this end, he at least embraced the task.[71]

With respect to treason, Billings marched in lockstep with his Union veteran contemporaries, many of whom published commemorative literature in the form of regimental histories and celebratory activities. This was true especially in regard to the Grand Army of the Republic and other veterans' organizations. Billings's comments on treason were remarkably similar to GAR bylaws both at the national and state level. Department "rules and regulations" aimed to "maintain true allegiance to the United States of America, based upon a paramount respect for, and fidelity to, its Constitution and laws, to discountenance whatever tends to weaken loyalty, incites to insurrection, treason, or rebellion, or in any manner impairs the efficiency and permanency of our free institutions."[72] Presumably, the sensibilities that would eventually dovetail with the national veterans' organization had moved Billings to enlist to preserve law, order, and, one might also assume, the virtues of a democratic republic. Modern historians tend to agree that Civil War soldiers enlisted for a wide range of reasons. Union soldiers could have enlisted for adventure or money, because of societal pressures, or on account of their loathing of a perceived "slavocracy" threatening the free institutions of the republic. But most important, many enlisted, especially early in the war, because of their earnest desire to preserve law, order, and, of course, Union. This motivating factor would naturally include an antipathy toward southern treason, which persisted throughout the war and helped frame many veterans' postwar commentary, including Billings's *Hardtack and Coffee*.[73]

Regimental historians during the last third of the nineteenth century likewise framed their histories as a fight to preserve the Union and the Constitution and suppress the treasonous aims of their wayward countrymen. Luther Tracy Townsend, author of the 15th New Hampshire's regimental history, offered a typical example in observing, "We need not proceed in this review of what then appeared, and appears still, to be Southern treason." W. W. H. Davis wrote of the patriotism expressed by his regiment in the first year after Confederate surrender: "None bore more faithful allegiance to the great cause of the Constitution and Union than the 104th Pennsylvania Infantry Regiment." Pennsylvania veteran Osceola Lewis wrote in 1866 that his regiment "went forth to the field of action upon the sole conviction that duty called them; and at a period when the iron strength and patriotism of the country was called forth without pecuniary or other inducements." Writing in a similar fashion in the 1880s concerning the initial rush to the colors in 1861, New York veteran Charles H. Cowtan outlined the impulses of the loyal North. "Patriotic and earnest men at the North," he stated, "saw looming up a war between the seceding states and those still loyal to the Union, and began to devise a means to assist the Government in the impending struggle . . . the mighty heart of the people seemed to pulsate with patriotism and love for the government which had been founded and maintained by the blood of our fathers."[74]

Billings's own writings mirrored many of these ideas. Reflecting on the Peninsula campaign of 1862 in his history of the 10th Massachusetts Battery, he noted, "Thousands of the flower of the nation's youth who, burning with the most ardent of patriotism had been marshalled in the ranks of the magnificent Army of the Potomac." Sounding very much like U. S. Grant, Billings paid some tribute to his former enemies by acknowledging their fortitude. Yet he did so while rejecting the Rebel cause and lauding his own: "The good deeds of the Battery have not been unduly magnified. . . . Nor have I intended to underrate the caliber of our antagonists . . . there must be at least two parties to a well contested field, and I firmly believe that no braver men were ever banded in an unrighteous cause than constituted the Rebel Army of Northern Virginia." *Hardtack and Coffee* readers, encountering Billings's recollection of community enlistment efforts in 1861, would have found the sentiment quite familiar. "Sometimes the patriotism of such a gathering," remembered Billings, "would be wrought up so intensely by waving banners, martial and vocal music, and burning eloquence, that a town's [enlistment] quota would be filled in less than an hour. . . . Any man or woman who lived in those thrilling early war days will never forget them. The spirit of patriotism was a fever-heat, and animated both sexes of all ages."[75]

Billings's readers would have found the addresses delivered at various monument dedications in the 1880s quite familiar as well. Sounding a tone strikingly similar to that found in the pages of *Hardtack and Coffee,* New Jersey governor Robert Stockton Green addressed the veterans of the 13th New Jersey Infantry attending their monument dedication at Gettysburg in 1887. "[This] was a war of principle; it was a war of devotion to the country and for the perpetuity of the Union. . . ," he remarked, "so long as the dead sentinels keep their watch and ward, so long will the integrity of the Union be established and never again will the supremacy of the Government under the Constitution be assailed." The following year at Gettysburg, Col. William A. Potter conjured the spirit of patriotism at the monument dedication to the 12th New Jersey Infantry: "Our best monument will be that a mighty nation . . . shall hold our patriotism and our cause beyond comparison—sacred. Our services and deeds stand for patriotism, loyalty, devotion to the highest interests of the whole country." But it was treason that really struck a chord at monument dedications and other veterans' speaking engagements, much as it did in Billings's commentary in *Hardtack and Coffee.* C. L. Sumbardo, speaking before his fellow veteran officers in Minnesota, noted, "The firing upon Fort Sumter was an act of audacity prompted by treason as damnable as can be found in the world's history.[76]

Billings affirmed that the presence of this sentiment existed during the war and persisted among a loyal public who sought a hasty victory and a restoration of the Union. Even the reverses of 1861 at Manassas Junction and the failure of Army of the Potomac commander George B. McClellan to capture Richmond the following summer did not deter the northern public. And 1862 saw the expression "'all quiet along the Potomac' . . . come to be used as a by-word of reproach," and "Public Sentiment was . . . making itself felt." Billings sensed the anxiety felt by a patriotic nation when the commanding brass let slip an expedient victory: "'Why don't the army move?' was the oft-repeated question which gave to the propounder no satisfactory answer, because to him, with the public pulse at fever-beat, no answer was satisfactory."[77]

Billings's understanding of the manifestations of patriotism among soldiers and civilians in 1861–62 gave him the space to slight those who lagged behind the initial rush to arms or paid for a substitute. "For patriotism unstimulated by hope of reward saw high-water mark in 1861," he wrote, "and rapidly receded in succeeding years, so that whereas men enlisted in 1861 and early in '62 because they wanted to go, and without hope of reward, later in '62 towns and individuals began to offer bounties to stimulate lagging enlistments." As Billings explained in the subsequent passages, these bounties provided the justification for some veterans to engage in "hazing" of raw recruits, something Billings did not particularly embrace unless recruits capitalizing on bounties brought it upon themselves. Though Billings thought that many "did good service . . . others became deserters immediately after enlisting." As for those "men of means" who paid their way out of military service by hiring a substitute "as allotted by law, to go in their stead," Billings offered a simple conclusion: "patriotism failed to set them in motion."[78] Commemorative literature published in the 1880s, including monument dedication speeches, regimental histories, and Billings's *Hardtack and Coffee,* resounded with nods to loyal citizens' patriotic fervor, the condemnation of treason, and the devotion to Union—both during and after the war.

John D. Billings's *Hardtack and Coffee* continues to merit attention from a range of readers interested in the military side of the Civil War. Most obviously, it retains a special position among veterans' literary efforts because it chronicled, in great detail, the day-to-day activities of men in the ranks. Scholars, history "buffs" and other enthusiasts, and living historians seeking to understand the experiences of the common soldier continue to mine its pages. But *Hardtack and Coffee* possesses value beyond Billings's attention to the daily world of regular Union soldiers—to the tents, and the bugs, and the corps badges, and similar things. It takes on sectional themes found in veterans' commemorative literature written in the last third of the nineteenth century, addressing issues with which readers of that literature would have been well acquainted. Billings wrote about slavery and its role in secession, about ideology and patriotism, and he rejected treason. He referred to Confederates as the enemy and harshly criticized policies of generosity that he believed weakened the Union cause.[79] In short, *Hardtack and Coffee* afforded readers a window into what Civil War soldiers experienced on the march and in camp, but also into what soldiers thought about the issues that pushed Americans to kill each other in great profusion between 1861 and 1865.

In terms of Civil War memory, *Hardtack and Coffee* reflects a pervasive attitude among veterans who commemorated their fight as a righteous cause worthy of praise despite reconciliatory literary efforts in the late nineteenth century that dismissed or overlooked sectional divisions. Any reader from the wartime generation who tackled *Hardtack and Coffee* would have recognized the sentiments expressed in many Union monument dedicatory speeches—as well as in the pages of Grant's and Sherman's memoirs and in regimental histories and other commemorative literature produced by veterans. They would have noted the patriotism, the fight against slavery, and, perhaps most important, the acknowledgment that southerners who established and fought for the Confederacy had committed treason against the Union. Today, scholars and other readers would do well to understand that *Hardtack and Coffee* provides a revealing look at Union veterans' commemorative culture as well as its wealth of detail about soldier life.

NOTES

1. John D. Billings, *Hardtack and Coffee: The Unwritten Story of Army Life* (Boston: George M. Smith, 1887), v. Billings refers to a "popular hotel in the White Mountains." One might assume that he is referring to the White Mountains of New Hampshire. Regarding Billings's rank, service records indicate that John D. Billings enlisted as a private and mustered out as a private. See "Billings, John D., 10th Independent Battery, Massachusetts Light Artillery," accessed October 1, 2019, The Civil War Soldiers and Sailors System (database), National Park Service, US Department of the Interior, https://www.nps.gov/civilwar/soldiers -and-sailors-database.htm.

2. Billings, *Hardtack and Coffee,* v.

3. Earlier in the 1880s, a Confederate veteran published his own account of life in the army in camp and on campaign, noting: "The historian who essays to write the 'grand movements' will hardly stop to tell how the hungry private fried his bacon, baked his biscuit, and smoked his pipe." See Carlton McCarthy, *Detailed Minutiae of Soldier Life in the Army of Northern Virginia, 1861–1865* (Richmond, VA: C. McCarthy, 1882), 16.

4. Billings, *Hardtack and Coffee,* 122.

5. This essay will discuss Billings's work in the context of two types of Civil War literature: popular war narratives published for a national audience (general histories) that appeared in various magazines and other publications beginning in the 1880s, and veteran commemorative literature written in support of a specific cause. I argue that scholars have not always effectively discerned a difference between the two.

6. Numerous scholars have held that Civil War veteran commemorative literature and other veterans' activities in the late nineteenth and early twentieth centuries notably avoided divisive sectional issues in the name of sectional reconciliation. See for example Paul H. Buck, *The Road to Reunion, 1865–1900* (Boston: Little, Brown, 1937); Gaines M. Foster, *Ghosts of the*

Confederacy: Defeat, the Lost Cause, and the Emergence of the New South (New York: Oxford University Press, 1987); Stuart McConnell, *Glorious Contentment: The Grand Army of the Republic, 1865–1900* (Chapel Hill: University of North Carolina Press, 1992): Nina Silber, *The Romance of Reunion: Northerners and the South, 1865–1900* (Chapel Hill: University of North Carolina Press, 1993). The most prominent of these studies is David W. Blight, *Race and Reunion: The Civil War in American Memory* (Cambridge, MA: Harvard University Press, 2001). Blight notes that white supremacists "locked arms with reconciliationists of many kinds, and by the turn of the century delivered the country a segregated memory of the Civil War on Southern terms" (p. 2). More recently, others have challenged the ubiquitous presence of a reconciliationist sentiment by noting the lingering sectional animosities of Civil War veterans from both the North and South despite nods to reconciliation in commemorative literature. For scholarly challenges to Blight and others, see Barbara A. Gannon, *The Won Cause: Black and White Comradeship in the Grand Army of the Republic* (Chapel Hill: University of North Carolina Press, 2011); M. Keith Harris, *Across the Bloody Chasm: The Culture of Commemoration among Civil War Veterans* (Baton Rouge: Louisiana State University Press, 2014); Caroline E. Janney, *Remembering the Civil War: Reunion and the Limits of Reconciliation* (Chapel Hill: University of North Carolina Press, 2013).

7. Billings, *Hardtack and Coffee,* vi.

8. Since the mid-twentieth century, a number of scholars have written studies on the common Civil War soldier, all of which seek to explain why men fought in the Civil War, by illuminating the experiences, motivations, and sentiments of the average enlisted man in the Union and Confederacy. Their efforts have engaged such questions as nationalism, ideology, and duty. See Bell Irvin Wiley, *The Life of Johnny Reb: The Common Soldier of the Confederacy* (Indianapolis: Bobbs-Merrill, 1943); Bell Irvin Wiley, *The Life of Billy Yank: The Common Soldier of the Union* (Indianapolis: Bobbs-Merrill, 1952); James M. McPherson, *For Cause and Comrades: Why Men Fought in the Civil War* (New York: Oxford University Press, 1997). More recently, Peter S. Carmichael has emphasized not *what* soldiers thought but rather *how* they thought. "In many cases, the connections between soldiers' thought and action appear mechanical and static," he argues, "because they fail to adequately account for the ways that beliefs and actions rose spontaneously out of particular conditions. The contingencies of soldiering, above all else, are often lost when ideological comments are extracted as transparent statements as to why men fought." (Peter S. Carmichael, *The War for the Common Soldier: How Men Thought, Fought, and Survived in Civil War Armies* [Chapel Hill: University of North Carolina Press, 2018], 10–11.) Recent scholars also have noted challenges to, and competing interpretations of, nationalism, patriotism, and the meaning of loyalty as it emerged along class, gender, ethnic, and religious lines. See for example Robert M. Sandow, ed., *Contested Loyalty: Debates over Patriotism in the Civil War North* (New York: Fordham University Press, 2018). Others argue that education and the understanding of "character" as an idealized standard of behavior contributed to nationalism among the educated elite specifically. See Kanisorn Wongsrichanalai, *Northern Character: College-Educated New Englanders, Honor, Nationalism, and Leadership in the Civil War Era* (New York: Fordham University Press, 2016). The latest trend in veteran scholarship—the co-called "dark turn"—broadens the scope of study to emphasize trauma suffered, both physical and psychological, by combat veterans and others who lived through the hardships of war. See David Silkenat, *Moments of Despair:*

Suicide, Divorce and Debt in Civil War Era North Carolina (Chapel Hill: University of North Carolina Press, 2011); Brian Matthew Jordan, *Marching Home: Union Veterans and Their Unending Civil War* (New York: Liveright Publishing, 2015); Diane Miller Sommerville, *Aberration of Mind: Suicide and Suffering in the Civil War Era South* (Chapel Hill: University of North Carolina Press, 2018); Sarah Handley-Cousins, *Bodies in Blue: Disability in the Civil War North* (Athens: University of Georgia Press, 2019).

9. Billings, *Hardtack and Coffee*, vi.

10. Henry Steele Commager, *The Blue and the Gray*, 2 vols. (Indianapolis: Bobbs-Merrill, 1950), 1:287.

11. Billings, *Hardtack and Coffee*, 51–52.

12. Billings, *Hardtack and Coffee*, 47, 62.

13. On the differences between a "good" and "bad" death in the context of the Civil War, see Drew Gilpin Faust, *This Republic of Suffering: Death and the American Civil War* (New York: Vintage Books, 2008). On disease in the Union Army and the reporting of disease in soldiers' letters, see Wiley, *The Life of Billy Yank*, especially Chapter 6.

14. Billings, *Hardtack and Coffee*, 175.

15. Billings, *Hardtack and Coffee*, 141. For a personal account of a Union surgeon who dealt regularly with diseased soldiers, see Christopher E. Loperfido, *Death, Disease, and Life at War: The Civil War Letters of Surgeon James D. Benton, 111th and 98th New York Infantry Regiments, 1862–1865* (El Dorado Hills, CA: Savas Beatie, 2018).

16. Billings, *Hardtack and Coffee*, 108.

17. Billings, *Hardtack and Coffee*, 110, 115.

18. Billings, *Hardtack and Coffee*, 113.

19. Billings, *Hardtack and Coffee*, 117, 124, 138.

20. Billings, *Hardtack and Coffee*, 81, 80, 82.

21. Billings, *Hardtack and Coffee*, 76–77.

22. Billings, *Hardtack and Coffee*, 269, 77, 134. For an account of the community building in winter quarters, see James A. Davis, *Music Along the Rapidan: Civil War Soldiers, Music, and Community during Winter Quarters, Virginia* (Lincoln: University of Nebraska Press, 2014).

23. Billings, *Hardtack and Coffee*, 196, 75, 217.

24. Janney, *Remembering the Civil War*, 165.

25. Robert Underwood Johnson and Clarence Clough Buel, eds., *Battles and Leaders of the Civil War*, 4 vols. (New York: The Century Company, 1887–88). The four-volume set, complete with illustrations, sold over 75,000 copies. See Blight, *Race and Reunion*, 431n10. *Battles and Leaders* has gone through multiple printings.

26. The standard number of Civil War deaths accepted by historians has stood at 620,000 for decades. See James M. McPherson, *Battle Cry of Freedom: The Civil War Era* (New York: Oxford University Press, 1988), 854. Recently, after a meticulous review of census data, historian J. David Hacker recalculated and revised the number of Civil War deaths. Hacker pronounced 750,000 to be the likely total but suggested the figure could be closer to 850,000. See J. David Hacker, "A Census-Based Count of the Civil War Dead," *Civil War History* 57 (December 2011): 307–48.

27. See William T. Sherman, *Memoirs of General William T. Sherman, by Himself*, 2 vols. (New York: D. Appleton, 1875); Ulysses S. Grant, *Personal Memoirs of Ulysses S. Grant*, 2 vols.

(New York: Charles L. Webster, 1885–86); Benjamin F. Butler, *Autobiography and Personal Reminiscences of Major-General Benjamin F. Butler: Butler's Book* (Boston: A. M. Thayer, 1892). On veteran commemorative literature and its implications in a postwar nation, see Harris, *Across the Bloody Chasm.* Recently, one scholar has pointed out how many veterans felt marginalized and demanded, through the written word, that Americans recognized their value as American citizens. See Benjamin Cooper, *Veteran Americans: Literature and Citizenship from Revolution to Reconstruction* (Amherst, MA: University of Boston Press, 2018).

28. Robert B. Beath, *History of the Grand Army of the Republic* (New York: Press of Willis McDonald, 1889), 27–28; 256. *Manual for the Guidance of the Grand Army of the Republic* (n.p.: n.p., 1881), 40.

29. On veterans' organizations, see Mary R. Dearing, *Veterans in Politics: The Story of the G.A.R.* (Baton Rouge: Louisiana State University Press, 1952); McConnell, *Glorious Contentment;* Gannon, *The Won Cause.* On tributes to the dead specifically, see John R. Neff, *Honoring the Civil War Dead: Commemoration and the Problem of Reconciliation* (Lawrence: University Press of Kansas, 2005).

30. For a list of GAR Department of Massachusetts past commanders and GAR activities, see *Journal of the Forty-sixth Annual Encampment Department of Massachusetts Grand Army of the Republic, Boston, Mass., April 2 and 3, 1912* (Boston: Wright and Potter Printing, 1912), 120, 165, 167, 182, 184.

31. *The Society of the Army of the Potomac: Report of the Ninth Annual Re-Union at Springfield, Mass, June 5, 1878* (New York: McGowan & Slipper, 1878), 42; *The Society of the Army of the Potomac: Report of the Twenty-Eighth Annual Re-Union at Troy, New York, August 20th and 21st, 1897* (New York: McGowan & Slipper, 1897), 109–10.

32. D. M. Gilmore, "Cavalry: Its Uses and Value as Illustrated by Reference to the Engagements at Kelly's Ford and Gettysburg," in Edward D. Neill, D.D., ed., *Glimpses of the Nation's Struggle: Papers Read before the Minnesota Commandery of the Military Order of the Loyal Legion of the United States, 1887–1890* (St. Paul, MN: St Paul Book and Stationery, 1890), 38–51; Allen B. Morse, "Address at the Annual Banquet of the Michigan Commandery of the Loyal Legion," in *War Papers Read Before the Michigan Commandery of the Military Order of the Loyal Legion of the United States* (Detroit: James H. Stone, 1898), 316–19.

33. A cursory review of any Grand Army of the Republic publication reveals the strictly business side of veterans' affairs. See for example *Journal of the Twenty-Third Annual Session of the National Encampment Grand Army of the Republic, Milwaukee, Wis., August 28th, 29th and 30th, 1889* (St. Louis: A. Whipple, Printer, 1889); *Journal of the Nineteenth Annual Session of the National Encampment, Grand Army of the Republic, Portland, Maine, June 24th and 25th, 1885* (Toledo, OH: Montgomery and Vrooman, Printers, 1885).

34. Ezra D. Simons, *A Regimental History: The One Hundred and Twenty-Fifth New York State Volunteers* (New York: Ezra D. Simons), xv.

35. Peter C. Luebke, "'To Transmit and Perpetuate the Fruits of This Victory': Union Regimental Histories and the Great Rebellion in Immediate Retrospect," in Gary W. Gallagher and Elizabeth R. Varon, eds., *New Perspectives on the Union War* (New York: Fordham University Press, 2019), 186–99. David Blight conspicuously neglects regimentals in *Race and Reunion.* For a corrective, see Janney, *Remembering the Civil War,* and Harris, *Across the Bloody Chasm.*

36. Luebke, "'To Transmit and Perpetuate the Fruits of This Victory,'" 187.

37. McPherson, *For Cause and Comrades,* ix.

38. On Union regimentals and the issue of slavery, see for example Leander W. Cogswell, *A History of the Eleventh New Hampshire Volunteer Infantry in the Rebellion War, 1861–1865* (Concord, NH: Republican Press Association, 1891), 260, 269, 348.

39. An exception, as mentioned earlier, was Carlton McCarthy's *Detailed Minutiae of Soldier Life in the Army of Northern Virginia.*

40. McPherson, *For Cause and Comrades,* 10–11. Sam Watkins first published *"Co. Aytch"* serially in the Columbia [TN] *Herald,* his hometown newspaper, in 1881 and 1882, under circumstances similar to Billings's. Watkins sought to offer a story overlooked by the "'big bugs,' Generals and renowned historians." See Sam Watkins, *"Co. Aytch" Maury Grays, First Tennessee Regiment; or, A Side Show of the Big Show* (Nashville, TN: Cumberland Presbyterian Pub. House, 1882), vii–viii, 5. Watkins's book has been reprinted many times.

41. Bruce Catton, *Mr. Lincoln's Army* (Garden City, NY: Doubleday, 1951); Jeffrey N. Lash, *A Politician Turned General: The Civil War Career of Stephen Augustus Hurlbut* (Kent, OH: The Kent State University Press), 215; Uzal W. Ent, *The Pennsylvania Reserves in the Civil War: A Comprehensive History* (Jefferson, NC: McFarland, 2014), 24; Larry Logue, *The Civil War Soldier: A Historical Reader* (New York: NYU Press, 2002), 107n54.

42. Marc Jordan Ben-Meir, *The Sons of Joshua: The Story of the Jewish Contribution to the Confederacy* (Bloomington, IN: Xlibris Corporation, 2012), 61; Tim Cook, *The U.S. Civil War on the Front Lines* (N. Mankato, MN: Capstone Press, 2014), no page number; Patricia Tichenor Westfall, *Mother of the Bride: A Molly West Mystery* (New York: St. Martin's Press, 1998), 231.

43. On reenactors, see Tony Horwitz, *Confederates in the Attic: Dispatches from the Unfinished Civil War* (New York: Pantheon Books, 1998). Horwitz's book partially recounts his travels around various Civil War battlefields and other sites of historical interest, often accompanied by living historian Robert Lee Hodge. Hodge, Horwitz claims, is a "hard core" reenactor. On an episode of my podcast, "The Rogue Historian," Hodge noted that much of what Horwitz published "sensationalized" the reenacting hobby. See "A Conversation with Robert Lee Hodge," "The Rogue Historian Podcast with Keith Harris," Episode #53, accessed July 15, 2019, https://theroguehistorian.com/the-rogue-historian-podcast/2019/7/8/episode-53-a-conversation-with-robert-lee-hodge.

44. Telephone interview with John Heckman, July 7, 2019; telephone interview with Larry Kelsey, July 9, 2019.

45. John D. Billings, *The History of the Tenth Massachusetts Battery of Light Artillery in the War of the Rebellion: Formerly of the Third Corps, And Afterwards of Hancock's Second Corps, Army of the Potomac, 1862–1865* (Boston: Hall & Whiting, 1881). The book was reprinted as *The History of the Tenth Massachusetts Battery of Light Artillery in the War of the Rebellion* (Boston: Arakelyan Press, 1909). For battle descriptions in the 1909 edition, see 44, 158, 194–95, 320. Historian Noah Andre Trudeau used Billings's regimental history to help understand the opening artillery salvos at Petersburg in 1864, noting that the Tenth "fired the first known shells to have been thrown into the city." (Noah Andre Trudeau, *The Last Citadel: Petersburg, June 1864–April 1865* [1991; reprint, New York: Savas Beatie, 2014], 88.)

46. Scholars almost universally cite Billings as a source for Civil War "detail" such as uniforms, tents, and commonplace military accoutrements. None of these scholars, in any significant way, addresses Billings's postwar reflections on sectionalism, commitment to cause,

or sentiments concerning his Confederate enemy. Scholars who deal specifically with late nineteenth-century Civil War memory more often than not leave Billings out altogether.

47. Billings, *Hardtack and Coffee*, 15–16, 18. Billings does not allocate much attention to the institution of slavery in his regimental history, except to note its "deadening influence" on the southern plantation economy. However, in ways similar to how he observed black people in *Hardtack and Coffee*, he did note the activities of black people he encountered. "They danced, sang, and even prayed their satisfaction in the most fervent manner." See Billings, *The History of the Tenth Massachusetts Battery* (1909 edition), 109, 428.

48. Billings, *Hardtack and Coffee*, 20.

49. Billings, *Hardtack and Coffee*, 24.

50. Billings, *Hardtack and Coffee*, 21–22, 249.

51. Robert Gould Shaw, who eventually would command the storied Massachusetts 54th Infantry Regiment, noted upon hearing news of the Emancipation Proclamation in September 1862: "So the 'Proclamation of Emancipation' has come at last . . . I can't see what practical good it can do now. Wherever our army has been, there remain no slaves, and the Proclamation will not free them where we don't go." (Russell Duncan, ed., *Blue-Eyed Child of Fortune: The Civil War Letters of Colonel Robert Gould Shaw* [Athens: The University of Georgia Press, 1992], 245.) On self-emancipation, see Ira Berlin and others, *Free at Last: A Documentary History of Slavery, Freedom, and the Civil War* (New York: The New Press, 1992); David Williams, *I Freed Myself: African American Self-Emancipation in the Civil War Era* (New York: Cambridge University Press, 2014).

52. Billings, *Hardtack and Coffee*, 369.

53. Today, many Confederate apologists claim that the presence of black men with Confederate armies necessarily means that they willingly supported the Confederacy, even as combat soldiers. While there were indeed blacks performing various duties in Confederate camps and on campaign, there is no evidence that they willingly embraced the Confederate cause. For a thorough refutation of the persistent myth of the so-called "black Confederate," see Kevin M. Levin, *Searching for Black Confederates: The Civil War's Most Persistent Myth* (Chapel Hill: University of North Carolina Press, 2019).

54. In his regimental history, Billings likewise ignored the specifics of the Emancipation Proclamation, though he did suggest, on the basis of observing estates of wealthy Virginians in 1862, that the institution of slavery had an adverse effect on agricultural enterprises. Further, he twice mentioned the twin causes of Union and freedom, though he did not elaborate with analysis. (Billings, *History of the Tenth Massachusetts Battery* [1909 edition], 109, 230, 321.)

55. Billings, *Hardtack and Coffee*, 286–87.

56. Billings, *Hardtack and Coffee*, 287–88.

57. Billings, *Hardtack and Coffee*, 245, 266, 366. On the USCT more generally, see Dudley Taylor Cornish, *The Sable Arm: Black Troops in the Union Army 1861–1865* (New York: Longmans, Green, 1956); Joseph T. Glatthaar, *Forged in Battle: The Civil War Alliance of Black Soldiers and White Officers* (New York: The Free Press, 1990).

58. Wiley, *The Life of Billy Yank*, 42–43, 109, 121.

59. McPherson, *For Cause and Comrades*, 19, 118–19.

60. Buck, *Road to Reunion*, 114; Edward Tabor Linenthal, *Sacred Ground: Americans and Their Battlefield* (Urbana: University of Illinois Press, 1991), 90–93; McConnell, *Glorious Con-*

tentment, 181. This reconciliationist sentiment, according to Gaines M. Foster, lasted well into the twentieth century.

61. Blight, *Race and Reunion.*

62. For an excellent study of lingering wartime animosity that examines Union veterans who mourned the loss of their comrades while basking in the so-called "cause victorious," see Neff, *Honoring the Civil War Dead.* On the 1913 Blue-Gray Reunion at Gettysburg, see Foster, *Ghosts of the Confederacy,* 193–94.

63. McPherson, *For Cause and Comrades,* 11.

64. Billings, *Hardtack and Coffee,* 270.

65. Billings, *Hardtack and Coffee,* 234, 351, 280, 60. In a reconciliationist context, referring to former adversaries as "the enemy" could, in effect, weaken postwar national bonds across sections. Veterans were well aware of this. See Harris, *Across the Bloody Chasm,* especially the introduction.

66. Billings, *The History of the Tenth Massachusetts Battery* (1909 edition), 313, 110, 171.

67. Billings, *Hardtack and Coffee,* 19.

68. Billings, *The History of the Tenth Massachusetts Battery* (1909 edition), 173.

69. Harris, *Across the Bloody Chasm,* 42 (and chapter two). Scholars have published an enormous amount of work on the origins and legacy of the so-called Confederate "Lost Cause." See for example Foster, *Ghosts of the Confederacy;* Rollin G. Osterweis, *The Myth of the Lost Cause, 1865–1900* (Hamden, CT: Archon Books, 1973); Gary W. Gallagher, *Lee and His Generals in War and Memory* (Baton Rouge: Louisiana State University Press, 1998), especially chapter ten titled "Jubal A. Early, the Lost Cause, and Civil War History: A Persistent Legacy"; William C. Davis, *The Cause Lost: Myths and Realities of the Confederacy* (Lawrence: University Press of Kansas, 1996).

70. Billings, *Hardtack and Coffee,* 210, 19, 18.

71. *New York Times,* May 31, 1895; Billings, *Hardtack and Coffee,* 250–51.

72. Robert B. Beath, *The Grand Army Blue-Book Containing the Rules and Regulations of the Grand Army of the Republic* (Philadelphia: Burk & McFetridge, Printers, 1886), 2.

73. McPherson's *For Cause and Comrades* devotes considerable attention to what motivated soldiers to enlist. Studies of World War II and the Vietnam era, based on testimony from both conflicts, minimized the soldiers' commitment to ideology, especially when connected to patriotism. "Questionnaires administered by social scientists to American soldiers," McPherson observes, "found that their 'convictions about the war and its aims' ranked low among various reasons for fighting. . . . American soldiers in Vietnam dismissed ideological and patriotic rhetoric as 'a crock,' 'crap,' 'a joke.'" But applying this model to Civil War soldiers and veterans, concludes McPherson, is problematic when one considers the abundant evidence to the contrary (pp. 90–91).

74. Luther Tracy Townsend, *History of the Sixteenth Regiment, New Hampshire Volunteers* (Washington, DC: Norman T. Elliott, Printer and Publisher, 1897), 15; W. W. H. Davis, *History of the 104th Pennsylvania Regiment, August 22nd, 1861, to September 30th, 1864* (Philadelphia: Jas. B. Rogers, Printer, 1866), preface. Osceola Lewis, *History of the One Hundred and Thirty Eighth Pennsylvania Volunteer Regiment* (Norristown, PA: Wills, Iredell, & Jenkins, 1866), 14; Charles W. Cowtan, *Services of the Tenth New York Volunteers (National Zouaves) in the War of the Rebellion* (New York: Charles H. Ludwig, 1882), 11–12, 18.

75. Billings, *The History of the Tenth Massachusetts Battery* (1909 edition), 17, 437–38; Billings, *Hardtack and Coffee*, 41–42.

76. Robert Stockton Green, "Governor Green's Address, July 1, 1887," and William A. Potter, "Address of William A. Potter, June 30, 1888," in *State of New Jersey Final Report of the Gettysburg Battlefield Commission, 1891* (1891; reprint, Hightstown, NJ: Longstreet House, 1997), 31, 84; C. L. Sumbardo, "Address of Captain C. L. Sumbardo," in Edward D. Neill, ed., *Glimpses of the Nation's Struggle: Papers Read Before the Minnesota Commandery of the Loyal Legion of the United States, 1889–1892* (New York: D. D. Merrill, 1893), 41.

77. Billings, *Hardtack and Coffee*, 253.

78. Billings, *Hardtack and Coffee*, 214–15.

79. Billings believed that orders designed to protect Confederate civilian property, and by extension to dampen bitterness toward the United States among those in rebellion, undermined the Union war effort. "Such tender regard for Rebel property," he claimed, "only strengthened the enemy and weakened the cause of the Union. . . ." By the end of the conflict, he added, few US soldiers opposed harsh forms of foraging in the rebellious states. (Billings, *Hardtack and Coffee*, 231.)

Elizabeth Bacon Custer in the mid-1880s, about the time she published *Boots and Saddles, or Life In Dakota With General Custer*. Courtesy of the Little Bighorn Battlefield National Monument.

One Widow's Wars

The Civil War, Reconstruction, and the West in
Elizabeth Bacon Custer's Memoirs

CECILY N. ZANDER

Elizabeth Bacon Custer's writings on life in the US Army can help historians answer fundamental questions about how nineteenth-century Americans interpreted the changes of their era. Though her works are often dismissed as biased defenses of her husband's career, Libbie, as she was known to her circle of friends, thought her memoirs could be useful for an entirely different reason. The opening sentence of the first book she published about her life, *Boots and Saddles, Or Life in Dakota With General Custer,* explained, "[o]ne of the motives that have actuated me in recalling these simple annals of our daily life has been to give a glimpse to civilians of garrison and camp life—about which they seem to have such a very imperfect knowledge." She continued, saying, "this ignorance exists especially with reference to anything pertaining to the cavalry, which is almost invariably stationed on the extreme frontier."[1]

In addition to giving civilians an invaluable portrait of garrison and camp life, Libbie Custer's memoirs offer an informative account of the way nineteenth-century Americans situated western expansion and related events on the American frontier to those of the Civil War and Reconstruction. The memoirs have never been utilized in this way, largely because until recently the field of Civil War history seldom focused closely on the West. Along with this new geographic focus, historians also have begun to question the chronological boundaries of the Civil War and Reconstruction, another subject Custer's writings help illuminate. Anyone interested in first-hand testimony about the institution most closely involved with waging war, managing peace, and expanding the nation after the Civil War should take seriously Libbie Custer's writings.

Libbie Custer and Her Books

Custer was born Elizabeth Clift Bacon on April 8, 1842, in Monroe, Michigan, on the western shore of Lake Erie. Tragedy marked her early life. She dealt with the death of two infant sisters and an older brother in her first decade. As the only surviving child of Daniel Bacon, a well-respected judge in Monroe, and Eleanor Sophia Page, Libbie experienced fierce protection from her parents. Libbie's mother insisted that her daughter pay special attention to the study of scripture, believing deeply in the teachings of the Bible and the Presbyterian Church. Surviving accounts suggest Libbie's independent personality chafed against her mother's efforts to keep her safe and confined to the home. Before Libbie reached her teenage years, Eleanor Bacon succumbed to dysentery, leaving Libbie and her father the only surviving members of a family that once had numbered six.

Daniel Bacon approached his new life as a widower and single parent by sending his daughter to live at the local preparatory school, Boyd's Seminary, while he boarded at the Exchange Hotel. For four years following her mother's death, Libbie studied at the seminary, admitting in her diary that she traded her status as a motherless child for favors and "for not doing anything I didn't want to do!" By all accounts, she excelled at the school. But her father withdrew her from the Seminary in 1858, hoping a change of scenery might help better manage the grief over her mother's death she still confessed to her diary. Judge Bacon sent Libbie to stay with his sister in Auburn, New York, where she attended the Young Ladies Institute.[2]

The New York sabbatical lasted only one year, at the end of which Libbie returned to Monroe. Her father welcomed her home with an introduction to his new wife, a local widow named Rhoda Wells Pitts. Libbie, her father, and her new stepmother moved back into the old Bacon home, where Libbie and Rhoda formed a close bond. An unknown illness prevented Libbie from beginning her final two years at Boyd's Seminary in 1859–60. In the fall of 1860, she reentered Boyd's, intending to graduate in 1862. Her final years at school were clouded by the onset of the Civil War and the departure of many of Monroe's young men to the front. In the spring of 1862, as Union forces celebrated success in the Western Theater under Ulysses S. Grant, Libbie prepared to give the valedictory address to her graduating class. The following fall, she met George Armstrong Custer, a young lieutenant then making a name for himself on the staff of Maj. Gen. George B. McClellan.[3]

Libbie and George shared a brief courtship, characterized by a deep intensity of feeling expressed by both parties. Daniel Bacon disapproved of his daughter's choice of beau until Maj. Gen. Alfred Pleasonton helped secure Captain Custer's promotion to brigadier general in the summer of 1863, and the new cavalry commander went on to distinguish himself in the Gettysburg campaign. Prior to Custer's great triumph on the third day of that July battle, Judge Bacon had forbidden the West Point graduate from entering his home or corresponding with his daughter. When Custer returned to Monroe in the fall of 1863, he finally secured permission to court Libbie—and less than four months later, on February 9, 1864, the pair married. Libbie immediately began preparations to accompany her husband east, where she planned to attach herself to him as closely as possible. Custer's subsequent role with Maj. Gen. Philip H. Sheridan's campaign in the Shenandoah Valley made frequent contact difficult, leaving Libbie in Washington, DC, for most of the war's final year. From the war's conclusion to the end of her association with the regular army, Libbie's three memoirs tell her life's story.

The memoirs' first editions appeared over the course of five years: *Boots and Saddles, or Life In Dakota With General Custer* (New York: Harper and Brothers, 1885); *Tenting on the Plains, or General Custer in Kansas and Texas* (New York: C. L. Webster, 1887); and *Following the Guidon* (New York: Harper and Brothers, 1890). Due to what she considered poor sales of *Boots and Saddles* at Harper's, Libbie published *Tenting on the Plains* with Webster in a 702-page edition. Webster reprinted the book in 1889, 1893, 1897, and 1915, when the original copyright expired. As the longest of the three memoirs, *Tenting on the Plains* also appeared in several abridged versions, beginning in 1893 with a 403-page version. In 1895, five years after issuing *Following the Guidon*, Harper's reprinted the 403-page edition, thus insuring readers access to Custer's complete trilogy from one press. Libbie found an audience in the United States as well as in London, where her works appeared in several editions from Sampson Low, Marston and Company (*Boots and Saddles* in 1885, *Tenting* in 1888 [full version] and 1893 [abridged], *Gui-*

don in 1890). In its first year of publication, *Boots and Saddles* sold 15,000 copies and was reprinted four times, with further editions in 1899 and 1902, as well as a 1907 edition that included George Custer's farewell address to his troops at the end of the Civil War and an appendix of Custer's letters. *Following the Guidon* received reissues by Harper's in 1891 and 1901.[4]

Libbie's memoirs demonstrate how she made sense of the momentous changes taking place in the United States between 1861 and 1876. Two posthumous publications of her writings that contain Civil War materials exclusively and the three memoirs dealing largely with the postwar years compose a rich body of evidence. Of primary importance to the narration of the Civil War, Reconstruction, and events in the West is *Tenting on the Plains; or, General Custer in Kansas and Texas* (1887), which deals with the end of the Civil War, Reconstruction, and Custer's western military service. Supplemental evidence from *Following the Guidon* (1890) and *Boots and Saddles; or, Life in Dakota with General Custer* (1885) fleshes out the analysis. Taken as a whole, Libbie's writings can help historians explore fundamental questions about how nineteenth-century Americans interpreted their era.

Many biographers of the Custer family have placed her writings alongside those of notable professional widows of her era—women such as La-Salle Corbell Pickett and Jessie Benton Frémont—who created heroic narratives of their dead husband's lives.[5] Carol K. Bleser and Lesley J. Gordon call Libbie a "model widow" in their edited collection dealing with Civil War husband-and-wife relationships. The editors conclude that Libbie's sole purpose after her husband's death became "promoting a man and creating a myth," just like Confederate widows LaSalle Pickett and Mary Anna Jackson. Shirley Leckie contends that "after decades of revising her husband on paper . . . she lost much of her ability to separate fact from myth in the popular sense." Leckie fails to acknowledge that Libbie wrote her three memoirs within two decades of the events she sought to describe, rendering the biographer's broadside somewhat toothless, and bolstering the case for analysis of the books beyond the George Custer narrative.[6]

Libbie's handling of the Little Bighorn understandably contributes to negative perceptions of her authorial intention. That element of Libbie's memoirs stands as a stout defense of a husband who probably disobeyed orders and endangered his command in the process of committing one of the best-known military blunders in American history. Her determination to finesse George Custer's actions at the Little Big Horn, however, did not extend to her views about the Civil War, the West, and Reconstruction. Indeed, it is only with historical distance and a fresh analytical lens that their considerable value divorced from the Little Big Horn becomes clear.[7]

Paul Andrew Hutton's assessment of Libbie's writings typifies scholarly representations of the books as little more than hagiography. "Custer emerged from her books," Hutton wrote in reference to Libbie's three memoirs, "as a man who found it impossible to hold a grudge, who was devoted to his family, loved children . . . a saintly hero who was entirely capable of accomplishing all deeds attributed to him." In a reader designed to provide primary and secondary materials on Custer's career, Hutton chose not to include any of Libbie's writing. In his Pulitzer Prize–winning biography of George Custer, T. J. Stiles references Libbie's memoirs on 80 occasions in 1,230 footnotes. Many of Stiles's citations deal with George Custer's relationship with Eliza, the African American cook and housekeeper the cavalry officer first employed during the Civil War. Stiles corrects Libbie's choice to render Eliza's speech in dialect because it strikes him as "both uninformative and egregiously condescending." In another instance, Stiles justifies his decision to quote from the memoirs by saying he found their sentiment "authentic."[8]

Critical historiographical treatment of Libbie's work represents an overcorrection. Because Libbie controlled the narrative of her husband's career until her death in 1933—and outlived all but one officer who participated in the 1876 campaign that culminated in the fight at Greasy Grass—historians have assumed she prevented any conflicting narratives of the fight from reaching a public audience. Robert M. Utley claimed, for example, that Libbie had been "ever present in the background of the controversies" over the Custer fight. Jane R. Stewart claimed that Libbie sometimes intervened directly with publishers to prevent anti-Custer material from appearing in print.[9]

To be sure, Libbie rebuked authors who charged Custer with misconduct, and some, such as Cyrus Townsend Brady, fought back. "Mrs. Custer's zeal in defense of her husband, which I admire," Brady explained in a public letter to *The New York Times* in 1904, "has led her into error." Brady defended his credibility as the author of *Indian Fights and Fighters,* and underscored the fact that others had charged Custer with misconduct before his account. "Nor am I the originator of the charge that Gen. Custer deliberately planned to 'cut loose' from Gen. Terry," he explained in his defense, saying, "that charge has been made many times and most prominently by Major Gen. Robert P. Hughes in *The Journal of the Military Service Institution* for January, 1896." While accounts in contradiction of Libbie existed long before her death, historians have blamed her for covering up the "truth" of the Custer fight, leading to a widespread rejection of her memoirs as valuable historical texts.[10]

Unlike present-day historians, Mark Twain and Charles L. Webster believed Libbie's writing could add value to their stable of memoirs from Civil War luminaries such as Ulysses S. Grant, William Tecumseh Sherman, and Philip H. Sheridan. In fact, Webster included Libbie's second memoir, *Tenting on the Plains,* in their "Shoulder Strap" series of Civil War reminiscences, which featured the three most prominent Union generals as well as another text shepherded to publication by a Union officer's widow—Almira Russell Hancock's *Reminiscences of Winfield Scott Hancock.* Twain initially hoped to offer Webster's subscribers a reprint of *Boots and Saddles,* packaged alongside a reprint of George Custer's *My Life on the Plains.* On December 30, 1886, he suggested to Charles Webster that if *Boots and Saddles* and *My Life on the Plains* were "put into one volume" and nothing was said "about their being second-hand, we could risk 25 cents per copy on it—& I would like to do it for *her* sake, for she needs money."[11] Eventually, Twain offered Libbie a $5,000 advance to publish a new memoir, plus royalties that eventually totaled $1,825.46.[12] Unlike Hancock and McClellan, Libbie did not edit material written by her husband for publication—which sets her apart from the war's notable professional widows.

Though initially positive, the partnership with Webster's proved to be an unhappy one. In addition to being delinquent in paying Libbie a check for her royalties, Twain's firm pushed printing of *Tenting on the Plains* to the end of 1887, setting off a chain reaction of decreased sales and an attempt by Libbie to purchase the rights to the book back from the firm so she could publish it with a house that would promote it. Twain excoriated his partner Fred J. Hall for "balling up" the Custer memoir with Twain's own *Library of Humor* and Samuel S. Cox's *Diversions of a Diplomat in Turkey,* which Twain preferred to promote over Libbie's volume.[13] When Frederick J. Hall reported *Tenting on the Plains* "printed and paid for" on December 24, 1887, Twain shot back: "What did you print the Custer book for?" By December 29, Twain's temper had cooled and he wrote Hall to say he thought "it will be best not to bind the Custer book for some months yet, as it cannot now be canvassed, and we can use the money to better advantage in other ways."[14]

By July 1888, Twain admitted slow sales of Libbie's book. Earlier that summer, Frederick Hall failed to hearten Twain about *Tenting on the Plains'* prospects, when he explained the publishing firm had only recently "gotten rid of" some recent inventory, including "a little over 100 Custer, all within the last two weeks."[15] The slow start for Libbie's memoir caused Twain to instruct the firm to turn down a memoir manuscript from the soon to be commanding general of the USArmy, Nelson Miles: "If we can't sell the Custer book we can't sell any smaller reputation's book."[16] Despite Twain's disillusion with the memoir, The New York Free Circulating Library reported in 1890 that the works of Mrs. Custer were in high demand among their readers, second in popularity only to Charles Carleton Coffin's *Boys of '61.*[17]

The circulating appeal of Libbie's book reflected the widespread positive reception her works received from contemporaries. Reviews and notices serve as another indication of the historical importance of the memoirs beyond their glorification of George Custer. Reviewers across the globe, in fact, devoted almost no attention to Libbie's portrait of her husband, instead focusing on the broad subject matter covered in her works. London's *Morning Post* captured the sentiment of many reviewers of *Tenting on the Plains,* saying the book could have benefited from some excisions. Nevertheless, the reviewer noted, "much that is interesting in her account of life in Texas, where, fortunately, there was a long spell of peaceful, if rough and ready existence, before the general was called away on his duty against the Indians." The review concluded, "As a picture of American military life after the Civil War, 'Tenting on the Plains' is deserving of a wide circulation." London reviewers also praised *Boots and Saddles,* affirming "on the march, in the villages of friendly Indians, or in garrison . . . Mrs. Custer heard and saw much that was worthy of record."[18]

American reviewers also lauded Libbie's three memoirs for their attention to the details of frontier life, saying relatively little about her treatment of her husband's career. In part, reviewers still subscribed to the heroic image of Custer propagated after his defeat at the Little Bighorn, but on the whole, Libbie's depictions of frontier life captured the majority of their attention. "One often reads what men in more pompous style tell of military life," the critic for *The New York Times* explained in his review of *Following the Guidon,* "but it is rarer to have a woman who, following the guidon, gives us in detail her every-day experiences." Women's magazines gave special notice to Libbie's memoirs, with *Harper's Bazaar* offering appreciation in a review of *Boots and Saddles*. "One finds himself not thinking so much of the fact that Mrs. Custer wrote this book as of the thought that Mrs. Custer lived this life," the magazine observed, "as she is original and different from all around her, her book is also unlike any autobiography ever before given the public."[19]

Libbie Custer chose to weave the Civil War into her frontier stories and her views of the connections between postwar Reconstruction and the role of the army in the American West. This focus speaks to a growing field of historical inquiry defined by two key questions. First, what was the relationship between the events historians typically include in their narrative of the Civil War and simultaneous events occurring in the western territories?[20] Second, did the war truly end at Appomattox, or should Reconstruction and western expansion be included in a new narrative of the "Long Civil War"? Libbie Custer provides evidence relating to both of these questions. Her opinion is especially valuable because she wrote with the advantage of firsthand experience of the events encompassed in this new historiography. If historians want to know how nineteenth-century Americans would have explained the relationship among the Civil War, Reconstruction, and the Far West, they would do well to consult Libbie Custer's writings.[21]

The Civil War

Libbie Custer's Civil War writings help to demonstrate how Americans made the transition from four years of intense sectional fighting to postbellum life. Libbie's experiences of the war's closing events underscore her belief that the conflict ended with the surrender of the Confederate armies, while signaling her transition from life among volunteers to life with the regular army. She opened *Tenting on the Plains,* her memoir of the immediate postwar years, with a biographical sketch of her husband's life that includes her most extensive commentary on his Civil War experiences. Though not the primary focus of any of Libbie's memoirs, the Civil War figures in her work. Collections of her Civil War memories and letters appeared posthumously. The first, *The Custer Story: The Life and Intimate Letters of General George A. Custer and His Wife Elizabeth,* edited by Marguerite Merington, appeared seventeen years after Libbie's death. Merington claimed that late in her life

Libbie "occupied her time making notes of Civil War happenings for which her books had held no place." Merington lamented that "these notes could not be put into publishable form, for they betokened failing hand and waning strength, though a clear memory for things gone by." A personal friend of Libbie's, Merington used her editorial hand to shape the letters exchanged between Custer and his bride into a tale of tragic romance.[22]

In 1994, Arlene Reynolds discovered what she believed to be Libbie's unfinished manuscript about the Civil War. Tucked among the reams of writing Libbie had donated to the Little Bighorn National Battlefield were notes that represented her "War Book." Transcribed by Reynolds, the material amounted to approximately 170 pages of recollections and correspondence. Taking nothing away from the archival and editorial service Reynolds rendered, any conscientious reader would realize that many of the stories in the "War Book" appear as vignettes throughout the frontier memoirs. Libbie clearly set out to expand on many of the stories about the war related to her by George Custer, but Reynolds's collection makes clear that writing about the war was never Libbie's great strength. Perhaps she never felt a compulsion to defend her husband's Civil War career, which offered far less potential for public criticism than his postbellum military record.[23]

Unlike many Civil War participants who later wrote about the conflict, Libbie never made systematic use of notes or published materials related to the war. In regard to her memoir draft, she admitted, "there are no dates, no statistics and, alas I fear, no information that would be valuable to a historian." Libbie also emphasized that she had never kept a personal diary of her experiences with the army at any point during her association with the institution. "When the most interesting portions of our life were passing," she wrote, "each day represented such a struggle on my part to endure the fatigues and hardships that I had no energy left to write a line when the evening came." Libbie further noted that as she committed to writing her Civil War reminiscences "I may have repeated myself but I never look in books about my husband and have forgotten what I've written." In sum, Libbie's comments suggest that her later attempts to write about the Civil War, while interesting, are impressionistic at best.[24]

While she was not present for her husband's battlefield endeavors, Libbie did witness the closing acts of the war. The role George Custer played in the Grand Review of Union Armies on May 23, 1865, was conspicuous to say the least. Yet the most distinctive element of Custer's participation—a moment when he apparently lost control of his mount near the presidential reviewing stand—did not appear in Libbie's account of the great victory parade. Rather, Libbie chose to note that "he proudly led that superb body of men, the Third Division of Cavalry, in front of the grand stand, where sat the 'powers that be'" and described the achievements of the division, which captured "111 of the enemy's guns, sixty-five battle-flags, and upward of 10,000 prisoners of war, while they had never lost a flag, or failed to capture a gun for which they fought." Libbie's breathless tone would not seem out of place in the concluding paragraphs of many regimental histories describing the same parade as a lasting symbol of the war's conclusion.[25]

Libbie's decision to leave out the incident highlighted in nearly every newspaper account of the parade likely reflected her efforts to temper her husband's reputation for exhibitionism. George Custer more than justified public perception of his incorrigibility during the Grand Review. As the army moved steadily past the reviewing stand, Washington's *Evening Star* reported, "Suddenly a thrill ran through the vast assemblage as a magnificent stallion dashed madly down past the president." The rider, "General Custar [sic], with a large wreath hanging from his arm, his scabbard empty, and his long hair waving in the wind," was "vainly trying to check him." "On swept the horse, the throng rising from their seats in breathless suspense," which changed quickly into "a long loud cheer as the general checked his frightened steed and rode gracefully back to the head of his column." Libbie's scaled-back depiction of the parade may also have signaled her desire to begin the frontier portion of her memoir, rather than dwell extensively on events frequently covered by other participant-authors. She suggested her husband gave little thought to the Grand Review, as he hastened to bid farewell to his troops and make his way to Texas, where his mentor, Gen. Philip H. Sheridan, had requested he take command of western soldiers who had not yet completed the terms of their enlistments.[26]

"All I knew was, that Texas," Libbie wrote in reference to her change of station, "having been so outside of the limit where the armies marched and fought, was unhappily unaware that the war was over." Libbie's comment deals with the situation that confronted the US Army at the close of the Civil War. By the end of the conflict, few US soldiers had set foot in the Lone Star State. The number of United States Colored Troops recruited from Texas is a clear indication of the state's wartime isolation. The total of 47 (0.13 percent of the military-age black male population) for the entire state paled in comparison to the 24,052 (more than 30 percent) from its Union-occupied neighbor Louisiana. Instead of Federal soldiers, Civil War Texans confronted an influx of refugees from other parts of the Confederacy. These refugees sought an escape from the actual presence of Union armies along the Mississippi River and actively attempted to move their property, including many enslaved people, beyond the reach of potential military liberators. "It was considered expedient to fit out two detachments of cavalry," Libbie explained, "and start them on a march through the northern and southern portions of Texas, as a means of informing that isolated State that depredations and raids might come to an end."[27]

As the Custers prepared to move to Texas, they were surrounded by the closing acts of the Civil War. "The train in which we set out was crowded with a joyous, rollicking, irrepressible throng of discharged officers and soldiers," Libbie recalled, "going home to make their swords into ploughshares." The occasion of the war's conclusion meant "there was not a vein that was not bursting with joy. The swift blood rushed into the heart and out again, laden with one glad thought, 'The war is over!'" Libbie went on to describe a scene that played out in thousands of towns and cities across the country, touching the lives of countless Americans: "At the stations, soldiers tumbled out and rushed into some woman's waiting arms, while bands tooted excited welcomes," and then the crowds "stepped off in a mimic march, following the conquering heroes as they were lost to our sight down the street, going home." Libbie's description of throngs of citizen-soldiers vanishing from her view marks a divide in both the national experience of the Civil War and Libbie's own association with the army. The war of the volunteers had ended, and the work of the professionals would resume.[28]

Reconstruction and Reconciliation

The duty assigned to George Custer entailed keeping the peace between newly freed African Americans and white citizens in Texas. Libbie thought it "hard for the citizens who had remained at home to realize that war was over, and some were unwilling to believe there ever had been an emancipation proclamation." Libbie echoed Shakespeare in noting that while performing Reconstruction duty "the lives of the newly appointed United States officers were threatened daily, and it was an uneasy head that wore the gubernatorial crown." As a result, she pronounced "them braver men than many who had faced the enemy in battle. The unseen, lurking foe that hides under cover of darkness was their terror." Officers chafed at their tenuous position carrying out Reconstruction service. Brig. Gen. Samuel D. Sturgis, stationed in Texas at the same time as Custer, referred bluntly to his occupation responsibilities as "going entirely outside the duty of my profession." Historian Andrew F. Lang has made the critical point that the role of occupiers did not fit within the republican tradition of the army. "White Union occupiers feared that their service within the wartime Confederacy had transformed their identities as citizen-soldiers into arbiters of military governance," Lang writes, "accelerating their perceived detachment from the republican ethic."[29]

The Custers and other Union soldiers faced a defeated populace and a landscape transformed by four years of war. Libbie knew the part her husband had played in Ulysses S. Grant's directive regarding the Shenandoah Valley in 1864, to "eat out Virginia clean and clear as far as they go, so that crows flying over it for the balance of the season will have to carry their own provender with them." She took in the destruction of the South as she steamed down the Mississippi River toward New Orleans. "We wished, as we used to do in that beautiful Shenandoah Valley," she explained, "that if wars must come, the devastation of homes might be avoided; and I usually added, with one of the totally impracticable suggestions conjured up by a woman, that battles might be fought in desert places." Libbie confronted the postbellum southern landscape with some sadness, admitting that "General Custer had already taught me, even in those bitter times, now the war was over, I must not be adding fuel to a fire that both sides should strive to smother." Sympathy for the defeated Confederates, in other words, formed part of the process of sectional reunion.[30]

Libbie's emphasis on reconciliation, a current that runs through *Tenting on the Plains,* has escaped notice in discussions of the memoir, including scholarly introductions to reprints of the volume. In describing an encounter with Confederate general John Bell Hood on their steamboat journey to New Orleans, Libbie observed that both her husband and the one-time commander of the Texas Brigade and later the Army of Tennessee quickly put the animosity of the war behind them. Libbie related a story of General Hood's quest to find the best possible prosthetic leg, which had led the commander to try models from England, France, Germany, the Confederacy, and the Union. She happily noted that General Hood acknowledged, despite his previous sectional loyalty, "the Yankee leg was best of all." When the steamer arrived at Hood's destination, "General Custer carefully helped the maimed hero down the cabin stairs and over the gangway." Mutual respect between two military men served Libbie's reconciliation narrative. Not all former Confederates merited the same praise as General Hood, though Libbie retained sympathy for the defeated soldiers of the South. "In its early days the Seventh Cavalry was not the temperate regiment it afterward became," she wrote of her husband's most celebrated command; "there were a good many men who had served in the Confederate army, and had not a ray of patriotism in enlisting; it was merely a question of subsistence to them in their beggared condition." While she singled them out for their lack of patriotism, Libbie cast no aspersions on ex-Rebels' former loyalty.[31]

Libbie believed that many of the army's highest-ranking officers shared her husband's desire for an easy peace. "In retrospection," she wrote, "I like to think of the tact and tolerance of General Sherman, in those days of furious feeling on both sides, and the quiet manner in which he heard the Southern people decry the Yankees." Commending the general most famous for setting large swaths of the American South ablaze, Libbie related that "he knew of their impoverished and desolated homes, and realized . . . what sacrifices they had made; more than all, his sympathetic soul saw into the darkened lives of mothers, wives and sisters who had given, with their idea of patriotism, their loved ones to their country." She also related the story of an old friend to whom Sherman paid a visit on his return to St. Louis after the war. "She ran to the head of the stairs, and in an excited tone, asked if he for one moment expected she would so much as speak, to a Yankee," Libbie explained. "The General went on his peaceful way," she continued, "and I can recall with what cordiality she came to greet him later in the year or two that followed. No one could maintain wrath long against such imperturbable good-nature as General Sherman exhibited. He remembered a maxim that we all are apt to forget, 'Put yourself in his place.'"[32]

As the country took uneasy strides toward reunification, Libbie observed a regular army plagued by dissatisfaction in the ranks. Soldiers under her husband's command manifested rebelliousness and sometimes violence. Libbie recalled that "insubordination reached a point where it was almost uncontrollable. Reports were sent to General Sheridan, in command of the Department, and he replied to my husband, 'Use such summary measures as you deem proper to overcome the mutinous disposition of the individuals in your command.'" Libbie quoted an unnamed officer who underscored soldier resentment at being retained in service after the war ended. "Tired out with the long service, weary with an uncomfortable journey by river from Memphis, sweltering under a Gulf-coast sun, under orders to go farther and farther from home when the war was over," the officer wrote, "the one desire was to be mustered out and released from a service that became irksome and baleful when a prospect of crushing the enemy no longer existed." Libbie's repeated emphasis on the belief among soldiers that the Civil War had ended with the defeat of the Confederacy, corroborated in numerous accounts of the period, conveys two messages. It shows how nineteenth-century Americans categorized wartime and postwar service, and it reveals how quickly soldiers decided the work of reconstructing the Union was less critical than the task of preserving it.[33]

Libbie frequently described her husband's difficulty in keeping enlisted soldiers engaged and disciplined while occupying the Lone Star State. "Troops that had been serving in the West during the war were brought together at that point from all directions, and an effort was made to form them into a disciplined body," Libbie wrote, admitting, "this herculean task gave my husband great perplexity." Directly referencing her husband's correspondence, Libbie explained that Custer "did not entirely blame the men for the restlessness and insubordination they exhibited, as their comrades, who had enlisted only for the war, had gone home, and, of course, wrote back letters to their friends of the pleasures of reunion with their families and kindred." Complicating Custer's task, Libbie believed, was the fact that "some of the regiments had not known the smell of gunpowder during the entire war . . . [and] every order issued was met with growls and grumbling." The regimental historian of a unit attached to Custer's command confirmed Libbie's assessment. "There was growing discontent among the soldiers at being sent further south," Thomas S. Cogley of the Seventh Indiana Cavalry explained, "when, as they supposed, the war was over." Typical of the views of the volunteer citizen-soldier, Cogley aimed his ire at Custer, bitterly describing the general as a model of "the tyranny of the regular army."[34]

Libbie identified the monotony of peacetime service as a problem among both soldiers and officers, as national attention focused on Reconstruction. Garrisons at remote frontier posts endured perhaps the worst of this phenomenon. "There was no wild clamor of war to enable them to forget the absence of the commonest necessities of existence," Libbie recalled; "in Texas and Kansas, the life was often for months unattended by excitement of any description." "For my part I was constantly mystified as I considered how our officers, coming from all the wild enthusiasm of their Virginia life," she related, "could, as they expressed it, 'buckle down' to the dull, exhausting days of a monotonous march." "Conceive, if you can," Libbie urged her readers, "how these brave men felt themselves chained . . . there were not enough to admit of a charge on the enemy, and the defensive is an exasperating position for a soldier or frontiersman." The emphasis on the lack of military action for soldiers in Texas and Kansas underscores how differently Libbie understood those types of service as compared to the Civil War.[35]

Postwar changes in rank sometimes produced comical confusion. Libbie paid close attention to the consequences of demobilization and the shrinking of the peacetime military establishment. As restless soldiers confronted monotony, their officers experienced simultaneous demotions, which meant less status and, critically, less pay. "As I look back and consider what a descent the major-generals of the war made," Libbie wrote, "I wonder how they took the new order of things so calmly, or that they so readily adapted themselves to the positions they had filled before the firing on Sumter in 1861." "The immense amount of rank these new lieutenants and captains carried was amusing," she explained, "for those who had served in the war still held their titles when addressed unofficially, and it was, to all appearances, a regiment made up of generals, colonels and majors." Yet Libbie surely understood this to be one of the least surprising consequences of the Civil War's conclusion. Her husband, along with untold other officers, had experienced the loss of high volunteer rank and reversion to a much lower position in the small professional army—in his case, from major general to captain and eventually to lieutenant-colonel in June 1866. This transformation, carried out over less than two years, served as a clear marker that the army judged the war to be over.[36]

In her transition to army life, Libbie quickly perceived she also would have to face boredom if she intended to remain at her husband's side. "In the autumn [of 1866], the appointment to the Seventh Cavalry came, with orders to go to Fort Garland," she recalled. "One would have imagined, by the jubilant manner in which this official document was unfolded and read to me, that it was the inheritance of a principality," she wrote of her husband's response to a posting to the remote Colorado fort, which would take him away from duty in one of the army's Reconstruction districts. At the same time, she admitted, "the sober colors in this vivid picture meant a small, obscure post, then several hundred miles from any railroad, not much more than a handful of men to command, the most complete isolation, and no prospect of an active campaign, as it was far from the range of the warlike Indians."[37]

Libbie's premonition regarding a posting to Fort Garland proved correct. Writing in 1876, an officer sent to inspect Fort Garland pitied the soldiers posted to that frontier installation. An assignment in the West, William A. Rideing observed, "means to the soldier concerned several years of unproductive, unrewarded, and wholly unsatisfactory service." "Frontier life suggests, I know, a sort of poetic expansiveness to the inexperienced," he continued; "to the soldier, it usually involves, except in the case of an Indian war, a career of humdrum routine." Luckily for the Custers, orders quickly redirected them to Fort Leavenworth, where preparations for an Indian campaign to be directed by Custer's mentor, General Sheridan, were under way. The rolling swells of the Kansas prairie quickly replaced visions of Fort Garland and the towering mountain vistas of Colorado's San Luis Valley.[38]

Libbie perceived her husband's enthusiasm at the prospect of escaping Reconstruction duty. "When orders came for the 7th Cavalry to go into the field again," Libbie related in *Boots and Saddles,* "General Custer was delighted. The regiment was stationed in various parts of the South, on the very disagreeable duty of breaking up illicit distilleries and suppressing the Ku-klux." "It seemed," she continued, "an unsoldierly life, and it was certainly uncongenial." Nelson A. Miles, a volunteer officer during the war and colonel in the peacetime army who would win a reputation as an Indian fighter and eventually became commanding general of the army, also welcomed a transfer to the West. "It was a pleasure to be relieved of the anxieties and responsibilities of civil affairs," he explained about his Reconstruction assignment in North Carolina, "to hear nothing of the controversies incident to race prejudice, and to be once more engaged in strictly military duties."[39] Libbie manifested so little interest in Reconstruction that she saved fewer than 100 newspaper articles, out of a total of nearly 2,500, related to the era over her four decades of collecting ephemera.[40]

Libbie often compared her husband's postbellum military experiences to his Civil War service. One of the most diverting passages in *Tenting on the*

Plains discusses the strong personal relationships forged in active military service. When George Custer was ordered out of Texas to await his next assignment, the couple returned to Michigan, where Custer's wartime staff broke up. "How the General regretted [saying farewell to] them," Libbie lamented, "the men, scarce more than boys even then, had responded to every call to charge in his Michigan brigade, and afterward in the Third Cavalry Division. Some, wounded almost to death, had been carried from his side on the battle-field, as he feared, forever, and had returned with wounds still unhealed." Switching momentarily to her present, Libbie informed readers that "one of those valiant men has just died, suffering all these twenty-three years from his wound. . . ." But in "writing, speaking in public when he could, talking to those who surrounded him when he was too weak to do more," she believed, the soldier had helped keep alive the memory of her husband's Civil War service. For this Libbie expressed gratitude—seemingly reserved for those who helped preserve her perception of her husband's military heroism.[41]

Beyond the gratitude she felt for soldiers who recalled her husband's memory, Libbie appreciated the physical cost of the Civil War. In recounting injuries received by men who campaigned with her husband, she celebrated the soldiers' resilience in their postbellum pursuits. "[A]nother of our military family," she told her readers, "invalided by his eleven months' confinement in Libbie Prison, set his wan, white face toward the uncertain future before him, and began his bread-winning, his soul undaunted by his disabled body." She continued, "another—oh, what a brave boy he was!—took my husband's proffered aid, and received an appointment in the regular army." "He carried always, does now, a shattered arm, torn by a bullet while he was riding beside General Custer in Virginia," she related, but "that did not keep him from giving his splendid energy, his best and truest patriotism, to his country down in Texas even after the war, for he rode on long, exhausting campaigns after the Indians, his wound bleeding, his life sapped, his vitality slipping away with the pain that never left him day or night."[42]

Then, taking complete leave of her husband's story, Libbie issued an appeal to her readers. "It is to those who, like his young staff-officer, bear unhealed and painful wounds to their life's end that I wish to beg our people to give thought," she said in hinting that perhaps too many people had forgotten the men's wartime sacrifices. "We felt it rather a blessing, in one way, when a man was visibly maimed," she recalled, "for if a leg or an arm is gone, the empty sleeve or the halting gait keeps his country from forgetting that he has braved everything to protect her." Sticking to her reconciliationist tone, she added that "the men we sorrowed for were those who suffered silently; and there are more, North and South, than anyone dreams of, scattered all over our now fair and prosperous land." Speaking about internal afflictions experienced by veterans, Libbie described symptoms resembling modern PTSD: "Sometimes, after they die, it transpires that at the approach of every storm they have been obliged to stop work, enter into the seclusion of their rooms, and endure the racking, torturing pain, that began on the battle-field so long ago."[43]

Libbie continued by relating the cultural response to the veterans' plight. "When asked why they suffer without claiming the sympathy that does help us all," she remarked, "they sometimes reply that the war is too far back to tax anyone's memory or sympathy now." "Oftener," she lamented, "they attempt to ignore what they endure, and change the subject instantly." Pointing directly to the cultural silence surrounding veterans, Libbie believed "people would be surprised to know how many in the community, whom they daily touch in the jostle of life, are silent sufferers from wounds or incurable disease contracted during the war for the Union." Focusing exclusively on the veterans of the Civil War, Libbie asserted that "the monuments, tablets, memorials which are strewn with flowers and bathed with grateful tears, have often tribute that should be partly given to the double hero who bears on his bruised and broken body the torture of daily sacrifice for his country."[44]

The long aside about the physical and mental toll of the Civil War touches on several of the larger themes in Libbie's work. Throughout the passage, she singled out the war as removed from later conflicts involving the army, or at least offered it as the primary conflict for which veterans merited the praise and thanks of the nation. She did not distinguish between Union and Confederate veterans in reckoning the war's costs, another reconciliationist gesture on her part. Monuments and memorials were the purview of Civil War veterans, she also suggested, excluding veterans of the Indian wars from her discussion. For a woman who spent years with soldiers deployed to the West—and whose husband perished in a campaign against Indians—to ignore their sacrifices and their right to the gratitude of the nation points to her striking separation of frontier service and that against the Confederacy. Libbie's extended reflection on the cost of the Civil War provides an example of how most Americans differentiated between the Civil War's citizen-soldiers and the veterans of Indian wars who, as one of the latter remarked ruefully, were "never invited to join in the parade."[45]

Libbie's repeated returns to reconciliation in her memoirs of the postbellum years further underscore her perception of the Civil War's purpose. Her understanding mirrored George Custer's assertion to Daniel Bacon: "The Union—it was the Union we were fighting for!" The point of view adopted by the Custers aligned them with the vast majority of the loyal citizenry, both in the army and in civilian life. If the primary goal of the conflict was restoration of the republic, it made sense to seek ways to bring the former Rebels back into the national fold. Emancipation served as a means to the end of Union, rather than as a preeminent end in itself, for the Custers. In *Tenting on the Plains,* both Libbie's depiction of George Custer's cook, Eliza, and her disregard for the army's work in protecting newly freed African Americans in Texas underscore a rejection of the emancipation narrative of the conflict. Like most white Americans in the loyal states, neither Libbie nor George Custer could be considered an abolitionist, or even broadly antislavery. A life-long Democrat, Custer first gained notice on the staff of George McClellan and was a confirmed acolyte of "Little Mac's" politics and prosecution of a limited war for Union.[46]

In *Tenting on the Plains,* Libbie wove the story of the Custer's African American cook and servant Eliza throughout the narrative. Like many nineteenth-century authors, she rendered Eliza's speech in dialect and never accorded equal status to the only other woman who campaigned with the Custers. Throughout the text, Libbie limited Eliza's role to keeping house and cooking for the Custers and protecting and comforting Libbie when hardships arose. As a result, Eliza takes on many of the attributes of a mammy figure. Libbie's explanation for this depiction adds further interest to Eliza's role in the narrative. Libbie admitted that Eliza insisted she never spoke like a field hand and had spent enough time in the North after the end of slavery that her accent almost had disappeared. Despite this explanation, Libbie asked her readers for forgiveness when placing words like *"whar* and *thar"* in Eliza's mouth, calling the stylistic choice a *"lapsus linguae."*[47]

The only hint of the emancipation cause in Libbie's narrative comes from the mouth of Eliza. In the midst of a passage explaining how her husband met his long-time cook, Libbie allowed Eliza to explain why she sought work with the Union army. "I allus thought this," Eliza shared through Libbie's pen, "that I didn' set down to wait to have 'em all free me. I helped to free myself. I was all ready to step to the front whenever I was called upon, even if I didn't shoulder the musket." Without comment, Libbie also permitted Eliza to speak on the war's cause: "Everybody was excited over freedom, and I wanted to see how it was. Everybody keeps asking me why I left. I can't see why they can't recollect what war was for, and that we was all bound to try and see for ourselves how it was." Unlike Libbie, Eliza could recollect that her war had been one for freedom from slavery.[48]

Libbie's understanding of the army's role in the reconstruction of Texas also exposed her disregard for the preservation of the rights of newly freed-people. In Texas, "General Custer not only had his own Division to organize and discipline, but was constantly occupied in trying to establish some sort of harmony between the Confederate soldiers, the citizens, and his command." First mentioning the former Confederate soldiers, Libbie noted that "they came home obliged to begin the world again," making clear her sympathy for the difficulty they faced. "The negroes of the Red River country," she wrote, "were not an easy class to manage in days of slavery . . . it certainly was difficult to make them conform to the new state of affairs." "The colored man," she claimed, "inflated with freedom and reveling in idleness, would not accept common directions in labor." Blame for the failure of Reconstruction, in other words, lay not with former slaveholders, who were rebuilding their lives from the ground up, but rather with the former slaves. By singling out slaves in Louisiana and Texas as "the most ungovernable cases," Libbie dismissed abolition and emancipation and placed blame for violence in the region on newly freed people.[49]

The Frontier

Tenting on the Plains also contains Libbie's recollections of her first frontier experiences, as her husband moved from the duty of reconstructing the South to the work of constructing the West. Despite the relief of escaping distasteful Reconstruction duty, Libbie clarified that the prospect of a frontier assignment held its own drawbacks. When Custer accepted a formal posting to Kansas, his commitment to the regular army elicited praise from the highest US military authorities. "General Grant wrote his approval of General Custer's acceptance," wrote Libbie, who quoted from the general: "There was no officer in that branch of the service who had the confidence of General Sheridan to a greater degree than General Custer, and there is no officer in whose judgment I have greater faith than in Sheridan's." However flattering approval of the army's commanding general, Libbie sensed "the stagnation of peace was being felt by those who had lived a breathless four years at the front. However much they might rejoice that carnage had ceased and no more broken hearts need be dreaded, it was very hard to quiet themselves into a life of inaction." Perhaps because her husband briefly considered taking a position as a general in Mexico before reaffirming his commitment to the regular army, Libbie understood the desire of some soldiers to seek new wars. "No wonder our officers went to the Khedive for service," she wrote.[50]

The geography and political importance of the frontier forced Libbie to reorient a frame of reference shaped by the terrain over which Union and Confederate armies waged the Civil War. "My attention had been so concentrated on the war," she wrote in *Tenting on the Plains* of her impending move to Kansas, "that I found the map of Virginia had heretofore comprised the only important part of the United States to me, and it was difficult to realize that Kansas had a city of 25,000 inhabitants, with several daily papers." Libbie's admitted geographic shortcomings further illustrate the separation between the Civil War and the West in her memoirs. The map of Virginia, where the two most important Civil War armies had fought their campaigns and international attention had been focused for four grueling years, had represented, for Libbie, the only important part of the United States. Whatever lay beyond the boundaries of the Old Dominion remained out of sight and mind for the years of the war—the West, though growing and flourishing, existed beyond Libbie's understanding of the sectional conflict.[51]

As the Custers prepared for a change of station, the army experienced a transformation of its own. Libbie paid attention to the composition of the reconstituted regular army in the years following the Civil War. "The regiments looked well on the roster," she noted, "but there were in reality but few men. A regiment should number twelve hundred enlisted men; but at no time, unless during the war, does the recruiting officer attempt to fill it to the maximum; seventy men to a company is a large number." The army was crippled, she observed, by desertions, which "during the first years of the reorganization of the army after the war thinned the ranks constantly. Recruits could not be sent out fast enough to fill up the companies." On average, for the period 1865–77, one-third of the enlisted men in the regular army deserted annually. Because soldiers were expected to remain on their posts, the War Department stipulated that they perform the labor necessary for the upkeep and expansion of those military installations. As one infantryman in the ranks explained, "all this unpaid labor, carried out from day to day, month to month, by men enlisted for military service, created almost universal dissatisfaction and desertions became frequent."[52]

The isolation of frontier posts, and their constant need for upkeep, astonished Libbie. "I had either been afraid to confess my ignorance, or so assured there was but one variety of fort," she explained, "that Fort Riley came upon me as a great surprise. I supposed, of course, it would be exactly like Fortress Monroe, with stone walls, turrets for the sentinels, and a deep moat." Indicating the fear she felt as a consequence of being sent to the remote frontier, Libbie described a "vision of the enclosure where we would eventually live" as "a great comfort to me." "I could scarcely believe that the buildings," she recalled, "a story and a half high, placed around a parade-ground, were all there was of Fort Riley." Typical of almost all frontier forts Libbie would call home over the next decade, Fort Riley was exactly as Libbie described: an assemblage of barracks, small homes for officers and families, a mess and hospital, and a prison, with no palisade to protect the inhabitants from hostile attacks.[53]

Not only isolated, frontier posts also lacked opportunities for socialization that Libbie had grown accustomed to while living in Washington during the war. "There was very little social life in garrison that winter," she wrote, as "the officers were busy studying tactics, and accustoming themselves to the new order of affairs, so very different from their volunteer experience." As officers set about learning the duties of the regular army, George Custer settled down to military administration. "It is hard to imagine a greater change than from the wild excitement of the Virginia campaigns, the final scenes of the war," Libbie told her readers, "to the dullness of Fort Riley. Oh! how I used to feel when my husband's morning duties at the office were over, and he walked the floor of our room, saying, 'Libbie, what shall I do?'" Often the answer was hunting for game, or in later years when the Custers had learned the routines of frontier life, piano and the company of other officer's families or visiting friends from the East. Whatever activities filled the day, Libbie emphasized, they never matched the frenetic pace of the Civil War, especially for the perpetually active cavalry.[54]

Libbie betrayed disappointment that even when army brass selected her husband to go on campaign, he commanded a force greatly reduced from the period of the Civil War. "He endeavored to induce me to think, as he did," she wrote of her husband's attempt to assuage her fears of his leaving for service in the field, "that the Indians would be so impressed with the magnitude of the expedition, that, after the council, they would accept terms and abandon the war-path." Libbie recalled, "eight companies of our own regiment were going out, and these, with infantry and artillery, made a force of fourteen hundred men." She explained that "it was really a large expedition, for the Plains; but the recollections of the thousands of men in the Third Cavalry Division, which was the General's command during the war, made the expedition seem too small, even for safety." Though intending to illustrate her fear of the consequences of Indian campaigning with such a small force, Libbie also underscored the vast differences commanders of Civil War armies, or even divisions, experienced when sent for service on the plains.[55]

In *Following the Guidon,* Libbie offered her readers a description of a typical day on campaign in her husband's regiment. Her account points to several tasks the regular army performed, most of which had nothing to do with waging conventional war. "Concise as is the record," she wrote, "[the army] served to point the way for many a tired pioneer who came after; for, on his map, compiled from these smaller ones, were the locations of places where he could stop for wood and water." As guides and explorers, in other words, the army filled in the map of the West. "In geological research," like the sort performed by her husband in the 1875 Black Hills Expedition, Libbie approvingly noted that "the officers of our army have been of incalculable use to their Government. They explored the Indian infested countries long before the colleges or Government sent out scientists for the purpose. The remains of fishes, serpents, birds, crocodiles, lizards, turtles, bats, etc., were gathered by our officers and sent to the East."[56]

The army did important work, Libbie realized, but "there was often a weary sigh among the youngsters who had no war record, and who longed to make some sort of soldier's name for themselves." Circumstances offered frontier soldiers no real war, no way to gain access to promotion or win the admiration of the nation. "Many a time the question was asked," she related, "what was the good of galloping after foes who knew the country thoroughly, who were mounted on the fleetest, hardiest animals in the world . . . who each day could be bountifully fed . . . without being hampered with a train of supplies." It was clearly a career of frustration, as Libbie noted: "They had marched and countermarched over the country so constantly that the wit of the regiment said to the engineer officer who made the daily map: 'Why fool with that? Just take the pattern supplement of the Harper's Bazar and no better map of our marches could be found.'" Though presented as wit, the soldier's conclusion underscored a pall of futility hanging over an army that lacked the clear purpose of 1861 to 1865.[57]

A few observations about the reception of Libbie's books will provide context for how other nineteenth-century Americans also separated the Civil War, Reconstruction, and western expansion. On April 15, 1888, *The New York Sun* published an approving notice for *Tenting on the Plains,* counting among the book's merits its "animated pictures of garrison life, of hunting on the plains, or encounters with hostile Indians." *The Critic,* a weekly periodical, had one quibble with *Tenting on the Plains*—the volume's bulk. The book would have been "more enticing, if it had been given two volumes," the reviewer determined, "especially as the first half deals with Custer in Texas and the second half with Custer in Kansas, with no necessary connection between the two." The *Critic's* review confirmed that Libbie's contemporaries joined her in distinguishing between Reconstruction and frontier service.[58]

The final word will fall to Chicago's *Dial,* a popular journal of literary criticism. The reviewer opened with the close of the Civil War, just as Libbie had done. *Tenting on the Plains,* it informed interested readers, "deals with the forgotten sequel." "While most of the boys in blue went back to their firesides and occupations of peace," the overview continued, "some of them were obliged to remain in the disordered States of the South or hurry off to new service on the Western frontier." Libbie Custer had the privilege, the reviewer wrote, "of seeing a half-settled country in a transition state between war and peace." "It was a part of our history that has no parallel; and it is fortunate that of the few women who participated in it there was one sufficiently gifted in the art of expression to give us its imperishable picture," the review admitted, celebrating everything but Libbie's characterization of her husband in its glowing assessment of the book.[59]

The review in *Dial* is an important reminder that Libbie Custer's memoirs, so often dismissed as mere hagiography of little historical value, contain one of the few firsthand historical accounts of American life in transition between the Civil War, Reconstruction, and the western frontier. In her writing, Libbie sought to delineate among three separate wars, believing that the part she and her husband had to play in each was different. Libbie Custer's importance to the literature of the American Civil War era is not, on its surface, obvious. But as historians attempt to revise long accepted narratives and search for broad patterns relating to the most important period in the nation's history, they can find a great deal of value in the memoirs of Libbie Custer. If willing to see Libbie not as a professional widow, or a mythmaker, but as an often perceptive observer, historians will discover a rich vein of testimony that reflects the spirit with which Libbie Custer lived her life.

NOTES

1. Elizabeth Custer, *Boots and Saddles, Or Life in Dakota with General Custer* (New York: Harper and Brothers, 1885), 1. For the purposes of this essay, quoted material will be taken from original editions of Libbie Custer's memoirs. The author wishes to thank Gary W. Gallagher and Stephen B. Cushman for their support of this essay, as well as Charles and Joan Zander, who could not have known how important childhood visits to historical places would be, but who made this piece possible.

2. Libbie Custer quoted in Jeffry D. Wert, *Custer: The Controversial Life of George Armstrong Custer* (New York: Touchstone, 1996), 63.

3. Biographical information on Libbie drawn from Wert, *Custer;* Shirley A. Leckie, *Elizabeth Bacon Custer and the Making of a Myth* (Norman: University of Oklahoma Press, 1993); and Marguerite Merington, *The Custer Story* (New York: Devin-Adair, 1950).

4. For sales figures, see Paul Andrew Hutton, "From Little Bighorn to Little Big Man: The Changing Image of Western Hero in Popular Culture," in *The Custer Reader* (Lincoln: University of Nebraska Press, 1992), 395–423. General bibliographical information can be found in the introductions to the University of Oklahoma Press reprints of all three of Elizabeth Custer's memoirs, all with introductions by Jane R. Stewart. The reprints were issued as part of the Western Frontier Library (*Boots and Saddles* [1961], number 17; *Tenting* in three volumes [1971], numbers 46, 47, and 48; *Guidon* [1966], number 33). Stewart's introductions were largely biographical, summarizing the content of the memoirs and discussing Libbie as a professional widow. The Bison Books imprint at the University of Nebraska Press also reprinted *Following the Guidon* in 1994, with an introduction by Shirley Leckie, in direct competition with a 1994 Oklahoma University Press reprint with foreword by Robert M. Utley.

5. See Lesley J. Gordon, *General George E. Pickett in Life and Legend* (Chapel Hill: University of North Carolina Press, 1998); Gary W. Gallagher, "A Widow and Her Soldier: LaSalle

Corbell Pickett as Author of the George E. Pickett Letters," *The Virginia Magazine of History and Biography* 94 (July 1986); Caroline E. Janney, "'One of the Best Loved, North and South': The Appropriation of National Reconciliation by LaSalle Corbell Pickett," *The Virginia Magazine of History and Biography* 116 (December 2008); Sally Denton, *Passion and Principle: John and Jessie Fremont, the Couple Whose Power, Politics, and Love Shaped Nineteenth-Century America* (New York: Bloomsbury, 2007). For the fullest treatment of Libbie in this vein, see Shirley A. Leckie, *Elizabeth Bacon Custer and the Making of a Myth* (Norman: University of Oklahoma Press, 1993).

6. Carol K. Bleser and Lesley J. Gordon, eds., *Intimate Strategies of the Civil War: Military Commanders and Their Wives* (New York: Oxford University Press, 2001), xviii–xviv. Gordon reiterates her categorization of Libbie as a professional widow in *General George E. Pickett in Life and Legend,* 238n3. Gordon also places Helen Dortch Longstreet and Varina Davis in league with Libbie (Leckie, *Elizabeth Bacon Custer,* xxiii).

7. The question of disobedience centers on whether or not Gen. Alfred Terry's orders specifically required Custer and Col. John Gibbon to link forces on June 26, 1876. If there is any consensus in Little Bighorn historiography, it is that the two commands were to unite, as Terry explained in his report following the campaign: "Lieutenant-Colonel Custer should keep still further to the south before turning toward that river [the Little Big Horn] . . . in order, by a longer march, to give time for Colonel Gibbon's column to come up." See copy of Alfred Terry's November 21, 1876, report to the secretary of war in Cyrus Townsend Brady, *Indian Fights and Fighters* (1904; reprint, Lincoln: University of Nebraska Pres, 1971), 225. Robert G. Athearn affirmed in *High Country Empire* (Lincoln: University of Nebraska Press, 1960) that because of "his supreme eagerness to win additional military fame he neglected to consider the magnitude of the enemy's forces" (118–19). Dean of Custer studies Robert M. Utley contends that Custer, suffering from a recent humiliation at the hands of President Grant, rushed into battle, disobeying orders and losing to a superior Indian force. (Utley, *Cavalier in Buckskin: George Armstrong Custer and the Western Military Frontier* [Norman: University of Oklahoma Press, 1988].)

8. Hutton, "Little Bighorn to Little Big Man," in *The Custer Reader,* 400; T. J. Stiles, *Custer's Trials: A Life on the Frontier of a New America* (New York: Alfred A. Knopf, 2015), 489n66, 487n50. Hutton's utter dismissal of Libbie Custer sends a clear message about scholarly opinion of her memoirs.

9. Utley, *Cavalier in Buckskin,* 8; Jane R. Stewart, "Introduction," in Custer, *Following the Guidon* (1890; reprint, University of Oklahoma Press, 1966), xiv. Utley reduces the historical value of Libbie Custer's memoirs to "intimate portrayals of a saintly husband and an idyllic marriage."

10. *The New York Times,* December 7, 1904. In her introduction to the 1971 reprint of *Tenting on the Plains,* Jane R. Stewart observes that "it was almost an axiom among students of the Battle of the Little Big Horn that the full truth of the battle would never be known as long as Mrs. Custer lived." Stewart also notes that the only officer present for the 1876 Sioux campaign to outlive Libbie was Charles Varnum, a second lieutenant in charge of the Indian scouts. See Jane R. Stewart, "Introduction," in Custer, *Tenting on the Plains* (1887; reprint, 1971), xxix.

11. Samuel Charles Webster, ed., *Mark Twain: Business Man* (New York: Little, Brown, 1946), 371. In the same letter, Twain instructed Webster to offer Gen. John A. Logan 40 percent of the profits on all sales of his memoir to entice the man who briefly commanded the Army of the Tennessee to publish with their firm.

12. This is the best guess based on a slightly cryptic chart in Frederick Anderson, ed., *Mark Twain's Notebooks and Journals, Volume 3 (1883–1891)* (Berkeley: University of California Press, 1979), 307. The figure for royalties is confirmed in Lewis Leary, ed., *Mark Twain's Correspondence with Henry Huttleston Rogers, 1893–1909* (Berkeley: University of California Press, 1969), 237. It may also be of interest to note that George B. McClellan's wife Ellen, with the aid of editor William C. Prime, negotiated $10,000 for her manuscript. In the same period of correspondence in which Twain discussed publication of a memoir with Libbie, he instructed Charles Webster to offer Gen. John A. Logan's widow, Mary Simmerson Cunningham Logan, half the profits of a proposed memoir. This was more than Twain had initially offered the general, but following his death in 1886, Twain appeared eager to obtain the reminiscences of the Illinois officer. Mrs. Logan never sold the manuscript. See Webster, ed., *Mark Twain: Business Man,* 372.

13. Twain told Frederick Hall to hold back the Custer book after his partner informed him, "the Cox book is going very well and our Agents have just started on it." This fact convinced Hall and Twain not to push the Custer book. See Hamlin Hill, ed., *Mark Twain's Letters to His Publishers, 1867–1894* (Berkeley: University of California Press, 1967), 240.

14. Anderson, ed., *Mark Twain's Notebooks and Journals, Volume 3,* 360.

15. Anderson, ed., *Mark Twain's Notebooks and Journals, Volume 3,* 390.

16. Hill, ed., *Mark Twain's Letters to His Publishers,* 253, 246.

17. *The Critic: A Weekly Review of Literature and the Arts* (New York), January 11, 1890, 23.

18. *The Morning Post* (London, England), August 22, 1888; June 2, 1885.

19. *The New York Times,* August 31, 1890; *Harper's Bazaar,* May 23, 1885, 339–40.

20. Several notable scholars compose the new school of thought that asserts a relationship among events in the American West, the Civil War, and the reconstruction of the former Confederacy. In 2003, Elliot West proposed the concept of a Greater Reconstruction in "Reconstructing Race," *Western Historical Quarterly* 3 (Spring 2003): 6–26. See also Elliot West, *The Last Indian War: The Nez Perce Story* (New York: Oxford University Press, 2009). West argued that the concept of a "National" era, under the umbrella term of Reconstruction, does a disservice to the history of more than half the nation, which is ignored in traditional narratives of the period. West instead suggested that Reconstruction should be expanded chronologically, in addition to geographically. West's Reconstruction involved both reunion (the traditional Reconstruction of the prewar Union) and the consolidation of national control in the West, including the military defeat of resistant Indians. Scholars such as Ari Kelman, Megan Kate Nelson, and Heather Cox Richardson argue for the American West's centrality to the causes and outcomes of the Civil War, in addition to Reconstruction. See Ari Kelman, *A Misplaced Massacre: Struggling Over the Memory of Sand Creek* (Cambridge, MA: Harvard University Press, 2013); Adam Arenson and Andrew R. Graybill, ed., *Civil War Wests: Testing the Limits of the United States* (Berkeley: University of California Press, 2015); Heather Cox Richardson, *West from Appomattox: The Reconstruction of America after the Civil War* (New

Haven, CT: Yale University Press, 2008); and Richard White, *The Republic for Which It Stands: The United States during Reconstruction and the Gilded Age, 1865–1896* (New York: Oxford University Press, 2017).

21. One of the most prominent historians dealing with a chronological expansion of the Civil War is Gregory Downs, who writes that after Appomattox the federal government could not declare the Civil War at an end without forfeiting the extraconstitutional war powers that it believed would allow the promise of emancipation to be realized. (Gregory P. Downs, *After Appomattox: Military Occupation and the Ends of War* [Cambridge, MA: Harvard University Press, 2015].) In this, Downs echoes the perspective of Avery O. Craven, who wrote in 1969 that "the American Civil War did not end at Appomattox" because he believed "until the Negro's place in American life was fixed, the war was not over." (Avery O. Craven, *Reconstruction: The Ending of the Civil War* [New York: Holt, Rinehart & Winston, 1969], 1–2.) William A. Blair has noted that in modern military parlance Downs's armies of occupation were a necessary response to an insurgency. Blair concludes that "the situation caused the U.S. Army to conduct small wars—low-intensity incursions and constabulary actions—that kept the conflict alive." (William A. Blair, "Finding the Ending of America's Civil War," *The American Historical Review* 120 [December 2015]: 1755].) Andrew F. Lang has suggested in *In the Wake of War: Military Occupation, Emancipation, and Civil War America* (Baton Rouge: Louisiana State University Press, 2017) that post–Civil War armies are best defined as a garrison force. The classic conceptualization, and the one most evident in Libbie Custer's writing, is Edward M. Coffman's characterization of the frontier army as a constabulary force. (Edward M. Coffman, *The Old Army: A Portrait of the American Army in Peacetime, 1784–1898* [New York: Oxford University Press, 1986], 171.)

22. Marguerite Merington, ed., *The Custer Story: The Life and Intimate Letters of General George A. Custer and His Wife Elizabeth* (1950; reprint, Lincoln, NE: Bison Books, 1987), xi.

23. Arlene Reynolds, ed., *The Civil War Memories of Elizabeth Bacon Custer* (Austin: University of Texas Press, 1994), xi–xv (for Reynolds's editorial remarks).

24. Reynolds, ed., *The Civil War Memories of Elizabeth Bacon Custer,* 2. It is difficult to recover how Libbie generally prepared her memoirs for publication. Her insistence on not using notes is corroborated by Stewart in the latter's introduction to the 1971 reprint of *Tenting on the Plains.* Libbie did excerpt published military orders, printed speeches, and letters written by her husband in the memoirs, often when reciting the course of military events that she did not witness. (Reynolds, *Civil War Memories,* 1, 2.) In reference to relying on notes, Libbie may have been commenting on other memoirs written and published by army wives, most specifically Margaret Irvin Carrington, who dedicated her memoir to "Lieutenant-General Sherman . . . whose suggestions at Fort Kearney, in the spring of 1866, were adopted, in preserving a daily record of the events of a peculiarly eventful journey." (Margaret Irvin Carrington, *Absaraka, Home of the Crows: Being the Experience of an Officer's Wife on the Plains* [Philadelphia: J. B. Lippincott, 1868], iii; Custer, *Boots and Saddles,* 141). According to historian Robert A. Murray, Col. Henry E. Carrington, husband to Margaret Carrington and later, following Margaret's death, Frances Carrington, edited and rewrote large portions of Margaret's *Absaraka* and Frances's *My Army Life and the Fort Phil Kearny Massacre* (Philadelphia: J. B. Lippincott, 1910) to improve his own image and defend his conduct in the aftermath of the

1866 Fetterman Fight. Prior to the Little Bighorn, the defeat of Capt. William J. Fetterman and his 68-man command represented the worst suffered by the regular army at the hands of Native Americans. See Robert A. Murray, *The Army on the Powder River* (Bellevue, NE: The Old Army Press, 1969), 9. Though both Carrington memoirs were produced by army wives, the intervention of Colonel Carrington in their composition further distinguishes Libbie's memoirs as works independent of her husband's control.

25. Custer, *Tenting on the Plains,* 27–28.

26. *The Evening Star* (Washington, DC), May 23, 1865.

27. Custer, *Tenting on the Plains,* 31–32; Gary W. Gallagher, *The Union War* (Cambridge, MA: Harvard University Press, 2012), 146.

28. Custer, *Tenting on the Plains,* 32.

29. Custer, *Tenting on the Plains,* 218–19; S. D. Sturgis to R. F. Halsted, April 13, 1866, US House of Representatives, *House Executive Document No. 57,* 40th Congress, Second Session, 1867–68 (Washington: Government Printing Office, 1868), 123; Andrew F. Lang, "Republicanism, Race, and Reconstruction: The Ethos of Military Occupation in Civil War America," *Journal of the Civil War Era* 4 (December 2014): 563. The Shakespearean allusion is to *Henry IV, Part 2,* Act 3, Scene 1.

30. US War Department, *The War of the Rebellion: A Compilation of the Official Records of the Union and Confederate Armie*s, 127 vols., index, and atlas (Washington: GPO, 1880–1901), ser. 1, vol. 37, pt. 2, 301; Custer, *Tenting on the Plains,* 55, 57.

31. Custer, *Tenting on the Plains,* 58, 693–94.

32. Custer, *Tenting on the Plains,* 602–4.

33. Custer, *Tenting on the Plains,* 98, 99; Libbie appears to have taken this passage from an article titled "Sentenced and Shot" published in *The Western Monthly* in November 1870. Written by R. S. Sheppard, the article provided a description of the postbellum Second Cavalry.

34. Custer, *Tenting on the Plains,* 93; Thomas S. Cogley, *History of the Seventh Indiana Cavalry Volunteers, and the expeditions, campaigns, raids, marches, and battles of the armies with which it was connected, with biographical sketches of Brevet Major General John P. C. Shanks, and of Brevet Brig. Gen. Thomas M. Browne, and other officers of the regiment; with an account of the burning of the steamer Sultana on the Mississippi River, and of the capture, trial, conviction and execution of Dick Davis, the guerrilla* (1876; reprint, Dayton, OH: Morningside Press, 1991), 171–72. Cogley suggested that his entire regiment loathed Custer and Libbie and accused the general of forcing soldiers "to perform menial services for her and himself, which was an express violation of the law," adding that he believed his unit had been forced to march to Texas "simply to retain dandy officers like Custer, a little longer in authority" (pp. 172, 174).

35. Custer, *Tenting on the Plains,* 144, 145, 363–64.

36. Custer, *Tenting on the Plains,* 325, 430; Francis B. Heitman, *Historical Register and Dictionary of the United States Army: From Its Organization, September 29, 1789, to March 2, 1903,* 2 vols. (Washington: GPO, 1903), 1:348.

37. Custer, *Tenting on the Plains,* 326–27.

38. William H. Rideing, *Appleton's Journal,* April 29, 1876, p. 564.

39. Custer, *Boots and* Saddles, 11; Nelson A. Miles, *Serving the Republic: Memoir of the Civil and Military Life of Nelson A. Miles* (New York: Harper and Brothers, 1911), 111.

40. In the collection of more than 2,550 articles Libbie willed to the Little Big Horn Battle-field museum, she explicitly described how she arranged the items to order her life's experi-ences. The fewer than 100 accounts dealing extensively with Reconstruction focus primarily on Custer's participation in Andrew Johnson's 1866 "Swing Around the Circle" campaign. Some 530 articles touch on the Civil War explicitly, with 135 offering direct assessments of Custer's wartime generalship. The rest of the Civil War pieces are typical newspaper fodder—veterans rehashing command decisions they disagreed with, biographical sketches of the war's famous commanders, and human-interest stories written by civilians who encountered the war in their daily lives. The Civil War collection also contains eighty-one accounts of Abraham Lincoln's assassination, an intriguing sideline that suggests Libbie was interested in the martyrdom of prominent figures and the public's hero worship of such individuals. The author would like to thank Cindy Hagen of the Little Bighorn Battlefield National Monument for her assistance with this vast collection of Libbie Custer materials—and for her general good cheer in helping a new Custer researcher find her bearings on the Montana prairie.

41. Custer, *Tenting on the Plains*, 298–99.

42. Custer, *Tenting on the Plains*, 299.

43. Custer, *Tenting on the Plains*, 302–3.

44. Custer, *Tenting on the Plains*, 303.

45. *Winners of the West*, January 1926.

46. Merington, ed., *The Custer Story*, 56. In *Boots and Saddles*, Libbie tells the story of a steamer on the Missouri River near Bismarck, North Dakota, that looked in danger of running aground on one of the river's wide and shifting sandbars. Though launched almost ten years after the war's conclusion, the ship had been christened *The Union*, and in the moment of crisis Libbie recalled the ship's captain declaring, "*The Union* must be preserved." (Custer, *Boots and Saddles*, 155.) For analysis of the meaning of Union to the loyal citizenry, see Gal-lagher, *The Union War*; for astute analysis of George B. McClellan's conception of Union and a limited war, see Stephen W. Sears, *Landscape Turned Red: The Battle of Antietam* (New Haven, CT: Ticknor and Fields, 1983), especially chapter 1, titled "The Limits of a Limited War." See also Ethan S. Rafuse, *McClellan's War: The Failure of Moderation in the Struggle for the Union* (Bloomington: Indiana University Press, 2005).

47. Custer, *Tenting on the Plains*, 40.

48. Custer, *Tenting on the Plains*, 41, 40.

49. Custer, *Tenting on the Plains*, 106–7.

50. Custer, *Tenting on the Plains*, 309.

51. Custer, *Tenting on the Plains*, 327.

52. Custer, *Tenting on the Plains*, 358; Leo E. Oliva, *Fort Union and the Frontier Army in the Southwest: A Historic Resource Study, Fort Union National Monument, Fort Union, New Mexico* (Santa Fe, NM: Southwest Cultural Resources Center, 1993), https://www.nps.gov/parkhis-tory/online_books/foun/index.htm; Douglas C. McChristian, *Regular Army O!: Soldiering on the Western Frontier, 1865–1891* (Norman: University of Oklahoma Press, 2017), 400.

53. Custer, *Tenting on the Plains*, 366–67.

54. Custer, *Tenting on the Plains*, 405, 408.

55. Custer, *Tenting on the Plains*, 484.

56. Custer, *Following the Guidon,* 4, 71.

57. Custer, *Following the Guidon,* 5.

58. *New York Sun,* April 15, 1888; *The Critic: A Weekly Review of Literature and the Arts,* May 19, 1888.

59. *The Dial; A Semi-Monthly Journal of Literary Criticism, Discussion, and Information,* May 1888, 13.

Robert E. Lee flanked by his son George Washington Custis (*left*) and Walter
Herron Taylor (*right*) in Richmond, Virginia, shortly after the Confederate surrender
at Appomattox in April 1865. Library of Congress, Prints and Photographs
Division, reproduction number LC-DIG-cwpb-06234.

Proximity and Numbers

Walter H. Taylor Shapes Confederate History and Memory

GARY W. GALLAGHER

Photographer Mathew Brady persuaded Robert E. Lee to sit for a series of portraits at the general's residence in Richmond, Virginia, a week after Appomattox. In one of the images, a seated Lee peers directly at the camera, his face showing the strain of recent events. Flanking Lee, each with one hand on the back of his chair, are the general's son Custis and Walter Herron Taylor, former assistant adjutant general of the Army of Northern Virginia. Both younger men look away from the probing lens, adding to the impact of Lee's intense visage. The three figures, all dressed in Confederate uniforms, offer a striking study of soldiers in the immediate aftermath of a failed and bloody effort to establish a slaveholding republic.[1]

Taylor had served on Lee's staff through the entire conflict. He not only observed his commander in camp and battle but also, as part of his duties at headquarters, oversaw preparation of the monthly returns that charted levels of manpower in the Army of Northern Virginia. Unique proximity to Lee and an unexcelled grasp of the army's fluctuating strength conferred upon Taylor a large measure of authority among former Confederates. His two books, *Four Years with General Lee; Being a Summary of the Most Important Events Touching the Career of General Robert E. Lee, in the War between the States; Together with an Authoritative Statement of the Strength of the Army which He Commanded in the Field,* and *General Lee, His Campaigns in Virginia, 1861–1865, with Personal Reminiscences,* published in 1877 and 1906 respectively, were widely cited by ex-Confederates and later by innumerable historians.[2] Taylor's volumes figured prominently in two major elements of the Lost Cause interpretation of the war: first, the depiction of Lee as a general of enviable character and unrivaled ability; and second, the fixation on superior Union manpower as the factor that rendered US triumph inevitable and made Lee's victories all the more admirable. Lee himself, who for a time after Appomattox planned to write a history of his army, turned to Taylor as the arbiter of questions relating to statistics. Beyond Lee, noted the historian Douglas Southall Freeman, "Colonel Taylor became in time an unofficial court of appeals on controversies related to the Army of Northern Virginia."[3]

Fortunately for historians, Taylor left a large set of letters, most of them written to Elizabeth Selden "Bettie" Saunders, whom he courted through the war and married in early April 1865. Material in the letters allows a comparison of Taylor's attitudes and observations in the midst of events with what he chose to put into his books, which in turn sheds light on the degree to which some elements of the Lost Cause had firm roots in the war. In *Four Years with General Lee,* Taylor alluded to using the wartime letters in preparing his text. "Reverting to the notes from which I have previously quoted," he observed, "I append additional extracts, whose only value, if any they have, is derived from the fact that they were written by one who was brought into daily and intimate relations with General Lee, and whose position made him thoroughly informed as to all matters of routine in the Army of Northern Virginia. . . ." Extracts from the letters possessed additional importance, continued Taylor, because "their tone may be regarded as in some measure indicative of the spirit and temper of that army; and the intimations of contemplated changes or probable movements therein made, as the reflex of the views and opinions of General Lee as to what was regarded as expedient or probable." Elsewhere, Taylor affirmed, "I have written as if under the supervision of General Lee himself, . . . and this conviction has been present to my mind as a controlling force through my entire narrative."[4]

These passages from *Four Years with General Lee* suggest that readers may infer much about Lee's motivations and strategic thinking from Taylor's books. In combination with the general's own letters and postwar interviews while president of Washington College, Taylor's narratives bring readers into the highest councils of the most important Confederate military figure and army. Maj. Giles B. Cooke, whose time on Lee's staff overlapped with Taylor's for the last six months of the war, aptly characterized the dynamic between his former comrade and their chief. Summoning memories of an earlier military relationship, Cooke wrote of Taylor: "His intimate relations with General Lee, resembling the friendship between General Washington and Alexander Hamilton, for four years as his personal aid and adjutant general had much to do with the shaping of Colonel Taylor's after life and enabled him to write of 'Four Years with General Lee' and 'General Lee, 1861–65.'"[5]

This essay begins with a review of Taylor's military career but does not attempt a full evaluation of his two books. It focuses more narrowly on how Taylor's writings shaped the development of Lee's reputation as a man and soldier and on how his assessment of comparative numbers helped buttress the Lost Cause memory of the war. Beyond these two topics, Taylor's books offer much useful information about campaigns and many of Lee's lieutenants, as well as well-crafted narrative passages. The long interval between publication of the books also highlights how attitudes among former Confederates solidified with the passage of time. Most obviously, Taylor's treatment of James Longstreet took on a much more negative cast between 1877 and 1906, though he never echoed the vitriolic cant evident in the writings of Jubal Early and others who sought to make "Old Pete" the scapegoat at Gettysburg and traitor to the South.[6] Of all the officers in the Army of Northern Virginia who wrote books about the war, only Edward Porter Alexander excels Taylor in evidential and interpretive value for modern readers.

Walter H. Taylor's Civil War

Taylor was born on June 13, 1838, in Norfolk, Virginia, and reared in a family prominent among that city's business community. He attended private schools before entering, in 1853, the Virginia Military Institute in Lexington, where he excelled in mathematics and other subjects. He withdrew from V.M.I. in the fall of 1855 upon learning his father had succumbed to yellow fever during an epidemic that swept through Norfolk. Although Col. Francis H. Smith, superintendent of the Institute, sought to make it possible for Taylor to complete his schooling, the young man replied that his family needed him. The next five years brought several changes. The Panic of 1857 and lingering effects from the yellow fever epidemic hampered Norfolk's economy, forcing the sale of the family's company in the winter of 1857. Taylor worked variously as a clerk with the Bank of Virginia, an auditor with the Norfolk and Petersburg Railroad, and, beginning in March 1859, first accountant for the Bank of Virginia.[7]

John Brown's raid on Harpers Ferry in October 1859 opened another chapter in Taylor's career. As with many other young Virginians, he responded to events at Harpers Ferry by joining a volunteer militia company. Elected orderly sergeant of Norfolk's "Southern Guard," which soon became part of Virginia's 54th Regiment of Militia, he watched national events race toward the election of 1860 and its disruptive aftermath. In mid-April 1861, the firing on Fort Sumter and Abraham Lincoln's call for 75,000 volunteers to put down the rebellion prompted Virginia to join the seven Deep South states that had seceded during the winter of 1860–61. Taylor's company mustered into state service on April 30 as Company G of the 6th Virginia Infantry, with Walter holding a second lieutenant's commission.[8]

Shortly thereafter, R. L. Page, first cousin of R. E. Lee and Taylor's uncle by marriage, recommended his young kinsman for advancement. Taylor matter-of-factly described the resultant posting to Lee's staff: "On the 2nd day of May, 1861, in obedience to telegraphic orders from Governor Letcher, I repaired to Richmond, and was at once assigned to duty at the headquarters of the Army of Virginia." Promotion to captain of Virginia forces on May 31, 1861, preceded the offer of a first lieutenancy of infantry in the Confederate States Army to rank from July 16, 1861. Once in national service, Taylor advanced to captain on December 10, 1861, to major of cavalry on April 21, 1862, and, finally, to lieutenant colonel on January 15, 1864, finishing the war at that rank. Brig. Gen. Gilbert Moxley Sorrel, for much of the war a member of James Longstreet's staff, voiced a common judgment about Taylor by those who saw him in action. Although Lee had no formal chief of staff, wrote Sorrel in his memoirs, the "officer practically nearest its duties was his extremely efficient adjutant, W. H. Taylor," and a better officer "could not be found for this important post."[9]

Taylor's wartime letters, which extend from May 1862 through March 1865, reveal that service on Lee's staff involved an overwhelming burden of work and frequent frustration as well as satisfaction from close association with a respected superior. Lee detested paperwork and quickly perceived that Taylor, the youngest member of his staff, possessed formidable bureaucratic gifts. A mounting tide of forms and other documents crossed Taylor's desk, as Lee increasingly relied on him to assure the efficient flow of paper at headquarters.[10] Loath to assemble a large staff, Lee ran the Army of

Northern Virginia with a relative handful of officers, an element of his military personality that historians have criticized. Taylor sometimes bridled at the volume of work and his chief's refusal to enlarge the staff—as well as at an absence of praise from Lee. In August 1863, for example, he complained to Bettie Saunders that while other generals had "ten, twenty, & thirty Ajt Generals, this army has only one and I assure you at times I can hardly stand up under the pressure of work." Taylor further unburdened himself, and invited Bettie's solicitude, by assuring her that he "never worked so hard to please any one, and with so little effect as with General Lee. He is so *unappreciative*." Professing not to "care a great deal for rank," Taylor nonetheless wanted "to hear that I please *my general*. When every body else on the staff goes on leave of absences and I cannot, I am not satisfied to have *others* say 'tis because my presence here is necessary. I want *him* to tell me, then I'll be satisfied." Three months later, Taylor urged one of his sisters to visit Mrs. Lee, calling her "very sweet and attractive. I feel that I could love her. I *don't think* I could entertain the same for the Gen'l."[11]

Vexation could give way to grateful remarks when Lee displayed kindness toward Taylor. In August 1864, the "General and I lost temper with each other," recounted Taylor, ". . . he is so unreasonable and provoking at times. I might serve under him ten years to come and couldn't *love* him at the end of that period." But the next morning "he presented me with a peach, so I have been somewhat appeased. You know that is my favorite fruit. Ah! but he is a queer old genius. I suppose it is so with all great men." Earlier that year, feeling oppressed by what he considered an unfair division of labor among Lee's staffers that required performance of "duties not legitimately mine," Taylor conceded that "there is much virtue in a *soft word*—it does more than turn away wrath, it comforts and encourages. The General has just looked in upon me and kindly enquired if I had a sore throat. . . , remarking at the same time that I should take some exercise & must ride out every day." Mingling gratitude with complaint, Taylor closed: "It is kind of him thus to think of me, but the Chief forgets that if I were to run off daily, I alone would suffer because of the necessary accumulation of work during my pleasure taking."[12]

"The Tycoon," as Taylor and others in Lee's official family sometimes called him, did appreciate his young aide. Taylor claimed otherwise in late 1863, grousing that "Genl. Lee will not push us up tho every body else goes. I have given over all expectations of being more than a Major—certainly as long as his say governs the matter." In fact, Lee expected each officer to do his full duty and exercised restraint in singling out members of his staff for public praise. Yet in January 1863 he spoke glowingly of Taylor in supporting his promotion to lieutenant colonel: "He is intelligent, industrious, and acquainted in the discharge of his duties, and his character irreproachable—I know of no better person for the appointment." During the last winter of the war, while Taylor enjoyed a rare break from headquarters drudgery, Lee realized how much correspondence and other material crossed the young man's desk. "Whilst [I was] away," noted Taylor upon his return to the army, "the General had a taste of what I had to do & since my return has insisted on dividing the labor. He told me he had often thought I had too much to do and he did not wish me to do all the work."[13]

As with many ambitious officers assigned to staff duty, Taylor longed to take a more active role on the battlefield. He may have looked to Lee as a model in this regard. During the war with Mexico, he surely knew, Lee had rendered notable service in the field while a member of Winfield Scott's staff. A few opportunities came Taylor's way. Late in the afternoon on May 10, 1864, word reached army headquarters that a Union assault had breached the western face of the Mule Shoe salient at Spotsylvania. Lee mounted to go to the point of danger, but Taylor and others held him back. "Then you must see to it that the ground is recovered," insisted the general, whereupon the staff spurred into action. Taylor hurried toward the fighting, where he took up a standard and joined other officers in directing a successful counterattack. Almost ten months later along the White Oak Road outside Petersburg, Taylor again responded to a Federal threat with daring behavior under fire. A Union attack had just taken possession of the road, recalled a witness, when "a fine looking young man distinguished for his superb gallantry, rode up." Galloping ahead between the lines, Taylor waved his hat and shouted, "Come ahead boys!" "The frenzy of battle seemed to have taken possession of the Southerners," Taylor wrote after the war, "and I never took part in nor witnessed a more spirited and successful assault."[14]

Taylor's wartime letters anticipated his later attention to relative Union and Confederate strength in the Eastern Theater. After Chancellorsville, he informed his sister that the previous week had been most eventful. "The operations of this army under Genl Lee during that time," he assured her, "will compare favorably with the most brilliant engagements ever recorded. When I consider our numerical weakness, our limited resources and the great strength & equipments of the enemy, I am astonished at the result."

Writing to Bettie Saunders three months later, he made this point even more forcefully: "At Chancellorsville, one of our most sanguinary engagements, the Yankees had over three to our one, & indeed Posterity will be astounded when the real facts are made known and our comparative weakness in numbers is exposed to public view." Taylor's discussion of the retreat from Pennsylvania following the battle of Gettysburg also featured numbers. After the failure of the Pickett-Pettigrew attack on July 3, he stated to his brother Richard, "it was deemed inexpedient to make any more attempts to carry this place by assault. It was beyond our strength, simply this. If we had have had say 10,000 more men, we would have forced them back." He further predicted to Richard that people would be astonished "when the *facts* of this war are made known to see against what *odds* this little army contended. Even you would be surprised if I were to give you the figures of the Yankee army and our own."[15]

Yet Taylor's comments about Chancellorsville demonstrate that he did not see the Union's preponderant strength as necessarily decisive—which went against the Lost Cause convention that Confederates battled gallantly against impossible odds in a war they never could have won. Indeed, optimism despite intimidating odds surfaced repeatedly in Taylor's correspondence. He expressed no fear of U. S. Grant's stronger force at the outset of the Overland campaign, even imagining that if "Grant's army is demolished, I don't think there is a doubt but that peace will be declared before the end of the year." After a month's carnage that included the battles of the Wilderness and Spotsylvania, he urged Bettie to "think nothing about our numerical weakness when compared with Grant's army. Recently we have recd something less than several thousand reinforcements and have plenty of men to manage the enemy. Indeed we begin to feel almost comfortable." As late as mid-February 1865, just six weeks before Appomattox and with Confederate manpower ebbing markedly, Taylor reiterated his belief that "the courage and endurance of this old army is unimpaired and with God's help we will always prove more than a match for Grant, and I really believe he can never take Richmond by force of arms."[16]

Faith in Lee's leadership undergirded Taylor's predictions of victory against the odds. The Army of Northern Virginia's "great Captain" fashioned triumphs such as Chancellorsville, while the absence of an equivalent Rebel commander in the Western Theater proved disastrous. "Now our troops in the West are in every respect equals of those here in Virga," Taylor noted in

August 1863: "Why is it then that we never succeed there? Simply because they need a leader." In early May 1864, when news reached Confederate headquarters that Maj. Gen. Ambrose E. Burnside's Ninth Corps had reinforced Grant's army along the Rappahannock River, Taylor expected "to hear that the last 'onward' has commenced." Whatever Grant's final strength, he prophesied Confederate success: "If all our army is placed under G[en]1 Lee's control, I have no fear of the result." Lee's obvious piety, thought the equally devout Taylor, contributed to his effective leadership. "In this respect our Chief sets a noble example," recorded Taylor in March 1864. "He attends the meetings of the chaplains and in many ways tries . . . to inculcate lessons of morality and piety among the troops."[17]

Unlike many Lost Cause writers, Taylor leavened praise of Lee with considerable criticism. Apart from carping about issues related to workload and supervisory coldness, the wartime letters highlight instances of Lee's striving too hard to maintain an image of patriotic sacrifice. Lee habitually refused to set up headquarters in comfortable houses or to seek special rations, mandating that he and the staff make do with tents and simple food. From camp near Orange Court House in November 1863, Taylor groused that the "General has declined the house proffered him by the Council. We knew he would." Five days before Christmas that year, with Lee visiting his family in Richmond, came a more pointed observation. "Christmas is near so it would be but natural for him to remain with his family during the week," began Taylor mildly to set up his barb, "but it will be more in accordance with his peculiar character, if he leaves for the Army just before the great anniversary to show how self-denying he is."[18]

Matters of policy and military decisions also spawned occasional friction. Taylor opposed arming enslaved men and placing them in Confederate service, something Lee publicly endorsed in the early winter of 1865. "My notions are still the same," he confided to Bettie in language laced with sarcasm, "but I cannot presume to place them in opposition to the well considered and mature views of so many of my wise superiors." As a staunch supporter of slavery (though he almost never mentioned the institution in his private correspondence), it saddened him "to reflect that the time honoured institutions will be no more, that the whole social organization of the South is to be revolutionized. But I suppose it is all right and we will have to be reconciled."[19] Taylor also thought Lee sometimes deferred too much to civilian superiors, which rendered him timid in his young staff officer's mind. With Confederate fortunes declining rapidly in February 1865, Taylor favored consolidating more authority in Lee. "We need a strong hand now," he insisted: "There can be no trifling, no halting or hesitation now without ruin. Our old Chief is too law abiding, too slow, too retiring for these times, that is to dare & do what I deem necessary. . . ." Backing off a bit, Taylor concluded that "nevertheless he is the best we have, certainly the greatest captain and in his own safe & sure way will yet, I trust, carry us through this greatest trial yet."[20]

Admiration for the Army of Northern Virginia constitutes a final theme in Taylor's wartime correspondence. With Lee at its head and "Stonewall" Jackson and James Longstreet his principal subordinates, the army reached apogee. The infantry repeatedly impressed Taylor, as in the bitter action at Antietam that "taught us the value of our men, who can even when weary with constant marching & fighting & when on short rations, contend with and resist three times their own number." Each test deepened an organic, familial bond that produced results on the battlefield. Taylor's profound feeling for the army, as well as a warm regard for James Longstreet's crucial role, showed vividly in his letters from the spring of 1864. Grant would "call to his assistance every available man," averred Taylor: "But if we can only get old Longstreet with that portion of our *family* now under him, we will be able to meet successfully all that Grant can collect." When Longstreet and two divisions of his First Corps returned to Virginia after months in Tennessee, Taylor gushed that the army had never been "in better trim than now. There is no overweening confidence, but a calm, firm & positive determination to be victorious, with God's help. I am proud of our army, and am almost anxious for the signal for the next & greatest struggle." Then, revisiting familial imagery, he closed with an emotional flourish: "A portion of *our family* has been returned to us. Old Pete Longstreet is with us and all seems propitious."[21]

Taylor's Confederate career closed with the sitting for Mathew Brady on the back porch of Lee's residence in Richmond. He returned to Norfolk and built an enviable reputation in business, banking, and civic affairs. A conservative Democrat, he held a seat in the state senate between 1869 and 1873 and opposed Radical Republicans and later the Readjuster Party in Virginia. Taylor participated in a range of veterans' activities, serving as the first corresponding secretary of the Association of the Army of Northern Virginia (founded in 1870 in Richmond with Jubal A. Early as its president) and later joining the United Confederate Veterans. Stricken by cancer in old age, he died in Norfolk on March 1, 1916. An obituary in the *Richmond Times-Dispatch* indicated how closely Virginians and other former Confederates identified Taylor with his old chief, observing that Taylor's "books, his work in later years, his service to the community will live after him. But after those will live what may be carved on his tomb: 'He was the adjutant of Lee.'"[22]

Proximity to Lee

Taylor fully grasped that his presence at army headquarters positioned him as a trustworthy authority regarding Lee. The first sentence in *Four Years with General Lee* established his unimpeachable credentials. "It was my peculiar privilege," he told readers, "to occupy the position of a confidential staff-officer with General Lee during the entire period of the War for Southern Independence. From the time he assumed the duties of the position of general-in-chief of the Army of Virginia ... and in all his campaigns, when in command of the Army of Northern Virginia—I had the honor to be at his side." The preface to *General Lee, His Campaigns in Virginia, 1861–1865* amplified the point. "I have been so frequently urged to write more in detail concerning the matters of which I have personal knowledge, and especially of General Lee," stated Taylor, "that I have concluded to publish them, in the hope that they may contribute in some degree to the clearer understanding of the events and operations in Virginia ... and as an humble tribute to the noble character of the Great Commander who so often led the Confederate troops to victory."[23]

Testimony from the pen of a witness so close to Lee supplied anecdotes and observations that Lost Cause authors and orators used to portray a Christian warrior whose conception of duty, self-control, humility, personal bearing, and military sagacity invited unreserved admiration. Neither of Taylor's books revisited the less attractive elements of Lee's personality evident in the wartime letters. Both muted the ways in which Taylor's opinions about military questions sometimes diverged from those of his superior. Overall, Lee emerged from the books as a less complex, more thoroughly heroic figure.

Taylor provided his fullest physical description of Lee in the opening pages of his second book. Not yet assigned to a specific post, he happened to see his future superior while eating breakfast at the Spotswood Hotel in

Richmond. Taylor found himself "at once attracted and greatly impressed by his appearance." Lee struck him as "then at the zenith of his physical beauty. Admirably proportioned, of graceful and dignified carriage, with strikingly handsome features, bright and penetrating eyes, his iron-gray hair closely cut, his face cleanly shaved except a mustache, he appeared every inch a soldier and a man born to command." This passage echoed many similarly effusive recollections of meeting the general for the first time, including the British officer A. J. L. Fremantle's. "General Lee is, almost without exception, the handsomest man of his age I ever saw," wrote Fremantle in his diary on June 30, 1863. "He is fifty-six years old, tall, broad-shouldered, very well made, well set up—a thorough soldier in appearance; and his manners are most courteous and full of dignity. He is a perfect gentleman in every respect."[24]

Few of Lee's attributes elicited more comment from former Confederates than his devotion to duty. Indeed, perhaps Lee's best-known "quotation," allegedly written to his son Custis in 1852 and still widely repeated, is: "Duty is the sublimest word in the English language." Although Lee never penned those words, he did comment often about duty. Taylor dealt with duty in *Four Years*, employing an anecdote featuring the death of Lee's second daughter, Anne Carter "Annie" Lee. Entering the commanding general's tent one morning in the aftermath of the 1862 Maryland campaign, he "was startled and shocked to see him overcome with grief, an open letter in his hands. That letter contained the sad intelligence of his daughter's death." Earlier that morning, Lee had addressed "matters of army routine upon which his judgment and action were desired." This episode, thought Taylor, "illustrates one of the noblest traits of the character of that noble man." As the "father of a tenderly-loved daughter" but also the commander of "an important and active army," Lee faced a cruel choice. "Lee the man must give way to Lee the patriot and soldier," affirmed Taylor, because "Duty first, was the rule of his life, and his every thought, word, and action was made to square with duty's inexorable demands."[25]

Taylor used instances of Lee's losing his temper—moments he had criticized in letters during the war—to commend his chief's self-discipline and generosity of spirit. "Scarcely less to be admired than his sublime devotion to duty was his remarkable self-control," insisted Taylor, a trait that allowed the general to restrain "strong passions" by "complete subjection to his will and conscience." Those at headquarters appreciated that "the occasional cropping-out of temper, which we, who were constantly near him, witnessed, only showed how great was his habitual self-command." In one flare-up between Lee and Taylor, the general "manifested his ill-humor by a little nervous twist or jerk of the neck and head, peculiar to himself, accompanied by some harshness of manner." When his aide replied in kind, Lee sought to soothe ruffled feelings: "Colonel Taylor, when I lose my temper, don't you let it make you angry." The episode taught Taylor, and by extension his readers, a lesson about magnanimity in the general who, "great and glorious in his humility, condescended to occupy the same plane with his youthful subaltern, and to reason with him as an equal, frankly acknowledging his own imperfections, but kindly reminding the inferior at the same time of his duty and position."[26]

Lee presided over a congenial headquarters in Taylor's telling, a place of warmth, humor, and mutual respect free of tensions evident in some of the wartime letters. Countering what he termed a prevalent idea that Lee's austerity made him difficult to approach, Taylor limned a commander of "much dignity" whose "intercourse with those around him was marked by a suavity of manner that removed all restraint and invited closer fellow-ship." There existed "between General Lee and his military family a degree of *camaraderie* that was perfectly delightful. Our conversation, especially at table, was free from restraint, unreserved as between equals, and often of a bright and jocular vein." Lee's own sense of humor included a habit "of teasing those about him in a mild way."[27]

Similarly, Taylor converted Lee's penchant for maintaining a spartan headquarters, which irked him during the war, into a virtue. A passage in *General Lee* offers evidence of a spare environment. "All the appointments were of the simplest kind," wrote Taylor, with "table furniture . . . of tin," "the regular army ration, supplemented by such additions from the country as could be procured by our steward by the use of a little money," and little "use of spirituous liquors." Taylor saw Lee drink wine only once in four years—while at Petersburg. Overall, "General Lee never availed himself of the advantages of his position to obtain dainties for his table or any personal comfort for himself."[28]

Both Taylor's books yield insights into Lee's conception of how the war should be waged and his style of generalship. From the outset, Lee expected a long conflict that would demand a massive application of Confederate resources—exemplified by his wish in 1861 that soldiers, rather than enlisting for a year, be "mustered in *for the war*." Lee accepted that Union superiority of men and matériel dictated a broad defensive strategy for the Confederacy, whose smaller armies stood no chance of utterly defeating the United States. But he favored a course that weakened Union morale by winning victories on the battlefield to create "dissatisfaction and pecuniary distress" in the United States and make "the people weary of the struggle." A sound national defensive policy, believed Lee, required taking "the aggressive when good opportunity offered; and by delivering an effective blow to the enemy, not only to inflict upon him serious loss, but at the same time to thwart his designs of invasion, derange the plan of campaign contemplate by him, and thus prolong the conflict." Taylor might have added that the Army of Northern Virginia's victories buoyed Confederate civilian morale at the same time they eroded support for the war north of the Potomac River.[29]

Time and again in both books, Taylor captured an ethos at Confederate headquarters that prized movement, maintaining the initiative, and taking audacious risks. In the wake of the Seven Days, with John Pope's Union Army of Virginia operating near Warrenton and George B. McClellan's Army of the Potomac still menacing Richmond, the "occasion demanded celerity and audacity." Lee responded with a daring division of his army that resulted in victory at Second Bull Run. "There could be no more conclusive vindication of the strategy of General Lee," stated Taylor, "than the success that attended his plans in this particular case." Chancellorsville showcased Lee at his boldest, dividing the Army of Northern Virginia to outmaneuver a compliant Joseph Hooker. "Acting on the defensive," began Taylor in *General Lee,* "he swiftly and vigorously assumes the offensive. Because unexpected, the counterstroke would be so much the more effective." To offset intimidating odds, Lee pursued "a plan that infuses dash and enthusiasm into his columns and so adds greatly to the weight of the impact of their blows upon their adversaries." In May 1864, General Grant and the Federals "doubtless expected" Lee would "manoeuvre to avoid a general engagement, and, by 'masterly retreat,' retard the progress of his enemy." Instead, perceiving the enemy's design, "General Lee advanced to attack him. . . . and took the initiative in what was destined to be a prolonged and bitter struggle." A month's carnage—"from the Wilderness to James River—ended, with Victory perched upon the banner of General Lee." Even when hunkered down in the trenches at Petersburg, "Reduced in numbers . . . and limited as it was in supplies of all kinds," Lee's army "nevertheless dealt many vigorous and destructive blows to its adversary, and contributed much to its already imperishable renown."[30]

Taylor singled out two aspects of Lee's leadership for criticism. The first became part of Lost Cause orthodoxy and, in the work of Douglas Southall Freeman and others, remained prominent well into the twentieth century. In *Four Years,* Taylor observed, in considered language, that "it may perhaps be claimed . . . that he was too careful of the personal feelings of his subordinate commanders, too fearful of wounding their pride, and too solicitous for their reputation." Having made his mild criticism, Taylor, in effect, attributed the shortcoming to one of Lee's larger virtues: "The world already knows he was at all times to take upon his own shoulders the responsibility for failure or mishap, and thus shield those from censure who had really failed to execute his orders or designs." Freeman followed Taylor's lead on this dimension of Lee's behavior: "His consideration for others, the virtue of the gentleman, had been his vice as a soldier."[31]

The second of Lee's weaknesses concerned his conception of proper military/civilian relationships. Reprising sentiments from his letter to Bettie Saunders dated February 20, 1865, Taylor accused Lee of buckling to civilian pressure. "It may be said," he wrote in *Four Years,* "that he was too law-abiding, too subordinate to his superiors in civil authority—those who managed the governmental machinery." Under normal circumstances a proper stance for soldiers in a democratic republic, this deference to politicians, posited Taylor, proved deleterious in "extraordinary times" when "in some matters, ordinary rules were extraordinary evils. General Lee should have been supreme in all matters touching the movements and discipline of his army. . . ." Interference from Richmond—and Taylor likely had Jefferson Davis, the various secretaries of war, and Congress in mind—trammeled Lee in promoting subordinates, determining strategic movements, and in other ways. By the time Lee was made general-in-chief in early February 1865, his enlarged authority made no difference because "the end was then near at hand, and the affairs of the South hopeless."[32]

Taylor seldom mentioned slavery and African Americans in his books, limiting his comments to the war's causation and the question of arming black men in the Confederacy. He blamed the war on a minority in the free states who sought to destroy slavery, terming Abraham Lincoln "what was called in the South a Black Republican, of pronounced type, thoroughly imbued with the ideas and teachings of the abolitionists, always on the antislavery side. . . ." Regarding possible black military service, public sentiment in the Confederacy "became reconciled to the enlistment of negroes as soldiers." In vintage Lost Cause style, Taylor painted a picture in *General Lee* of enslaved people who "were universally loyal and their conduct in all respects admirable," adding that "individually, alongside their masters and encouraged by them, they would have made good soldiers and rendered good service." Taylor closed with a brutally invidious comparison almost universally embraced in the Jim Crow South. African Americans observed "the bounds of perfect and unfaltering respect for the white race" while enslaved, but after emancipation "their conception of freedom is unbridled license, and their tendency to a life of idleness, immorality, and crime is truly sad and disheartening."[33]

Both *Four Years* and *General Lee* support the foundational Lost Cause tenet that the Army of Northern Virginia and its commander succumbed only when ground down by more powerful Union forces. For Taylor, the time between the Seven Days and Appomattox featured stirring Confederate victories and some standoffs but no unequivocal defeats. On the battlefields of Antietam and Gettysburg, contests that by almost any measure would be reckoned Union triumphs, Taylor stressed that Lee's men held their ground at the end of fighting. He labeled Antietam a battle that left both sides exhausted and neither able "to claim a victory." After Gettysburg, the "lack of supplies and of ammunition alone" constrained Lee "to abandon the enemy's front and recross the Potomac." The surrender in Wilmer McLean's parlor on April 9, 1865, wrote Taylor somewhat obscurely in *Four Years,* "terminated the career of the Army of Northern Virginia—an army that was never vanquished; but that, in obedience to the orders of its trusted commander, who was himself yielding obedience to the dictates of a pure and lofty sense of duty to his men and those dependent on them, laid down its arms, and furled the standards never lowered in defeat." *General Lee* presented a more direct assertion: "Attrition had done its work—the career of the Army of Northern Virginia was closed and its banners furled; but the record of its achievements glows with undiminished splendor and constrains the admiration of the world."[34]

Taylor and the Question of Numbers

Taylor's most substantial contribution to Confederate historiography rested on his authority regarding troop strengths in the Army of Northern Virginia. Observations about superior Union manpower formed a leitmotif in his wartime letters, and the goal of establishing comparative Confederate and Union numbers in the Eastern Theater lay at the heart of his decision to write *Four Years* and continued, to a lesser degree, in the preparation of *General Lee*. Many former Confederates, most notably his old commander, turned to Taylor when pursuing information about numbers.

Lee's General Order No. 9, dated April 10, 1865, laid the groundwork for subsequent explanations for Confederate failure. Drafted by Lt. Col. Charles Marshall of Lee's staff, the order quickly became a touchstone for former Confederates. "After four years of arduous service," read the first sentence, "marked by unsurpassed courage and fortitude, the Army of Northern Virginia has been compelled to yield to overwhelming numbers and resources." In these twenty-seven words, the order articulated two fundamental parts of the Lost Cause interpretation of the war—a determined soldiery fought gallantly, and they failed only because of the enemy's limitless men and matériel. Those themes, as Taylor's letters indicate, had deep roots in the war, which gave them additional credibility among defeated Rebels seeking something positive in a shattering defeat that destroyed their slavery-based social system and killed 30 percent of the Confederacy's military-age white men.[35]

A letter from Lee in late July 1865 directed Taylor's attention toward numbers. Lee planned to write a history of the Army of Northern Virginia that would address what he considered salient features of the conflict, a project complicated by the fact that he had lost most of his official papers during the chaotic retreat from Richmond to Appomattox. "I am desirous that the bravery of the Army of N. Va shall be correctly transmitted to posterity," he informed Taylor, ". . . . & I am anxious to collect the necessary data for the history of the campaigns in Vrga from the commencement of its organization to its final surrender. I am particularly anxious that its actual strength in the different battles it has fought, be correctly stated." Lacking the wartime records, Lee hoped Taylor's familiarity with the army's bimonthly returns would allow him to "state with some confidence its effective strength at each of the great battles it has fought, in Inft Cavy & Arty.

You may also have some memoranda within your reach that would assist your memory. Please give me at least the benefit of your recollection." Taylor turned to Thomas White, a clerk who had compiled the field returns at headquarters, to supply the information Lee sought. White replied with a series of estimates, copies of which went to Lee and Taylor. Lee wrote Taylor again in November 1865, remarking that some of White's figures for Confederate strengths seemed too high. Lieutenant Colonel Marshall also had shared his recollections on the topic. "When I get yours," Lee remarked, "I shall have to make a just average. I have made no progress as yet in writing, and very little in collecting information."[36]

Although Lee never published anything about his army, Taylor honored his old chief's request relating to numbers. He presented his findings in 1877 in the *Southern Historical Society Papers* and, most fully, in *Four Years*. In doing so, he contributed to an often-rancorous debate that pitted former Confederates led by Jubal A. Early, who played up the disparity in numbers against Union officers, including Adam Badeau of U. S. Grant's staff, who minimized the Federal advantage.[37] Introductory comments in *Four Years* laid out Taylor's purpose and sources. The book supplied a "comparative statement of the strength of the Confederate and Federal armies that were engaged in the operations in Virginia." Taylor could "speak with confidence of the numerical strength of Confederate forces" because he had "for a long time supervised the preparation of the official returns of the Army of Northern Virginia" and had "been permitted to make a recent examination of a number of those returns, now on file in the archive-office of the War Department at Washington." His figures for Federal strength rested on "official documents emanating from the officers and authorities of the United States Government."[38] Other Union sources, unnamed in Taylor's preface but evident in his text and notes, included William Swinton's *Campaigns of the Army of the Potomac: A Critical History of Operations in Virginia, Maryland and Pennsylvania from the Commencement to the Close of the War, 1861–5* (1866) and reports of proceedings from Congress's Joint Committee on the Conduct of the War.

Taylor's labors benefited from "very kind and courteous treatment . . . at the hands of officials of the War Department, who extended to me every facility for the accomplishment of my purpose." Anticipating skepticism among ex-Confederates about the federal recordkeepers, he assured "former comrades-in-arms of the evident purpose of the Government authorities charged with the custody of these records to discard all sectional bias ... and to preserve faithfully and impartially all documents now in their custody." Staking out reconciliationist ground that would be increasingly popular later in the century, Taylor hoped the American people soon would "contemplate all that was manly, all that was virtuous, all that was noble, all that was praiseworthy, in the recent struggle between the sections, whether developed on the side of the North or that of the South. . . ." As for himself, "I claim that my only aim has been historical accuracy."[39]

Taylor presented the results of his research in twenty-three pages of tables. His figures, not unexpectedly, showed that Lee never fought on equal terms against any of the seven Union generals who opposed him in major engagements. The relative numbers were closest at the Seven Days (80,762 CS, 105,000 US), and Second Bull Run (49,077 CS, 74,578 US), farthest apart at Chancellorsville (57,000 CS, 132,000 US) and in the Overland campaign (64,000 CS, 141,000 US). Taylor believed he had so performed his work "as to command the confidence of all." The disparity in strength at several battles likely would startle some readers, he ventured, though his numbers rested "on incontrovertible evidence." Harkening back to many statements from his wartime letters, and perfectly aligned with Lost Cause advocacy, Taylor averred that the gap in numbers "makes pardonable the emotions of pride with which the soldier of the Army of Northern Virginia points to the achievements of that incomparable body of soldiery, under its peerless and immortal leader."[40]

Numbers occupied far less of Taylor's attention in *General Lee* than in *Four Years*. By 1906, he knew the idea of vastly outnumbered Confederates had long been a matter of faith in the South and become widely accepted across much of the rest of the nation and abroad as well. Taylor's preface in *General Lee* alluded to his first book as an attempt to establish "the fact of the great numerical odds against which the army under General Lee had to contend in its encounters with the Federal armies opposed to it." He had taken on that project out of loyalty to his old commander. "General Lee had expressed a purpose to do this," wrote Taylor, "and after his death, before its accomplishment, the duty seemed logically to devolve upon me." The narrative in *General Lee* gave relative strengths in the course of examining various campaigns—sometimes merely reprinting sections from *Four Years*—but did not dwell on statistics. One of the reprinted passages used numbers in comparing Lee and Grant during the Overland campaign. Only by keeping in mind that Grant crossed the Rapidan River in early May with 140,000 men to Lee's 64,000, warned Taylor, could readers appreciate that "brilliant genius made amends for paucity of numbers, and proved more than a match for brute force, as illustrated in the hammering policy of General Grant."[41]

Any attempt to pinpoint strengths on a Civil War battlefield invites frustration in trying to make sense of different categories of soldiers—"present for duty," "effective strength," and "engaged strength"—that participants, as well as later historians, defined differently. Entire books have been devoted to establishing numbers for a single campaign, and modern monographs on the same battle can disagree about both soldiers available for action and casualties.[42] Thomas L. Livermore's *Numbers and Losses in the Civil War in America, 1861–1865,* compiled by a former officer in the 5th New Hampshire Infantry and published in 1900, stood as the standard source on strengths and casualties for many decades. Livermore's computations, like Taylor's, depended on available materials but yielded different totals in many cases—almost always narrowing the gap between Union and Confederate strength. Livermore had the benefit of the *Official Records,* the massive set of documents published by the War Department between 1880 and 1901. He also had in mind Lost Cause assertions. "It is a part of human nature," observed Livermore dryly, "which persuades the losers in war to believe that the result must have come from a great disparity in numbers." The world acknowledged Confederate valor, he added, and "exaggerated statements of numbers cannot further exalt it."[43]

Taylor could not know how future historians would revise or sustain his numbers. He came very close with some of his estimates and missed the mark with others—as did Livermore and all writers, Union and Confederate, from the Civil War generation. The following figures for seven important campaigns show Taylor's and Livermore's estimates followed by a third from recent scholarly work:

- Seven Days—Taylor 80,762 CS/105,000 US, Livermore 88,113 CS/ 91,169 US, Burton 89,772 CS/88,870 US

- Second Bull Run—Taylor 49,077 CS/74,578 US, Livermore 48,527 CS/ 75,696 US, Long 48,500 CS/75,000 US

- Antietam—Taylor 35,255 CS/87,164 US, Livermore 51,844 CS/75,316 US, Hartwig 38,095 CS/72,727 US

- Fredericksburg—Taylor 78,288 CS/113,000 US, Livermore 72,497 CS/ 113,987 US, O'Reilly 78,000 CS/135,000 US

- Chancellorsville—Taylor 57,000 CS/132,000 US, Livermore 57,352 CS/ 97,382 US, Furgurson 60,892 CS/133,868 US

- Gettysburg—Taylor 62,000 CS/105,000 US, Livermore 75,054 CS/ 83,298 US, Busey and Martin 71,699 CS/93,921 US

- Outset of Overland campaign—Taylor 64,000 CS/141,000 US, Livermore 61,025 CS/101,895 US, Young 66,000 CS/118,000 US[44]

These comparative figures demonstrate that Taylor's estimates of Confederate strength are generally accurate, with the margin of error exceeding 10 percent only for Gettysburg. They align especially well with recent scholarship for Second Bull Run and Fredericksburg but underestimate Lee's manpower at the Seven Days by 9,010 (10 percent), Antietam by 2,840 (7.5 percent), Chancellorsville by 3,892 (6.4 percent), Gettysburg by 9,699 (13.5 percent), and the opening of the Overland campaign by 2,000 (3 percent). In contrast, Taylor's Union estimates in four cases significantly exceed those in recent scholarship—by 16,130 (18 percent) at the Seven Days, 14,437 (20 percent) at Antietam, 11,079 (11.7 percent) at Gettysburg, and 23,000 (19.5 percent) at the opening of the Overland campaign. He undercounted Union forces at Fredericksburg by 22,000 (16 percent) and at Chancellorsville by 1,868 (1.3 percent) and got Second Bull Run right. Taylor's inflated Union strengths at Antietam, Gettysburg, and on the eve of the Overland campaign certainly assisted his, and R. E. Lee's, desire to cast the Army of Northern Virginia as a gallant underdog. Together with Chancellorsville, where even during the war people in the United States and the Confederacy knew Hooker vastly outnumbered Lee, these three campaigns served as lynchpins in Taylor's overall argument. It is worth noting that Livermore's numbers similarly deviated from recent scholarship, and countered Lost Cause claims, by undercounting Union strength at Antietam by 13,749 (36 percent), at Gettysburg by 10,623 (11.3 percent), and at Chancellorsville by 36,486 (27 percent).[45]

One last number from *Four Years* got to the heart of the Lost Cause case for overwhelming Union power. Taylor placed it in the second line of his dedication, guaranteeing that readers would see it before getting to the main text:

TO THE
EIGHT THOUSAND VETERANS
(THE SURVIVING HEROES OF THE ARMY OF NORTHERN VIRGINIA)
WHO, IN LINE OF BATTLE,
ON THE 9TH DAY OF APRIL, 1865,
WERE REPORTED PRESENT FOR DUTY,
THE FOLLOWING PAGES ARE RESPECTFULLY DEDICATED

The dedication would have evoked, for untold ex-Confederates, Lee's tribute to "the brave survivors of so many hard fought battles, who have remained steadfast to the last" in General Order No. 9 at Appomattox. Taylor chose 8,000, rather than, in his words, the "number of men and officers paroled [at Appomattox] . . . in round numbers between twenty-six and twenty-seven thousand." He probably took the smaller number from Lee's report to Jefferson Davis on April 12, which stated that on the morning of the 9th, "according to the reports of the ordnance officers, there were seven thousand eight hundred and ninety-two (7,892) organized infantry with arms, with an average of seventy-five (75) rounds of ammunition per man." This figure suggests an army that had broken down completely by April 9, with thousands of soldiers near Appomattox Court House who shortly would sign paroles but were unfit for duty. More important for Taylor's purposes, the number 8,000 conjures images of a corporal's guard, loyal to the end, as U. S. Grant's powerful encircling armies closed in.[46]

Reception and Reputation

Taylor's two books quickly became staples in the Lost Cause canon. A notice in the December 1877 issue of *Southern Historical Society Papers* unsurprisingly pronounced *Four Years* a "book of historic value, and which settles the question of relative numbers engaged in all of the great battles of the two armies." Taylor had contributed a piece to the *SHSP* earlier that year offering his opinion about why the Confederacy lost. "The solution to this point, in my judgment," he wrote just before *Four Years* came out, "is summed up in the simple sentence: *Paucity of men and resources.*" A later, longer review in *SHSP* mentioned Taylor's authority as a member of Lee's staff, calling *Four Years* a "book which must have the widest circulation, and go down to posterity as of highest authority on the points which it treats." The reviewer hoped "this book will meet with such general favor as to induce the accomplished author to write a *full* history of the campaigns of the Army of Northern Virginia." *Confederate Veteran,* the official publication of the largest organization of ex-Rebel soldiers, provided its readership with a delayed review of *General Lee* in 1913. "The book impresses me as the most satisfactory account of the military achievements of General Lee against overwhelming odds of men and resources," it read, and the "official relations of the author with General Lee stamp his statements with authority as thoroughly trustworthy." Beyond its use of numbers, the volume featured "delightful reminiscences, which bring out some of the most pleasing features of the hero's character—his magnanimity, his genial humor, his tender sympathy, and his personal magnetism."[47]

Former Confederates who wrote about the war often praised Taylor and quoted from his books. They used his numbers in their accounts of specific military operations and relied on his observations about Lee's personal behavior and character. Three examples, one each from the 1880s, 1890s, and early twentieth century, suggest Taylor's influence. In *Memoirs of Robert E. Lee,* Armistead L. Long, who served on Lee's staff in 1861–63, quoted "some incidents from Colonel Taylor's *Four Years with General Lee* as illustrative of his [Lee's] strong power over his feelings even on the most trying occasions." Long selected the passages relating to Annie Lee's death and to Lee's apologizing after exhibiting some "harshness of manner" toward Taylor. J. William Jones, a Confederate chaplain, editor of the *SHSP,* and author of two widely circulated books about Lee, invoked *Four Years* and Taylor as an "invaluable book" and an "able and efficient adjutant general" in an article challenging Adam Badeau and others who wrote from a Federal perspective. Robert Stiles, a major of artillery, cited Taylor's estimates of strength repeatedly in his popular memoir, describing *Four Years* at one point as an "invaluable work, so frequently referred to." Regarding comparative numbers, Stiles thought Taylor and Jubal Early "better informed on the subject than any other man."[48]

Members of the Lee family also referenced *Four Years.* Robert E. Lee Jr., the general's youngest son, published *Recollections and Letters of General Robert E. Lee* in 1904, reprinting excerpts from *Four Years* concerning, among other topics, the 1861 operations in western Virginia, the Overland campaign, and the last phase of the war. Fitzhugh Lee, the general's nephew and a major general of cavalry in the Army of Northern Virginia, earlier had depended on Taylor's "valuable work" in writing *General Lee*, a biography published in 1894. Fitz Lee devoted part of his discussion of strengths at Gettysburg to Taylor's method of establishing numbers, including how he "after the war, examined the Federal archives with much care."[49]

Douglas Southall Freeman's widely influential studies of Lee and the Army of Northern Virginia carried Taylor's name and role in the war forward well into the twentieth century. *R. E. Lee: A Biography,* a massive and unwaveringly admiring effort that won the first of Freeman's two Pulitzer Prizes, deemed Taylor's wartime letters and other papers "the most important source of collateral [manuscript] material on the military career of General Lee." *Four Years* and *General Lee*—both used the wartime letters extensively—showed "the weakness of the Army of Northern Virginia at different stages of military operations," preserved "certain of the most significant anecdotes of Lee," and related "some very intelligent observations on Lee's strategy." Freeman's *The South to Posterity: An Introduction to the Writing of Confederate History,* written after the biography, further vouched for Taylor's intimate knowledge about the strength of Lee's army; moreover, "Many incidents that have become a part of every life of Lee appeared for the first time in Taylor." Overall, added Freeman, Taylor's "conclusions seldom are subject to dispute, because he possessed a memory that was both tenacious and accurate." Many of Taylor's conclusions informed Freeman's own summary assessments of Lee as a soldier and a man—that, to give three examples, the general manifested a "wise devotion to the offensive" and a "well-considered daring" but allowed "excessive amiability" to color his decisions regarding subordinates.[50]

In the twenty-first century, historians must decide how best to use writings produced by the wartime generation. Alert to Lost Cause ideology, they gauge value of different kinds. They know, for instance, that an account unreliable on details about a wartime episode nonetheless can help document how memory traditions developed. Some titles can yield benefits of both kinds. Walter Taylor's books invite this kind of scrutiny. Elizabeth Brown Pryor, a biographer of Lee, judged Taylor's first book and his letters in a historiographical essay: "In 1877, aide Walter Taylor published a memoir, *Four Years with General Lee,* that upheld the Lost Cause tradition. It was superseded more than a century later by the publication of Taylor's far more candid and critical wartime letters." David J. Eicher, a historian and bibliographer, agreed that "Lee was never at fault according to Taylor, and errors were always made by others." But he concluded that *General Lee* provides useful "interpretations of Lee's attitudes about tactics and subordinate commanders" and "includes much material about the personal traits of Lee and of Taylor himself and stands up well to analysis from other sources." Taylor's books continue to be cited by historians interested in both Lee and his campaigns and how they were celebrated by advocates of the Lost Cause stream of memory.[51]

Walter H. Taylor's books reflect the experiences of their author and the times in which they were written. In conjunction with his published wartime letters, they enable readers to contemplate both the history and memory of the nation's most profoundly disruptive event. Although Taylor's narrative skill has not been the focus of this essay, it is worth noting that *Four Years* and *General Lee* can transport readers to specific moments in a way possible only with well-crafted eyewitness accounts. One such passage concerns the fall of Richmond in early April 1865. Taylor married Bettie Saunders just after midnight on April 3 and then hastened to rejoin the army. His account in *General Lee* recalls specific sights and sounds, anger toward triumphant Union forces, and the pain of emotional partings:

> There was universal gloom and despair at the thought that at the next rising of the sun the detested Federal soldiers would take possession of the city and occupy its streets. The transportation companies were busily engaged in arranging for the removal of the public stores and of the archives of the government. A fire in the lower part of the city was fiercely raging, and added greatly to the excitement. Somewhere near four o'clock on the morning of the 3d of April I bade farewell to all my dear ones, and in company with my brother-in-law, Colonel John S. Saunders, proceeded toward Mayo's Bridge, which we crossed to the south side of the James in the lurid glare of the fire and within the sound of several heavy explosions that we took to be the final scene in the career of the Confederate navy, then disappearing in smoke on the James River near Rocketts.[52]

Two weeks after escaping from the chaos in Richmond, Taylor was back in the city posing for Mathew Brady as Lee stared at the camera. The resulting image froze him in time, beside his commander, as he had been during

the war and would be in the two books he contributed to the literary record
of the Confederacy.

NOTES

1. Lee at first refused Brady's request, but Mrs. Lee helped convince him to pose for what
one historian of Civil War photography has deemed "several of the most popular and most
recognizable photographs of Lee ever taken." (Bob Zeller, *The Blue and the Gray in Black and
White: A History of Civil War Photography* [Westport, CT: Praeger, 2005], 165, 167.)

2. *Four Years with General Lee* was published in New York by D. Appleton, with a second
printing in 1878. Indiana University Press reprinted the book in hardcover and paperback
editions (Bloomington, 1962, 1997) without the long subtitle and with an introduction by
James I. Robertson Jr. *General Lee: His Campaigns in Virginia* was printed by Braunworth
Press of Brooklyn and distributed by Nusbaum Book and News of Norfolk. Taylor had first
approached Doubleday-Page of New York; however, demands that he revise his manuscript
extensively, including a drastic reduction of the sections "which have to do wholly or chiefly
with military affairs," prompted him to publish the book himself. The Morningside Bookshop
of Dayton, Ohio, issued a hardcover reprint in 1975, and the University of Nebraska Press a
paperback edition, with an introduction by Gary W. Gallagher, in 1994. Robert K. Krick kindly
provided information about Taylor's dealings with Doubleday-Page as well as other details
about the first edition (Krick to Gary W. Gallagher, October 21, 2019).

3. Douglas Southall Freeman, *The South to Posterity: An Introduction to the Writing of
Confederate History* (1939; reprint, Baton Rouge: Louisiana State University Press, 1998), 65.

4. Taylor, *Four Years*, 16, 188.

5. Giles B. Cook[e], "Col. W. H. Taylor, A. A. G. Army of Northern Virginia: An Appreciation," in *Confederate Veteran* 24 (May 1916): 234–35. For a good selection of Lee's wartime cor-
respondence, see *The Wartime Papers of R. E. Lee*, ed. Clifford Dowdey and Louis H. Manarin
(Boston: Little, Brown, 1961), and *Lee's Dispatches: Unpublished Letters of General Robert E.
Lee, C.S.A., to Jefferson Davis and the War Department of the Confederate States of America,
1862–1865*, ed. Douglas Southall Freeman and Grady McWhiney (1915; revised edition, New
York: Putnam's, 1957). For Lee's postwar interviews with William Allan (1868, 1870), Clifford
Gordon (1868), and William Preston Johnston (1868, 1870), see Gary W. Gallagher, ed., *Lee
the Soldier* (Lincoln: University of Nebraska Press, 1996), 3–34.

6. The immense, often combative, literature on responsibility for Confederate defeat at
Gettysburg can be mind-numbing. The early stage of the debates played out in the pages of
J. William Jones and others, eds., *Southern Historical Society Papers*, 52 vols. (Richmond,
VA: The Society, 1876–1959) [hereafter cited as *SHSP*], where Jubal Early's controlling hand
often was evident. Taylor contributed four pieces to the *SHSP*: "Memorandum of Colonel
Walter H. Taylor, of General Lee's Staff," 4:2 (August 1877): 80–87; "Second Paper by Colonel
Walter H. Taylor, of General Lee's Staff," 4:3 (September 1877): 124–39; "Numerical Strength
of the Armies at Gettysburg," 5:5 (May 1878): 239–41; and "Colonel Taylor's Reply to the Count
of Paris," 5:5 (May 1878): 242–46. For Taylor's discussions of Longstreet at Gettysburg in his
books, see *Four Years with General Lee*, 97–110, and *General Lee*, 194–209.

7. Taylor's class rankings and other information relating to his career at the Institute may be found in his file in the V.M.I. Archives, Preston Library, Virginia Military Institute, Lexington. His reasons for deciding not to return to V.M.I. are set forth in Walter H. Taylor to My Dear Friend [Francis H. Smith], September 24, 1855, V.M.I. Archives. On Taylor's activities after leaving V.M.I., see Emanuel Meyer, "Walter Herron Taylor and His Era," unpublished M.A. thesis, Old Dominion University, 1984, 21–28.

8. Meyer, "Walter Herron Taylor," 30–36.

9. Taylor, *Four Years*, 11; Walter Herron Taylor, Compiled Service Record, M331, roll 243, National Archives, Washington, DC. [hereafter cited as Taylor CSR]; G. Moxley Sorrel, *Recollections of a Confederate Staff Officer* (New York and Washington: Neale Publishing, 1905), 68–69. Taylor's promotion to major in the cavalry is an odd facet of his Confederate service about which the records offer no further details. For an excellent discussion of Confederate staff positions, see Robert E. L. Krick, *Staff Officers in Gray: A Biographical Register of the Staff Officers in the Army of Northern Virginia* (Chapel Hill: University of North Carolina Press, 2003), 2–35.

10. See Taylor CSR for documents that reveal the scale of paperwork at headquarters. For example, a requisition dated September 22, 1863, requested six reams of letter paper, two thousand official envelopes, one thousand letter envelopes, and three boxes of pens. Taylor's justification for this order was a curt "supply exhausted."

11. Taylor to Elizabeth S. Saunders, August 8, 1863, Taylor to My dear Sister, November 14, 1863, in Walter H. Taylor, *Lee's Adjutant: The Wartime Letters of Colonel Walter Herron Taylor, 1862–1865,* ed. R. Lockwood Tower (Columbia: University of South Carolina Press, 1995), 68–69, 84. For a critique of Lee's inadequate staff by an officer who served as his chief of ordnance between June and September 1862, see Edward Porter Alexander, *Fighting for the Confederacy: The Personal Recollections of General Edward Porter Alexander,* ed. Gary W. Gallagher (Chapel Hill: University of North Carolina Press, 1989), 236, 273, 419.

12. Taylor to Elizabeth S. Saunders, August 15, January 28, 1864, in Taylor, *Lee's Adjutant,* 182, 109. Taylor's allusion to a *"soft word"* drew on Proverbs 15:1, which in the King James Version reads: "A soft answer turneth away wrath; but grievous words stir up anger."

13. Taylor to Elizabeth S. Saunders, November 15, 1863, February 5, 1865, in Taylor, *Lee's Adjutant,* 89, 220; R. E. Lee to Confederate War Department, January 7, 1863, Lee Family Digital Archive, Stratford Hall, Virginia, accessed June 13, 2020, https://leefamilyarchive. org/9-family-papers/142-robert-e-lee-recommendation-for-walter-h-taylor-1863-january-7. Abraham Lincoln's young secretaries also referred to him as "the tycoon." See for example John Hay, *At Lincoln's Side: John Hay's Civil War Correspondence and Selected Writings,* ed. Michael Burlingame (Carbondale: Southern Illinois University Press, 2000), 48.

14. Taylor, *General Lee,* 240 (Spotsylvania), 270 (White Oak Road); R. Lockwood Tower, "Introduction," in Taylor, *Lee's Adjutant,* 18, 20. Douglas Southall Freeman, *R. E. Lee: A Biography,* 4 vols. (New York: Charles Scribner's Sons, 1935–36), 3:131–34, misidentifies the first episode as part of the fighting on May 12 at Spotsylvania. For an account that attributes somewhat improbable language to Taylor at White Oak Road, see *Confederate Veteran* 7 (October 1899): 464. In this version, Taylor "rode out in front of the line, waved his hat, and cried: 'Come ahead men! God bless you! I love every one of you!'"

15. Taylor to My dear Sister, May 8, 1863, Taylor to Elizabeth S. Saunders, August 15, 1863 [?], Taylor to Richard C. Taylor, July 17, 1863, in Taylor, *Lee's Adjutant,* 53, 62, 69–70.

16. Taylor to Elizabeth S. Saunders, May 1, June 1, 1864, February 16, 1865, in Taylor, *Lee's Adjutant,* 158, 165, 223–24.

17. Taylor to Elizabeth S. Saunders, August 15, 1863 [?], May 1, 1864, March 25, 1864, in Taylor, *Lee's Adjutant,* 69–70, 158, 144. For representative evidence of Taylor's own piety, see 42, 50–51, 113.

18. Taylor to My dear Sister, November 14, 1863, Taylor to Elizabeth S. Saunders, December 20, 1863, in Taylor, *Lee's Adjutant,* 83, 101.

19. Taylor to Elizabeth S. Saunders, February 16, 1865, in Taylor, *Lee's Adjutant,* 223–24. On the topic of arming enslaved men in the Confederacy, see Robert F. Durden, *The Gray and the Black: The Confederate Debate on Emancipation* (Baton Rouge: Louisiana State University Press, 1972); Bruce Levine, *Confederate Emancipation: Southern Plans to Free and Arm Slaves during the Civil War* (New York: Oxford University Press, 2006); and Philip D. Dillard, *Jefferson Davis's Final Campaign: Confederate Nationalism and the Fight to Arm Slaves* (Macon, GA: Mercer University Press, 2017). Only Dillard refers to Taylor's opposition, though Durden includes a letter to Taylor from the colonel of an Alabama regiment stating that a majority of his command "are willing to take the negroes in the ranks with them" (220–21).

20. Taylor to Elizabeth S. Saunders, February 20, 1865, in Taylor, *Lee's Adjutant,* 225. Many Confederates favored granting Lee far greater power as the war went on. For examples, see Gary W. Gallagher, *The Confederate War* (Cambridge, MA: Harvard University Press, 1997), 88.

21. Taylor to Elizabeth S. Saunders, April 3, 24, 1864, in Taylor, *Lee's Adjutant,* 148, 155. For a contemporary account of the emotional reaction to Longstreet's return to the Army of Northern Virginia in April 1864, see R. to the editor of *The Daily South Carolinian,* May 1, 1864, printed in *The Daily South Carolinian* (Columbia), May 10, 1864.

22. Meyer, "Walter Herron Taylor," chronicles Taylor's various postwar activities. The obituary from the *Richmond Times-Dispatch* is quoted in *Confederate Veteran* 24 (May 1916): 235.

23. Taylor, *Four Years,* [4]; Taylor, *General Lee,* v–vi.

24. Taylor, *General Lee,* 21–22; Arthur James Lyon Fremantle, *Three Months in the Southern States: April–June 1863* (1863; reprint, Lincoln: University of Nebraska Press, 1991), 248. Fremantle's diary, first published in Great Britain, reached American audiences in New York and Mobile editions in 1864. Extracts from the diary were published in September 1863 in *Blackwood's Edinburgh Magazine* and reprinted verbatim as an appendix to Edward A. Pollard's *Southern History of the War: The Second Year of the War* (New York: Charles B. Richardson, 1863), 326–74.

25. Taylor, *Four Years,* 76–77. On the bogus quotation about duty, see Freeman, *R. E. Lee,* 1:316n47, and Sean Heuston, "The Most Famous Thing Robert E. Lee Never Said: Duty, Forgery, and Cultural Amnesia," *Journal of American Studies* 48 (November 2014). A perusal of websites on June 16, 2020, revealed many that treated the quotation as valid, among them HistoryNet (https://www.historynet.com/robert-e-lee-quotes) and ForbesQuotes (https://www.forbes.com/quotes/8025/).

26. Taylor, *Four Years,* 77–78 (Taylor repeated this anecdote in *General Lee,* 156–57). Edward Porter Alexander also referred to Lee's habit of jerking his head when upset, calling it

"that peculiar little shake of his head which he used when he was worried, & which we used to call snapping at his ear." (Alexander, *Fighting for the Confederacy,* 389–90.)

27. Taylor, *General Lee,* 157.

28. Taylor, *General Lee,* 157–58.

29. Taylor, *Four Years,* 11–12, 90. A number of historians have argued that Lee's aggressiveness cost the Confederacy so much manpower it shortened, rather than extended, the war and thus hastened Union victory. Others have countered that his strategy came close to breaking civilian morale in the United States. For a sampling of opinions from the 1860s through the end of the twentieth century about Lee's generalship, see the essays in Gallagher, ed., *Lee the Soldier.*

30. Taylor, *General Lee,* 97, 166; Taylor, *Four Years,* 126, 140.

31. Taylor, *Four Years,* 147; Freeman, *R. E. Lee,* 4:168. On the question of Lee's ability to deal forthrightly with officers who failed, see Gary W. Gallagher, *Lee and His Army in Confederate History* (Chapel Hill: University of North Carolina Press, 2001), 191–219.

32. Taylor, *Four Years,* 147–48.

33. Taylor, *General Lee,* 8, 266–67.

34. Taylor, *General Lee,* 137, 211; Taylor, *Four Years,* 153. Taylor was neither the first nor the last former Confederate to argue that Lee's army was not defeated but merely worn out. In a widely disseminated speech delivered in January 1872, Jubal Early claimed the Army of Northern Virginia "had been gradually worn down by the combined agencies of numbers, steam-power, railroads, mechanisms, and all the resources of physical science." (Jubal A. Early, *The Campaigns of Gen. Robert E. Lee. An Address by Lieut. General Jubal A. Early, before Washington and Lee University, January 19th, 1872* [1872], reprinted in Gallagher, *Lee the Soldier,* quotation on p. 67.)

35. Lee, *Wartime Letters,* 934–95. The Confederacy mobilized approximately 900,000 soldiers out of a white population of 5,500,000 and lost 260,000–300,000 dead. For the traditional estimate of Confederate fatalities, see E. B. Long, *The Civil War Day by Day: An Almanac, 1861–1865* (Garden City, NY: Doubleday, 1971), 711. For an argument revising the numbers upward, see J. David Hacker, "A Census-Based Count of the Civil War Dead," *Civil War History* 57 (December 2011): 307–48.

36. Lee to Taylor, July 31, 1865, Lee Digital Archive, accessed June 19, 2020, https://leefamily archive.org/papers/letters/transcripts-W&L/w231.htmlLee; Lee to Taylor, November 2, 1865, reproduced in Taylor, *Four Years,* 157–61. White's numbers are in Taylor, *Four Years,* 157–60. Lee sent requests for copies of reports and other information to a number of former subordinates. On his plans to write about the war in Virginia, see Allen W. Moger, "General Lee's Unwritten 'History of the Army of Northern Virginia,'" *Virginia Magazine of History and Biography* 71 (July 1963): 341–63. On his influence regarding Lost Cause arguments, see Gary W. Gallagher, "Shaping Public Memory of the Civil War: Robert E. Lee, Jubal A. Early, and Douglas Southall Freeman," in Gallagher, *Lee and His Army,* 255–58.

37. For an exchange between Early and Badeau, see Jubal A. Early, *The Relative Strength of the Armies of Gen'ls Lee and Grant. Reply of Gen. Early to the Letter of Gen. Badeau to the London Standard* (n.p.: n.p., [1870]), and William A. Blair, "Grant's Second Civil War: The Battle for Historical Memory," in Gary W. Gallagher, ed., *The Spotsylvania Campaign* (Chapel Hill: University of North Carolina Press, 1998), 230–36.

38. Taylor, *Four Years,* [5].

39. Taylor, *Four Years,* 163, 188.

40. Taylor, *Four Years,* 55, 62, 83, 136, 188. The tables are on pp. 164–86.

41. Taylor, *General Lee,* [5], 231 (reprinting a passage from p. 125 of *Four Years*).

42. For two impressive examples of dealing with strengths and casualties, see John W. Busey and David G. Martin, *Regimental Strengths and Losses at Gettysburg,* 4th edition (Hightstown, NJ: Longstreet House, 2005), and Alfred C. Young III, *Lee's Army during the Overland Campaign: A Numerical Study* (Baton Rouge: Louisiana State University Press, 2013). For different totals in scholarly monographs, see Edwin B. Coddington, *The Gettysburg Campaign: A Study in Command* (New York: Charles Scribner's Sons, 1968) and Stephen W. Sears, *Gettysburg* (Boston: Houghton, Mifflin, 2003), both of which reflect careful scholarship. Coddington places Confederate casualties at "20,451 officers and men, and very likely more" (p. 536) and Sears at 22,626 (p. 498). Patricia L. Faust, ed., *Historical Times Illustrated Encyclopedia of the Civil War* (New York: Harper and Row, 1986), a standard reference work, gives the total as 28,063 (p. 307).

43. Thomas L. Livermore, *Numbers and Losses in the Civil War in America, 1861–1865* (Boston: Houghton, Mifflin, 1900), 2–3. Livermore mentioned Jubal Early and other Confederates in his text but not Taylor or *Four Years.* US War Department, *The War of the Rebellion: A Compilation of the Official Records of the Union and Confederate Armies,* 127 vols., index, and atlas (Washington: Government Printing Office, 1880–1901), popularly known as the *Official Records,* included many documents Taylor had examined in manuscript.

44. For Taylor's numbers, see *Four Years,* 53–55 (Seven Days), 61–62 (Second Bull Run), 73 (Antietam), 83 (Chancellorsville), 113 (Gettysburg), 136 (outset of Overland campaign), and *General Lee,* 145–46 (Fredericksburg). Livermore's estimates are in *Numbers and Losses,* 84–85 (Seven Days), 88–89 (Second Bull Run), 92–93 (Antietam), 96–97 (Fredericksburg), 98–99 (Chancellorsville), 102–03 (Gettysburg), 110–11 (outset of Overland campaign). For the scholarly estimates, see Brian K, Burton, *Extraordinary Circumstances: The Seven Days Battles* (Bloomington: Indiana University Press, 2001), 402–3; Long, *Civil War Day by Day,* 258 (Second Bull Run); D. Scott Hartwig, *To Antietam Creek: The Maryland Campaign of September 1862* (Baltimore: Johns Hopkins University Press, 2012), [678–80]; Francis Augustin O'Reilly, *The Fredericksburg Campaign: Winter War on the Rappahannock* (Baton Rouge: Louisiana State University Press, 2003), 7; Ernest B. Furgurson, *Chancellorsville 1863: The Souls of the Brave* (New York: Alfred A. Knopf, 1992), 364–65; Busey and Martin, *Regimental Strengths and Losses at Gettysburg,* 16, 169; Young, *Lee's Army,* 2, 12.

45. Wartime testimony regarding Hooker's huge advantage in numbers includes Horace Greeley's famous reaction to news of the Union retreat. "My God! It is horrible—horrible," exclaimed the editor of the *New York Tribune,* "and to think of it, 130,000 magnificent soldiers so cut to pieces by less than 60,000 half-starved ragamuffins." (J. Cutler Andrews, *The North Reports the Civil War* [Pittsburgh: University of Pittsburgh Press, 1955], 369.)

46. Taylor, *Four Years,* [3], 154; R. E. Lee to Jefferson Davis, April 12, 1865, in Lee, *Wartime Papers,* 937. For a discussion of how many Confederates fought, laid down arms, and were paroled at Appomattox, which includes attention to Taylor's dedication in *Four Years,* see Chris M. Calkins, *The Final Bivouac: The Surrender Parade at Appomattox and the Disbanding of the Armies, April 10–May 20, 1865,* 2nd edition (Lynchburg, VA: H. E. Howard, 1988), 216–17.

47. "Books Received," in *SHSP* 4:6 (December 1877): 320; Taylor, "Memorandum of Colonel Walter H. Taylor," in *SHSP* 4:2 (August 1877): 80–81; "Book Notices," in *SHSP* 5:1 (January–February 1878): 95–96; James H. McNeilly, "General Lee's Virginia Campaigns," *Confederate Veteran* 21 (July 1913): 360.

48. A. L. Long, *Memoirs of Robert E. Lee: His Military and Personal History, Embracing a Large Amount of Information Hitherto Unpublished* (New York: J. M. Stoddart, 1886), 222–24; J. William Jones, "Relative Forces of Lee and Grant. On Their Summer Campaign of 1864," *Confederate Veteran* 7 (December 1899): 555; Robert Stiles, *Four Years under Marse Robert* (New York and Washington: Neale Publishing, 1903), 262, 92–93. Jones's *Personal Reminiscences, Anecdotes, and Letters of Gen. Robert E. Lee* (New York: D. Appleton, 1874) and *Life and Letters of Robert Edward Lee, Soldier and Man* (New York and Washington: Neale Publishing, 1906), both hagiographical, went through many printings.

49. Robert E. Lee Jr., *Recollections and Letters of General Robert E. Lee* (New York: Doubleday, Page, 1904), 51–52 (western Virginia), 129 (Overland campaign), 155, 162 (end of the war); Fitzhugh Lee, *General Lee* (New York: D. Appleton, 1894), 166 (note), 301–2. Other notable Confederate memoirs that quote from Taylor include G. Moxley Sorrel's *Recollections of a Confederate Staff Officer* (cited in note 9 above), H. B. McClellan's *The Life and Campaigns of Major-General J. E. B. Stuart, Commander of the Cavalry of the Army of Northern Virginia* (1885), Edward Porter Alexander's *Military Memoirs of a Confederate: A Critical Narrative* (1907), and McHenry Howard's *Recollections of a Maryland Confederate Soldier and Staff Officer under Johnston, Jackson and Lee* (1914).

50. Freeman, *R. E. Lee*, 4:552–53; Freeman, *The South to Posterity*, 64–65. See chapters 11 and 28 of volume 4 of *R. E. Lee* for Freeman's summary assessments.

51. Elizabeth Pryor Brown, "Robert E. Lee," in Aaron Sheehan-Dean, ed., *A Companion to the U. S. Civil War*, 2 vols. (Malden, MA: John Wiley and Sons, 2014), 2:657; David J. Eicher, *The Civil War in Books: An Analytical Bibliography* (Urbana: University of Illinois Press, 1997), 111–12. For examples of works that quote Taylor's books regarding the substance of Lee's actions and attitudes, see Gordon C. Rhea, *Cold Harbor: Grant and Lee, May 26–June 3, 1864* (Baton Rouge: Louisiana State University Press, 2002), and Brian Holden Reid, *Robert E. Lee: Icon for a Nation* (London: Weidenfeld & Nicolson, 2005). On Taylor and the Lost Cause, see Thomas L. Connelly's pioneering *The Marble Man: Robert E. Lee and His Image in American Society* (New York: Alfred A. Knopf, 1977), 47–50. For a discussion of Taylor's handling of Confederate numbers, see Young, *Lee's Army*, 3, 218.

52. Taylor, *General Lee*, 278. Taylor's brother John Cowdery Taylor wrote about the wedding, setting the time precisely: "Sunday April 2nd 65, came the evacuation of Richmond. Oh harrowing time!—Walter was married Sunday night 12 ½ o'c." (Transcription kindly provided by Mary Roy Edwards on November 14, 2007.)

CONTRIBUTORS

WILLIAM A. BLAIR is Walter and Helen P. Ferree Professor of Middle American History Emeritus at Penn State University.

STEPHEN B. CUSHMAN is Robert C. Taylor Professor of English at the University of Virginia.

GARY W. GALLAGHER is John L. Nau III Professor of History Emeritus at the University of Virginia.

J. MATTHEW GALLMAN is professor of history at the University of Florida.

SARAH E. GARDNER is professor of history and director of Southern Studies at Mercer University.

M. KEITH HARRIS teaches at a private high school in Los Angeles and is the host of The Rogue Historian Podcast.

ELIZABETH R. VARON is Langbourne M. Williams Professor of History at the University of Virginia.

CECILY N. ZANDER is a postdoctoral fellow at the Center for Presidential History at Southern Methodist University.

INDEX

Aaron, Daniel, 92

Abolition, 55, 169, 209–10

Abolitionists, 52, 62; in Great Britain, 58; publications banned in US mail, 61; political antislavery movement, 67, 74; Garrisonians, 71, 74; immediatism, 71; expenses of, 73

Adams, Henry, 80

Adams, John Quincy, 60

African Americans, 68, 72–73; role in emancipation, 77; white soldier views of, 210–11

African Methodist Episcopal Church, 70

Alcott, Louisa May, 103, 104, 117n47, 157; *Hospital Sketches,* 103, 104

Alden, Henry Mills, 108–9

Alexander, Edward Porter, 18, 37, 263

American Anti-Slavery Society, 60–61, 72, 74

American Missionary Association, 58

American Party, 74, 75–76, 81

American Revolution, 68, 70

Andersonville, GA, 107

Andrew, John A., 210

Antietam (battle), 22, 28, 123, 124, 125, 136, 150–51, 176, 271, 275; troop strengths, 279

Appomattox Courthouse, VA, 23, 32, 43, 77, 123, 185, 261, 262, 275; in writings of James Longstreet, 23–24; number of surrendered troops, 281

Atlanta, GA, 26, 40

Atlanta Constitution (newspaper), 12, 19, 20, 21, 22, 38

Aristotle, 125

Army Life in a Black Regiment, 104

Army of Northern Virginia, 13, 124, 261; First Corps, 3, 13, 18, 30, 40, 176, 267, 269; staff officers of, 264–65; as national institution, 269, 273; troop strengths, 276, 279–80

Army of the Potomac, 17, 123, 124, 126, 128, 134, 136, 143, 148, 176; Fifth Corps, 207; Ninth Corps, 268; troop strengths, 276, 279–80

Army of Virginia, 273

Articles of Confederation, 64

Ashton, Diane, 112

Association of the Army of Northern Virginia, 269

Atlanta campaign, 138

Atlantic Monthly, 104, 108, 124, 128

Bacon, Daniel, 230, 231

Badeau, Adam, 182, 183, 277, 282

Bailey, Gamaliel, 59

Baker, Edward D., 169

Ball's Bluff (battle), 136, 140

Bancroft, George, 58

Banneker, Benjamin, 69

Barlow, Arabella, 172, 173

Barlow, Francis, Channing, 172, 172

Barnum, P. T., 128–29, 130, 177